Karl Peinkofer - Fritz Tannigel

HANDBOOK OF PERCUSSION INSTRUMENTS

Their Characteristics and Playing Techniques, with Illustrations and Musical Examples from the Literature

Translated from the original German by
Kurt and Else Stone

SCHOTT
LONDON   NEW YORK   MAINZ

Exclusive Representation for the United States
BELWIN-MILLS PUBLISHING CORP.
MELVILLE, NEW YORK 11746

AP 406

Library of Congress Catalog Number: 76-000330

Copyright © 1969 B. Schott's Söhne, Mainz. BSS 42 191
English translation Copyright © 1976 B. Schott's Söhne, Mainz
Pictorial Reproductions: Georg Gehringer GmbH, Kaiserslautern
Printed in U.S.A.

AP 406

CONTENTS

PREFACE 7
    Names of Percussion Instruments in English-German-Italian-French 10
    Common Abbreviations and Symbols for Percussion Instruments 17
    Table of Beaters, with Illustrations, Measurements, and Uses 19

INTRODUCTION 31
GENERAL OBSERVATIONS 31

INSTRUMENTS WITH DEFINITE PITCH

    Timpani or Kettle Drums 35

    Wooden-Bar Instruments 41
        Xylophone 45
        Keyboard Xylophone 46
        Marimba, Xylorimba 47
        Bass Xylophone 48
        Trough Xylophone 49

    Metal-Bar Instruments 51
        Glockenspiel or Orchestra Bells 52
        Keyboard Glockenspiel 55
        Celesta 56
        Vibraphone 56
        Metallophones; Campanelli giapponese; Loo-Jon 58

    Lithophones (Stone-Disk Instruments) 59

    Metal Instruments
        Crotales or Antique Cymbals 60
        Gong 62
        Steel Drums 63
        Bells and Chimes 64
            Large Bronze Bells 65
            Bell Substitutes: Calottes; Piano-String Bells (Grail Bells) 66
            Electro-Acoustical Bells; *Ondes Martenot; Mixtur-Trautonium* 66
            Bell Plates 67
            Orchestral Chimes (Tubular Chimes) 69
        Tubaphone (Tubuscampanophone) 71

    Glass Instruments
        Sets of Tuned Glass Vessels 72
            Musical Glasses 72
            Glass Harp 72
            Glass Harmonica 73
            Tuned Bottles 73

    Miscellaneous Instruments
        Flexatone; Musical Saw; Sansa; Kalimba; Marimbula 74

Miscellaneous Instruments *(Cont'd)*
    Slide Whistle (Lotos Flute, Swanee Whistle) 78
    The Piano as Percussion Instrument 79
    Bar Instruments of the Orff *Schulwerk* 80

INSTRUMENTS WITH INDEFINITE PITCH

Introduction 83
Skin Membranophones
    Drums 84
        Tambourin Provençal (Tabor) 84
        Long Drum (with snares) 85
        Parade Drum *(Basler Trommel)* 86
        Military Drum (Field Drum, Street Drum, etc.) 87
        Tenor Drum (Without snares) 88
        Snare Drum 88
        Bass Drum 94
        Frame Drum (Tambourine without jingles) 97
        American Indian Drums 98
        Boobam 99
        Tambourine 100
    String or Friction Drums 103
        Pasteboard Rattle *(Waldteufel)* 103
        Lion's Roar *(Brummtopf)* 104
    Hand Drums 105
        Arabian Hand Drum *(Darabucca)* 105
        Bongo Drums 106
        Conga Drums 108
        Tablas and Banyas 110
    Tom-Toms 111
        Chinese Tom-Toms 112
        O-Daiko (Japanese) 113
        Taiko (Japanese) 113
        Modern Tom-Toms 114
        Roto Toms 115
    Timbales 116

Struck Idiophones 118
    Triangle 118
    Cymbals 119
        Clash Cymbals; Suspended Cymbals; Sizzle Cymbal; Hi-Hat;
        Chinese Cymbals
    Tamtams; Cast Tamtam; Water Gong 126
        Sarténes 128
        Tchanchiki or *Atari-gane* 129
    Animal Bells; Herd Bells *(Almglocken)*; Cowbells; Metal Blocks;
        Herd Bells without Clappers *(Cencerro)* 130
    Small Bells; Hand Bells; Doorbells; Turkish
        Crescent; Bell Tree; Sanctus Bells; Sarna Bell; Ship's Bell 132
    Japanese Temple Bell *(Dobači)* 135
    Anvil; Steel Plates (Steel Disks); Automobile Brake Drums 136
    Switch 138
    Clappers 138
        Hands; Wooden Clappers; Whip or Slapstick; Small Boards (Bones);
          Bak; Strung Clappers *(Bin-Zasara)*; Concussion Blocks *(Hyoshigi)*
        Claves 141
        Castanets 142
    Finger Cymbals; Cymbal Tongs 144

    Wooden Drums 145
        Tubular Wood Blocks 146
        Rectangular Wood Blocks 146
        Temple Blocks 147
        Mokubio 148
        Slit Drums 149
        Log Drum 149
        Wood-Plate Drum (Wooden Tom-Tom); Wooden Barrel (Sake Barrel) . . 150
        Wooden Board 151
    Hammer 151

Scraped Instruments 152
    Ratchet 152
    Güiro (Gourd Scraper) 153
    Sapo Cubana or Bambú Brasileño (Bamboo Scraper) 154
    Reco-Reco (Wooden Scraper) 155
    Washboard; Metal Rasp (Metal Scraper) 155

Rattling Instruments 156
    Beaten Rattles 157
        Sistrum; Spurs 157
        Pandereta Brasileño; Wasamba Rattle 158
        Jawbone (Quijada); Vibra Slap 159
        Cabaza; Angklung 160
        Rattle Drum; Chinese Paper Drum 161
    Container Rattles 162
        Round Bells; Sleigh Bells 162
        Ghungrü (Indian Bell Strap); Maracas 163
        Mexican Bean 164
        Metal Rattles; Chocallos; Ganza; Sandbox; Sand Rattle; Marbles 165
    Row Rattles 166
        Fruit Husk Rattle; Chains; Chain Rattles 166
        Bamboo (Wood) Chimes; Glass Chimes; Disk Chimes (Shell Chimes) 167
    Foil Rattles 168
    Bumbass 169

IMITATIVE INSTRUMENTS
    Cuckoo, Nightingale, and Quail Calls, etc. 170
    Hoofbeats 171
    Toy Trumpets; Sand Blocks (Steam Engine); Automobile Horns; Signal
        Whistles; Mouth Siren; Siren; Fog Horn, etc. 171
    Wind Machines; Thunder Sheet; Rain Machine 172
    Cannon, Rifle, and Pistol Shots; Popgun 174
    Office Machines and Other Noises 175

List of Latin-American Instruments and their Possible Substitutions 177

APPENDIX
    Musical Examples 180
    Bibliography 238
    Index 240
    Acknowledgments and Credits 257
    Table of Ranges . . . . fold-out

PREFACE

The *Handbook of Percussion Instruments* is designed to provide today's practicing musician and music student, and especially today's percussionist, with a comprehensive survey of the entire arsenal of percussion resources he is likely to encounter in his professional life.

Among the subjects covered are:
-- Classification of the instruments into basic groups;
-- Detailed descriptions of the construction of each instrument including many Latin-American, Afro-American, and East-Asian instruments;
-- A brief tracing of the origin and history of each instrument;
-- The ranges of all pitched instruments;
-- The most commonly used beaters, etc., for each instrument, as well as the less common ones;
-- The essential playing techniques for each instrument;
-- The way the instruments have been used in the most significant compositions of the orchestral and operatic repertoire (detailed references);
-- Over 100 musical examples (mostly complete score pages) from the literature, showing how the instruments appear in context;
-- A special listing of Latin-American percussion instruments, and how to substitute for those that are unavailable;
-- An English-German-Italian-French glossary;
-- A special listing of the percussion instruments used in the Orff *Schulwerk*;
-- Photographic illustrations of virtually all instruments covered.

The roots of the music of Western civilization may be traced to a mixture of oriental elements with elements of the music of ancient Greece.

As Western (European) music developed, ingredients of non-Western cultures continued to influence it throughout the centuries, and still do. One of the consequences of these continuous influences has been that our musical instruments have undergone numerous changes, not only because of technical improvements, but especially to meet new tastes. In addition, many of the non-Western instruments not only inspired timbral changes in Western instruments, but were often added *as such* to the instrumental resources of the Western musical world.

Another way of tracing the history of percussion instruments in Western music is to trace the stylistic development of the music itself. We then find that throughout most of the 19th century and before, the primary focus in all music was on melody and harmony, while rhythm and timbre (among other elements) remained in relatively subordinate positions. Consequently, there was little need for percussion instruments, except as a means of reinforcement.

In the late 19th and early 20th centuries, however, we observe the emergence of a pronounced interest in timbral aspects of music (late Romanticism and Impressionism), and with it a considerable emphasis on percussion effects. This trend grew to unimagined prominence during the second half of the 20th century, i.e., in the music of our own era.

There are at least three reasons for this development:

1) Our present contemporary (concert) music, characterized by extremely complex rhythms and unprecedented preoccupation with timbres, requires a much stronger emphasis on percussive sounds than had ever been known in Western music. As a result, the percussion sections of our orchestras, and even of our chamber ensembles, have grown enormously in the number and variety of instruments used and in the commensurate proficiency of their performers.

2) The world-wide proliferation of jazz and its successors has brought into the Western

musical environment a large number of hitherto unknown, or at least unused, instruments and rhythms of African and Latin-American origin. Moreover, these new stylistic features of jazz made inroads into a fair amount of "serious" music, in America as well as abroad, thus adding still more new instruments to the orchestral percussion section.

3) Once the influx of African and Latin-American (Afro-American) instruments and sounds had spread and become a familiar phenomenon, instruments and playing techniques from other continents, especially from East Asia, also made their appearance, further enriching our percussion resources.

The orchestral percussion section, thus, after its modest beginnings during the Baroque and Classical periods, has by now become an absolutely essential ingredient of our era's musical sound palette. In fact, today's typical orchestral percussion section has become an entity of timbres and techniques so complete and complex that many independent, self-sufficient percussion ensembles with their own musical literature have arisen throughout the Western world.

It is in recognition of these facts and circumstances that the present book was conceived.

The authors would like to take this opportunity to give cordial thanks to all those who have so kindly assisted them in their work.

Munich 1969

Fritz Tannigel
Member of the
Bavarian Radio Orchestra
Munich

Karl Peinkofer
Member of the
Bavarian State Orchestra
Munich

TRANSLATORS' NOTE

Translating a book--any book--on percussion instruments is a difficult task because of the incredible lack of uniformity in percussion terminology. Whether it is a matter of beaters (or mallets or sticks, etc.) or drums (field drum, tenor drum, side drum, parade drum, etc.) or bells (cowbells, herd bells, animal bells, etc.), almost each choice of a specific term is a gamble. It will please some and offend others. All we can say for ourselves is that at least we have tried to be consistent.

Another problem are the measurements. Exact equivalents of the German lengths and weights would often have become so cumbersome that we considered it more practical to settle for approximations instead.

Finally there are the foreign-language titles of operas and programmatic works. We have retained the original languages except in works that seemed to us to be better, or at least equally well known by their English titles. Thus, Orff's *Der Mond* appears as *The Moon* because American performances have used an English libretto. Wagner's operas, on the other hand, appear with their original titles because they are practically always performed in German.

Our sincere thanks go out to William and Dorothea Hays, and to Lynne H. Richter, each of whom in his or her own way has been of invaluable assistance in the translation. Equally sincere thanks are due to the authors who patiently unravelled for us many knotty problems, in addition to providing a good many new entries not yet contained in the German edition.

Cornwall Bridge, Connecticut 1975   Else and Kurt Stone

NAMES OF PERCUSSION INSTRUMENTS IN ENGLISH-GERMAN-ITALIAN-FRENCH

The following table contains names of percussion instruments commonly used. For translations of frequently encountered performance instructions, such as damped, bowed, without snares, with soft mallets, with the hands, etc., pertinent dictionaries should be consulted.

The names of the instruments appear here in the order in which they are discussed in the book. For alphabetical listings see the Index.

ENGLISH	GERMAN	ITALIAN	FRENCH
Timpani Kettle Drums	die Pauken die Kesselpauken	i timpani	les timbales
Xylophone	das Xylophon	lo xilofono il silofono	le xylophone
Keyboard Xylophone	das Klaviaturxylophon	lo xilofono a tastiera il silofono a tastiera	le xylophone à clavier
Xylorimba Xylomarimba	die Xylomarimba	la xilomarimba la silomarimba	la xylomarimba la xylorimba
Marimba Marimbaphone	das Marimbaphon	il marimbafono la marimba	le marimbaphone
Bass Xylophone	das Bassxylophon	lo xilofono basso il silofono basso	le xylophone basse
Trough Xylophone	das Trogxylophon das Resonanzkastenxylophon	lo xilofono in cassetta di risonanza	le xylophone à cassette-résonance
Glockenspiel Orchestra Bells	das Glockenspiel das Stabglockenspiel	i campanelli	le glockenspiel le (jeu de) timbres
Carillon Chimes Bells	das Turmglockenspiel	il gariglione il cariglione la soneria di campane	le carillon
Keyboard Glockenspiel	das Klaviaturglockenspiel	i campanelli a tastiera	les (jeux de) timbres à clavier le glockenspiel à clavier
Celesta	die Celesta	la celesta	la célesta
Vibraphone or Vibes Vibraharp	das Vibraphon	il vibrafono	le vibraphone
Metallophone	das Metallophon	il metallofono	le métallophone
Loo-Jon	das Loo-Jon	il loo-jon	le loo-jon
Lithophone Stone Disks	das Lithophon das Steinspiel	il litofono la lastra di sasso	le lithophone
Antique Cymbals Crotales Greek Cymbals	die Zimbeln	i cimbali antichi i crotali	les cymbales antiques les crotales

ENGLISH	GERMAN	ITALIAN	FRENCH
(Domed) Gong	der (Buckel-)Gong	il gong	le gong
Steel Drum	die Trinidad Gongtrommel die Stahltrommel die Blechtrommel die Calypsotrommel	il tamburo d'acciaio	le tambour d'acier
(Church) Bell (Steeple) Bell	die (tiefe) Glocke	la campana (grave)	la (grande) cloche
Bell Plate	die Plattenglocke	la campana in lastra di metallo	la cloche en lame de métal
Tubular Bell(s) Tubular Chimes	die Röhrenglocke(n) das Röhrenglockenspiel	la campana tubolare le campane tubolari	le(s) tube(s) de cloche(s)
Tubaphone	das Tubaphon das Tubuscampanophon	il tubofono	le tubaphone
Tuned Glasses Glass Harmonica Glass Harp	das Gläserspiel die Glasharmonika die Glasharfe	i bicchieri di vetro l'armonica di vetro	les coupes de verre l'harmonica de verre les verres choqués
Tuned Bottles	das Bouteillophon das Flaschenspiel	il suono di bottiglia	le bouteillophone
Flexatone	das Flexaton	il flessatono	le flexatone
Musical Saw	die (singende) Säge die Spielsäge	la sega (cantante)	la scie musicale
Slide Whistle Lotos Flute Swanee Whistle Swanee Piccolo	die Lotosflöte die Stempelflöte die Ziehpfeife	il flauto a culisse	la jazzo-flûte le sifflet à coulisse
Piano Strings (struck)	die Klaviersaiten (geschlagen)	le corde di pianoforte (percosse) or (battute)	les cordes du piano (frappées)
Tambourin Provençal Tabor	die provenzalische Trommel	il tamburo provenzale	le tambourin (provençal)
Long Drum (with snares) (Mercenary Soldiers' Drum)	die Rührtrommel (tief) (die Landsknechtstrommel)	il tamburo basso il gran tamburo vecchio la cassa rullante	le grand tambour
Field Drum	die Rührtrommel (hoch)	il tamburo rullante con corde	la caisse roulante (avec cordes)
Parade Drum	die Basler Trommel die Paradetrommel	il tamburo di Basilea	le tambour d'empire
Military Drum Side Drum	die Militärtrommel	il tamburo militare	le tambour (militaire)
Tenor Drum (without snares)	die Wirbeltrommel die Rolltrommel die Tenortrommel die Rührtrommel ohne Saiten	il tamburo rullante senza corde	la caisse roulante or le tambour roulant (sans timbre) or (sans cordes)

ENGLISH	GERMAN	ITALIAN	FRENCH
Snare Drum	die Kleine Trommel	il tamburo piccolo il tamburo alto *or* chiara il tamburino	la caisse claire
Bass Drum Big Drum	die Grosse Trommel	la grancassa *or* gran cassa catuba	la grosse caisse
Gong Drum	die einfellige Grosse Trommel	la grancassa a una pelle	la grosse caisse à une seule peau
Frame Drum *or* Dance Drum Tambourine without jingles	die Rahmentrommel das Tamburin ohne Schellen	il tamburino senza cimbali	le tambour sur cadre
American Indian Drum	die indianische Trommel	il tamburo indiano (d'America)	le tambour indien (américain)
Boobam	das Boo-Bam die Bambustrommel	il boo-bam	le boo-bam
Tambourine	die Schellentrommel das Tamburin	il tamburello (basco) il tamburino il tamburo basco	le tambour de basque
Pasteboard Rattle	der Waldteufel	(il diavolo di bosco)* (il tamburo di frizione)	le bourdon** le tambour à friction le diable des bois*
Friction Drum String Drum Lion's Roar	der Brummtopf die Reibtrommel	il buttibu la caccavella	le tambour à friction le tambour à corde
Arabian Hand Drum Darabucca	die arabische Trommel die Darabukka *or* Derbuka	il tamburo arabo	le tambour arabe la derbouka
Bongos *or* Bongo Drums Cuban Tom-Toms	die Bongo-Trommeln die Bongos	i bongos i bonghi	les bongos
Conga (Drum) Tumbadora African Drum	die Conga(-Trommel) die Tumba	la conga la tumba	la conga la tumba
Tablas (Indian Drums)	die Tabla-Trommeln die Tablas	le tablas	les tablas
Chinese Tom-Tom (Modern) Tom-Tom Jazz Tom-Tom	das (chinesische) Tom-Tom Tom-Tom das (Jazz-) Tom-Tom	il tom tom (cinese) il tom tom	le tom-tom (chinois) le tom-tom
O-Daiko (Japanese)	das O-Daiko	l'o-daiko	l'o-daiko
Taiko (Japanese)	das Taiko	il taiko	le taiko
Timbales	die (lateinamerikanischen) Timbales	i timbales latino-americani i timpanetti	les timbales cubaines

*Translation by the authors.
**see Curt Sachs: *Reallexikon der Musikinstrumente*.

ENGLISH	GERMAN	ITALIAN	FRENCH
Triangle	der Triangel	il triangolo	le triangle
Cymbals (pair) Crash (Clash) Cymbals	die (türkischen) Becken (paarweise)	i piatti (a due) i cinelli	les cymbales (à 2)
(Suspended) Cymbal	das Becken (hängend) *or* (auf Ständer)	il piatto (sospeso)	la cymbale (suspendue)
Chinese Cymbal	das chinesische Becken	il piatto cinese	la cymbale chinoise
Hi-Hat (High-Hat) Pedal *or* Foot Cymbal(s)	die Becken mit Fussmaschine die Charleston-Becken-maschine die Fussbecken das Hi-Hat	il hi-hat i piatti a pedale	les cymbales à pédale
Tamtam (Malaysian)	das Tamtam	il tamtam	le tam-tam
Sarténes (Spanish)	die Sarténes	i sartenes	les sartènes
Cowbells (Herd Cowbells) Animal Bells Alpine Herd Bells	die Herdenglocken das Geläute die Almglocken	lo scampanellio da gregge le campane da pastore	le bruit de sonnailles des troupeaux
Cowbell (without Clapper) Cencerro	die Kuhglocke (ohne Klöppel)	il cencerro il campanaccio (di metallo)	le cencerro le bloc (de) métal
Small Bell (bowl-shaped) Dinner Bell	das Schalenglöckchen die Tischglocke	il sonaglio	la clochette la sonnette de table
Hand Bells	das Handglockenspiel	i sonagli a mano	les clochettes à mains
Bell Tree (Turkish) Crescent	der Schellenbaum	l'albero di sonagli la barra di sospensione con i sonagli	le chapeau chinois
Sanctus Bells	die Messklingeln	le campanelle da messa	les clochettes pour la messe
Sarna Bell (Elephant Bell)	die Elefantenglocke		
Alarm Bell Storm Bell Ship's Bell	die Alarmglocke die Sturmglocke die Schiffsglocke	la campana d'allarme il campanello d'allarme	le tocsin
Dobači Japanese Temple Bell	Dobači die Tempelglocke	Dobači	Dobači
Anvil (Metal Block)	der Amboss (der Metallblock)	l'incudine (il blocco di metallo)	l'enclume (le bloc de métal)
Steel Plate *or* Metal Disk	die Metallplatte	la lastra di metallo	la plaque de métal
(Automobile) Brake Drums	die Auto-brake-drums	gli auto-brake-drums	les auto-brake-drums
Switch	die Rute	la verga	la verge

ENGLISH	GERMAN	ITALIAN	FRENCH
(Wooden) Clapper Slapstick Whip	die Klapper das Klappholz die Peitsche *or* der Peitschenknall	la frusta	le fouet
Bones	die Bones die Beinklapper *or* die Knochenklapper	la taletta il suono di osso	la tablette
Board Clappers	die (amerikanische) Brettchenklapper	la tabella	la cliquette
Strung Clapper Bin-Zasara	die Reihenklapper die Bin-Sasara	la bin-sasara	la bin-sasara
Concussion Blocks Hyoshigi (Japanese)	die Gegenschlagblöcke die Hyoshigi	gli hyoshigi	les hyoshigi
Claves Cuban sticks	die Claves die Gegenschlagstäbe	i claves i legnetti	les claves
Castanets	die Kastagnetten	le castagnette le nacchere	les castagnettes
Finger Cymbals (Crotales)	die Fingerzimbeln die Krotalen	i crotali i cimbalini	les crotales
Cymbal Tongs Metal Castanets	die Gabelbecken die Metallkastagnetten	le castagnette di ferro	les castagnettes de fer

Wood Drum
Wood Block
Tubular Wood Blocks
	die Holztrommel
	der Holzblock
	die Röhrenholztrommel
		la cassa di legno
		la cassettina (di
		  legno)
		la nacchera
		  cilindrica
			le bloc de bois
			le bloc en bois
			le bloc de bois
			  (cylindrique)

Rectangular Wood Block Chinese Wood Block	die Holzblocktrommel das Holz-Tom-Tom	il (blocco di) legno il teschio cinese	le bloc chinois
Temple Block Korean Block	der Tempelblock	la campana di legno il blocco di legno coreano	le temple-bloc

Slit Drum
Jungle Wood Drum
(Small) Log Drum
	die Schlitztrommel	il tamburo di legno
		  africano
			le tambour de bois
			  (africain)

Log Drum	die Log-Drum	il log-drum	le log-drum

Wood-Plate Drum
(Wooden Tom-Tom)
	die Holzplattentrommel	il tamburo di legno
		  pelle
			le tambour en peau
			  de bois

Wooden Board	das Schlagbrett	la tavola di legno	la table de bois
Barrel Drum *or* Wooden Barrel	das Holzfass	il barile di legno	le baril de bois
Sake Barrel (Drum)	das Sakefass	il barile di sake	le baril de sake
Hammer	der Hammer(schlag)	il martello	le marteau le coup de marteau

ENGLISH	GERMAN	ITALIAN	FRENCH
Ratchet	die Ratsche die Knarre die Schnarre	la raganella	la crécelle
Guíro Gourd or Gourd Scraper Guaracha	der Guíro die Kürbisraspel	il guíro	le guíro le guitcharo
Sapo Cubana Bamboo Scraper Bambú Brasileño	das Sapo cubana die Bambusraspel	il sapo cubana	le sapo cubana
Reco-Reco Wooden Scraper or Scratcher Rasp	das Reco-Reco die Holzraspel	il reco reco il reso reso il lero lero	le reco reco la râpe de bois
Raspador Metal (Metal Scraper) Washboard	die Metallraspel das Waschbrett	la raspa di metallo la tavola da lavare	la râpe de métal
Sistrum	das Sistrum	la sistra	le sistre
Spurs	die Sporen	gli sproni or speroni	les éperons
Sleigh Bells Harness Bells Bunched Sleigh Bells Ghungrü (Indian Bell Strap)	die (Roll)schellen das Schellenbündel das indische Schellenband	la sonagliera i sonagli	les grelots
Pandereta Brasileño	die Stabpandereta	il pandereta brasiliano	la pandéréta brésilienne
Wasamba (Rattle) Quijada Jawbone (of an ass)	die Wasamba-Rassel die Quijada die Schlagrassel	la wasamba la quijada la mascella d'asino	la wasamba la quijada
Cabaza Gourd Rattle	die Cabaza die Kürbisraspel	la cabaza	la cabaza
Angklung (Javanese) (Bamboo Rattle)	das Angklung die Gitterrassel	l'angklung	l'angklung
Maracas	die Maracas die Rumbakugeln	i maracas	les maracas
Mexican Bean	die Mexican Bean or die Schotenrassel		
Metal or Tin Rattle Metal-Container Rattle	die Metallgefässrassel	il maraca di metallo	le maraca de métal
Chocallo or Chucalho Brazilian Bamboo Shaker Tubo	das Schüttelrohr das Tubo	 il bambù brasiliano il tubo	le chocalho le bambou brésilien le tubo
Sandbox	die Sandrassel	l'arenaiuolo	le sablier
Iron Chains	die Kettenrassel	la catena	la chaîne

(Suspended) Bamboo
  Chimes
Wood Wind Chimes
Japanese Wood Chimes
	die (hängenden)
	  Bambusrohre
	die Holz-Windglocken
		il bambù sospeso
		i tubi di bambù
			le bambou suspendu

ENGLISH	GERMAN	ITALIAN	FRENCH
Glass Wind Chimes	die (hängenden) Glasstäbe	le bacchette di vetro sospese	les baguettes de verre suspendues
Glass Chimes	die Glas-Windglocken		
Shell Chimes	die Muschel-Windglocken		
Foil Rattle	die Metallfolie	il foglio di metallo	le bruit de tôle
Bumbass	der Bumbass	il bumbass	basse de flandres
Bladder and Strings			
Cuckoo Call	der Kuckucksruf	il cuculo	le coucou
Nightingale	der Nachtigallenschlag	l'usignuolo	le sifflet imité du rossignol
Bird Whistle	die Vogelpfeife	gli uccelli	le sifflet d'oiseau
Coconut Shells	die Kokosnuss-Schalen	le noce di cocco	les coquilles noix de coco
Hoofbeats	das Hufgetrappel		les pas de cheval
Toy Trumpet	das Rufhorn	il grido di corno	le corne d'appel
	die Kindertrompete		
Sand Blocks	die Sandblöcke		
Sand Paper	das Sandpapier	la carta sabbiata *or* vetrata	le papier de verre
Automobile Horn	die Autohupe	il clacson	le klaxon
Taxi Horn (Motor Horn)			la trompe d'auto
Signal Whistle	die Signalpfeife	il fischio	le sifflet signal
Police Whistle	die Polizeiflöte		
Pea Whistle	die Trillerpfeife	il fischietto a pallina	le sifflet à roulette
(Mouth) Siren	die Sirenenpfeife	il fischio sirena	le sifflet sirène
(Police) Siren	die Sirene	la sirena	la sirène (aigue)
Fog Horn	das Nebelhorn	la sirena bassa	la trompe de brume
Wind Machine	die Windmaschine	la macchina dal vento	la machine à vent
	das Aeolophon		l'éoliphone
Thunder Sheet	das Donnerblech	la lastra dal tuono i tuoni	la tôle pour imiter le tonnerre
Rain Machine	die Regenmaschine	l'effetto di pioggia	le prisme de pluie
Surf Maschine	das Regenprisma		
Cannon Shot	die Kanone	il cannone	le canon
Pistol Shot	der Pistolenschuss	la pistolettata	le coup de pistolet
	der Revolver	la rivoltella	le revolver
Pop Gun	der Flaschenkorkenknall	stappare la bottiglia	le coup de bouchon
Typewriter	die Schreibmaschine	la macchina da scrivere	la machine à écrire

Common Abbreviations and Symbols of Percussion Instruments

Name of Instrument	Abbreviation	Symbol
Timpani	Timp.	
Xylophone	Xyl.	
Keyboard Xylophone	Kbd. Xyl.	
Marimba	Mar.	
Bass Xylophone	Bass Xyl.	
Tenor Xylophone	Ten. Xyl.	
Glockenspiel	Glsp.	
Keyboard Glockenspiel	Kbd. Glsp.	
Celesta	Cel.	
Vibraphone	Vibes	
Metallophone (Vibraphone with motor off)	Metalloph. (Vibes w. motor off)	
Crotales (Antique Cymbals)	Crot. (Ant. Cymb.)	
Gong	Gong	
Large Bell(s)	Bell(s)	
Bell Plate(s)	Bell Pl.	
Tubular Chimes	Chimes	
Tubaphone	Tubaph.	
Musical Glasses	Mus. Gl.	
Flexatone	Flex.	
Musical Saw	Mus. Saw	
Slide Whistle	Sl. Wh.	
Long Drum	L. Dr.	
Tambourin Provençal	Tamb. Prov.	
Military Drum	Milit. Dr.	

Tenor Drum	Ten. Dr.	
Snare Drum	S. D.	
Bass Drum	B. D.	
Tambourine	Tamb.	
Bongo	Bongo	
Conga	Conga	
Chinese Tom-Toms	Chin. Tom-T.	
Modern Tom-Toms	Tom-T. or T.-T.	
Timbales	Timb.	
Triangle	Trgl.	
[Clash] Cymbals	Cymb.	
Suspended Cymbals	S. Cymb.	
Hi-Hat	Hi-Hat	
Chinese Cymbal	Chin. Cymb.	
Tamtam	Tamt.	
Cowbells, Herd Bells, *Almglocken*	Cowb., Herd B.	
Metal Block	Met. Bl.	
Board Clapper	Bd. Clp.	
Claves	Clav.	
Castanets, Handle Castanets	Cast., Handle Cast.	
Cymbal Tongs	Cymb. Tongs	
Wood Block, Slit Drum	W. B.	
Temple Block	T. B.	
Ratchet	Ratch.	
Guíro	Guíro	
Jingles, Sleigh Bells	Jingles	
Maracas	Marac.	

TABLE OF BEATERS, WITH ILLUSTRATIONS

Size, Character, and Illustrations of Beaters with their Common and Less Common Uses.

In addition to the sounding parts of the instruments themselves, the beaters, i.e., the means by which these parts are made to sound, are of considerable timbral importance to a majority of percussion instruments.

The independent development and proliferation of percussion beaters is particularly evident in today's availability of a large number of beaters that can be used for playing several different instruments instead of being integral parts of specific instruments only. We speak here of the beaters as such, not as components of any particular percussion instruments.

The various types of beaters are classified into the following five groups according to their construction and names:

1. Beaters:
   Beaters having as basic characteristics suitably long handles of wood or cane with ball-shaped, eliptical, or disk-shaped heads of various materials possessing different degrees of softness or hardness. Heads also may be wrapped, covered, or padded.

2. Hammers or Mallets:
   Hammers or *Mallets* differing from beaters by having a hammer-like beating part of wood, horn, metal, or synthetic material, any of which may or may not be covered or padded.

3a. Sticks:
   Sticks tapered towards their points and usually having small beater heads.*

3b. Rods:
   Rods, cylindrical, of metal or wood in various lengths and thicknesses.

4. Metal Clappers:
   Metal Clappers similar to clappers in cast bells.

5. Switches and Brushes:
   Switches and *Brushes* characterized by a flexible, resilient beating part.

---

*Transl. note: The reader should not be confused by the fact that in American usage the term "stick" is applied rather loosely, as in the case of "drum stick." We speak of side drum "sticks," and correctly so, but we also refer to bass drum and timpani "sticks" although strictly speaking they are beaters or mallets.

Illustration	Name Material (Measurements)	Instruments for which the respective beaters are commonly used -- Common --	Other instruments playable with the respective beaters, though only if specifically indicated -- Not Common --
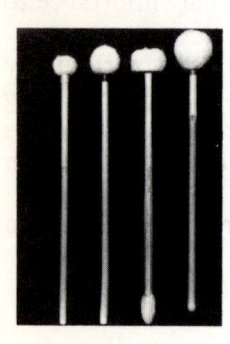	Timpani Beaters: Soft-felt beaters or pairs of beaters with cores of different sizes and degrees of hardness, covered with soft felt of various degrees of thickness and density. Diam. of head ca. 2.5 - 4.5 cm Length of handle ca. 30 - 35 cm	Timpani Bass Drum (rolls) Frame Drum Chinese Tom-Tom Loo-jon	Vibraphone Metallophone Marimbaphone Bass Xylophone Piano Strings Long Drum without snares Tenor Drum without snares Snare Drum without snares Bass Drum Boobam Bongo Drum Conga Drum Modern Tom-Toms Timbales Cymbals Small Tamtam Animal Bells mounted on stand
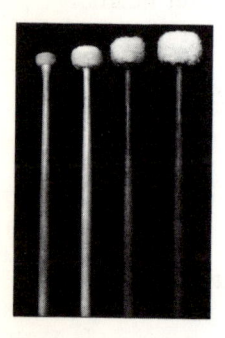	Beaters with heads consisting of several flannel disks. Diam. of head ca. 2.5 - 5 cm Length of handle ca. 30 - 32 cm Sponge Beaters (now generally replaced by soft-felt beaters)	Timpani	as above
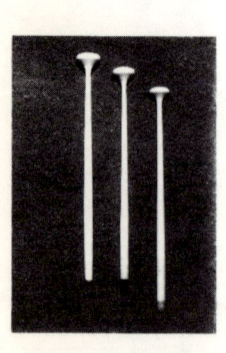	Wooden Timpani Beaters: Heads of hardwood, usually wound with straps of roughened leather, or with a leather band around the edge of the head. Diam. of head ca. 2.5 - 3.3 cm Length of handle ca. 30 - 32 cm	Timpani (in Baroque music)	Timpani (if wooden mallets are indicated) Metallophone (hard) Vibraphone (hard)

Illustration	Name Material (Measurements)	Instruments for which the respective beaters are commonly used -- Common --	Other instruments playable with the respective beaters, though only if specifically indicated -- Not Common --

	Hard-Felt Beaters:
	Heads of hard felt.
	Diam. of head
	ca. 2 - 5 cm
	Length of handle
	ca. 30 - 35 cm
		Small Tamtams
		Tamtam (rolls)
		Suspended Cymbals
		  (rolls)
		Slit Drums
			Timpani
			Xylomarimba
			Marimbaphone
			Trough Xylophone
			Vibraphone
			Metallophone
			Piano Strings
			Bass Drum
			Drums without snares
			Tambourine
			  mounted on stand
			Hand Drums
			Tom-Toms
			Timbales
			Suspended Cymbals
			  (individual beats)
			Herd Bells (Almglocken)
			  mounted on stand
			Wood Blocks

	Hands:
	con la (or *colla*)
	mano (with the hand)
		Hand Drums
		  Arabian Hand
		    Drums
		      (Darabuccas)
		  Bongo Drums
		  Conga Drums
		  Tablas
		  Tambourine
		  Glass Harp
			Timpani
			Drums
			Tom-Toms
			Tamtam *(ppp)*
			Cymbal *(ppp)*

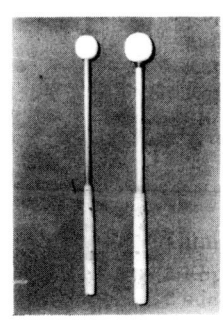

Illustration	Name Material (Measurements)	Instruments for which the respective beaters are commonly used -- Common --	Other instruments playable with the respective beaters, though only if specifically indicated – Not Common --
1 2 3	Xylophone Mallets: 1 Eliptical heads of wood or synthetics; 2 As above, covered with thin leather. Diam. of head ca. 2.2 - 2.5 cm Length of head ca. 3 - 3.2 cm Length of handle ca. 27.5 - 29 cm	Xylophone	Bar Instruments (upper range) Lithophone *(p)* Sets of Tuned Glass Vessels Tubaphone Tuned Bottles Piano Strings Skin Membranophones Wood Blocks Cymbals Herd Bells (Almglocken) mounted on stand
	Bass Xylophone Mallets: 3 Head of wood or synthetics, covered with soft felt. Diam. of head ca. 5 cm Length of handle ca. 30 - 34 cm	Bass Xylophone	Marimbaphone Vibraphone Metallophone

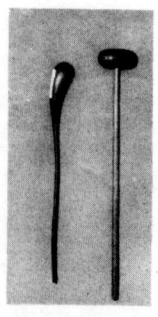

Illustration	Name	Common	Not Common
1 2	1 Spoon Beater (sometimes padded with leather). Total length ca. 23 - 24 cm	Four-row Xylophone Four-row Tubaphone	
	2 Small Wooden Hammer Diam. of head ca. 2 cm Length of head ca. 4 cm Length of handle ca. 26 cm	Two-row Tubaphone	Glockenspiel of light metal

Illustration	Name Material (Measurements)	Instruments for which the respective beaters are commonly used -- Common --	Other instruments playable with the respective beaters, though only if specifically indicated -- Not Common --
1 2 3 4	Glockenspiel Beaters: 1 Small Brass hammers with beater tips of buffalo horn or synthetics. Diam. of head ca. 1.5 - 1.7 cm Length of head ca. 4 cm Length of handle ca. 24 - 28 cm	Glockenspiel Lithophone (f) Wood Blocks Temple Blocks	
	2 Round plastic heads. Diam. of head ca. 2.4 cm Length of handle ca. 26 cm		
	3 Small wooden hammer. Diam. of head ca. 1.6 cm Length of head ca. 4 cm. Length of handle 25 cm	Glockenspiel of light metal	
	4 Mallets with metal heads. Diam. of head ca. 1.3 - 1.8 cm Length of handle 26 cm	Glockenspiel (substituting for keyboard glockenspiel)	Vibraphone Lithophone Tubular Chimes Small Cast Bells Suspended Cymbals Crotales

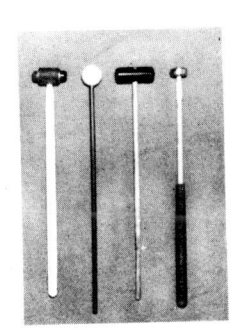

Illustration	Name / Material / (Measurements)	Instruments for which the respective beaters are commonly used -- Common --	Other instruments playable with the respective beaters, though only if specifically indicated -- Not Common --
1 2	**Hammers for Tubular Chimes:** Hammers of wood or synthetics. 1 partly padded with rawhide;	Tubular Chimes	
	2 partly padded with felt. Diam. of head ca. 3 - 4.5 cm Length of head ca. 8 - 10 cm Length of handle 25 - 30 cm	Tubular Chimes	
1 2 3	**Vibraphone Mallets:** 1 Heads of rubber;	Vibraphone	Marimbaphone
	2 Same as 1 but wound with wool yarn in 3-4 different degrees of thickness. Diam. of head ca. 2.8 - 3.3 cm Length of head ca. 3.5 - 4.3 cm Length of handle ca. 31 - 35 cm	Metallophone Loo-jon	Xylorimba Bass Xylophone Metallophone Cymbals (soft) Small Tamtam Animal Bells (soft) mounted on stand Log Drum (soft)
	3 Heads of hard rubber or synthetics. Diam. of head ca. 2.5 cm Width of head ca. 2 cm Length of handle ca. 31 - 35 cm	Vibraphone (hard)	

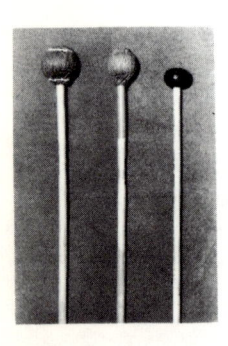

Illustration	Name Material (Measurements)	Instruments for which the respective beaters are commonly used -- Common --	Other instruments playable with the respective beaters, though only if specifically indicated -- Not Common --
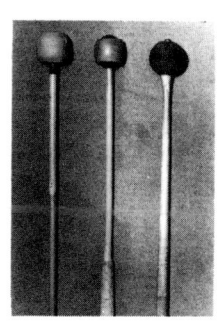 1 2 3	Rubber Mallets: 1 Heads of wood or 2 Heads of synthetics, covered with rubber tubing in different degrees of thickness. Diam. of head ca. 2.5 - 3.3 cm Length of handle ca. 28 - 35 cm	Marimbaphone Xylorimba Trough Xylophone Metallophone Vibraphone (in the (orchestra) Animal Bells mounted on stand	Xylophone Piano Strings Crotales Suspended Cymbals Wood Blocks Tambourine mounted on stand
	Mallets with Solid-Rubber Heads: 3 (sometimes covered with thin, soft felt). Diam. of head ca. 3.4 - 4 cm Length of handle ca. 30 - 33 cm	Bass Xylophone *(f)* Bass Metallophone Log Drum	
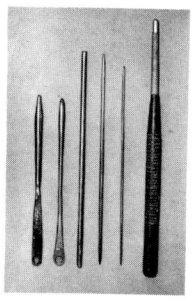 1a b c d e 2	Metal Rods: 1 a) to e) in different sizes and thicknesses. Diam. of rod ca. 2 - 6 mm Length of rod ca. 16 - 21 cm	Triangle	Glockenspiel Vibraphone Loo-jon Piano Strings Single Crotales Cymbals Tamtam Animal Bells mounted on stand Metal Block Scrapers
	2 Metal Rod, with cloth or leather-wound grip. Total length 25 cm	Triangle (soft)	

Illustration	Name Material (Measurements)	Instruments for which the respective beaters are commonly used -- Common --	Other instruments playable with the respective beaters, though only if specifically indicated – Not Common --
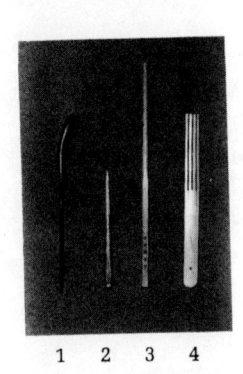 1 2 3 4	1, 2, 3: Small wooden or plastic sticks for beating or scraping. 4: Cane scraper (bamboo or rattan). Length ca. 16 - 23 cm	3 Guíro 2, 3, 4 Reco-Reco 2, 3, 4 Sapo Cubana	1 Triangle

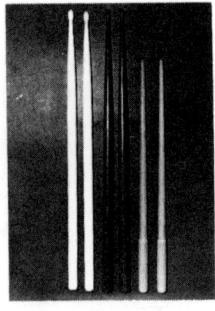 1 2 3	Drum Sticks:
	1 Wooden
	or
	2 Plastic sticks.
	Diam. of head ca. 6 - 20 mm
	Total length ca. 32 - 39 cm
		Long Drum
		Tambourin Provençal
		Tenor Drum
		Parade Drum
		  (*Basler Trommel*)
		Military Drum
		Snare Drums
		Modern Tom-Toms
			Timpani
			Bass Drum
			Tambourine
			  mounted on stand
			Boobam
			Suspended Cymbals
			Metal Block
			Wood Blocks
			Tubular Chimes

	3 Sticks for Timbales: Small, light, wooden sticks. Length ca. 30 - 36 cm	Timbales	Skin instruments without snares
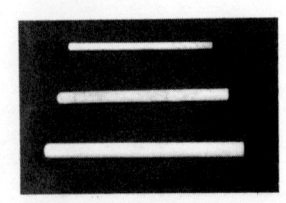	Round Wooden Sticks. Diam. of stick ca. 1 - 3 cm Length ca. 30 - 43 cm	Taiko Sake Barrel Slit Drum (hard) Wood Plate	Skin instruments without snares

Illustration	Name Material (Measurements)	Instruments for which the respective beaters are commonly used -- Common --	Other instruments playable with the respective beaters, though only if specifically indicated -- Not Common --
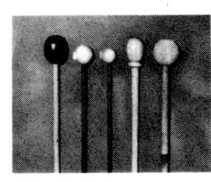 1 2a b 3 4	**Wooden Mallets:** 1 Wooden or plastic heads covered with thin leather. Diam. of head ca. 2.8 - 3 cm Length of handle ca. 31 cm	Suspended Cymbal	
	2a) b) Wooden-headed mallet. Diam. of head ca. 2.3 cm and smaller Length of handle ca. 26 cm	Tuned Glass Vessels	Tubular Chimes Piano Strings Skin instruments without snares Cymbals Cowbell Wood Plate
	3 Mallet with elongated wooden head. Diam. of head ca. 2 cm Length of handle ca. 30 cm	*Tambourin Provençal*	
	4 Mallet with cork head. Diam. of head ca. 2.5 - 3.5 cm Length of handle ca. 30 - 35 cm		Piano Strings Skin instruments without snares
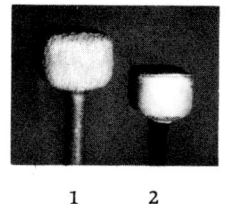 1 2	**Bass Drum Mallets:** 1 Large-headed wooden mallet covered with lambskin or soft felt. Diam. of head ca. 8 - 9 cm Length of handle ca. 30 cm	Bass Drum	Tamtam Large Suspended Cymbal Large Tom-Tom Sound Board of Concert Grand Body of Harp
	2 Mailloche (older type of mallet, used in military music) with leather-covered wooden head. Diam. of head ca. 5- 7 cm Length of handle ca. 24 - 28 cm		

Illustration	Name Material (Measurements)	Instruments for which the respective beaters are commonly used -- Common --	Other instruments playable with the respective beaters, though only if specifically indicated -- Not Common --
1 2	Tamtam Mallets: 1 Mallet with large, hard-felt head. Diam. of head ca. 6 - 10 cm Length of handle ca. 30 - 34 cm 2 Disk-shaped mallet with heavy wooden or metal core covered with leather or felt. Diam. of head ca. 12 - 15 cm Length of handle ca. 31 cm	Tamtam	Gong Bell Plates
1 2	Mallet for Domed Gongs: 1 With round head or 2 with heavy, hammer-like head of wood, plastic, or metal, thickly padded with felt. Diam. of round head ca. 13 cm Diam. of hammer head ca. 5 - 7 cm Length of hammer head 12 - 15 cm Length of handle ca. 28 - 34 cm	Gong	Large Bell Plates Large Tamtam
	Mallets for Bell Plates: Large, heavy wooden hammer, or metal head padded with felt. Length of head ca. 19 - 27 cm Length of handle ca. 31 - 34 cm Weight ca. 400-1400 grams	Bell Plates	Gong

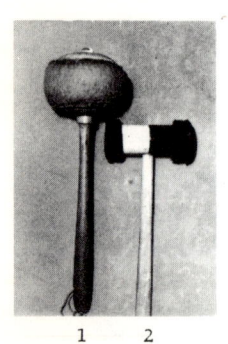

Illustration	Name Material (Measurements)	Instruments for which the respective beaters are commonly used -- Common --	Other instruments playable with the respective beaters, though only if specifically indicated -- Not Common --
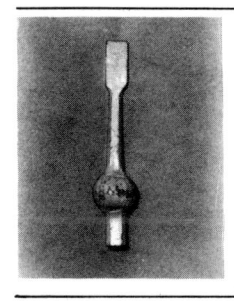	Metal Clapper. Length ca. 20 - 25 cm Weight (according to size of bell) up to 1.5 kg	Cast Bells	
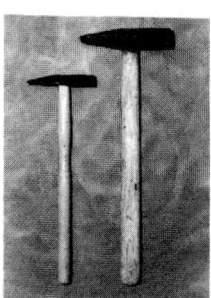	Hammers: Metal hammers, light to medium heavy. Diam. of head ca. 1.3 - 2.8 cm Length of head ca. 8 - 12 cm Length of handle ca. 24 - 27 cm	Anvil Metal Plates	Tubular Chimes Bronze Bells
	Small hardwood hammer, sometimes padded with leather. Length of head ca. 13 cm Length of handle ca. 28 cm		Piano Strings

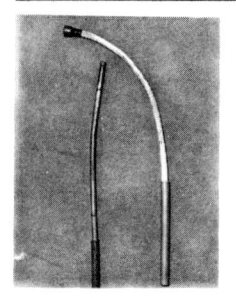	Switches:
	1 Cane switch.
	  Diam. ca. 9 mm
	  Length ca. 38 cm
			Skin of Bass Drum

	2 Janissary switch.
	  Diam. ca. 9 mm
	  Length ca. 50 cm
			Skin of Bass Drum

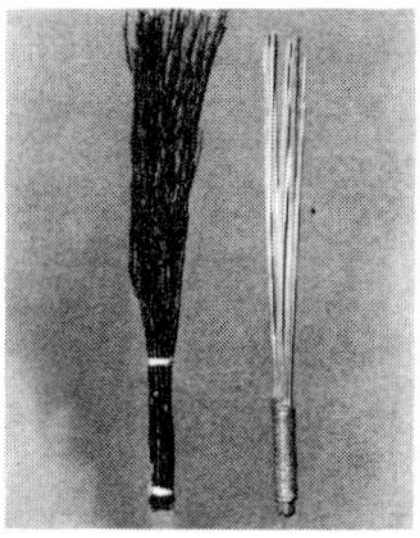	3 Birch brush (brush of twigs). Length ca. 60 cm	Shell of Bass Drum	Skin of Bass Drum
	4 Brush of split bamboo. Length ca. 60 cm	Shell of Bass Drum	Skin of Bass Drum

Illustration	Name Material (Measurements)	Instruments for which the respective beaters are commonly used -- Common --	Other instruments playable with the respective beaters, though only if specifically indicated -- Not Common --
1 2	Brushes: 1 Brush of sheet-metal strips (lamellae) with handle. Total length ca. 40 cm		Tamtam Cymbals Timpani Bass Drum Tom-Toms
	2 Wire Brush, i.e., brush of thin, flexible steel wires gathered in the handle. Total length ca. 32 cm		Timpani Piano Strings Drums Suspended Cymbals Tamtam

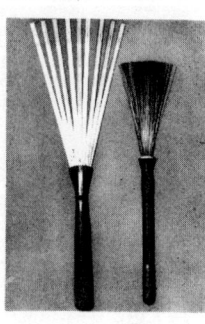

INTRODUCTION

Musical instruments generally are classified into five principal groups:

Group I Idiophones

The self-sounding instruments: instruments whose sound comes from their own material without assistance from other materials such as membranes or strings.

By taking into consideration the means of sound production, this principal group, which includes a large number of percussion instruments, may be subdivided as follows:

- A. Idiophones struck directly:
  1. Idiophones struck together (clappers, pairs of cymbals).
  2. Idiophones struck singly (wooden-bar instruments such as xylophones; metal-bar instruments such as marimbas; bells, gongs, triangles, single cymbals, wood blocks).
- B. Idiophones struck indirectly:
  1. Shaken idiophones (rattles).
  2. Scraped idiophones (ratchets, rasps).
- C. Bowed or stroked idiophones (glass harmonica, musical saw).
- D. Plucked idiophones (Sansa, Marimbula, Jew's-Harp).

Group II Membranophones

Sound is produced by stretched membranes vibrating transversely. Instruments are sounded by striking (timpani, drums), by friction (friction or string drums), or by being hummed into (mirliton or kazoo).

Group III Chordophones

Included here are all instruments whose principal means of sound production comes from strings under tension (stringed instruments--plucked or bowed--and keyboard string instruments).

Group IV Aerophones

Sound is produced by vibrating columns of air (wind instruments).

Group V Electrophones

Into this group fall instruments using electronic means of amplification (electric guitar, electric bass, electric chimes) as well as purely electronic instruments (*Trautonium, ondes Martenot,* synthesizers).

General Observations

In practice, percussion instruments are traditionally divided into two principal groups. The first includes those instruments whose notation always requires a fixed pitch; the second includes those either not requiring fixed pitches or, according to the wishes of the composer, both fixed and unfixed pitches.

Thus, the first group is called "instruments with definite pitch;" the second group, "instruments with indefinite pitch," although these designations do not always conform to the actual facts.

For example, some of the instruments found in a percussion section, such as bird calls and the wind machine, are not really instruments of percussion in its literal meaning. They are included here, however, because of their traditional association with true percussion instruments.

A percussionist, thus, is also expected to blow the slide whistle, play the glass harmonica, or take on any other contraptions that produce sounds or noises required for the compositions to be performed.

Precise, unambiguous terminology is essential for the designation of those percussion instruments whose original names have assumed new meanings in the course of time.

Frequently the confusion is compounded by composers inventing their own terminology or choosing wrong designations for certain instruments.

In many cases it is no longer possible to correct such instances in a strictly musicological sense since certain misnomers have, over the years, become accepted here and there.

Among such misnomers falls, for example, the tamtam (Malaysian-African *tammittam* meaning "drum") which we, in our musical world, consider to be a gong with indefinite pitch, while "gong" generally is considered by us to be an instrument with definite pitch (domed gong). Further adding to the confusion is the fact that the small, high-sounding tamtam is sometimes called gong in order to differentiate it from the large tamtam.

An especially graphic example is the name *tambourin* which for some reason is widely used as the name for the tambourine. Only in French-speaking areas is *tambourin* used to designate the cylindrical long drum of the Provençals, while the tambourine there is called *tambour de basque*.

In Italian, the diminution of *tamburo* is *tamburino*, which explains why certain Italian scores of older vintage, to avoid confusion, use *tamburo piccolo* for the small drum. Often, the proper instrument can only be determined by examining the entire score.

In older music various names were used which later were replaced by new ones, often brought about by a change in the construction of the instrument in question. For example, *sistro* (Italian) was changed to *campanelli; jeux de timbres* (French) to *glockenspiel;* resonaphone (English) to marimba.

In some cases it is impossible to ascertain precisely the proper choice of instrument--much is open to discussion and must be left to the musical intuition of the performer.

The circular skins (membranes) of the membranophones generally produce only very tightly knit, dissonant vibration patterns resulting in noise-like sounds which are more or less blurred in pitch. Even so, it is quite easy, and sometimes also quite necessary, to bring most of the tunable membranophones to at least an approximation of definite pitch (more about this further on). The only membranophone among all percussion instruments that is notated with fixed pitches is the timpano or kettle drum. Its kettle, designed for controlled resonance, its precise tuning mechanism, the careful choice of its skin, and the use by the player of the most effective beating spot all help to achieve a pure-pitched tone.

Bronze bells, small bowl-shaped bells *(Schalenglöckchen),* anvil, metal block, and herd-cowbells *(Almglocken)* are usually classified as percussion instruments with indefinite pitch since they frequently produce a predominantly noise-like sound, and also because the listener tends to identify them with their usual non-musical functions. Cowbells, for example, are treated as percussion instruments with indefinite pitch although some cowbells have quite clear pitches when played with soft beaters. Therefore, in order not to produce the wrong kind of sound in certain compositions, it is advisable to select suitably pitched bells, even though no pitches are notated. In other words, here, too, exceptions have to be taken into account.

Sleigh bells, classified as rattle instruments, can also be quite precise in sound if the bells are sorted according to pitch instead of being thrown together indiscriminately as is usually the case.

Among the wood blocks, the temple blocks, although designed to produce fairly specific pitches, are too imprecise and blurred to make pitch notation feasible.

The Classical era did not as a rule specify the use of beaters; the means of playing were always only those typical for the instrument in question. Berlioz was the first to tell the performer specifically which beaters to use (when he deemed it necessary): for example, wooden or sponge beaters for timpani and cymbals, or perhaps timpani beaters for the bass drum. This practice gained adherents and eventually led to giving specific names to different beaters. Moreover, with the growing number of instruments a similarly growing variety of beaters was developed, each designed for a specific percussion instrument.

The choice of material, form, size, and weight of percussion beaters depends upon requirements dictated by the nature of the instrument involved, the desired volume of sound, the intended sound quality, and the necessary techniques of playing. All effort should be made, however, to "dematerialize" the sound of beaters as much as possible, i.e., to eliminate non-musical noises, especially for instruments with wooden or metal bars (such as xylophones and marimbas), and for bells, gongs, cymbals, and triangles, or any other vibrating instruments consisting of hard material.

In compositions requiring a large number of percussion instruments, changes of beaters often must be made so quickly that written instructions cannot be read easily. Instead, special signs and symbols have proved useful, which should be listed in a table at the beginning of a pertinent composition.

Examples -- Henze: *Elegy* (Mus. Ex. 1), *Antifone* (Mus. Ex. 3a).

If a change of beaters is not possible because of the rapid succession of instruments to be played, the question invariably arises as to the appropriate choice of beaters which will work on all the instruments involved. This is especially important in percussion solos, and it is often left to the ingenuity of the performer to find just the right beaters--even to make them himself if need be.

Examples -- Antoniou: *Epilog* (Mus. Ex. 4).

The table on page 19 shows which beaters may be used for specific percussion instruments.

In addition to the use of unusual kinds of beaters and equally unusual beating spots, instructions for specific ways of beating have also increased, especially, for example, in the case of drums beaten by hand. Here, again, the use of symbols is helpful.

Many percussion instruments often are referred to as "dry" instruments because they produce very short, dry sounds (xylophones, high drums, etc.). In writing for these instruments the actual brevity of their sounds is usually disregarded to facilitate reading. Conversely, percussion instruments capable of prolonged ringing (cymbals, tamtams, etc.) are often notated with shorter note-values than the actual duration of their sounds calls for in given situations, such as in orchestral tutti places. The players must be careful to determine the appropriate durations of the reverbarations in such instances and not damp too soon (if at all!) any instruments capable of sustained sound.

The notation for instruments with indefinite pitch is tied neither to a key signature nor to a specific staff system. For ease in reading, the notation should if at all possible conform to the order of the approximate pitches of the instruments indicated.

Example -- Berio: *Circles* (Mus. Ex. 2).

On the five-line staff, note-heads for traditional percussion instruments are usually placed as follows: triangle, tambourine, castanets, etc., are placed on, above, or between the two upper lines; snare drums on the third line; drums without snares on the second lowest line; cymbals between the second lowest and third lines; the bass drum on the lowest line; and the tamtam below the lowest line. In works calling for a percussion section of several players the percussion parts should be notated in the form of a condensed score. Such scoring makes it possible to effect quick changes in the division of the instruments among the performers, as well as each performer's changes from instrument to instrument, while separate parts for each instrument often necessitate cumbersome set-ups and arrangements. If at all feasible, staves for instruments with definite pitch should be placed above those for instruments with indefinite pitch.

Example -- Henze: *Antifone* (Mus. Ex. 3b).

Compositions in which the performer has been given a large number of instruments to handle should, for the sake of legibility, not contain a staff system too extensive nor too widely spread apart.

Example -- Berio: *Circles* (Mus. Ex. 2).

A system of notation presenting a visual appearance too far removed from what is customary, using numerous invented signs, and concerned mostly with presenting an interesting graphic picture, forces the performer to write out his own legible version if he does not want to spend an unreasonable amount of time deciphering and learning his part.

Written instructions regarding dynamics, size, construction of instruments, playing techniques, and types of beaters have come into use in an attempt to meet the heightened requirements of performance. In general it is very difficult to set hard and fast standards because many things must be considered. Among the problems which thus impose themselves upon the percussion section are: the size of the instruments involved, the acoustics of the hall, the purpose of the musical event, the composer's as well as the conductor's concepts of sound, the number of players and their proficiency, and so forth.

It must be noted, furthermore, that an exact mental image cannot be formed purely from a description of sounds--this can be worked out only at the instrument itself. Today the leading music schools nearly everywhere have increased their collections of percussion instruments and brought them to such a high standard that anyone seriously interested in the field of percussion is able to study it.

Instruments with Definite Pitch

Timpani or Kettle Drums

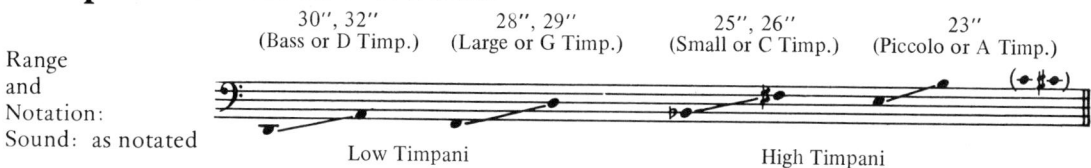

Range and Notation:
Sound: as notated

30", 32" (Bass or D Timp.)   28", 29" (Large or G Timp.)   25", 26" (Small or C Timp.)   23" (Piccolo or A Timp.)

Low Timpani   High Timpani

Common beaters: timpani beaters (different sizes of beaters with heads of soft felt or flannel)

Less common: wooden beaters (wooden heads covered with leather)
drum sticks
wire brushes
by hand (*con la* or *colla mano*)

History. The membranophones called timpani are of ancient Asiatic origin. The first timpani must have been made of clay and later of wood, covered with skins tied by ropes. Throughout the Orient, and spreading as far as India, timpani were usually used in pairs, tuned a fourth or fifth apart, to accompany straight trumpets and buysines.

In Europe--at first in Spain and southern Italy--very small timpani of Arabic origin appeared during the crusades and into the 13th century. The player carried them either by handles or attached to his belt in pairs, and they are still used in this way as drum-like instruments in the Islamic world.

The first large timpani of the modern Occidental type reached western Europe by way of Hungary and Poland in the middle of the 15th century. Closely associated with trumpets, they established themselves firmly in the musical life of the Renaissance courts. Gradually they became the dominant skin-membrane instruments everywhere, reaching the peak of their usefulness and importance in the large orchestras of the Classical and Romantic periods.

Construction, Pitch Range, and Notation. The truncated conical kettle, open at the top, is nowadays usually made of copper sheeting. The open top is covered with skin wound over a hoop so that its tension--and therefore its tuning--can be regulated mechanically. At the bottom of the kettle is a smaller round opening providing for equalization of air pressure during playing.

Especially prepared, tanned calf skin is preferable over all other animal skins for the batter head. A strip about the width of a man's hand, called a "backbone," runs across the center of the skin, constituting a natural thickening.

For some years now, batter heads of synthetic material have been used on timpani. These so-called plastic heads are bonded onto the hoop and have the advantage of being much less sensitive to climatic conditions, nor do they require the special concern for the "backbone," since plastic heads do not have any. It is not easy, however, to convert instruments covered with calf skin to plastic, because a plastic head requires a kettle with a specially built rim.

Orchestras have always used at least two timpani: low and high. Today there usually are at least two low and two high drums at the timpanist's disposal, to which more may be added in special cases. The pitch of a normal pair of timpani, i.e., a G drum (28" or 29") and a C drum (25" or 26"), ranges from about F to f-sharp. For higher pitches, up to about b, a specially built drum is used--the so-called high A drum or piccolo timpano (23"). Its smaller diameter and special mechanism make possible a greater degree of skin tension.

Examples for the use of the A drum -- Stravinsky: *Les noces, Le Sacre du printemps;*

Piston: Violin Concerto; Orff: *Die Bernauerin, Antigonae, Trionfi* (Mus. Ex. 15), *Oedipus;* Hartmann: 7th Symphony (Mus. Ex. 11).

It is difficult to go beyond pitches above b, even on the specially designed piccolo timpani. For such pitches small, one-headed drums such as bongos are best suited.

Examples for the use of timpani above b -- Britten's ballet *The Prince of the Pagodes* (c-sharp^1 - d^1); Milhaud's *La création du monde* (d^1 - f-sharp^1 -- Mus. Ex. 12)

The so-called D or bass timpano (30"-32") produces low pitches down to about D. Such a large drum needs a "well-rested" head because skin that has been frequently stretched to its full limit becomes impure in the lower pitches. Similarly, timpani that have been used for high pitches should not be tuned below d if a clear pitch is desired.

The nomenclature "G drum" and "C drum" goes back to the time before Beethoven when timpani were always notated G and c (dominant and tonic), while the actual ("concert") pitch--for example, A and d--was given at the beginning of the work, just as with transposed instruments.

Types of Timpani. Timpani are classified according to their tuning devices. There are four basic types. First, the hand-screw timpani, designed in the 16th century and tuned by turning six or eight screws or even more, depending on the design. The screws were turned either with tuning keys or with wing nuts. Composers were forced to take this time-consuming tuning operation into account. For example, in Verdi's compositions up to 1874, tunings are found in the timpani parts which do not always conform to the key signature of the composition, solely because proper retuning could not be accomplished in the time available.

Screw Timpano

The development of compositional technique toward progressive chromaticism virtually demanded the construction of timpani with centralized tuning. G. Kramer, royal court timpanist in Munich, was the first to invent a device to operate all the tuning screws at once (1812). Numerous types of machine timpani have since been developed, of which the lever timpani are the most widespread. They are still used in smaller orchestras and as supplementary drums in larger ones. The lever timpani have all the tuning screws combined in a central thread so that only a main screw needs to be manipulated, either with a master lever or with a crank. Within the limits of the possible pitch range of the instrument any desired changes may thus be obtained by operating only one device.

Lever Timpano

The rotary-tuned timpani represent another system, first built in 1821 by J. C. N. Stumpff in Amsterdam. In this type the kettle is mounted on a stand equipped with a central spindle which, as the entire kettle is rotated, functions as a main tuning screw. A variety of tunings are easily accomplished but there is the disadvantage that the beating spot keeps changing as the kettle is rotated. It is therefore impossible to avoid playing occasionally on the less desirable beating spots such as the "backbone" which vibrates poorly.

Rotary-Tuned Timpano

The pedal timpani, invented by Pittrich in 1872 and continuously improved ever since, must be considered the best solution to date because it permits a relatively quick tuning by means of a pedal operated by pressure of the timpanist's foot. This makes it possible to change the tuning not only during short rests but also while playing. The desired pitch can be read from a gauge coordinated with the pedal. The percussion sections of present-day orchestras are usually equipped with modern timpani of this type.

Pedal Timpani

It is difficult, however, to achieve precise tunings with the pedal because of the different degrees of flexibility of the skins and the climatic influences upon them: the wider the required interval of retuning, the greater the difficulty. The timpanist is forced, therefore, to recheck the tuning again and again by tapping his finger softly on the drum head--insofar as rest-counting will permit.

For retuning a set of more than two timpani it is essential to estimate the minimum time needed for the transfer of the foot from pedal to pedal, and for the reading of the pitch gauge of each drum.

Altering the tuning immediately after striking produces a change in the reverberations equal to a glissando. One way of doing this is first to strike the initial, notated pitch, and thereafter to press down the pedal until the second (final) notated pitch has been reached. This rather delicate effect is only practical in solo playing; in an orchestral context it is not audible. A glissando produced in this manner, but progressing from a high pitch to a low one, is only very faintly perceptible and therefore even less useful. A second type of glissando may be produced while rolling and is effective going either from low pitch to high or *vice versa,* and at any dynamic level.

Examples for timpano glissandi -- Bartók: Music for Strings, Percussion, and Celesta, Violin Concerto, Sonata for Two Pianos and Percussion; Egk: *Die chinesische Nachtigall;* Morton Gould: *Latin-American Symphonette;* Henze: *Elegy* (Mus. Ex. 8), *Il re cervo* (Mus. Ex. 9); Kotoński: *Musique en relief* (Mus. Ex. 77).

Sound Factors. The fullness and purity of the sound of a kettle drum depend chiefly upon a select, even-textured calf skin tuned by the six or more tuning screws with which each drum is equipped. Even the most minute unevenness in the sound of the skin must be eliminated through fine-tuning, which is difficult and requires careful and tedious listening. This fine-tuning operation must be repeated at intervals, depending on how much the instruments are used. Naturally, climatic conditions also play a large part as far as sound is concerned: dry heat or cold cause the skin to contract and will impair both sound and tuning, while high humidity (as for example in full concert halls*) slackens the skins excessively.

Trans. note: Not to mention tropical climate.

Another important factor affecting sound is the choice of the so-called beating spot. Generally this spot lies about a hand's width from the rim and equidistant from the end points of the "backbone" of the skin. Adherence to the exact position of the beating spot limits the imprecision in pitch caused by dissonant sound components (partials), especially in the lower register. The closer to the center the head is struck, the more imprecise the pitch; struck in the exact center of the head, timpani become muffled.

The unique quality of the clear, vibrant sound of the timpani -- possessed by no other skin membranophone--is the result of the impact sound as well as the subsequent reverberation. The duration of the reverberation decreases in direct proportion to the degree of increased tension of the drum head, i.e., of the height of the pitch.

The instruction *timpani coperti* originally meant to cover the skin with a piece of cloth before playing. Nowadays a felt disk the size of the palm of a hand is placed on the drum head, opposite the beating spot. By this procedure the reverberations after the stroke are damped, and a dull, dry sound results (Orff: *Antigonae* -- Mus. Ex. 97).

Types of Beaters and Techniques of Playing. Until the beginning of the 18th century the guild timpanists used beaters with wooden heads covered with leather. Further developments led to the use of beaters having heads made of several flannel disks of different sizes and pressed together.

Since the time of Berlioz the instruction "with sponge beater" has often been found whenever exceptionally soft strokes were wanted. The beater heads are made of Mediterranean sponges cut into round shapes and covered with fabric.

The best sound quality with the least amount of beating noise is obtained from beaters with heads of soft merino-wool felt on Tonkinese reed sticks. These beaters, developed by outstanding timpanists, are manufactured with heads of several sizes and degrees of hardness and are the most widely used today. Differences in sound depend on the materials used for the heads and on the quality and strength of the handles. There are "piano" and "forte" beaters; "Bruckner" and "Wagner" beaters for full but soft sound; and "microphone" beaters for light, accentuated sound. The choice of beaters is determined not only by the type of sound desired but also by the existing acoustical conditions and the quality of both the timpani and their heads.

Today a professional timpanist has about a half-dozen different kinds of beaters at his disposal--the choice depends upon the individual timpanist. In addition there are the so-called wooden beaters which are indicated expressly for passages needing strongly accented, crackling and popping sounds.

Examples using wooden beaters -- Berlioz: *Symphonie fantastique;* Stravinsky: *The Firebird;* R. Strauss: *Salome, Elektra, Der Rosenkavalier;* Mahler: 7th Symphony (Mus. Ex. 13); Henze: *Elegy* (Mus. Ex. 30); Orff: *Antigonae* (Mus. Ex. 37).

In the music of the Baroque era (ca. 1580-1760) a combination of trumpets and timpani is often encountered, having been taken over from court usage. The drum style typical of that kind of music requires the wooden beaters of the time with their disk-like heads covered with a thin band of leather (see Ill. p. 20).

Illustrations in theoretical works of the early Baroque show that round-headed beaters covered with soft material or with leather were also used.

Example -- Jacques Philidor le cadet: *Partition de plusieurs marches* -- 1705 (Mus. Ex. 14).

Special effects such as the following occur only rarely: tapping with the fingertips *(colla mano)* -- Orff: *Die Bernauerin* (Mus. Ex. 54) and G. Gordon: *The Rake's Progress;* playing with drum sticks or with the handles of beaters -- Bartók: Violin Concerto; Orff: *Trionfi* (Mus. Ex. 15); W. Thärichen: Timpani Concerto.

Timpani technique depends essentially upon the correct training of the joints and muscles, especially those of the hands, arms, and shoulders. Study, lasting many years, begins with the basic concepts of simple beating on a pair of timpani and progresses to rolls and finally to the execution of the most difficult etudes and solo pieces on four timpani. In addition the student must learn the Classical and contemporary orchestral repertory--by no means limited to four timpani--progressing in technical difficulty. At the outset he is tested for both rhythm and ear training (pitch) because he must be able, eventually, to tune his timpani under all possible circumstances, even while counting rests and hearing "wrong" and contradictory harmonies in the orchestra.

The execution of a series of beats over several timpani requires not only an accurate aim, attained by practice, but also a sure touch to obtain the proper dynamics.

Examples -- Hartmann: 6th Symphony (Mus. Ex. 17); Henze: *Elegy* (Mus. Ex. 10).

The sound of the timpani is sustained by means of the roll: a rapid succession of strokes with two alternating beaters at any dynamic level. The shortest possible reverberations after simple beats or ends of rolls are achieved by damping the drum head with the extended fingers of one hand. A succession of staccato beats is achieved by using beaters with small, hard heads which produce a strong and precise attack.

Examples --Bartók: Music for Strings, Percussion, and Celesta.

Use. There are two possible ways to set up the timpani in the orchestra: either the high drum stands to the right of the player and the low drum to the left, following the lay-out of keyboard instruments and of those percussion instruments arranged like keyboards (xylophone, glockenspiel, etc.); or else in reverse order, with the high drum to the left and the low drum to the right. The latter arrangement is preferred by many timpanists for reasons of beating technique, sound, and last but not least, tradition.

A few examples from orchestral literature will serve as a survey of the many diverse possibilities of playing the timpani.

During the Classical era timpani, as a rule, were used in pairs only. Scores calling for three and more timpani are rare. Examples -- Mozart's Serenade, K. 187/188 (with four timpani) and the Symphony (with eight timpani) by Johann Wilhelm Hertel (1726-1789). Later on, Meyerbeer (1791-1864) used four timpani in the operas *Le prophète, L'africaine,* and *Robert le diable,* thus requiring the timpanist to have a good deal of technical skill. Wagner, in several of his works, makes possible a variety of drum tunings by calling for two timpanists with two to three drums each *(Lohengrin, The Ring, Parsifal).*

Assembling numerous pairs of timpani, as was done by Berlioz in his *Symphonie fantastique* with three to four timpanists, and in his Requiem with eight timpanists (sixteen timpani in various tunings), has remained the exception (see Mus. Ex. 5). A few examples of the use of two and three timpanists may be found in contemporary music, such as in Stravinsky's *Le Sacre du printemps* (Mus. Ex. 6); Berg's *Wozzeck,* and Three Pieces for Orchestra; Orff's *Trionfi* and *Antigonae* (Mus. Ex. 37); and Hartmann's 8th Symphony (Mus. Ex. 7).

Solo literature for the timpani includes concerti for timpani with keyboard or orchestral accompaniment by O. Gerster, K. Striegler, F. Büttner, W. Thärichen, R. Parris, H. Cowell, A. Tcherepnin, and K. H. Köper; the Solo Sonata by D. Jones; the Concertino for Solo Timpani, Strings, and Winds by F. Donatoni; and the Concertino for Solo Timpani and Percussion by H. Konietzny. Solo pieces for timpani and percussion with keyboard or orchestral accompaniment have been written by Bozza, Delerue, Dervaux, Desportes, Passerone, Petit, and Tomasi. Elliott Carter wrote Eight Pieces for Four Timpani (one player) (1950, 1966). Contemporary chamber music also uses timpani in a virtuoso manner (see Britten: Nocturne -- Mus. Ex. 16). The best known example is probably Bartók's Sonata for Two Pianos and Percussion.

WOODEN-BAR INSTRUMENTS

Range of the entire group as well as individual ranges (the ranges are categorized according to hard and soft beaters).

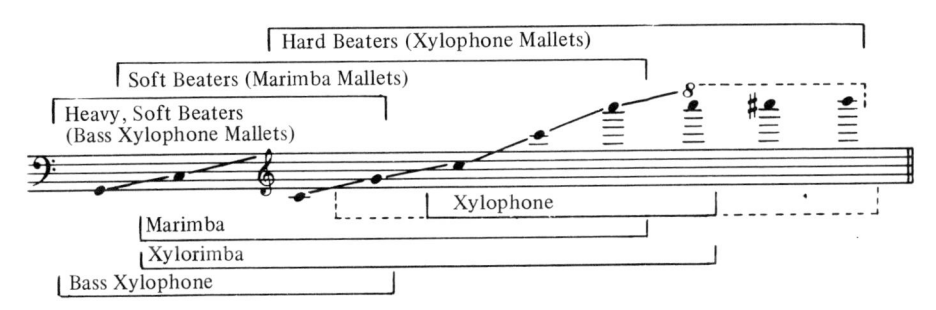

Xylophone

Range and notation:

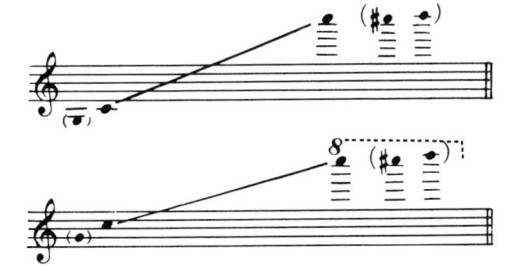

Sound: one octave higher

Common beaters: xylophone mallets--wooden heads (round or egg-shaped) covered with thin leather
mallets with heavy wooden heads for hard, sharp sounds
Less common: wooden-headed mallets covered with rubber
mallets wound with wool yarn

Keyboard Xylophone

Range and notation: same as xylophone

Sound: Same as xylophone

Marimba

Range and notation:

Sound: as notated

Common beaters: rubber covered mallets
mallets wound with wool yarn
soft-felt padded mallets

Less common: xylophone mallets

Xylorimba

Range and notation:

Sound: a) as notated

b) one octave higher

Common beaters: for high range–xylophone mallets
for low range–-marimba mallets

Less common: same as for xylophone and marimba in the corresponding ranges

Bass Xylophone

Range and notation:

Sound: as notated

Common beaters: mallets with heavy heads of soft, solid rubber
large wooden-headed mallets wrapped with soft felt strips

Less common: mallets wound with wool yarn
soft-felt timpani mallets

Trough Xylophone (Orff)

Soprano

Range and notation:

Sound: as notated

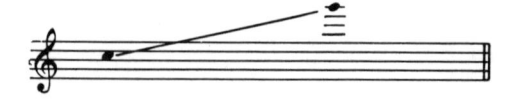

Common beaters: xylophone mallets

Less common: same as for xylophone

Tenor

Range and notation:

Sound: as notated

Common beaters: wooden-headed mallets covered with rubber
hard-felt mallets

Less common: xylophone mallets

History. Instruments with wooden bars (xylophones) originated in Southeast Asia. Their further development, so rich in forms, took place both there and in Africa.

It may be assumed that these instruments spread from the Southeast to Europe during the 15th century, and that their form was simple: portable instruments used by wandering musicians.

The modern term *xylophone* (from the Greek meaning "wood sounder") first appeared at the beginning of the 19th century and denoted an instrument consisting of a row of wooden bars.

The earliest pictorial evidence of the xylophone is found in a woodcut from the collection *Totentanz* (Dance of Death--1511) by Holbein the younger, depicting Death carrying the instrument hanging from a shoulder strap.

This type of instrument underwent very little further development, in contrast to the non-European xylophones with their resonators in the form of boxes, gourds, or bamboo tubes. After 1830 the European form became more widely known in western Europe through wandering folk musicians and was heard at public performances and popular concerts. With its use in the art music of the mid-19th century, the xylophone began to develop into an accepted orchestral instrument.

Early examples of its use – H.C. Lumbye (1810-1874): *Traumbilder;* Saint-Saëns: *Danse macabre* (1874); Humperdinck: *Hänsel und Gretel* (1892), *Die Königskinder* (1898); Puccini: *La Bohème* (1896); Pfitzner: *Die Rose vom Liebesgarten* (1900); R. Strauss: *Salome* (1905).

The European xylophone, nonetheless, retained its medieval arrangement of bars without resonators until years after World War I.

Four-Row Xylophone

Construction. The first xylophones of the type without resonators consisted of only two or three primitive rows of bars. The developed type has 30 to 37 tuned wooden bars arranged scalewise in four rows lying on cross supports consisting of wound straw ropes. The two inner rows produce a G-major scale while the two outer rows fill in the chromatic half-steps. The range may extend from c^2 to e^5 but is often less wide, from about e^2 to c^5.

The bars are usually of rosewood and were originally cylindrical. Since the 17th century, however, they have been cut with square corners and a slightly arched top side. The "wood and straw instrument," as Humperdinck and Richard Strauss still referred to it, is beaten with a pair of light, spoon-like beaters of hardwood or horn.

Use. While the xylophone was originally designed to serve as a virtuoso instrument for the performance of bravura solos, composers had to realize that the more limited proficiency of the average orchestra percussionists made it advisable to avoid, as far as possible, wide skips and passages requiring the use of two mallets with one hand. However, the so-called four-row xylophone is still played for brilliancy and dexterity by soloists and ensemble performers on the music hall stage and in similar contexts.

The xylophone now in use in most orchestras is the American two-row type with resonators. Its development may be traced from its Asiatic origins, across Africa, to America. The original (Asiatic) form of all xylophones -- crude, thick boards of seasoned wood, spread on the player's lap and struck with pestle-like beaters -- led to the subsequent stage, the cross-support xylophone *(Holmxylophon)*, and finally to the type with resonators. According to Curt Sachs the *Holmxylophon* is the form which was taken from Asia to East Africa. It had up to 19 bars laid out on cross supports, usually banana stalks, and was played with two, four, and even eight hands. Early types of resonators were earthen bowls on which the bars were either laid or pinned. Next followed the xylophones with gourd resonators under each bar, the gourds having been selected according to size to amplify the sound of the respective bars.

Gamelan Instruments from Indonesia (Java): Trough Xylophones, Gongs, Sets of Gongs

In Asia the predominant xylophones are those with trough resonators (trough xylophones); Bali, however, also has xylophones with correspondingly scaled bamboo tubes to catch and strengthen the tone. In Asia the individual resonators have generally remained confined to instruments of the metallophone type.

The days of the slave trade brought the marimba -- as the Southeast African natives called the "gourd xylophone" -- to America where it found a new sphere of activity in Latin-American folk-dance music.

Its further development, leading to the modern resonator-type instrument, began when Western jazz and dance musicians "discovered" the marimba and used it for their own purposes.

Construction. While the bars of the exotic xylophone lie side by side in a single row, those of the modern instrument are placed chromatically, corresponding to the arrangement of keyboards.

Hard, well-seasoned wood, preferably of the rosewood type, is best suited as material for the bars. The bars have holes width-wise at their nodal points in the first and third quarter of each bar and are strung on soft strings. They no longer lie on straw or felt cross-supports but instead hang freely above the resonators, separated from one another by rubber-covered dividers. The resonators are made of metal or plastic and are measured exactly in order to amplify properly the vibrations of each bar.

In practice the total range of approximately five and one-half octaves of the entire xylophone group is divided into several instruments of differing but overlapping ranges.

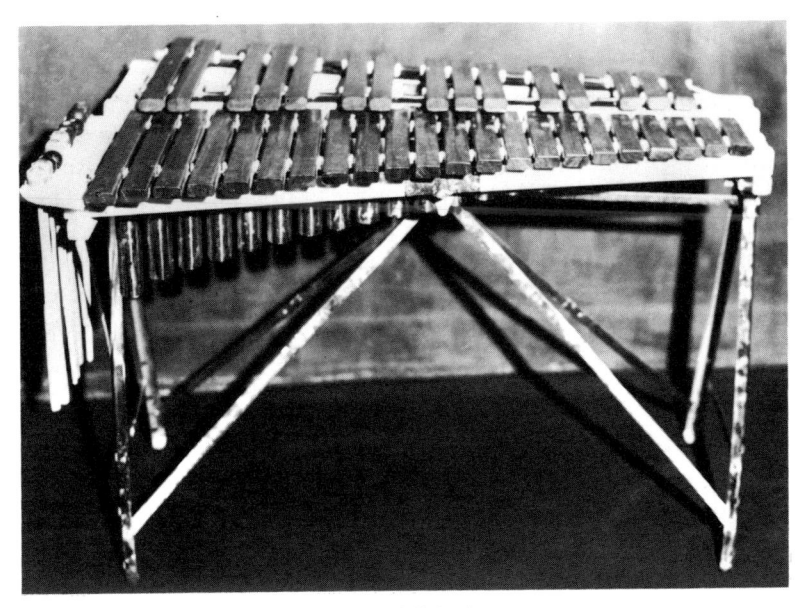

Orchestral Xylophone

Xylophone

The range of the instrument identified simply as "xylophone" is identical with that of the old four-row wood and straw instrument: three highest octaves, from c^2 to c^5, occasionally extended by a few tones above and below. Only seldom is it realized that the xylophone is a transposing instrument; it sounds one octave higher than notated. Contemporary composers have extended the normal xylophone range downward by about one octave to f^1 and sometimes even to c^1, the lowest tone on which hard-headed mallets can be used.

Examples -- Roussell: Suite in F (xylorimba range of f^1 - f^3); Berg: *Wozzeck* (c^1 - e^4), Three Pieces for Orchestra; Boulez: *Le marteau sans maître* (f^1 - f^4); and others.

The acoustical characteristics of the xylophone's tone color make it difficult, especially for an untrained ear, to recognize the octave in which its hollow, dry tones are sounding. Errors as to the exact octave may be avoided if one follows the example of Alban Berg and adds to the xylophone part the instruction "sound as notated" (see *Wozzeck*) or "sounds one octave higher" (see Three Pieces for Orchestra).

The sharp, direct sound of the xylophone penetrates easily, even in thick orchestrations. Its traditional use is therefore confined mostly to a few staccato interjections and short solo passages.

Technique of Playing. The execution of all sorts of scales, passage work, broken chords, sequences, and trills is limited more or less to what one hand playing staccato can perform on a keyboard instrument. In addition, fast glissandi on the C-major row of bars sound very well. The tremolo (rolling on a single tone) is used not only for its own quality of sound but also to prolong a tone, since the bars, once struck, do not reverberate.

Double notes and chords of three and four tones, when written for a single player, considerably slow down the speed of playing. Four-note chords, for example, require two mallets in each hand and a corresponding manipulation of the hands for each change of interval. This technique is used more frequently on the marimba and vibraphone than on the xylophone (see *Modern School for Xylophone* by Morris Goldenberg).

Polyphonic passages may be executed by several performers on one or more xylophones.

Examples -- Egk: *Joan von Zarissa* (2 performers); Hartmann: 3rd Symphony (2 xylophones), 6th, 7th, and 8th Symphonies (2-3 xylophones, 4 performers).

Beaters. Mallets with small, egg-shaped heads, such as those used in Latin America, are currently preferred over beaters with round heads. Because their weight is balanced more effectively they produce an extremely powerful sound. They are made of particularly heavy, exotic woods (*lignum vitae,* ebony) or else of synthetic material of corresponding weight and hardness. The heads are covered with thin leather to avoid hard, clattering strokes. Mallets with heavy wooden heads must be used if especially dry, sharp passages are desired. Strong, light leather coverings are recommended for playing the low tones of the xylorimba. To obtain a marimba-like sound in low ranges, sections of soft rubber tubing are pulled over the normal mallet heads. Best suited for mallet handles are Tonkinese canes, 6 - 7 mm (1/4" - 5/16") in diameter and about 28 cm (11 3/16") long, and if possible equipped with thin cork handles.

Increasing numbers of 20th-century composers have become attracted to the xylophone whose tone color greatly enriches the orchestral palette. In recent times composers have also used it in chamber music, assigning parts of the greatest technical difficulty to it.

Examples of interesting xylophone literature -- Stravinsky: *The Firebird, Petrouchka, Les noces* (Mus. Ex. 19); R. Strauss: *Schlagobers, Die schweigsame Frau;* Hindemith: Chamber Music No. 1; Bartók: *The Wooden Prince, The Miraculous Mandarin,* Music for Strings, Percussion, and Celesta, Sonata for Two Pianos and Percussion; Kodály: *Háry János;* Gershwin: *Piano Concerto in F, Porgy and Bess;* Egk: *Peer Gynt;* Orff: *Antigonae, Oedipus* (Mus. Ex. 28); Hartmann: *Simplicius Simplicissimus,* 2nd Symphony, 6th Symphony (Mus. Ex. 20), 7th Symphony, 8th Symphony (Mus. Exx. 23 and 27), Concerto for Piano, Winds, and Percussion; Fortner: Symphony; Shostakovich: 5th, 6th, and 7th Symphonies; Prokofiev: *Alexander Nevsky,* 7th Symphony; Khatchaturian: *Gayane;* Heinrich Sutermeister: *Raskolnikov;* Britten: *The Prince of the Pagodes;* Theodor Berger: *Concerto manuale;* Armin Schibler: Concerto for Percussion and Orchestra; Messiaen: *Oiseaux exotiques* (Mus. Ex. 29).

Keyboard Xylophone

The range of the keyboard xylophone is approximately the same as that of the xylophone. The wooden bars are struck on the bottom side by hammers connected to a keyboard. The construction and the playing mode allow for very little differentiation or resonance. The advantage of the instrument lies in the possibility of executing two-handed pianistic passages, tremolos, thick chords, and tone clusters. (See Ill. on p. 47.)

The origin of the keyboard xylophone goes back to the 17th century. At that time the carillons of Holland, Flanders, and northern France had already reached a high stage of development and could be played from a keyboard modeled after that of the organ. Since the keyboard glockenspiel and the celesta have found their way into the orchestra, the keyboard xylophone, constructed similarly, has also been used occasionally. However, it is difficult, these days, to find an instrument in playable condition.

Keyboard Xylophone

Example -- Bartók: *Bluebeard's Castle* (Mus. Ex. 21).

Marimba

The range c - c^4 of this instrument duplicates the two lower octaves of the xylophone (c^2 - c^4).

Marimbas with an extension to five octaves (to c^5) cover the entire xylophone range. Pierre Boulez asks for such a xylorimba in *"pli selon pli"* by the term *grande xylophone*, notated one octave lower and played by two performers.

Xylorimba (five-octave type)

Because of its smooth timbre the marimba does not have the penetrating power and loudness of the xylophone. Rolls or tremolos in low ranges blend into one another, similar to soft timpani rolls. Harder mallets make possible more accentuated playing, especially in the range that duplicates that of the xylophone on which a sound of considerably greater carrying power can be achieved.

Technique of Playing. It corresponds to that of the xylophone, although the larger size of the bars does not permit exactly the same muscular movements. On the other hand, it facilitates playing with four mallets, a technique that has become highly developed through Latin-American music and jazz.

Beaters. The marimba belongs to that division of the family of wooden-bar instruments which is played only with soft mallets. As the lower bars grow longer and wider, the touch must grow softer but also weightier to bring the entire bar into complete vibration. In these low ranges -- especially in the very lowest parts -- a hard-headed mallet such as a xylophone mallet does not permit the wood to vibrate completely; it will only produce a clattering, undefined noise.

Marimba mallets have heads of hardwood, hard rubber, or synthetic materials of similar characteristics, pressed into a round shape (24 - 28 mm -- ca. 1" - 1 1/8" -- in diameter), and covered with a 2 to 3 mm (1/12" - 1/8") thick rubber tubing. In low registers and for especially soft tones, heads of hard felt or rubber wound with wool yarn are best. Microphone pickups sometimes require timpani beaters.

Usefulness of the marimba -- like that of the softly played vibraphone -- is greatest in transparent orchestrations and in chamber music and solo playing.

A forte sound of some carrying power can be achieved by grouping marimbas with other, similar instruments, such as trough xylophones. Such a combination is used by Orff in *Antigonae* and *Oedipus.*

Examples -- Janáček: *Jenufa, Kátja Kabanová;* Orff: *Antigonae, Oedipus, Trionfi;* Hartmann: Concerto for Piano, Winds, and Percussion, Concerto for Viola, 6th, 7th, and 8th Symphonies (Mus. Exx. 23 and 27), *Gesangsszene;* Henze: *Antifone* (Mus. Ex. 3a), *Ode an den Westwind, Elegy* (Mus. Ex. 30); Gould: *Latin-American Symphonette;* Boulez: *"pli selon pli," Le marteau sans maître;* Killmayer: Chamber Music for Jazz Instruments; Zimmermann: *Dialogue.*

Bass Xylophone

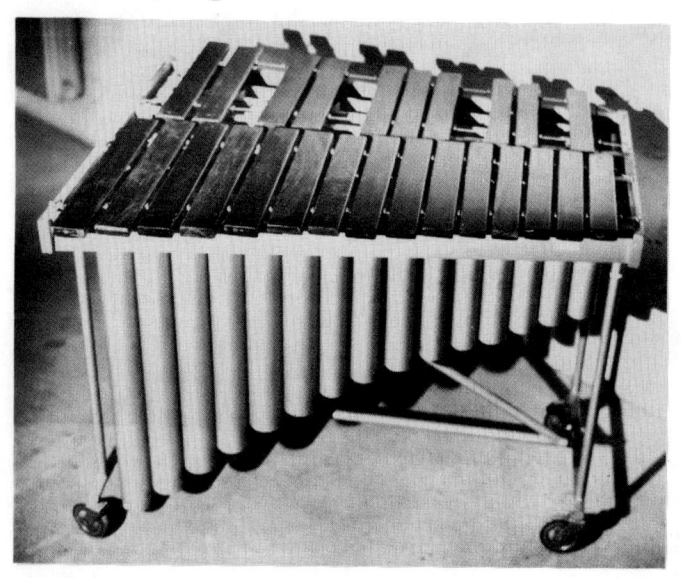

Bass Xylophone

The bass xylophone extends the range of the xylophones downward to G. In its upper range it overlaps that of the marimba, extending it to g^1. It is built along the same principles as the marimba, but because of its larger bars and resonators it has a somewhat awkward size. For example, the largest bar, G, is 53 cm (21 3/16") long and 6.5 cm (2 5/8") wide, and its corresponding resonator is 80 cm (32") long and 8 cm (3 3/16") in diameter.

The individual tones sound soft and hollow with little incisiveness. Although easily heard from nearby, the sound does not carry well; in other words, what was true of the lower registers of the marimba applies here to an even greater extent.

Tremolos can be achieved with large, soft timpani mallets. On the larger bars soft tremolos and rolls run together like low-pitched timpani rolls.

The bass xylophone requires mallets with soft but heavy, solid rubber heads approximately 3.5 cm (1 3/8") in diameter. Mallets with wooden or plastic heads padded with soft felt strips produce less volume but also no impact noise.

Electronic amplification is advisable if the instrument is to be used in a large orchestra.

The impetus for building a bass xylophone may well have originated with Puccini's opera *Turandot* which calls for such an unusual percussion instrument. Carl Orff uses it in his stage works *Die Bernauerin* (Mus. Ex. 24), *Antigonae* (Mus. Ex. 55), *Oedipus*, and *Prometheus*; Egk uses it in *Columbus*.

Trough Xylophone

Instruments of the trough xylophone type originated during the Middle Ages throughout an area extending from Burma, Thailand, and Cambodia to Old Java and Bali. They have been incorporated into the modern Western percussion section in a recreated form, thanks to the initiative of Carl Orff.

Tenor Trough Xylophone

Construction. The bars of the trough xylophone are arranged side by side in a single row across the slightly curved, open top of a long, narrow box, either in diatonic or in chromatic order. They rest with their nodal points upon the felt or foam-rubber padded edges of the resonator box or trough. Along one of the edges metal pins separate the bars from one another; along the other, the bars are held in place by single pins running through each bar. In this way the bars can easily be lifted off and exchanged with others--for example, a chromatic bar may be inserted into a diatonic instrument.

The most successful orchestral version of the trough xylophone also has a curved, cradle-shaped resonator box, but here the bars are *always* arranged chromatically, lying suspended on strings or on rubber cushions.

The letter-names of the tones are stamped into the individual bars and the C-major triad is given additional identification by colored markings.

The trough xylophone group, as it appears in Orff's orchestrations, is divided into several soprano and tenor instruments. While ordinary xylophones or marimbas may be substituted for the soprano trough xylophone, the tenor is irreplaceable because the required glissandi are possible only on its single-row arrangement of bars.

Examples -- Orff: *Catulli Carmina* (Mus. Ex. 25), *Antigonae* (Mus. Ex. 37), *Weihnachtsspiel* (Mus. Ex. 110).

The bass trough xylophone is too weak in sound for use in the orchestra. The volume in such a low register may, however, be increased considerably by the addition of resonator tubes of adequate size (see also Bass Xylophone, p. 48).

The volume of sound of a well-built tenor trough xylophone exceeds in many registers that of the marimba because its box-like shape greatly favors its resonance.

Performance, however, is hampered by the single-row arrangement of the bars, since the performer obviously cannot play difficult passage work and wide intervals. Such material must be given to instruments with bars in keyboard arrangement.

Beaters. Trough xylophones require mallets with felt, rubber, or wooden heads. Xylophone and marimba mallets are best suited.

METAL-BAR INSTRUMENTS

Range of the entire group, as well as individual ranges; ranges classified according to hard and soft beaters.

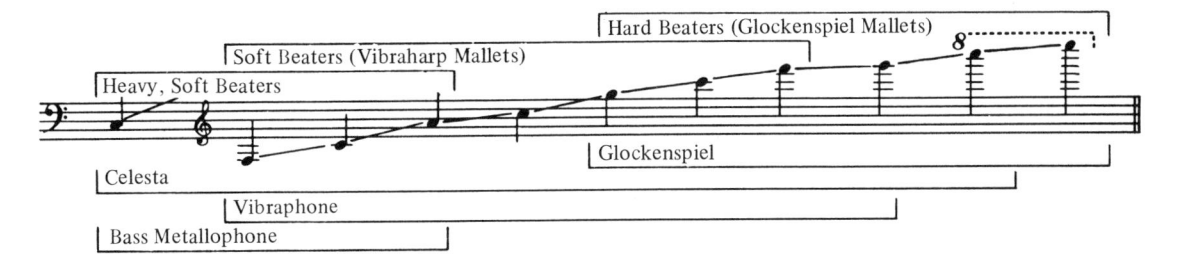

Glockenspiel (Orchestra Bells)

Range and notation:

or:

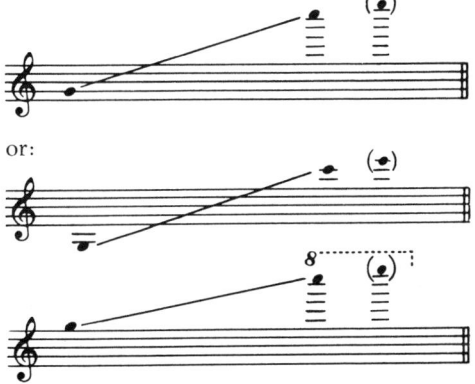

Sound: one (or two) octave(s) higher

Common beaters: glockenspiel mallets (brass-headed hammers into which are screwed interchangeable beating tips made of buffalo horn or plastic
metal-headed mallets

Less common: wooden mallets
glockenspiel bars
small beaters with heads of synthetic material covered with thin rubber tubing

Keyboard Glockenspiel

Range and notation:

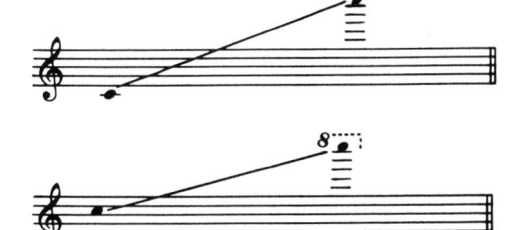

Sound: one octave higher

Celesta

Range and notation:

Sound: one octave higher

Vibraphone

Range and notation:
Sound: as noted

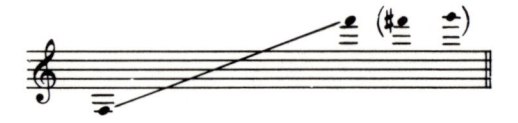

Common beaters: rubber-headed mallets wound with wool yarn in some 3 to 4 different degrees of hardness ranging from very soft to moderately hard (soft, medium, hard)
mallets with heads of hardwood or plastic and covered with 2 to 3 mm (1/12" to 1/8") thick rubber tubing

Less common: glockenspiel mallets
metal mallets
knitting needles
xylophone mallets (for extremely hard sound)
timpani mallets (for very soft, vague sound)
large wire brush

Metallophones

Range and notation:
Sound: as notated
(identical to the vibraphone with motor off)

Beaters: as for the vibraphone

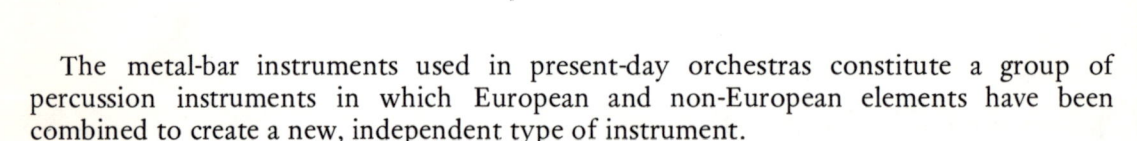

The metal-bar instruments used in present-day orchestras constitute a group of percussion instruments in which European and non-European elements have been combined to create a new, independent type of instrument.

Glockenspiel

Although the modern glockenspiel's metal-bar construction is only distantly related to the small bells of its medieval ancestor, the glockenspiel's characteristic sound and its name have changed very little, for which reason the old European small bells are rightly included among the predecessors of modern metal-bar instruments. It should not be overlooked, however, that the shapes of exotic metallophones have also had a strong influence on the physical appearance as well as the playing technique of present-day metal-bar instruments.

History. Small and even tiny bells have always existed wherever people were capable of working metal.

As prototypes we may consider the bells carved from wood or made from fruit husks. These were presumably the forerunners of bells found in Asia and Africa, which consist of thin sheets of iron bent together to form the cups. Cast and riveted iron bells (see animal or herd bells) evolved subsequently, as (on a higher level) did the foundry bells of varying sizes.

According to Curt Sachs's definition, glockenspiels consist of bells tuned scalewise and combined to form melodic instruments. Since the 8th century Western monks have built primitive glockenspiels called *cymbala* by fastening as many as 13 small bells to an iron rod and playing them with small metal hammers.

The development of mechanically played glockenspiels began in the 13th century, and in the 14th century there evolved in Holland and Flanders a large version, the carillon, which eventually became widely known. Today many churches and ceremonial buildings contain a set of tuned bells which can be played melodically by means of an ingenious mechanism. Neither the large tower-carillon nor the small mechanical type with its fine, delicate sound, as found in musical clocks, lends itself to use in concert music. Instead, the name glockenspiel was transferred to the metal-bar instrument which arose in Holland and whose origin is assumed to go back to the instruments of the native orchestras of Java. In the early 17th century the Dutch, as conquerors of a major part of the Malaysian archipelago, must have become acquainted with the *gamelan* orchestra and its trough-shaped metallophones *(gambang gangsa, saron)*. Their sound which is akin to that of the glockenspiel stimulated the building of bronze-bar instruments.

The original purpose of similar European instruments was to aid the Dutch bell masters in tuning their tower carillons and to serve as teaching aids. Later, keyboard-operated instruments evolved. By the end of the 17th century, when they were incorporated into organs as independent stops, glockenspiels already had mostly bronze or steel bars. In the score of J. S. Bach's* Alto Cantata No. 53, *Schlage doch, gewünschte Stunde,* we find the indication *Campanella in H E* (small bells in b and e).

Orchestral glockenspiels have a range of approximately two-and-one-half octaves. As an early example (1738) one might cite the carillon part in Handel's oratorio *Saul* (c^2 - g^4).

Orchestra Bells or (Orchestral) Glockenspiel

The glockenspiel most commonly used today in the orchestra is a metal-bar instrument and is considered part of the percussion section. It is built according to the principles of the metallophone.

Origin. It is possible that the bell lyra, which was introduced into the bands of the German infantry sometime after 1870, was the model for the orchestral glockenspiel. A small glockenspiel built into a box and having the approximate range of the bell lyra was part of the European salon orchestra at the turn of the century. It is this latter type, with an expanded range of almost three octaves (g^2 - e^5), which became the glockenspiel, also called orchestra bells, of the modern symphony orchestra.

Construction. The bars are made of a special kind of steel or, in cheaper and less satisfactory instruments, of light-weight metal. The ideal volume of sound requires bars of sufficient weight to produce proper vibrations; a minimum thickness of 8 mm (1/3") is essential. To achieve a clear, floating tone the bars should be suspended, in keyboard arrangement, on soft strings, either within the resonator box or above precisely scaled tubular resonators.

*It has not been established to date whether the work was actually written by Bach or by another 18th-century composer, Georg Melchior Hoffmann. (Trans.)

In order to avoid the impractical hand-damping of reverberating bars a pedal damper--similar to that of the vibraphone--is of great advantage. This attachment also makes it possible to play half-damped, i.e., with shortened reverberations.

Modern Orchestral Glockenspiel with Pedal Damper

Beaters. The glockenspiel is played with small hammers whose heads consist of strong, narrow brass tubes into which are screwed beating tips made of buffalo horn. The weight of the head of a normal mallet should be at least 30 grams (1 oz.) to elicit the best sound possible from a properly scaled orchestral glockenspiel. Lighter pairs of mallets of the same material are used for delicate as well as fast and difficult passages.

In order to be able to lay the mallets down quickly yet quietly the metal parts of their heads are best covered with thin felt or leather.

If glockenspiel mallets with round, plastic heads are used the heads must be weighted with metal in order to make them sufficiently heavy.

Soft sounds can be achieved through nuances of touch, but should never be attempted with the clattering wooden mallets occasionally called for in certain scores.

In his masterful way of discovering effective combinations of percussion sounds, Carl Orff invented a method of playing the glockenspiel with the sides of single glockenspiel bars so that their long edges strike several adjacent bars simultaneously in resiliant strokes. The result is a strident mixture of fundamentals and partials, which lends brilliance to certain tutti passages in Orff's *Trionfi, Antigonae,* and *Oedipus* (Mus. Ex. 28).

In *Antigonae* fortissimo glissandi covering more than one octave are executed with mallets having small round metal heads.

Paul Hindemith, in his Chamber Music No. 1, directs that one glockenspiel bar tuned to $f\sharp^2$ be suspended freely and struck. For this, too, it is expedient to use a mallet with a metal head.

Incidentally, whenever the sound and character of the keyboard glockenspiel is desired, mallets with small metal heads should be used.

Playing Technique and Use. The technique of playing the glockenspiel--like that of all percussion instruments with keyboard arrangement--demands considerable proficiency and the ability to produce a wide dynamic spectrum. In works of the Romantic period this has frequently led to playing passages originally written for keyboard glockenspiel on the orchestral glockenspiel, thus restricting the use of the former to chords and pianistic passages.

Examples -- Dukas: *L'apprenti sorcier;* Jolivet: Piano Concerto; Messiaen: *Oiseaux exotiques;* Glazunov: Violin Concerto.

The most resonant register of the orchestral glockenspiel, as well as that having the clearest tone and greatest carrying power, lies within the 3 and 4-line octaves. Players prefer it particularly for Romantic music, regardless of whether the original scoring actually calls for keyboard glockenspiel. The result has been to play the orchestral glockenspiel two octaves higher than notated unless expressly indicated otherwise, while the keyboard glockenspiel is transposed up only one octave.* Orchestral tutti places, such as in scores of Richard Strauss, are often doubled at the octave in order to achieve the greatest possible wealth of bell-like overtones.

Occasionally composers ask for two or more glockenspiels.

Examples -- Orff: *Trionfi, The Moon, Die Bernauerin, Antigonae;* Egk: *Joan von Zarissa, Peer Gynt;* Hartmann: 7th and 8th Symphonies.

Concerning the use of glockenspiel bars as substitutes for antique cymbals see the chapter on antique cymbals, p. 60.

Terminology. The names for glockenspiel in other languages are often misleading. Respighi called it *carillon* in *The Fountains of Rome*, while in *The Pines of Rome* he chose *campanelli* for the same instrument. The old Italian designation *sistro* also meant glockenspiel and must not be confused with *sistra,* meaning the sistrum.

Keyboard Glockenspiel

The development of the keyboard glockenspiel began even earlier than that of the orchestral glockenspiel described above. A glockenspiel with key action and with a compass of three octaves (c^2 - c^5) was built as early as 1791 for Mozart's *The Magic Flute.* There are, however, few other instances of the use of the glockenspiel in Classical music; only in the latter part of the 19th century did it begin to play an increasing role in the orchestra. As a rule it was played by a keyboard musician.

The metal bars of the keyboard glockenspiel are struck with the small metal heads of a hammer mechanism activated by keys. The modern version of the instrument has an action comparable to that of the piano so that the tone is damped whenever the corresponding key is released. This action can be negated, since the dampers for the entire instrument may be lifted all at once either by means of a hand stop or by pressure on a pedal similar to the damper pedal of the piano.

The compass of the keyboard glockenspiel is generally three octaves (c^2 - c^5), notated one octave lower. The instrument's metallic, pointed sound resembles that of small bells and has a unique charm but also a penetrating brilliance. Its dynamic range, however, is extremely narrow.

Keyboard Glockenspiel

Alban Berg, who always indicated the exact octave, calls for low glockenspiel tones from c^1 - c^4 (actual pitch) in his concert aria Der Wein. *Even the substitution of a metallophone cannot completely solve this problem.*

The keyboard glockenspiel has regained a certain prominence in a number of contemporary works.

Examples may be found in the works of Henze, Boulez, and others. Orff: *Oedipus* (Mus. Ex. 28); Messiaen: *Oiseaux exotiques* (Mus. Ex. 29); Henze: *Elegy* (Mus. Ex. 30).

Occasionally the keyboard glockenspiel as well as the orchestral glockenspiel are found side by side in the same score.

Examples -- Henri Tomasi: *Don Juan de Mañara;* Orff: *Oedipus* (Mus. Ex. 28); Zimmermann: *Contrasts.*

Celesta

The celesta, a steel-bar piano invented in 1886 by the Parisian instrument maker A. Mustel, may have resulted from an attempt to create a more delicate, softer tone quality than that produced by the glockenspiel. In appearance the celesta resembles the harmonium, and it has a range of five octaves ($c - c^5$). Parts for it are notated one octave below the actual pitch and are written on two staves, like piano music. Smaller instruments, more easily movable, are built with four octaves ($c^1 - c^5$) or with only three ($c^2 - c^5$).

Each of the celesta's steel bars lies across a small, wooden resonator box of commensurate size, and is struck with a felt-padded hammer activated by a key.

The celesta's fine, transparent sound added new, silvery tone colors to the orchestra and was thus quickly admitted into the scores of the period. Particularly striking examples may be found in Tchaikovsky's *Nutcracker Suite* (1892--Mus. Ex. 26); Charpentier's opera *Louise* (1900); and R. Strauss's *Salome* (1905).

The celesta quickly became an instrument in its own right; in fact, today it is no longer considered a member of the percussion section. Its refined mechanism and comparatively wide range permit the use of a pianistic technique, for which reason it is usually played by pianists.

Examples -- Hartmann: 6th Symphony (Mus. Ex. 20), 8th Symphony (Mus. Ex. 27); Henze: *Elegy* (Mus. Ex. 30); Bo Nilsson: *Ein irrender Sohn* (Mus. Ex. 89).

Vibraphone

The first metal-bar instrument capable of producing a tremolo by means of agitating the air inside its built-in resonance chambers, was constructed in the United States in 1907.

After World War I the instrument spread wherever American jazz and jazz-inspired educational music, etc., was played. Because of the vibraphone's soft, somewhat fuzzy vibrato quality it is considered best suited as a melody instrument, or is used for the resonantly vibrant chord progressions of relatively slow pieces of semi-Classical music. Its acceptance into serious scores has been slow and reluctant.

After World War II the potentialities of the instrument gradually became more and more apparent, particularly in educational and *Gebrauchsmusik* and in modern scores. As a result the vibraphone has by now gained a prominent position among clef-notated percussion instruments. This has led to a virtuosic playing technique -- developed chiefly by important American vibraphonists -- involving sophisticated pedalling as well as the use of specially designed beaters of different degrees of hardness, which make it possible to produce a secco tone quality not unlike that of the xylophone.

Vibraphone

Construction. The metal bars of the vibraphone were originally of bronze or steel. Today they are made of a special, very hard light-metal alloy. As in the marimba, they are suspended in keyboard order above metal resonator tubes.

Damping is made possible by means of a pedal which presses a felt-lined rail against the edges of the rows of metal bars. With the help of a small electric motor, thin metal disks, mounted on a spindle and located above each resonator tube, are set in vertical (sideways) rotation which causes a rapid pulsation of the air columns in the resonator tubes, resulting in a tremolo effect. The speed of this tremolo can be increased or decreased by changing the speed of the motor.

The customary range of vibraphones is three octaves (f - f^3) although composers exceed it occasionally.* It is possible, if necessary, to add the tones $f\sharp^3$ and g^3.

Example -- Henze: *Elegy* (Mus. Ex. 30).

Beaters. In large orchestras one generally uses rubber mallets, as for the marimba. In addition, sets of specific vibraphone beaters are needed in 3 to 4 different degrees of softness, their rubber heads wound more or less heavily with wool yarn.

The choice of softer or harder, as well as lighter or heavier beaters depends on the kind of metal bars used, the size of the instrument, the room, and possibly even the microphone placement if any, etc. Very hard beaters produce a strong impact noise and shrill overtones.

Long, sustained tones and chords require especially soft and commensurately heavy beaters, while rapid sections and virtuoso passages demand harder and lighter ones.

André Jolivet, in his Piano Concerto, asks that the vibraphone be played with *balais de metal.* Here a large metal brush (see Ill. on p. 30), produces good, clearly audible results.

Playing Technique and Use. The vibraphone requires the same agile technique with two and four mallets as the xylophone and the marimba. In addition the manipulation of the damper pedal demands extremely sensitive control because its task is to achieve, by way of almost imperceptibly subtle dampings, clarity in quick passages and harmony changes, as well as proper slurrings. Under no circumstances must there be audible interruptions of sound or noticeable impairments of tone quality due to abrupt or overly strong damping. Melodic phrasing (legato) is achieved through hand-damping of a tone immediately after, or together with, striking a new tone--a technique which usually is of considerable complexity and can only be carried out if there is enough time.

Examples -- Milhaud: Concerto for Vibraphone and Orchestra; Berg: *Lulu,* Three Pieces for Orchestra; Messiaen: *Turangalîla Symphony;* Egk: *Die chinesische Nachtigall, Die Zaubergeige, Irische Legende, Variations on a Caribbean Theme, Die Verlobung in San*

---

*Alban Berg, in Lulu, *calls for a range from c♯ to b^3, which cannot be played on a standard instrument. Attempts to substitute a glockenspiel or a bass metallophone are, unfortunately, none too satisfactory.*

Domingo; Fortner: *Der Wald;* Hartmann: Symphonies Nos. 2, 6, 7 and 8 (Mus. Exx. 23 & 27), Concerto for Piano, Winds, and Percussion, Concerto for Viola and Orchestra; Dallapiccola: *The Prisoner;* Henze: *Antifone* (Mus. Ex. 3a), Symphonic Etudes, *Elegy* (Mus. Ex. 30); Boulez: *Le marteau sans maître, "pli selon pli;"* R. Strauss: *Die Frau ohne Schatten* (vibraphone substitutes for glass harmonica); Kotoński: *Musique en relief* (vibraphone with half pedal--see Mus. Ex. 31); Bo Nilsson: *Ein irrender Sohn* (Mus. Ex. 89), *Reaktionen* (Mus. Ex. 50).

Sound-Characteristics. The vibraphone, somewhat like the marimba, is hardly able to prevail within an orchestral tutti. Its lower tones usually suffer from insufficient carrying power. Its middle, and especially its upper ranges do, however, penetrate a great deal better.

Metallophones, Campanelli Giapponese, Loo-jon

In the orchestra the vibraphone with motor off and resonators open may serve as a metallophone. Playing technique and beaters are the same; the vibraphone part is simply marked *senza vibrato* or "motor off" if a metallophone effect is wanted.

Examples – Orff: *Die Bernauerin, Catulli Carmina* (Mus. Ex. 25); Egk: *Joan von Zarissa;* Th. Berger: *Concerto manuale;* Killmayer: *Orfeo;* Britten: *The Prince of the Pagodes.*

Puccini, in *Madama Butterfly,* called for a Japanese metal-bar instrument which he named *Campanelli giapponese,* for whose four tones a special instrument was built, shaped and decorated in a Far-Eastern style so it could be used on stage.

Mascagni, likewise, asked for such an instrument in his opera *Iris* (1898). However, since it does not appear on stage, a vibraphone with motor off can be used.

Campanelli Giapponese

In modern times a bass metallophone called loo-jon was developed in America. It consists of a tall, rectangular resonator box of teak or rosewood, open at the top, and partitioned into as many resonance compartments as it has aluminum sound-plates. Thus, it would have 13 plates for a range of F - f (see Ill. on p. 59). Each of these plates, the largest of which measures 9 x 13 cm (3 5/8" x 5 3/16"), is fastened with screws to one of the padded rims of the sound partitions. By regulating the screws a modicum of fine-tuning can be attained.

The peculiar metallophone sound is produced with soft timpani sticks or vibraphone mallets. Since the instrument has only limited carrying power it is often used with electro-acoustic amplification or in recording studios (for example, for film music). Luciano Berio has used a loo-jon in *Circles* (Mus. Ex. 32).

Loo-jon

Lithophones (Stone-Disk Instruments)

Range and notation:

or:

Sound: one (two) octave(s) higher

Common beaters: glockenspiel mallet (for *ff*)
plastic beater
xylophone mallet (for *pp*)

Less common: metal beater

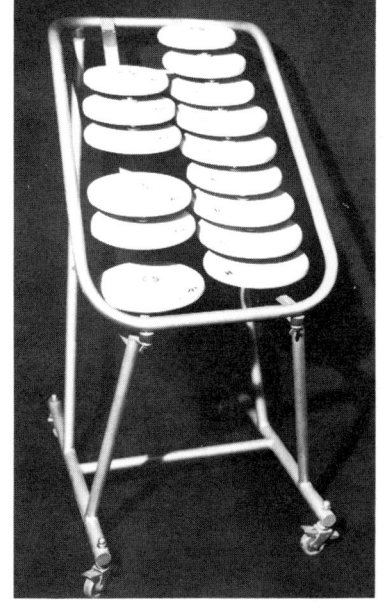

Lithophone

History. Carl Orff has revived an ancient, tuned stone-disk instrument of Sino-Indonesian origin for use in his compositions.

In the original Chinese version of this instrument, up to 24 tuned ringing-stones made of nephrite and shaped like obtuse angles with sides of unequal length were suspended in a frame. Their sound is assumed to have been clear, bright, long-sustained, and of considerable carrying power.

Construction. The lithophone of our time consists of round, chiseled slate disks *(Solnhofener Platten)* with a hole in the center, mounted on rubber-coated metal pegs, and arranged on a frame in overlapping chromatic order. The smallest and strongest disks produce the highest pitches. A c^4 is produced by a disk 2 cm (3/4") thick with a diameter of 21 cm (8 3/8"). A disk producing a^3 (lowest pitch) measures 1.8 x 21.5 cm (11/16" x 8 5/8"). The range cannot be extended downwards because larger disks are too likely to break when struck. (See Ill. on p. 59.)

Sound, Beaters, Playing Techniques. The secco sound of the instrument penetrates far and can be recognized by its strangely stone-like timbre. Its hard and glassy-clear sound quality exceeds even that of the upper range of the xylophone.

The beaters are hard; their weight depends on the desired loudness. Best suited are heavy glockenspiel mallets, and for softer sounds plastic or xylophone mallets. Metal heads in careless hands may break the disks. The strike point producing the fullest sound is in the rim area of the disk.

Since it is rather awkward to get from one strike point of the lithophone to another (because of the disk shapes and the way the disks are mounted) great agility is impossible. Except for this shortcoming, however, the lithophone's playing technique is identical with that of the wood and metal-bar instruments.

Examples – Orff: *Die Kluge, Die Bernauerin, Astutuli, Trionfi, Antigonae* (Mus. Ex. 33), *Oedipus* (Mus. Ex. 28); Kelemen: *Equilibres* (3 stone plates, 3 metal plates--Mus. Ex. 34).

METAL INSTRUMENTS

Crotales or Antique Cymbals (Finger Cymbals)

Range and notation:

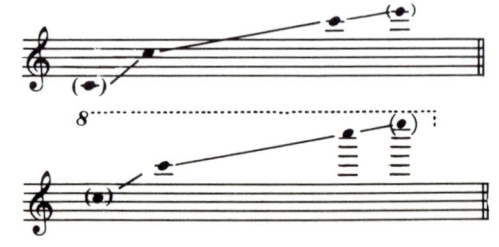

Actual sound: two octaves higher

Methods of playing - - common: in pairs, rim against rim
singly with metal beaters

- - less common: single cymbals with rubber beaters
with glockenspiel mallets
with wooden beaters

Crotales

History. The use of cymbals beaten in pairs--also called crotales--has been traced back as far as the Bronze Age. They have played significant roles in the cultural lives of the Far- and Near-Eastern peoples, Indians, Egyptians, Assyrians, Hebrews, Greeks, and Romans.

Some crotales were shaped like shallow bronze dishes whose rims vibrated while their much thicker and bulging centers remained still, thus permitting the instruments to be held by small chains or leather straps pulled through a center hole. Other variations of small cymbals, with cup or bowl-shaped bodies, are found to this day among the instruments of oriental peoples. Although almost bell-like in form, these instruments nevertheless belong to the crotales because they are played in pairs.

In spite of the fact that the poets have sung of oriental cymbals and that many old paintings show them, and in spite of the fact that wars and trade relations with the Orient during the Middle Ages must have acquainted Europeans with them, these small cymbals hardly ever made inroads into the European arsenal of instruments.

Berlioz discovered the shallow, dish-like cymbals in the Museum of Pompeii and introduced them into art music under the name *cymbals antiques.* Their subsequent use remained quite sporadic, however, because the technique of casting them was slow in developing.

As a result, new, small substitute cymbals were made of brass sheets. Unfortunately, however, their timbre in no way resembles that of the oriental cymbals. A sound much closer to the genuine cymbal timbre was produced by individual glockenspiel bars freely suspended from gut strings and struck with similar bars.

Construction. Today the instrument industry offers sets of paired antique cymbals cast from the finest bell bronze and having a compass of c^3 to e^5. The largest of these cymbals (c^3) has a diameter of ca. 12 cm (4 3/4") and a 4 mm (1/6") thick rim; the measurements of the smallest (e^5) are 6 cm (2 3/8") and 3 mm (1/8"), respectively.

Playing Technique and Use. The two cymbals are held by their leather loops (see Ill. on p. 60) and moved up and down in opposite directions: while one of them is briskly moved downwards it passes and touches with its lower edge the upper edge of the other one which is being moved upwards. In other words, they collide slightly while passing, touching only each other's edges and not rubbing each other, thus producing a clear, very bright, high, bell-like tone of metallic sharpness, which is capable of penetrating even a large orchestra.

Manipulation of the kind used in playing regular clash cymbals would only be proper if specifically called for as a special effect.

Examples -- Berlioz: *Symphonie Roméo et Juliette;* Johann Nepomuk David: Violin Concerto; Debussy: *L'après-midi d'un faune;* Ravel: *Alborada del gracioso;* Messiaen: *Turangalîla-Symphonie;* Stravinsky: *Les noces* (Mus. Ex. 36), *Le Sacre du printemps* (Mus. Ex. 35); Orff: *Antigonae* (Mus. Ex. 37); Jolivet: Piano Concerto.

Some composers have notated antique cymbals without specifying any pitch, perhaps merely aiming at the bright cymbal sound of oriental music. Here it is sufficient to use a cymbal pair with the highest possible pitch.

Examples -- Delibes: *Coppelia;* R. Strauss: *Josephslegende;* Orff: *The Moon, Die Kluge, Trionfi, Oedipus, Nänie und Dithyrambe;* Pfitzner: *Palestrina;* Britten: *The Prince of the Pagodes.*

Pierre Boulez, in *"pli selon pli,"* alternates normal playing with lightly pressured clashes which not only produce clatter but at the same time stop the reverberations. He uses the same effect in *Le visage nuptial.* In Henze's *Elegy* (Mus. Exx. 38 & 39) and *Antifone* (Mus. Ex. 67), crotales (antique cymbals) are to be struck with metal rods of different thicknesses and with rubber mallets. The last-mentioned procedure is only possible on the larger cymbals; the smaller ones do not have sufficient vibrating material to produce a tone in this way. If a set of several single antique cymbals is to be used, they may be mounted on a stand, in keyboard order, and struck with beaters. If enough cymbals are combined to cover the entire available pitch range one obtains a kind of crotalophone or cymbalphone reminiscent of medieval sets of small bells (see Ill. on p. 62).

Examples -- Messiaen: *Sept Haïkaï, Couleurs de la cité céleste*; Krenek: *Der Zauberspiegel.*

Cymbal Set (Zimbelspiel)

For tuned hand bells see page 132.

Gong

Range and notation:

Sound: as notated

Beaters: heavy mallets padded with felt or cloth

Gongs

As a general classification the term gong may stand for all instruments consisting of circular disks made of hammered bronze and bent more or less into the shape of a bowl. Their rims have holes for straps by which they are hung. They are struck in the center. Current practice uses the term gong only for instruments that produce a precise, clear tone because of the thickness of their metal and their wide flange, and because they are cast with a central protuberance or "dome". In this respect they differ from the tamtams whose sound is diffused into numerous partials due to their thinner metal and their lack of the gong's center dome.

Origin. Of all the countries that originally used domed gongs Java developed the best instruments as part of her renowned *gamelan* orchestras. Their sound is dark, rich, and pure; the giant gongs particularly sound incomparably majestic. Such gongs have a diameter of about one meter (40").

Construction. A Javanese gong in G has a diameter of about 68 cm (27 3/16"). Its dome measures 15 cm (6"), its average thickness is 1 cm (3/8"), and the width of its flange measures about 15 cm (6"). While Western music uses only an occasional single gong of low or medium pitch, Javanese sets of gongs may range all the way to c^3.

Method of Playing and Use. The gong is struck on the semispherical dome that bulges out from its center. The beater, heavily padded with felt or cloth, should have a weight corresponding to the size of the gong to assure full vibrations of the metal. The gong is damped by touching its dome with the hand.

Even though gongs, as well as the other instruments of the *gamelan* orchestra, must have been known in Europe as early as the 16th century, they did not appear in the orchestra prior to the 19th century, probably because of their rarity. The first composition calling for a gong seems to have been the opera *La princesse jaune* (1872) by Saint-Saëns (2 gongs, in e and g). Puccini asks for twelve gongs in *Madama Butterfly* and calls them *gong giapponese,* pitched A, B♭, B, c, d♭, d, e♭, e, f, f♯, g, and g♯. In *Turandot* he also calls for twelve gongs, this time indicating them as *gong chinese,* pitched A, B♭, c, d♭, d, e♭, e, f, g♭, and a (Mus. Ex. 40). In both works the gongs sound one octave higher than notated.

Richard Strauss enriched the score of *Die Frau ohne Schatten* with the exotic color of gong sounds on the pitches D♭, d♭, d♭^{1}, g♭, and b♭. The following works make use of the gong's timbre as such, i.e., simply as a new orchestral sound: Egk: *Columbus, Joan von Zarissa,* French Suite, *Die chinesische Nachtigall;* Orff: *Antigonae, Oedipus,* and *Prometheus.* A gong set of smaller, muted gongs is used by Cage and Harrison in *Double Music* (Mus. Ex. 91).

In the last three Orff works mentioned above, low-pitched gongs are particularly important. Since it is generally impossible to procure all these required gong pitches, even if a combination of private collections and museums is drawn upon, the gongs that are available may be complemented by large tamtams, low bell plates amplified by resonators, and bass piano strings struck with beaters.

If a gong is notated without clef it generally means that a tamtam is intended. Often this means a small tamtam not unlike the dinner gong that used to be part of the percussion set of salon orchestras.

Steel Drums

The steel drums of the native musicians of Trinidad may be considered a new variation of gong sets. At first they consisted of empty gasoline or oil drums into whose concave tops were hammered dents in various numbers, shapes, and sizes. The finished tops were then cut off, with part of the body of the drum still attached to act as a resonator, its length depending on the top's curvature and the number and sizes of the dents. Steel drums are played with padded beaters; their timbre lies somewhere between the marimba and the gong. Instruments with three or four large dents have resonators extending almost the full length of the drum and produce low, somewhat indistinct pitches. Tops with a greater number of smaller dents have shorter resonators and produce higher, more definite pitches.

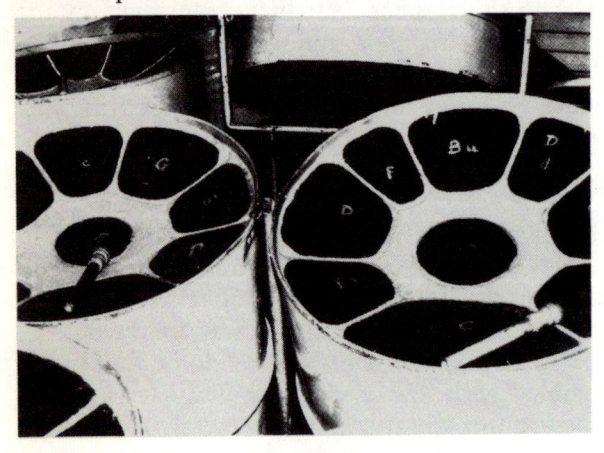

Steel Drums

Steel drums are either worn horizontally, suspended on straps from the player's neck and shoulders, or mounted on a frame. Groups of from 3 to 30 players perform popular music with brilliant virtuosity, some playing the tune, others taking care of rhythm and harmonies. A number of theater and dance orchestras in the United States use steel drums. The instruments are now manufactured commercially and sold in sets. For an example of a composition using steel drums see Haubenstock-Ramati: *Vermutungen über ein dunkles Haus* (Mus. Ex. 41).

BELLS AND CHIMES
Large Bronze Bells, Calottes, Piano-String Bells (Grail Bells), Electro-Acoustical Bells, Bells Recorded on Tape

Range and notation:

Sound: as notated

Beaters: clappers
         hammers

General Description, Origin, and History. According to Curt Sachs the bell consists of a percussion vessel (cup) with a sounding rim (lip) and a silent top (crown). Its history goes back to ancient Asia. Church bells in shapes and sizes as we know them today appeared throughout Europe from approximately the 13th century on, developing from forms resembling beehives or sugar loaves.

The art of bell casting reached a peak around the 15th century. The world's largest bell was cast in 1733 and is located in the Kremlin in Moscow. During the great fire there in 1811 it suffered heavy damage and has not been sounded since. It is about 6 meters (20') high, has a diameter of about 7 meters (23' 4"), weighs almost 200,000 kg (ca. 440,000 lbs.), and is said to have had great D as its fundamental.

Since the end of the 18th century, bells and chimes have been used both on stage and in the orchestra. The impossibility of installing large, cast bells with their enormous weight and their timbre designed to carry great distances, gave rise to the search for suitable substitutes. (A cast bell in c, for example, weighs at least 8,000 kg -- 17,600 lbs.)

Cast Bronze Bell

Construction. Most bells are made of bronze (78% copper and 22% tin) and are cast without forging. Not infrequently, however, other materials, such as steel, aluminum and nickel are also used. The centuries-old tradition of bell casting has developed specific names for the individual parts of a bell. Thus a bell is hung by the "crown" which is fastened to the "top plate" which, from its "shoulder," leads down to the "waist." The waist, in turn, leads down to the "hip" and then to the outer "sound bow" of the "mouth." The lowest part of the bell, from the sound bow to the "edge," is called the "lip." Opposite the outer sound bow, i.e., inside the bell, is the inner sound bow. The specific beater with which a bell is rung is called the "clapper."

Characteristics of Sound. Among the most important sounds that together result in the typical bell tone one must distinguish between the fundamental, which is the lowest audible sound, and the striking note, which lies one octave above the fundamental and is the clearest and most recognizable pitch. The striking note--the tone that denotes the bell's pitch--consists of a mixture of light, clear timbres, which comes about at the moment of greatest agitation by the clapper, and which is followed by the other components of the total bell sound, which become audible in varying degrees as the vibrations gradually die away. These different components do not, however, follow the normal series of partials -- a unique feature of bell sound, and one that makes it especially difficult to find suitable bell substitutes for use in the orchestra and on stage. Another characteristic of bell sound lies in the fact that its components occur not only as a tonal mixture, but also as distinct pitches of a consonant chord, so that one talks about bells being tuned in major or minor, respectively.

Various Bell Substitutes and Their Uses. While acceptable bell substitutes from c upward have been found, such as bell plates, square steel rods, tubular chimes, and small bronze bells, the simulation of low-pitched bells continues to be a problem. Composers, deceived by the strong and prominent low reverberations of bells, often venture far below the lowest possible pitches.

The first attempt at substitutes was made on the operatic stage of the 19th century with the so-called *calottes,* small semispherical bells shaped like skullcaps and hailing from the Middle Ages. Their shape survives today in the signal bells of electrical appliances. Boito, in his opera *Mefistofele* (1868), used as substitutes for bells five *calottes* cast in bronze, of equal thickness but different dimensions. He notated them C, D, E, F, and G, although the actual sound was one octave higher. The lowest bell (C) weighed about 100 kg (220 lbs.); the highest (G) about 30 kg (ca. 66 lbs.). This type of bell substitute did not, however, become widespread, perhaps because of the quality of its sound, perhaps because of difficulties of manufacture.

In Mussorgsky's *Boris Godunov* (1874) a low tamtam was used instead of low bells, and in his *Khovanshtchina* (in the Rimsky-Korsakov version) a piano was used playing diminished fifths in the lowest register to approach more closely the sound of low bells.

Grail Bells - - Four choirs of Strings (C, G, A, E) struck with large, felt-padded hammers (Munich, National Theatre)

Wagner's scoring four Grail bells in *Parsifal* (1879), tuned C, G, A, and E, led to the construction of a kind of giant dulcimer having string choirs of eight strings each, to be struck with large, felt-padded wooden hammers. Later a similar instrument was built for Bayreuth, but with keys which had to be struck with fists. In order to achieve an added metallic timbre, tuned gongs and metal plates were hung in large resonator barrels and played (struck) along with several of the afore-mentioned bell pianos.

A less complicated way of producing *Parsifal* bells is through electro-mechanical pick-up and amplification of piano strings: the four Grail-bell pitches are played in octaves of the great and contra ranges on a prepared piano or a strung steel frame.

Toward the end of the 1930's, at the suggestion of Clemens Krauss, a device was built in Munich to produce an imitation of low bells with the help of electronics. Tuned metal rods were placed in resonance chambers and struck by means of an electro-mechanical keyboard. The sound was then electronically amplified and fed into speakers (see Ill. on p. 67). Such a device for producing bell sounds can easily be built nowadays for any required pitch or series of pitches.

The rods of such an instrument must be struck with small, felt-padded hammers to produce a soft, rather gong-like bell sound which is reminiscent at times of old-fashioned grandfather clocks. Since these bell sounds are intended to convey the effect of distance, the speakers should always be placed far back on stage. Even so, the dynamic scale may range from pianissimo to a hall-filling fortissimo.

Examples -- R. Strauss: *Friedenstag* (Mus. Ex. 42); Puccini: *Tosca;* Pfitzner: *Palestrina;* Humperdinck: *Die Königskinder;* Janáček: *Out of a Death-House.*

The *ondes Martenot* as well as the *Mixtur-Trautonium* have proved to be good solutions to the bell problem. Both instruments are capable of producing bell sounds at any pitch and volume by means of a complex electronic apparatus. Since 1955 the *Mixtur-Trautonium* has occasionally been used in this way in *Parsifal* performances in Bayreuth.

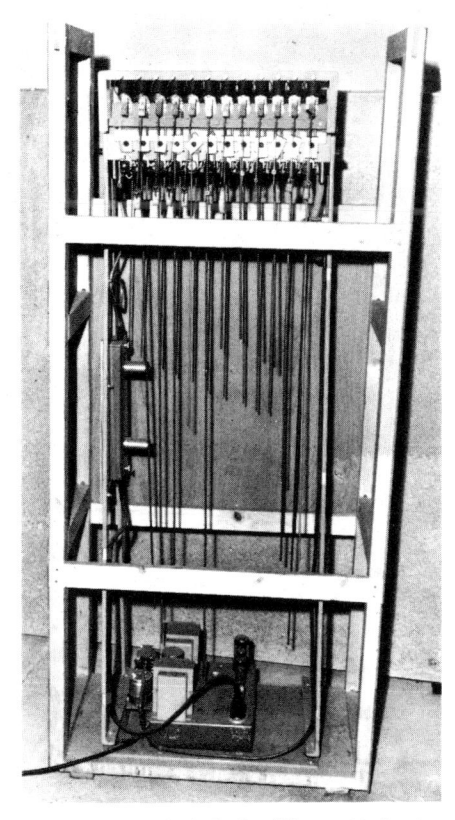

Electro-Acoustical Bells (Electro-Mechanically Activated)

Arthur Honegger, in *Jeanne d'Arc,* used the *ondes Martenot* to produce bell sounds.

Finally, there is the possibility of recording actual bells on tape and playing them back through amplifiers and speakers placed either on stage or elsewhere in the auditorium. This method is used mainly to obtain a background of bell sounds and is rarely notated precisely.

Examples -- Mussorgsky: *Boris Godunov* (Coronation Scene); Verdi: *Don Carlos* (in front of the church); Mahler: 6th Symphony (Mus. Ex. 86); Egk: *Columbus, Peer Gynt.* Wherever the structure of the score permits, individual, pre-taped bell sounds may be included, as, for example, the Kremlin Bell in Mussorgsky's *Khovanshtchina.*

Bell Plates

Range and Notation:

Sound: as notated

Common beaters: large, heavy wooden hammers or metal beaters with heavy felt or leather padding

Less common: heavy hard-felt beaters

Bell Plates with Resonators

Origin and Construction. Tuned plates of metal, used since ancient times in the civilizations of Asia, entered Western music as bell substitutes at the end of the 19th century.

Rectangular plates of aluminum or bronze -- or occasionally of steel -- with cord hangers to hold or otherwise suspend them, are struck with beaters having heavy felt or leather-padded wooden or metal heads.

The range of a three-octave set of bell plates is C to c^2 (g^2). A C-plate of aluminum measures about 100 x 75 cm (40" x 30") and weighs about 6 kg (ca. 13 1/4 lbs); a c^2-plate measures 28 x 25 cm (11 3/16" x 10"), weighs about 1 kg (2 lbs. 2½ ozs.), and is 6 mm (1/4") thick.

Each octave of plates is suspended from a semicircular frame: the lower row constitutes a C-major scale while the upper row contains the half-steps, in keyboard order.

Characteristics of Sound and Method of Playing. Bell plates convey not so much bell sounds with precise strike tones as sounds resembling distant bells. This is due to the predominantly low resonance-tones produced by striking the plates softly, a characteristic that must be taken into consideration when bell plates are used. The harder the padding of the beater, the more partials are brought out, eventually over-shadowing completely the plates' fundamentals.

The best strike points for the clearest possible fundamental are in the center or near the lower rim of the plate. Greater volume, but also a richer mixture of partials, results from striking the center of the lower or upper third of the plate.

Bell plates should only be struck moderately; if forced unduly, the result will be a disturbing clatter. For this reason the plates' volume of sound and carrying power--especially in the low range--are often insufficient. They can be increased, however, through the use of microphones and amplification. The most effective electro-acoustic amplification can be accomplished by attaching contact microphones to the plates. Weak, subtly calculated strokes can become very precise and rich in sound when transmitted over such a playback system, because it eliminates all extraneous noises likely to be picked up by an acoustic microphone. The lowest partials of a bell plate can be boosted with the help of a resonator shaped like an open barrel or box and placed with its opening toward the plate's surface. The size of the resonator depends on the size of the plate. This arrangement results in a considerable acoustic amplification of the bell plate's sound.

The speed of playing is limited because of the large size of the plates, their slowly developing sounds, and the heavy beater. Reverberations can be stopped by placing the hand on the upper edge of the plate. If less abrupt damping is desired the beater may be held against the plate.

Examples – Puccini: *Tosca* (E, F, B♭, f); Verdi: *Il Trovatore* (death knell in E♭); Pfitzner: *Palestrina* (F♯, G, c, e) and *Von deutscher Seele* (two low bell plates of any pitch); R. Strauss: *Also sprach Zarathustra* (E) and *Friedenstag* (C, E♭, a, e♭, g^1); Janáček: *Out of a Death-House;* Webern: Six Pieces for Orchestra, Op. 6 (low bells of unspecified pitch); Schönberg: *Die glückliche Hand* (tremolo on a low bell as a sound effect). For Pierre Boulez's *"pli selon pli"* a set of bell plates for two players must be constructed, having a compass of two octaves from C to c^1, thus taking on the role of a melodic orchestral instrument.

Orchestral Chimes (Tubular Chimes)

Range and notation:

Sound: as notated

Common beaters: rawhide mallets with wooden or plastic core

Less common: soft hammers
                  metal hammers
                  drum sticks
                  wooden mallets
                  triangle beaters

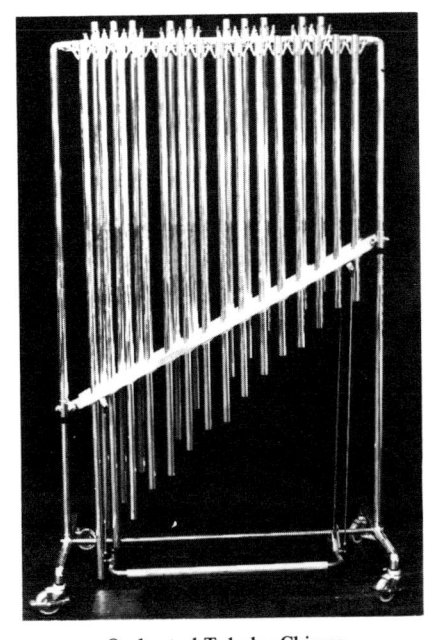

Orchestral Tubular Chimes

Origin and Construction. Sounding metal tubes go back to Asiatic origins. Since about 1885 they have served as bell substitutes in English orchestras, and soon thereafter they also appeared in orchestras of continental Europe. The earliest of these tubular chimes were cast in bronze, while today they are cut from industrially manufactured brass tubes.

The pitch of a tubular chime is determined by the length of the tube and the commensurate thickness of the metal. For example, a c^1 chime measures 155 cm (5'2") in length, an f^2 chime measures 76 cm (ca. 30 1/2"), and both have a diameter of 3.8 cm (ca. 1 1/2") and a metal thickness of 1.5 mm (3/32"). Chimes made especially for use on stage might have a metal thickness of up to 3 mm (3/16").

It is customary in continental Europe to hang individual chimes from a rack, in the order in which they are to be played in each composition. The damping is done by hand. In England and America, frames were first constructed in which the chimes hang in chromatic order (keyboard arrangement) and can be damped *in toto* by means of a pedal. This innovation emancipated the tubular chimes from the role of substitutes for regular bells to that of an independent instrument capable of playing melodic patterns in rapid tempo, half-damped, similar to the vibraphone in jazz. The widest possible compass of such a chromatic set of chimes ranges from f to f^2 (g^2); smaller instruments range from c^1 to f^2 or only to c^2.

Examples -- Britten: *The Turn of the Screw;* Boulez: *"pli selon pli;"* Hartmann: 7th and 8th Symphonies.

Method of Playing, Sound, and Uses. Chimes are played with pairs of hard wooden or plastic hammers covered with rawhide. Differences in tone quality are achieved through variations in the thickness of the leather and the weight of the hammers. Very soft tones require felt-padded hammers. The strike point for the purest bell-like tone is at the upper rim of the tube.

Example -- Henze: *Elegy* (Mus. Ex. 43).

An especially hard, metallic sound will result from using metal hammers. These are suitable only for high pitches.

Examples -- Copland: 3rd Symphony; Orff: *Antigonae.*

Webern, in his Six Pieces for Orchestra, Opus 6, calls for pianissimo chime tremolos played with rubber beaters. Actually, softly padded hammers would be more suitable. Scriabin, in *Le poème de l'extase,* Opus 54, asks for a forte tremolo on a *campane* in c^1, but it sounds better played one octave higher with normal hammers.

Orff, in *Trionfi* and *Oedipus,* indicates a glissando with wooden beaters or with a metal rod. Here the object is to create as shrill a sound as possible.

J. A. Riedl, in his Piece for Percussion, has the tubes played with triangle beaters and drum sticks, thus turning the bell sound more toward noise-like rattles. See also Kagel: *Anagrama* (Mus. Ex. 44).

Tubular chimes are preferable to bell plates whenever the clear and precise sound of small church bells is wanted. However, one generally plays one octave higher than notated. Particularly characteristic instances of such church-bell sounds are found in Verdi's *Il Trovatore* (Scene I), and *Un Ballo in maschera;* Mascagni's *Cavalleria rusticana;* Leoncavallo's *Pagliacci;* Ravel's *L'heure espagnole;* R. Strauss's *Die schweigsame Frau;* Puccini's *La Bohème.*

Tubular chimes without programmatic connotations, i.e., purely as timbre, are used in the following works -- Puccini: *Turandot;* Egk: *Peer Gynt, Abraxas,* and *Die Zaubergeige;* Hindemith: *Symphonic Metamorphosis* (Mus. Ex. 71), *Die Harmonie der Welt;* Th. Berger: *Symphonie chronique;* Orff: *Die Bernauerin, Trionfi, Antigonae, Oedipus* (Mus. Ex. 28); Henze: *Elegy* (Mus. Exx. 10, 30, 43), *Il re cervo* (Mus. Ex. 45); Messiaen: *Sept Haïkaï* (Mus. Ex. 88); Mamangakis: *Constructions* (Mus. Ex. 96); and others.

A set of high tubular chimes with a two-octave range of about c^2 to c^4 is used by Michael Gielen in *Pentaphonie* (Mus. Ex. 18). It is made of tubes having a considerably smaller diameter than ordinary tubular chimes, and consisting of the same alloy used for crotales. See also Henze: *Il re cervo* (Mus. Ex. 45).

Tubaphone (Tubuscampanophone)

Range and notation:

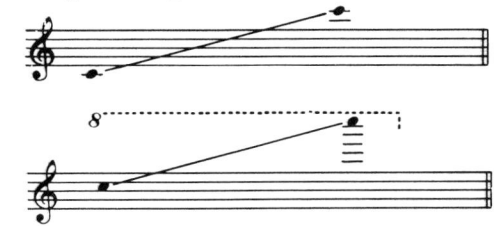

Sound: 2 octaves higher than notated:

Beaters: leather-padded wooden mallets
         small hardwood mallets

Origin and Construction. Before World War I, when the four-row xylophone with bars resting on straw pads was a favorite solo instrument in vaudeville, there appeared -- at first in England -- a complementary instrument called tubuscampanophone, or tubaphone for short.

Tubaphone

Instead of wooden bars it had brass or steel tubes with a diameter of 15 mm (5/8″). These tubes were of approximately the same length as the bars of the four-row xylophone and were arranged the same way. The instrument was played with spoon-like wooden mallets padded with leather, which brought forth metallic, hollow sounds having a slight vibrato. In the highest registers the sound was not unlike that of a glockenspiel.

The vibrato resulted from suspending the tubes on very thin cords, thus allowing them to swing back and forth slightly after having been struck.

Method of Playing and Uses. The tubaphone was played in the same manner as the four-row xylophone, for which reason the same or similar virtuoso pieces were played on either instrument.

The tubaphone did not, however, achieve the popularity and dissemination of the xylophone and was soon virtually forgotten. A later variation of the tubaphone with the tubes arranged in keyboard fashion failed to revitalize the instrument. Its use in serious music is rare.

Example -- Khatchaturian: *Gayané* (Mus. Ex. 46).

GLASS INSTRUMENTS (Sets of Tuned Glass Vessels)

Musical Glasses

Approximate range and notation:

Sound: as notated

Beaters: light beaters with wooden heads

Glass Harp

Range and notation:

Sound: as notated

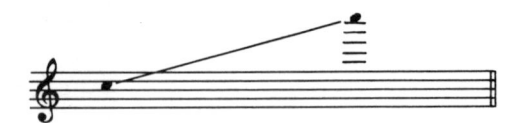

Played by rubbing with the fingers *(colla mano)*

Musical Glasses

    Thin-walled drinking glasses, standing on a cloth-covered base, can be made to produce sounds if struck at the rim with light, wooden-headed beaters. By pouring water into the glasses it is possible, within limits, to lower the indigenous pitch of each glass, even though this reduces the dynamic volume slightly. In using glasses of different sizes it is possible to arrange an entire scale. Needless to say, the glasses must be struck gently.
    Their delicate sound resembles that of small bells and, centuries ago, led to the construction of glass-bell instruments (musical glasses). Single glasses appear in Orff's *Schulwerk*, while in his stage work *The Moon* a two-part passage for six glasses tuned c^2, d^2, e^2, g^2, a^2, c^3 is included (Mus. Ex. 48).
    Another possibility of playing glasses is to rub the rims with finger tips moistened with vinegar. Sets of tuned glasses, called glass harps, were already known in the 18th century.

Glass Harmonica

Range and notation:

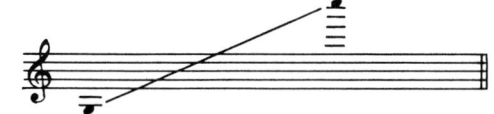

Sound: as notated

Played by rubbing with the fingers *(colla mano)*

In 1763, in London, Benjamin Franklin invented the glass harmonica, an instrument which soon was to enjoy great popularity, especially in Germany. It consisted of chromatically tuned glass bowls of decreasing diameters, mounted vertically on a spindle, and telescoped one into another to take up the least amount of space. Rotation was effected by means of a treadle, while the finger tips, held against the rims, caused the glass bowls to sound. The instrument -- usually in a case of precious wood -- had in its largest version a range of 3 1/2 octaves: $g - c^4$. The half-steps were identified by contrasting tints of glass.

After it was discovered that the glass harmonica greatly affected the nervous system of the player, the instrument, for which even Mozart, Beethoven, and their contemporaries had composed, gradually lost this rather eminent position, and by the end of the 19th century it could only be found in music halls and similar places of entertainment, for the performance of very simple, light music.

Richard Strauss chose the glass harmonica for the last scene of his opera *Die Frau ohne Schatten,* asking for chords containing up to eight tones. Since no glass harmonica was powerful enough to be effective in the context of a large orchestra, he himself suggested substitutes, first a reed organ, and later a vibraphone with two players.

The delicate sound of the glass harmonica, a sound that seems to hover in the air in glassy transparency, is capable of the softest, most subtle reverberations. Since the tones develop and fade slowly they do not lend themselves to fast playing: only slow, sustained, and rhythmically simple melodic passages are possible on the instrument. On the other hand, full chords can be performed very effectively.

Played with two hands by a single performer the instrument requires virtuoso agility, but if several players divide the phrases of a composition among themselves there is no problem.

Examples -- Orff: *Astutuli, Weihnachtsspiel, Oedipus* (Mux. Ex. 47), *Prometheus.*

Tuned Bottles

Range and notation:

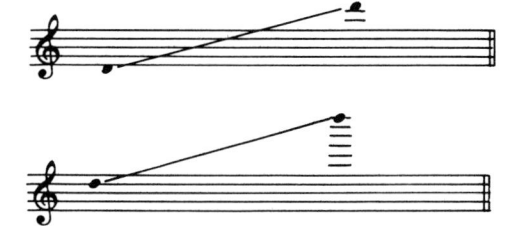

Sound: one octave higher than notated

Beaters: light, leather-padded xylophone beaters

Tuned Bottles

When Eric Satie wrote his ballet *Parade* in 1917 he incorporated -- inspired by Jean Cocteau -- sounds and noises from outside the field of music proper, such as the rattling of a roulette wheel, the clacking of a typewriter, and many others. From the stunt musicians of vaudeville he adopted the tuned bottles, also called *bouteillophone*. They consisted of a collection of empty bottles, selected individually by pitches, arranged by sizes from the smallest to the largest, fine-tuned if need be by adding water, and hung from a rack in scale order. They are best played with light, leather-padded xylophone beaters and demand the sureness of aim of a xylophone player. (See Mus. Ex. 49.)

Further examples -- Honegger: *Le dit des jeux du monde*; Nilsson: *Reaktionen* (5 empty bottles -- see Mus. Ex. 50).

MISCELLANEOUS INSTRUMENTS

Flexatone, Musical Saw, Sansa, Kalimba, Marimbula

According to Curt Sachs the flexatone, as well as the musical saw, appeared on the scene when vibrato and glissando were the hallmarks of American jazz. In the twenties they spread to Europe, and although they soon vanished from the music that had originally featured them, the flexatone attracted the attention of a few composers of serious music.

Flexatone

Range and notation:

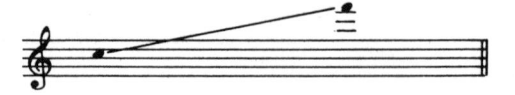

Sound: as notated

The flexatone consists of a steel blade or tongue which is struck on both sides by small, leather-padded wooden beaters attached to it by flexible steel wires. The tongue is fastened at its top edge to a frame, the bottom part of which functions as the handle of the instrument. While the hand that holds the instrument shakes it, thus causing the beaters to produce a tremolo, the thumb presses upon the narrow part of the tapered steel tongue. Differing degrees of thumb pressure alter the tongue's tension and thus lengthen or shorten its vibrating part. The greater the pressure and the higher the tension, the smaller the vibrating area and the higher the pitch. To achieve the desired pitch a good ear and a certain muscular sensitivity are required, since there are no means for pitch control other than the tensioning of the steel tongue.

The flexatone can only be played in tremolo fashion: individually struck tones are hardly possible.

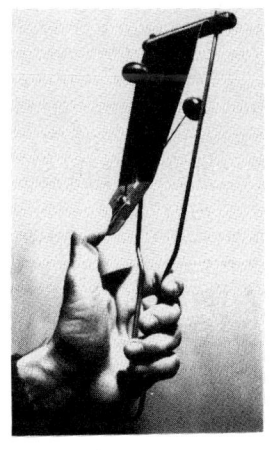

Flexatone

Shaking the flexatone vigorously, or less so, determines its volume of sound. Its dynamic range, however, is quite limited. Each tremolo pitch can be connected to the following one by way of a glissando. The sound of the flexatone has little resonance and is rather dry, shrill, and somewhat tinny and scurrilous.

Examples -- Schönberg: *Moses and Aaron* (Mus. Ex. 51); Berg: Three Pieces for Orchestra; Khatchaturian: Piano Concerto (Mus. Ex. 52).

Musical Saw

Range and notation:

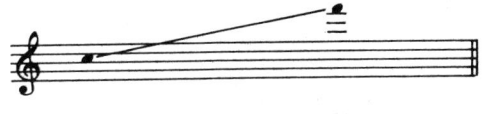

Sound: as notated

The tone production of the musical saw, like that of the flexatone, is based on the principle of a vibrating steel tongue. Unlike the flexatone, however, its whining tone is produced by passing a hair bow across the edge of a saw blade, causing it to vibrate. Differences of pitch are achieved by bending the blade. Only rarely is the musical saw played with a soft beater.

The musical saw is played by specialists who rarely are orchestra musicians. In cases where the notated range of the musical saw goes beyond the instrument's capability, an electric guitar played with a metal bar to produce tremolos and glissandi, an *ondes Martenot*, or a *Mixtur-Trautonium* may serve as a substitute.

Examples -- Honegger: *Antigone;* Mayuzumi: *Tonepleromas 55;* Henze: *Elegy.*

Sansa (Sanza, Zanza), Kalimba

Potential range -- within the
total range shown:
(but never more than 17
tones per instrument)

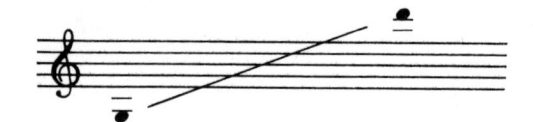

Sound: as notated

This fairly small instrument with plucked tongues of metal or wood has come to us from Black Africa where it is known by many different names, depending on the respective tribal languages (for example, *sandi, etingili, lun, lilimba, kasanga, ambira, djimba, ekende, ibeka, likembe, kankobele, mbira, nsimbi, pokido*). Along the Congo river the instrument is also known as the marimba, a name borrowed, of course, from the bar instrument. In (Latin-)America it became the marimbula, a larger counterpart of the sansa, with a much more extended compass.

The sansa consists of a wooden resonator whose shape may differ widely. A rectangular or trapezoidal body may be considered the basic type. However, one also finds round and oval forms, as well as boat and trough-shaped types. On the resonator surface that contains one or more sound holes are fastened several flat, tuned, tonguelike lamellae of metal (or of wood in more primitive instruments). The mounting of these tongues is basically similar in all types: the set of tongues is pressed onto two bridges by means of looped wires or of a wooden or metal crossrod, so that the free ends of the lamellae project slightly upwards from the body of the instrument. Short sounds (single or double tones, as well as series of tones) are produced by plucking the projecting, freely vibrating tongue ends with the thumbs, while both hands clasp the corpus of the instrument to hold it. Precise tuning can be accomplished by pushing the tongues in and out, thus shortening or lengthening their projecting (vibrating) segments.

The various African sansas do not necessarily possess the same number of tongues; from 7 to 15 different tone producing lamellae are used, depending on the size and origin of the instrument. The placement next to each other of shorter and longer tongues, i.e., of higher and lower tones, often seems quite arbitrary. In most cases, however, the lowest tones are placed in the center.

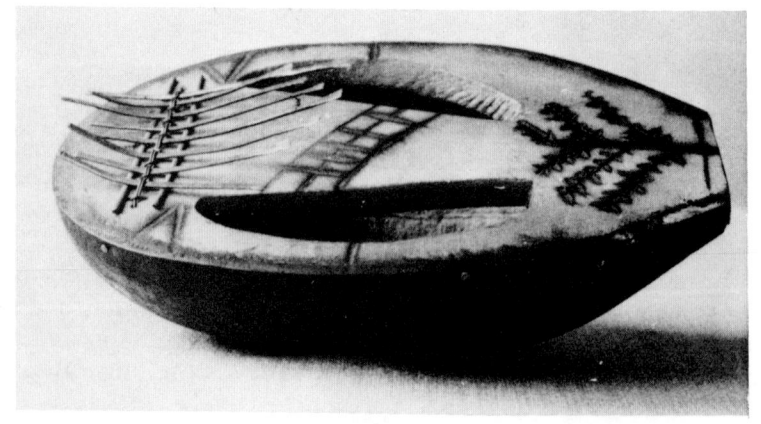

Sansa

In South Africa, an instrument related to the sansa is now manufactured in factories and called kalimba. It has 15 to 17 tuned steel tongues comprising a G major scale which rises from the center toward the outsides, with alternating tones right and left. Its tone quality is quite delicate, and the use of steel for the tongues produces relatively long reverberations. Its sound is not unlike that of a musical clock.

Kalimba

The measurements of the body of a trapezoidal kalimba are as follows:
    length: 18½ cm (7 3/8")
    width at the top: 10½ cm (4 3/16")
    at the bottom: 13 cm (5 3/16")
    depth: 3 cm (1 3/16")

Walter Haupt has used the sansa in *Lasermusik,* notated with graphics lacking specified pitches. The stereotyped succession of patterns is scored together with pizzicato violins which, likewise, are played by percussionists (in sansa fashion, so to speak). A toy hurdy-gurdy (*Kinderleier*) and a Jew's Harp (*Maultrommel*) are used as additional plucking instruments. (See Mus. Ex. 111)

Marimbula

Range and notation:

Sound: as notated

Beaters: fingertip
    steel needle
    wooden rod

The German firm of M. Grabmann has produced a marimbula modeled after its Latin-American ancestor, whose set of tongues. arranged in keyboard order (see Ill. on p. 78), comprises two octaves ($c - c^2$). The individual tongues of this instrument can be tuned the same way as those of the sansa.

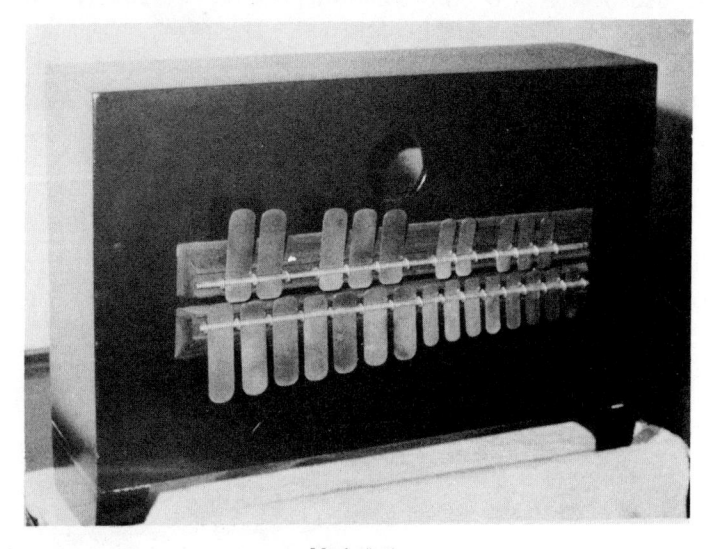

Marimbula

Measurements of the resonator
    length: 71 cm (28 3/8")
    width: 43 cm (17 3/16")
    depth: 20 cm (8")
Measurements of the tongues
 lowest tone (c) -- length: 10 ½ cm (4 3/16")
       width: 3 cm (1 3/16")
 highest tone (c^2) -- length: 6 cm (2 3/8")
       width: 2 cm (3/4")

Henze used the marimbula for the first time in *El Cimarron* and in *Heliogabalus Imperator*.

Slide Whistle (Lotos Flute, Swanee Whistle)

Range and notation:

Sound: as notated

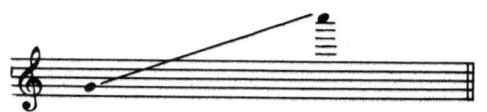

Characteristics, Origin, and Construction. The slide whistle is one of the instruments that owes its recent popularity to the prominence of vibrato in early jazz. Together with the flexatone it was relegated to the special effects of the percussion group. Its forebears are found in Asia and on the islands of the South Pacific. While the slide whistles of Papua may be as long as 2 meters (6'8"), the present-day instrument consists of a 28 cm (11 3/16") long cylindrical tube of ebony with a total diameter of about 3 cm (1 3/16") and a wall thickness of 6 mm (1/4"). The inner wall of the tube is lined with tin. A metal piston is moved up and down inside the tube with the help of an attached wire rod, thus shortening or lengthening the air column. The wire rod protrudes from the end of the whistle. The slide whistle is played with a recorder-type mouth piece. It is particularly popular in England where it is called Swanee whistle.

Characteristics of Sound. The sound of the slide whistle would be the same as that of the recorder were it not for the vibrato produced by the hand that moves the piston. This exaggerated vibrato, and the whistle's ability to produce a fast or slow glissando throughout its entire range, turned it into a "gag instrument" used to underline the action in comic as well as dramatic scenes in vaudeville, radio, and films.

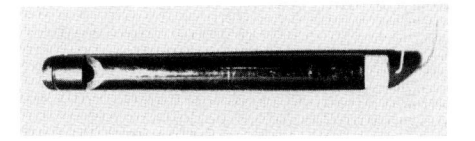

Slide Whistle

As with the flexatone, the slide whistle does not possess any points of reference for finding pitches; the player must rely exclusively on his ear and his manipulative sensitivity for the instrument. The slide whistle develops its greatest loudness from about g^2 up.

Uses. G. Gordon has used the slide whistle in his ballet *The Rake's Progress,* where it provides the voice for a miming female ballet singer. Isolated vibrato tones are played in Chabrier's *Souvenir de Munich* for orchestra, as arranged by I. Française.

Additional examples -- J. Homs: *Musica per A 6;* Ravel: *L'enfant et les sortilèges* (Mus. Ex. 53).

The Piano as Percussion Instrument

Range and notation: same as a concert grand

Beaters: bass drum beater
         timpani beaters
         hard-felt mallets with large and small heads
         rubber beaters
         cork beaters
         wooden beaters (large and small hammers) and bars
         drum sticks
         metal beaters and bars
         plectra (for plucking)
         wire brush and other brushes

Strings struck with beaters have been known for centuries, beginning with the various kinds of dulcimers. Piano strings, however, were probably not struck in this manner before the first Grail bells were constructed in 1879. In 1912 Henry Cowell first introduced his experiments with tone clusters played on the keys with flat hands and forearms; later he composed pieces in which the strings were played directly by the hands as if the piano were a harp. Further developments led to the use of beaters hitting the strings, and at times the strings themselves were prepared with the most diverse objects in order to change the normal piano sound into non-piano sounds, reverberations, rattles, and muted effects. Moreover, the sounding board and the frame also were used for the production of new sounds (cf. the music of John Cage, Mauricio Kagel, and others). Subsequently, Orff called for piano strings played with beaters in the *witch's scene* of *Die Bernauerin.* The objective was to create a mixture of dark and bright background noises by having members of the percussion section play tremolos with timpani beaters up and down the piano's bass and treble strings (Mus. Ex. 54).

In Orff's *Antigonae, Oedipus,* and *Prometheus,* individual tones as well as entire phrases and chords are to be played with beaters of various sizes and degrees of hardness (Mus. Ex. 55).

In order to find the proper tones among the many indistinguishable strings of the piano it is well to mark the dampers by pasting onto them small pieces of paper with letters. Beaters with small heads are preferable in the middle and upper registers because the strings are very close there. Best suited are small wooden hammers which may have felt padding on one side of the head and leather on the other. Orff, in his *Prometheus*, indicates that the string choirs should be struck with single cymbals, as well as with crotales, to create a mixture of high metal sounds with the sounds of the piano strings.

Bar Instruments of the Orff Schulwerk

Construction, ranges, and dynamic capacities of the instruments specially designed for Orff's *Schulwerk*, as well as their beaters, have been developed primarily for the musical education of the young. Even so, the quality of the instruments with large bars (bass xylophone and bass metallophone) is high enough to meet the requirements and sound quality of regular orchestra instruments. They may thus be used in this role as long as their ranges fit the compositions in question. Furthermore, the bars of all the *Schulwerk* instruments listed below can easily be lifted off, thus making it possible, through exchanges of certain half-tone bars, to provide for different diatonic scales.

Most suitable for playing glockenspiels and xylophones are small, round-headed wooden beaters which may be equipped with thin rubber rings or small felt pads for softer impacts.

Alto instruments are generally played with hard felt beaters whose heads have a diameter of about 2 cm (3/4").

For bass xylophone and bass metallophone, best results are achieved with orchestral rubber-head beaters wound with wool yarn.

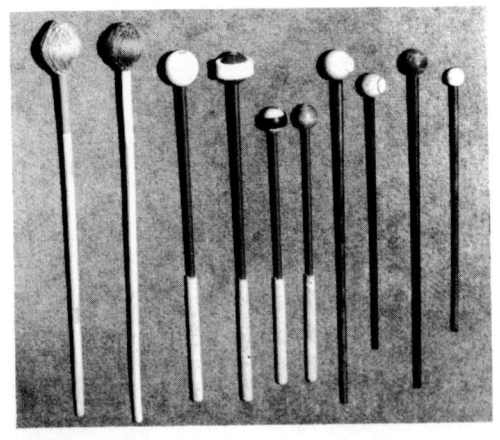

Beaters for the Orff Schulwerk Instruments

Soprano Glockenspiel

Range and notation:

(diatonic* or chromatic model)

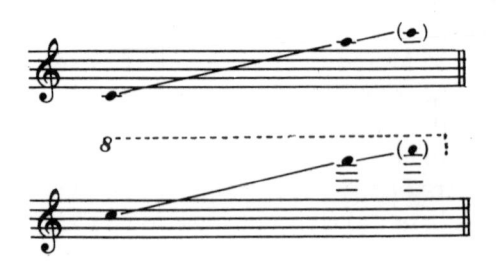

Soprano Glockenspiel

Sound: two octaves higher than notated

General information: Special *Schulwerk* beaters: wooden head with different strike surfaces -- one side for hard impacts; the other side with small felt pad or thin rubber ring for soft impacts.

* = C-major scale bars

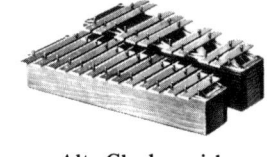

Alto Glockenspiel

Range and notation:
(diatonic* or chromatic model)

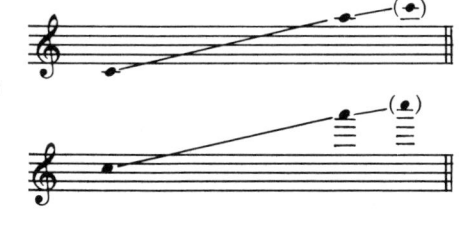

Sound: one octave higher than notated

Alto Glockenspiel

Beaters: same as Soprano Glockenspiel

Alto-Soprano Glockenspiel

Alto-Soprano Glockenspiel

This instrument is a combination of the two preceding glockenspiels.

Soprano Xylophone

Range and notation:
(diatonic* or chromatic model)

Sound: one octave higher than notated

Soprano Xylophone

Beaters -- common: small wooden-headed beaters
         -- less common: small hard-felt beaters

Alto Xylophone

Range and notation:
(diatonic* or chromatic model)

Alto Xylophone

Sound: as notated

Beaters -- common: small hard-felt beaters
         -- less common: small wooden-headed beaters

Alto-Soprano Xylophone

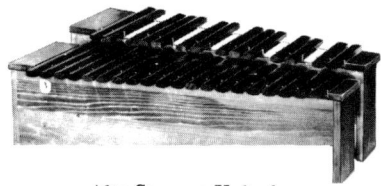

Alto-Soprano Xylophone

This instrument is a combination of the two preceding xylophones.

* = C-major scale bars

Bass Xylophone

Range and notation: 
(diatonic* or chromatic model)

Sound: as notated

Beaters: large hard-felt beaters
  beaters with rubber heads wound with wool yarn

Bass Xylophone

Soprano Metallophone

Range and notation: 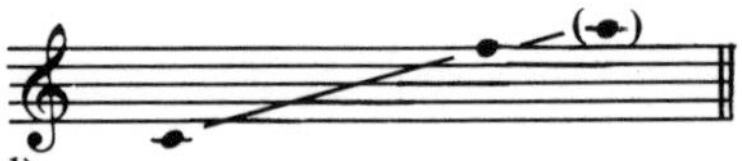
(diatonic* or chromatic model)

Sound: one octave higher than notated

Beaters: hard-felt beaters

Soprano Metallophone

Alto Metallophone

Range and notation: 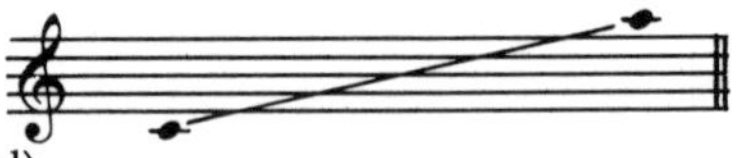
(diatonic* or chromatic model)

Sound: as notated

Beaters: large hard-felt beaters

Alto Metallophone

Alto-Soprano Metallophone

This instrument is a combination of the two preceding metallophones.

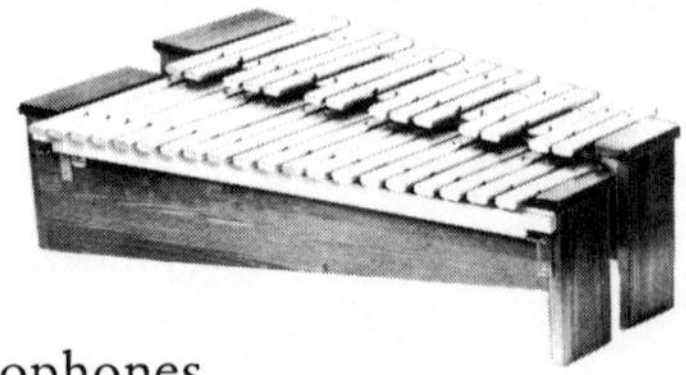

Alto-Soprano Metallophone

Bass Metallophone

Range and notation: 
(diatonic* or chromatic model)

Sound: as notated

Beaters: large hard-felt beaters
  beaters with rubber heads wound with wool yarn

Bass Metallophone

* = C-major scale bars

INSTRUMENTS WITH INDEFINITE PITCH

Introduction

The preceding section includes only one clef-notated skin membranophone: the timpano -- a traditional percussion instrument.

In more recent times other membranophones with controllable head tension and without snares or other auxiliary sounds have also been tuned to fixed pitches, such as the bass drum tuned to B♭ in Stravinsky's *Le Sacre du printemps.* In other instances it was not so much a matter of choice as of necessity to insist on fixed pitches so that the instruments could meet the harmonic and melodic requirements of the music, especially if the instrumentation was transparent. This applies primarily to membranophones with pitched skin sounds, where the pitches stand out clearly because of favorable conditions of resonance, especially if played with soft-headed beaters. Among these are frame drums such as in Chailley's *La Dame à la Licorne* (Mus. Ex. 64), bongos, and Latin-American timbales.

The current tendency to extract new sounds from the wealth of potential musical (as well as non-musical) sound sources around us, particularly from those with definite pitches, is enhanced by our ability to pick up sounds by electro-acoustic means and reproduce, amplify, and otherwise manipulate them electronically. Instruments with weak volume and limited carrying power as well as certain performance subtleties thus can now be brought out clearly and raised to the same levels of volume as those of other, stronger instruments. In fact, new skin membranophones have recently been built in the United States, specifically designed for use in recording studios for popular music. However, since they are still in the developmental stage their eventual quality and uses remain to be seen. Among these instruments are the tuned tom-toms (discussed under tom-tom sets in the chapter below) and the boobam, an instrument consisting of skin-covered segments of bamboo. A similar new instrument is the log drum, a tuned bass wood block belonging to the family of the slit drums.

Temple blocks have not yet been notated with clefs even though they are manufactured in clearly differentiated sets. Their timbre, however, precludes unambiguous pitch definition.

Bronze bells and small bowl-shaped bells *(Schalenglöckchen),* anvils, metal blocks, and cowbells are generally considered struck idiophones of indefinite pitch. However, even these instruments are often scored in precise tunings. In more recent scores one occasionally finds selected cowbells combined into sets and played with beaters.

Jingles, which belong to the family of rattles, can also be fairly clearly separated in sound if one arranges the many randomly combined jingle disks according to their pitches.

The angklung, which belongs to the beaten rattles, functions as a tuned melody instrument in the Far Eastern lands of its origin, while in Western civilization it is used as a rattle of indefinite pitch.

SKIN MEMBRANOPHONES (Drums)

Tambourin Provençal (Tabor); Long Drum; Parade Drum or Basler Trommel; Military Drum; Tenor Drum (without Snares); Snare Drum (Side Drum).

General Remarks. Skin-covered instruments with bowls, tubes, or frames as resonators have been part of ritual and cult since Antiquity. However, by the time they appeared in Western Europe, during the early Middle Ages, they were no longer restricted to ritual, and their tubular or cylindrical forms soon spread widely as folk and military instruments.

Their sizes and proportions have changed continually throughout their existence, depending on their respective functions. Around the turn of the 18th century they entered the orchestra. One of their earliest uses on the stage was in the opera *Alcyone* (1706) by Marin Marais of the Lully School. Subsequently, drums were developed chiefly within the context of military music and later also in the field of entertainment, and the orchestra took over the new drum types as they evolved.

The percussion inventory of today includes a considerable number of different kinds of cylindrical drums in a variety of sizes, thus making it possible to do justice to the intended timbres appropriate to music of different eras and civilizations. Often the date of origin of a composition and the musico-geographic background of the composer must act as guides for the proper choice of drums, since the indications in scores are not always sufficiently explicit. Borderline cases, as well as incorrect nomenclature due to a notorious confusion of concepts in this field, are frequent and must always be taken into consideration.

Tambourin Provençal (Tabor)

Common beaters: drum sticks
Less common: small soft-felt beaters
small hard-felt beaters
wire brushes

The primitive precursor of military drums is a smaller and lighter drum without snares and with only one skin: the tabor. This type of drum survives to this day as a folk instrument, the *tambourin provençal,* played by the *Galoubet* pipers of southern France. The small drum hangs by a cord from the wrist of the same hand that also holds the fife *(galoubet),* and is beaten with the player's other hand.

The body of the early *tambourin provençal* -- of light, fine wood adorned with carvings -- measures up to 70 cm (28") in depth and has a diameter of about 36 cm (14 3/8"). Instruments of this kind may have one skin or two and may or may not have one snare string lying across the batter head. In French operatic tradition *tambourins* without snares were preferred, and they have gradually become the norm in general usage.

The dimensions of the orchestral *tambourin provençal* are identical, by and large, with those of the early instruments, but they may be adjusted in size to fit the sound requirements of a given ensemble. Today the *tambourin* is considered, in a way, a forerunner of the tom-tom and is often used to fill a gap in a set of pitched drums. Its tone quality resembles that of a tenor drum or a long drum without snares. Its structural innovations over the years are similar to those of the latter (see Ill. on p. 85).

In the folk music of Provence the *tambourin* is played with a beater having a heavy, oval head (see Ill. on p. 27).

If used in combination with other drums -- all played by one performer -- each respective beater indication also applies to the *tambourin* (small drum sticks or felt beaters, etc.).

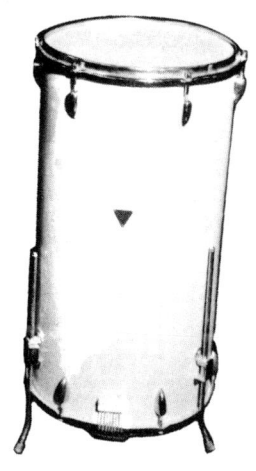

Orchestral *Tambourin Provençal*

Examples of general use -- Lully: *Amadis;* Massenet: *Le Cid;* Bizet: *Farandole* and *Pastorale* from *L'arlésienne suite;* Milhaud: *Suite française, Suite provençale* (Mus. Ex. 57), *Salade, La création du monde* (Mus. Ex. 58), Concerto for Percussion and Small Orchestra, *La mort d'un tyran* (Mus. Ex. 60); Messiaen: *Turangalîla-Symphonie;* Honegger: *Le roi David;* Jolivet: Concerto for Piano and Orchestra (*tambourin moyen, tambourin grave,* both struck at the rim with timpani beaters); Copland: *Appalachian Spring;* Stravinsky: *Petrouchka* (original version).

Long Drum (with Snares)

The designation long drum is applied chiefly to the large drums which in their original form were used together with fifes by the mercenary soldiers of the Middle Ages. Calf skins, mounted on narrow wooden hoops, are stretched across a wooden shell by means of pressure hoops and tightened with cords that run zigzag around the drum. The drum's shell measures about 50 to 75 cm (20″ to 30″) in depth and has a diameter of 40 to 50 cm (16″ to 20″). A few strong gut strings, stretched across the bottom of the snare head, provide the snare noise that blends with the dark, resonant sound of the drum proper.

Long Drum

In present-day orchestras a type of long drum is used which has approximately the same dimensions as its medieval forerunner. The cords for tightening the drumheads have been replaced with tensioning screws that permit rapid adjustments. The snares consist of 4 to 6 strong gut strings stetched against the lower surface of the snare head, which can be tightened or loosened by means of a mechanical device. The large cavity of the shell generates a strong resonance while the snares, being rather far from the batter head, are activated to a much lesser degree. This gives the drum its dark and muffled timbre which is, of course, increased further if the drum is played with snares off. Like the modern standing tom-toms the long drum stands on three adjustable feet which are attached to its shell and which prevent impairment of its sound (see Ill. on p. 85).

Examples -- Wagner: *Die Walküre, Lohengrin, Parsifal* (on stage), *Die Meistersinger* (on stage); R. Strauss: *Till Eulenspiegel, Der Rosenkavalier, Friedenstag;* Hindemith: *Mathis der Maler;* Egk: *Die Zaubergeige;* Orff: *Die Bernauerin* (Mus. Ex. 56); Paul Dessau: *In memoriam Bert Brecht* (3 long drums).

Parade Drum (Basler Trommel)

The parade drum is a smaller version of the long drum, with a wooden or metal shell. In order to achieve the highest possible head tension the drum requires very strong tensioning devices made of metal. The drum guilds of Basel prefer to this day the historical zigzag tension cords which cause high head tension and thus a brightly ringing tone. The heavy cords, however, do demand commensurate care and effort to assure equal tension at all times.

Old Parade Drums *(Basler Trommeln)*

After the Thirty Years' War (1618-1648) the depth of these large drums was gradually reduced, so that by the middle of the 18th century the average shell dimensions had come down to 40 x 40 cm (16" x 16"). This caused the dark, resonant sound to give way to the greater prominence of the snare noise: the sound typical of today's parade drum (also known as *Basler Trommel*). Subsequently the wooden shells were replaced by brass shells.

The modern orchestral parade drum with the standard measurements of 40 x 40 cm (16" x 16") possesses the same snares and tensioning devices as the larger long drum and has the same kind of feet, but may also be placed on a stand.

Examples -- Beethoven: *Wellington's Victory;* Mozart: *Contra Dances;* Frank Martin: *Der Cornet;* Honegger: *Deliciae Basilienses;* Liebermann: *Geigy Festival Concerto* for *Basler Trommel* and Orchestra (Mus. Ex. 59).

Parade Drum  Military Drum

Military Drum (Field Drum, Street Drum, etc.)

The tensioning-screw mechanism, invented in 1837, not only brought about faster, more efficient tightening of the drum heads, but also permitted a reduction of the drums' shells to a depth of about 30 cm (12") with a width of about 37 cm (ca. 15"). It was at the time of this innovation that the term military drum *(tambour)* was coined.

A subsequent desire for a lighter timbre and for easier handling caused the military drums of most European countries to grow still smaller. For example, the sizes of the Bavarian drums were reduced to a depth of only 22 cm (ca. 9"), and this as early as 1860. Naturally this development created a certain amount of confusion, with drum sizes differing from country to country.

It is important for military drums that their easy, crisp, and dry timbre be retained even though their resonance may vary according to their different shell depths. The heads, which are stretched across metal shells and are made very tight by the tensioning screws, should agitate at least eight gut or wound, plastic strings, which, to be fully effective, must lie closely against the skin of the snare head (as, in fact, they must in all types of snare drums). The snares can be applied and detached quickly and noiselessly with the help of a modern mechanism, the snare release.

The drum is placed on a stand which, being slightly slanted, enables the player to move quickly to other instruments.

Examples -- Beethoven: *Egmont;* Rossini: *La gazza ladra;* Auber: *Fra Diavolo;* Donizetti: *La fille du régiment;* Gounod: *Faust;* Rimsky-Korsakov: *Shéhérazade, Capriccio espagnol;* Charpentier: *Louise;* Puccini: *La Bohème* (drums on stage), *Tosca;*

Ravel: *Bolero, Alborada del gracioso;* Lalo: *Le roi d'Ys, Symphonie espagnole;* Debussy: *Fêtes, Iberia;* Kotoński: *Musique en relief* (Mus. Ex. 77).

Tenor Drum (without Snare)

In the early 19th century a snareless drum called tenor drum (German: *Wirbel-, Rollier-,* or *Tenortrommel;* French: *caisse roulante*) appeared in military bands. It had the same dimensions as the older wooden shell drums and was probably put together from discarded specimens. Its dark and somber roll furnished the background for the rhythms of the light-timbred snare drums. On the average it measured 30 to 40 cm (12" to 16") in depth and up to 46 cm (ca. 18") in width. The shell of the tenor drum is made of wood, and its dimensions are designed to achieve good resonance in order to assure a sonorous sound without the help of snares. The head-tensioning mechanism and the feet correspond to those of the drum types mentioned earlier. Berlioz used the *caisse roulante* in his *Requiem* (1837) with the instruction that it be tuned to B♭ and played with timpani beaters. It was Berlioz's opinion that Gluck already had this type of drum in mind for the chorus of the *Scythians* in his opera *Iphigenie en Tauride* (1779).

Tenor Drum *(caisse roulante)*

For today's composers this type of drum is rather superfluous since its timbral characteristics are practically identical to those of the parade drum with snares off, or to the modern tom-tom. In drum choirs, on the other hand, it still provides the timbral contrast to the snared parade and military drums and is often played with felt beaters.

In recent music we find the tenor drum in Milhaud: *Suite provençale;* Honegger: *Pacific 231;* Varèse: *Ionisation* (Mus. Ex. 109); Fortner: *The Creation;* Copland: 3rd Symphony; Britten: *The Prince of the Pagodes;* and others.

Snare Drum

Both the type and the name of the snare drum originated at the time when the small drum (snare drum) of the military bands was taken over by salon and dance orchestras and by jazz bands. In the course of this transfer the shell-depth of the military drum was gradually reduced to 20, 16, 14, and even 10 cm (approx. 8", 6", 5" and even

4″) while its diameter remained the same: 35 or 36 cm (about 14″).

The term snare drum became established in the beginning of the 20th century, even though the drum's size was still that of the small military drum. The Germans called it *Kleine Trommel*, the French called it *caisse claire*, and the Italians *tamburo piccolo* or *cassa chiara*. It is also known as side drum.

The standard version of a concert snare drum has a shell of metal or laminated wood, about 16 to 18 cm (ca. 6 1/2″ to 7 1/4″) in depth, with a modern mechanism for tightening the skins, and with a snare-release mechanism for the 8 to 12 wound, plastic snares. Shallower models are better suited for small instrumental ensembles or for sets of several snare drums in timbral gradations. The differences in sound result from adjusting the respective drum-head tensions to the different drum sizes. The drums are placed on stands in the same manner as the military drums.

The adoption of the snare drum by salon and dance orchestras did not serve it well: on the one hand it was reduced to providing nothing but accompaniments which in turn caused its players to lose their technical proficiency; on the other hand the ever greater reduction of the drum's shell depth robbed it of its original timbre since a very shallow resonance space can produce little more than a rather chirpy, papery sound. This sound deteriorated still further with the introduction of wire spirals in place of ordinary snares. The spirals, because of their easy response, were intended to help amateur players cover up their poor roll technique. However, such blankets of spiral snares blur the drums' beats which normally are exceptionally exact and terse, especially when they come in rapid succession. In addition, the spirals have the disadvantage of creating disturbing sympathetic vibrations when the pitches of other instruments correspond to those of the drum heads.

The recent introduction of synthetic drum heads to replace animal skins has had the advantage that these plastic heads are almost completely impervious to the influence of humidity or dryness and possess great tensile strength.

Snare Drums

The sound of snare drums with snares off is hard, dry, and of little resonance. The batter head is always tuned a bit tighter than the snare head, so that the sound of each remains distinct from the other. Drummers often prefer the modern tom-toms to the snare drum with snares off, even though these do not always meet the composers' intentions.

The term muffled drum, hailing from old military usage, requires covering the batter head with a cloth or disengaging the snares. Today the former is done only when expressly called for, while the latter is simply marked *senza corde* or *snares off.*

Examples -- Pfitzner: *Die Rose vom Liebesgarten;* Kotoński: *Musique en relief* (see Mus. Ex. on following page).

3 *Tamburi con corde, coperti* (cloth covered)

pp = soft beaters, ff = hard beaters, *) press roll = keep beater pressed against batter head so that it will continue to bounce a few times.

Recent compositions often call for sets of different types of drums of different sound quality, with and without snares, to be played by one or more performers. One of the best-known examples is Stravinsky's *L'histoire du soldat* (1918), which is scored for one bass drum, two snare drums of different sizes and pitches with snares off (*caisse claire sans timbre*), as well as a military drum (*tambour*) which, in the original version, was played with snares on throughout so that it could serve as the drum with the highest pitch.

In a later version, prepared for a recording, Stravinsky substituted tom-toms for the two snare drums with snares off, while the *tambour* -- though still the highest sounding drum -- was used with snares on only in the *Royal March* and *The Song of the Devil*.

Milhaud, in several of his works, used the following drums in tuned sequence: *caisse claire* (snare drum), *caisse roulante* (tenor drum), and *tambourin provençal* (Mus. Ex. 60). Ravel, in *Daphnis et Chloë*, contrasts a *caisse claire* (snare drum) with a *tambour* (military drum).

In Bartók's Sonata for Two Pianos and Percussion (1937), a snare drum with snares on and another with snares off are used, and in certain spots they are grouped with a bass drum played with wooden beaters.

Varèse, in his *Ionisation* (Mus. Ex. 109) uses *caisse roulante* (tenor drum), *caisse roulante avec timbre* (tenor drum with snares), *tambour militaire* (military drum), *caisse claire* (snare drum), *caisse claire détimbrée* (snare drum with snares off), and *tarol* (a very bright-sounding, shallow little drum, with a few gut snares).

Other compositions requiring sets of drums as part of the percussion section are Stravinsky: *Les noces* (Mus. Ex. 19); Hindemith: *Symphonic Metamorphosis;* Hartmann: Concerto for Piano, Wind Instruments, and Percussion, *Simplicius Simplicissimus*, 6th and 7th Symphonies; Henze: *Ode an den Westwind, Antifone;* Egk: *Die chinesische Nachtigall, Irische Legende;* Chavez: Toccata; Jolivet: Concerto for Ondes Martenot and Orchestra; Killmayer: *La tragedia di Orfeo;* Armin Schibler: Concerto for Percussion and Orchestra; Nono: *Canti di vita* with 8 *tamburi senza corde* (snare drums with snares off) and 4 *gran casse* (bass drums).

Beaters. Shapes and materials of drum sticks have changed with the times. The unwieldy beaters of the medieval mercenary soldiers were succeeded by the conically tapered sticks with their pea or olive-shaped points, as we know them today. These drum sticks are heavy or light, depending on whether they are used for large or small drums, and are made of exotic hardwood, mostly Brazilwood or ebony.

Drum sticks used by jazz drummers must be especially strong, particularly at the tip, because they are also used for beating the rim of the drum, as well as the suspended cymbal. A slender stick was developed which begins to taper towards its small head only in the final quarter of its total length. It is manufactured in several sizes with heads of different weights and shapes, and in orchestral use it has largely replaced earlier types.

A small-headed timpani mallet (*mailloche*) or a stick with a small hard-felt head may, if specifically called for, be used for snareless drums, as, for ex., in Stravinsky's *L'histoire du soldat, Marche Royale* (Mus. Ex. 62). The timpani mallets used in this way produce a somewhat flat tone, while the beaters with the hard-felt heads sound more precise, but also less delicate.

The technique of using wire brushes, singly and in pairs, originated with the jazz drummers. Modern composers of serious music occasionally adopt simple forms of this style of drumming, selected from the numerous jazz variants.

The brush consists of a bundle of very thin, flexible steel wires held together by a handle and spread evenly like a fan. A mechanical device, or a rubber ring, permits adjustments of the spread of the wires to the desired width which, for use on the snare drum, is most effective at 4 to 5 cm (1 5/8" to 2"). The drum is beaten with the ends of the wires which are brought down flat on the skin.

Use of wire brushes in pairs permits a rapid series of beats, up to the single-stroke roll. A stirring-motion of the brush produces a high pitched hiss which in the days of the silent movies was used to imitate the sound of steam locomotives and similar noises.

Examples of the use of the steel brush -- Gershwin: *Porgy and Bess;* Jolivet: Concerto for Ondes Martenot and Orchestra; Gordon: *The Rake's Progress;* Killmayer: *Rêveries* for Soprano, Piano, and Percussion, *La tragedia di Orfeo;* Weill: *Lost in the Stars;* Armin Schibler: Concerto for Percussion and Orchestra, Op. 63; Bo Nilsson: *Ein irrender Sohn* (Mus. Ex. 89).

Technique of Playing. Techniques of drum beating originated in the Middle Ages, around the 13th century, when mercenary troops were first supplied with fifes and drums. During the 15th and 16th centuries the large snare drums of the Swiss mercenaries emerged as the prototype of military snare drums; in fact, they were then widely known as the "Swiss." The honor to have preserved and developed the highly sophisticated military drum technique with its profuse repertory of embellishments belongs to the old established traditional drum guilds of Basel.

When the drum moved from the orchestra into smaller instrumental ensembles and was relegated to the role of accompanimental background, its technique of playing had to be adjusted to a reduced level of volume so that the drum sound would blend suitably into its new instrumental environment. Some of the subtleties of drum playing thus were lost.

Only in jazz music did percussion regain its soloistic role, and a modern, clear, yet colorful and virtuosic technique of beating has been the result. This technique has proved useful too to orchestral percussionists in view of the ever-growing acceptance of jazz-related elements into concert music and its fringe areas. The jazz drum technique, incidentally, has much in common with the virtuoso drum-corps style, the so-called Basel drum technique, which is particulary popular in English-speaking countries. In fact, many of the Basel techniques were taken over by American drummers in the early days of jazz.

A work such as the Geigy Festival Concerto for Drum *(Basler Trommel)* and Orchestra by Rolf Liebermann demands of the soloist great technical proficiency in this mode of playing.

In the Basel technique the strokes are always short and dry. The vitality and interest of this kind of drum playing rest on the continuous alternation of the two hands *(Applikatur)* as they produce a wide variety of effects, different dynamics, accents, grace notes, and rolls, through skillful handling of the beaters.

The fact that a drum stick, by means of finger pressure applied immediately upon striking, can bounce and produce another stroke of equal strength permits the execution of very rapid successions of beats.

Tamb mil. (Military Drum)

Examples — Henze: *Il re cervo*

The systematic alternation of single and double strokes is called paradiddle, a technique which not only enlivens the phrasing but makes possible rapid strokes while moving from instrument to instrument.

3 Tom-toms

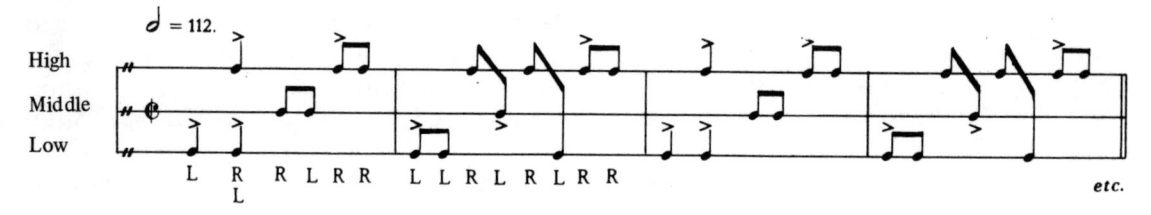

Example -- Latin-American Rhythmic Sequence

2 Tom-toms

Alto

Basso

Piatto (Cymbal)

Tamb. mil.
sul palco
(Military drum on stage)
(senza measure)

Example -- Henze: *Il re cervo*

The drummers of the Basel tradition believe that rolls consist of the fastest possible double-bounce strokes, while jazz drummers also employ the single-stroke roll (open roll), a rapid succession of single strokes brought about by means of a special finger technique.

The close or dense roll of orchestral drummers is produced by pressing the sticks upon the skin in rapid alternation and with good muscular control of fingers, arms, and hands. Thoughtful and diligent practice is essential to achieve an even and dynamically expressive roll in which no individual strokes can be discerned.

The single grace note is called a flam: a note struck immediately before the accented main note. Both strokes, the grace note as well as the main note, are always played with alternating hands.

The two-note grace, called the drag or the three-stroke ruff, consists of two small notes before the main note. It is executed by a double-bounce stroke played as lightly and fast as possible with one drum stick, followed immediately by the other stick playing the main note on the strong beat. The three-note grace, also called the four-stroke ruff or simply the ruff, requires a double-bounce stroke followed by a single stroke before the main note is struck. Successions of all of these strokes must be played as fast and evenly as possible.

In the four-note grace or five-stroke ruff two double-bounce strokes are played immediately before the main note

Single Grace Note or Flam:

| L R | L R | L R | L R |
| R L | R L | R L | R L |

Two-Note Grace or Three-Stroke Ruff, also called Drag:

| L L R | L L R | L L R | L L R |
| R R L | R R L | R R L | R R L |

Three-Note Grace or Four-Stroke Ruff:

| R R L R | R R L R | R R L R |
| L L R L | L L R L | L L R L |

Four-Note Grace or Five-Stroke Ruff:

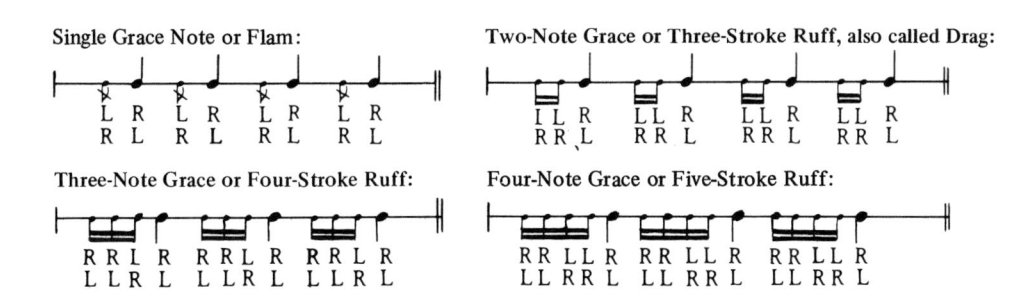

| R R L L R | R R L L R | R R L L R |
| L L R R L | L L R R L | L L R R L |

Two, three, and four-note graces are often played as upbeat rolls or press rolls, whereby the individual strokes that precede the main note become so fast that they can no longer be perceived as such. This execution is a hold-over from the era of dance and dinner music, when military-drum technique was considered too crude for such small orchestras, and means were sought to refine it. Even though these rolls deviate from the written notation they are considered justifiable under the circumstances and are used widely for the waltzes, polkas, and marches, etc., of that particular repertoire. It is important that this be kept in mind in connection with notation and interpretation of such music:

Notation:

Snare Drum

Possible Interpretation:

In this type of music the drum part is in fact often written in a simplified notation: the grace notes and rolls are omitted and their addition and execution left to the performer who improvises them in accordance with the melody line and the accents of the accompaniment:

Melody part

Notation: (Snare Drum)

Percussion (Bass Drum & Cymbal)

Suggested Interpretation:

The rim shot is a jazz-derived drum effect. One way of playing it is to strike the skin and the rim (hoop) simultaneously with one stick. (In British usage this is known as the "hoop-crack" -- Trsl.) Its execution demands a good aim, especially if the rim shot comes at the end of a roll. The resulting crack is startling -- not unlike a pistol shot.

Examples -- Varèse: *Ionisation;* Gould: *Latin-American Symphonette, Declaration Suite* (Mus. Ex. 103); Copland: 3rd Symphony; Killmayer: *Rêveries, La tragedia di Orfeo;* Armin Schibler: Concerto for Percussion and Orchestra.

Another version of the rim shot, also called stick rim shot or stick over stick, is to place one stick on the skin as well as on the rim and strike it with the shaft of the other stick. The effect is less explosive and contains more extraneous noise.

An effect rarely used is that of beating rhythms and rolls on the rim of the drum, as in

Daphnis et Chloé by Ravel *(caisse claire sur le bois)* and in *Mathis der Maler* by Hindemith. The wooden hoops of tenor and bass drums are best suited for this. Mahler, in his 6th Symphony, directs that the wooden hoop of the bass drum be struck with a small wooden stick (Mus. Ex. 63). In Maurice Ravel's orchestration of Mussorgsky's *Pictures at an Exhibition,* in the *Dance of the Chicks in their Shells,* the shell of a drum is to be struck with the tips of the drum sticks.

Bass Drum

Common beaters: large bass drum beater
timpani beaters in pairs (for rolls)

Less common: mallet with leather-padded head
hard-felt mallet
wooden-headed mallet
snare drum sticks
switch
wire brush
colla mano (with the hand)

History. With the introduction of Turkish Janissary music into the courts of Europe around the second half of the 18th century, a large drum with a new technique of playing entered Western music. The player carried the drum, or placed it on the floor, with its skin surfaces in vertical position, so that it could be struck on both sides. In the traditional Turkish bands this so-called Turkish drum, to this day, is struck on *one* of its skins (on the accented beat) with a wooden beater whose head is covered with cloth or leather, while the *other* skin is struck with a switch, either on the beat or after it. The new and exotic sounds of Janissary percussion, produced by bass drum, cymbal, and triangle, quickly gained wide-spread popularity. In the orchestra they first appeared in works of oriental flavor, such as Mozart's *Abduction from the Seraglio* (1782), or in works simulating military music of the period, such as Haydn's Military Symphony (1794 -- Mus. Ex. 61). Later these sets of percussion instruments lost the noisy background of the switch and the constant, automatic jangling of the triangle. In Spontini's opera *La Vestale* (1807) the bass drum was used for the first time in a way different from Janissary tradition. It was struck with a beater having a large cloth or leather-padded head, while a second performer had to play a pair of cymbals in the same rhythm. This practice obviated the necessity for mentioning the *piatti* in a *gran cassa* part, since it was understood that the cymbals would always have to play along with the bass drum. Only when the specific instruction *cassa sola* appeared was the bass drum to sound alone.

Since then, this custom has been followed in many scores, particularly in Italian music, such as the well-known examples in Verdi's *Rigoletto, Il Trovatore, La Traviata,* and *Un Ballo in maschera.* Only in later works, where individual rhythms and rolls were to be executed on the bass drum alone, did the indication *gran cassa* cease also to imply the *piatti,* so that it became necessary to use the more precise indication *gran cassa e piatti* if both were to play.

The task of playing the bass drum usually fell to a musician with little or no training in drum technique to speak of. He was therefore not expected to be able to play complicated rhythms, let alone rolls with two beaters. It is for this reason that Berlioz in his *Symphonie fantastique* expressly called for timpani players to execute the rolls on the bass drum, the only drum which, he wrote, sounds lower than the lowest kettle drum.

The music of the 20th century, however, demands of the bass drum player sensitivity for timbre and a good technique for playing rolls and other patterns, fully equal to that of a timpanist.

Construction and Use. The measurements of the bass drums used in orchestras and chamber groups differ widely; they depend primarily on the acoustics of the halls and the size of the ensembles. Many [European] orchestras still use the old bass drums with shells of about 65 cm (26″), which originally still had tensioning cords like those of the long drums. The tensioning screw mechanism introduced later permitted finer tuning and tension control for a more sonorous, full sound with good carrying power, aided additionally by the vibrating wood of the shell. Modern bass drums, made of plywood or brass, average 45 to 55 cm (18″ to 22″) in depth, with a diameter of 70 to 80 cm (28″ to 32″).

Orff, in *Die Bernauerin* (Mus. Ex. 56), *Antigonae, Oedipus,* and *Prometheus* (Mus. Ex. 72) uses two bass drums of contrasting timbre. Three bass drums of different sizes are used in the massive percussion ensemble of Varèse's *Ionisation* (Mus. Ex. 109).

The indigenous pitches of the two heads of the bass drum can be ascertained, as with any other drum, by striking close to the rim. Tuning should aim at a pitch best suited to the resonance of the instrument's shell. Depending on the sizes of the drums, the specific pitches of the batter head may be around E or, at the highest, G, while the other head should be tuned about one half-step lower to produce a round, full quality of sound.

A bass drum type particularly popular in British orchestras, the so-called gong drum, consists of a narrow wooden shell, at most 25 cm (10″) deep, with a diameter of about one and one-half meters (60″). It has only one skin which is tightened with tensioning screws. According to its construction it actually belongs to the frame drums which, to judge by ancient stone reliefs, already existed in pre-Christian eras at the courts of Chaldea and Egypt. They were almost as tall as a man. Today's gong drum, if played loudly, produces a sound of explosive force, while on softer levels it has less carrying power and is more akin to the smoother sound of the two-headed drum.

Bass Drum

The bass drum sounds best if suspended freely, or at least resting on horizontal straps, so that when it is struck its entire body can vibrate unimpaired. It should not be placed on a rigid stand, let alone on the floor. For best results it should be suspended in a swivel stand that permits turning the instrument to the slanted position most convenient for the player (see Ill. on p. 95).

Technique of Playing and Beaters. As a rule, single strokes should not be aimed at the center of the head since it does not vibrate well, but about one hand's width away from it. The direction of the stroke should be downward or grazing. Several different beaters are used for the bass drum when played in the orchestra. The customary bass drum beater has a wooden head, 6 to 8 cm (2 3/8" to 3 3/16") in diameter, which is covered with lambswool or thick, soft felt. It produces rich, sonorous single strokes from pianissimo to the strongest fortissimo. Mallets with similarly covered but smaller heads produce sounds that are less booming, thinner, and more sharply defined. A still harder sound results from the use of leather-covered wooden mallets taken over from the military band and called *mailloche* in French.

Examples -- Stravinsky: *L'histoire du soldat* (Mus. Ex. 62), *Le Sacre du printemps, Firebird.*

Rolls are executed with soft, large-headed timpani beaters; the beating point should be near the dark-sounding center of the skin. Timpani-like beats and rolls are played closer to the edge but are used only when specifically called for or when the bass drum is to sound at a specific pitch. Wooden mallets the size of xylophone mallets or cymbal beaters produce a dry, pointed, unpitched sound. This noisy quality becomes even more pronounced with drum sticks, while small hard-felt beaters reduce the noise of impact to some extent.

Examples -- Stravinsky: *L'histoire du soldat;* Orff: *Die Bernauerin* (Mus. Ex.24), *Antigonae, Trionfi* (Mus. Ex. 15); Bartók: Sonata for Two Pianos and Percussion.

Bartók, in one passage of his ballet *The Miraculous Mandarin,* has reverted to having the bass drum played with small sticks and mallets in a manner widely used not only in the folk music of the Orient but also in southeastern Europe, Asia, and Africa.

A smaller bass drum, played in the same manner as the Bartók drum, is the *tapan.* Its diameter is approximately 60 cm (24") and the depth of its shell about 50 cm (20"). Both heads of this drum are tightened with cords run through holes punched into the skins, instead of with pressure hoops. The tapan has been used by Milko Kelemen in the large percussion section of his *Composé.*

The whirring beat of the wire brush on the bass drum is as unmistakable as the swishing sound produced by stroking the drum head with the brush.

Examples -- Orff: *Antigonae;* Killmayer: *La tragedia di Orfeo.*

The bass drum can also be played *colla mano.* In Orff's *Oedipus,* for example, successions of somber-sounding strokes are produced by treating the bass drum as a member of a whole choir of hand-beaten skin instruments.

Bass drums for jazz and dance music must have a short, dry sound, for which reason small-sized drums are preferred, along with felt or cloth dampers for the skins and hard beater-heads for the pedals. Striking the drum by means of a pedal mechanism permits little if any differentiation in the attack, thus making the quality of sound dull and monotonous.

Heinrich Sutermeister, in his opera *Raskolnikov,* has used a bass drum with pedal mechanism to characterize honky-tonk music. Gershwin used it as a dance-band drum in *Porgy and Bess.*

Armin Schibler, in his Concerto for Percussion and Orchestra, uses the pedal to produce dry strokes on the bass drum, while he calls on the same performer to play other instruments with his hands.

Pedal Mechanism for the Bass Drum

Frame Drum
(Tambourine without Jingles, also called Dance Drum or Tambourine)

Beaters: soft-felt beaters
         hard-felt beaters
         drum sticks
         con la or *colla mano* (with the hand)

History and Construction. Frame drums are instruments whose shells consist of simple, usually narrow hoops with only one skin. While in the cylindrical drums the air mass enclosed within the shell vibrates sympathetically and amplifies the sound of the skin, the sound of the frame drum results almost exclusively from the skin's own vibrations, the resonance of the hoop being negligible.

Frame drums of various sizes were in use as early as the Babylonian and Egyptian civilizations. In Antiquity they were known as *tympanon*. Frame drums were also used both in their round and, less frequently, in their square forms in the ritual, dance, and folk music of Asia and America.

The tensioning of the skin, originally effected either with cords or by nailing the skins to small hoops, is accomplished in modern instruments by mechanical tensioning devices as used in snare drums. The diameters of instruments suitable for orchestral use range from about 25 to 60 cm (10" to 24"), and the hoop depths vary proportionately between ca. 4 to 8 cm (1 5/8" to 3 3/16"). The proper proportion of skin tension to drum size assures the most sonorous tone of the drum. A set of frame drums of different sizes will provide a sequence of different pitch levels. A soft beater, used without forcing, produces natural pitch levels clearly, while hard beaters bring forth more rattling, drumlike, unpitched sounds.

Playing Technique and Use. In popular music, frame drums are played with finger tips and the ball of the hand, often with extraordinarily exciting effect. The use of soft-felt beaters, on the other hand, elicits only very moderate dynamic degrees from this naturally quite soft instrument.

In general, the frame drum is held with one hand and played with the other, either with beaters or sticks, or *colla mano*, the same as the tambourine (see Ill. on p. 98).

If one player has to use several differently tuned frame drums, either by themselves or together with other percussion instruments, it is necessary to place or mount the instruments on special stands. This permits arrangements and techniques of playing similar to those described under timpani and other drum sets.

The frame drum is rarely used in the orchestra. In Jean Cocteau's ballet *La Dame à la Licorne* (The Lady and the Unicorn) with music by Chailley, simple rhythms, intended to simulate music of ancient times, occur for *tambour sur cadre* (indicated as *Tamb. basque sans castagnettes* -- Mus. Ex. 64). De Falla, in his marionette opera *El Retablo de Maese Pedro,* uses several tuned frame drums of different sizes, called *Pandéros*, the way the composer knew them from the famous Corpus Christi processions in Cadiz, the city of his birth, where the drums reach a diameter of one meter (40").

However, the part for tambourine without jingles in Gottlieb von Einem's opera *Dantons Tod* is usually played on a low-pitched drum without snares, rather than on a frame drum, in order to achieve the required volume.

The Orff *Schulwerk* uses frame drums of various sizes.

Frame Drum

American Indian Drums

Beaters: club-like mallets
beaters with built-in rattles

The primitive skin drums of the North American Indians are now found only in museums.

Drums of American Indians

North American instrument manufacturers do, however, produce sets of so-called Indian drums of the frame or tubular type in different sizes. One or two skins on a shell of wood or burnt clay are tightened with cords, and hard, rattling sounds are then produced with club-like mallets. The noisy strokes are often made even noisier by the use of beaters whose hollow heads are filled with pebbles or seeds acting as rattles.

Carlos Chávez, inspired by the drumming tradition of primitive Indians, includes simple strokes on an Indian drum in his *Sinfonía India*. In his Toccata for Percussion Instruments he uses two Indian drums, the smaller of which must have a high, sharp sound. Silvestre Revueltas combines an Indian drum with two tom-toms in *Sensemayá*. Werner Egk has added two Indian drums in the revised version of his opera *Columbus*. Two Indian drums also appear in Elliott Carter's *Pocahontas* (Mus. Ex. 65).

Bongos or conga drums may serve as substitutes for Indian drums although their skins hardly possess the required strength and thus can produce only an approximation of the genuine sound. Strong sticks or the shafts of heavy drum sticks are best-suited as beaters.

Boobam

The boobam, a new instrumental type which originated in North America, consists of bamboo sections of different lengths and diameters. One opening of each section is covered with skin while the other is left open.

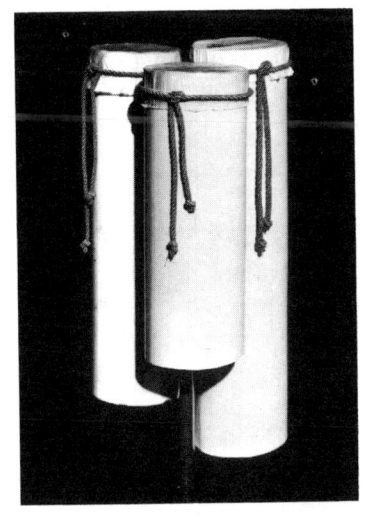

Boobam

Differences in sound do not result from the respective tensions of the skins but from the sizes of the bamboo resonators and their vibrating columns of air.

The tubes are suspended vertically either in groups of five to eight in contrasting tunings or in chromatic keyboard arrangement.

Set of Bamboo Boobams in Keyboard Order

The use of the boobam in the United States was at first confined to popular music, usually in combination with other unusual percussion instruments. Its use in recording studios as a special sound effect came later. This was partly a result of structural improvements consisting of the substitution of elongated, rectangular wooden resonators in place of the original bamboo tubes, their sizes depending on the respective pitches.

A circular frame, 8 cm (3 3/16″) in diameter, covered with a plastic skin, is placed on top of the resonator. Its pressure hoop is connected to the top of the resonator by screws which can be adjusted for the required skin tension.

Set of Rectangular Boobams in Keyboard Order

The boobam's range covers two octaves, from F to f^1. (The illustration shows a one-octave instrument.) The instrument is played with fingers or with soft beaters and often requires electro-acoustic amplification. Hard beaters or metal sticks produce a noisy, high-pitched skin sound which largely drowns out the pitches generated by the resonators.

Tambourine

Method of playing -- common: with the hand *(con la mano* or *colla mano)*

less common: hard-felt beaters
drum sticks
triangle beater

History. The tambourine is mentioned in the Old Testament and was also known to primitive Asiatic peoples. Medieval minstrels adopted it from the Romans. It also became the instrument of the Gypsies and spread to Spain and southern Italy where it has retained its role as a popular instrument for folk and dance music to this day. Around the year 1800 it gained a firm place in the Janissary music which the European military bands had taken over from the Turks, and soon thereafter it also appeared in the Classical orchestra where it was used to underline folk and dance elements.

The Spaniards call the tamburine *pandereta;* the French *tambour de basque.* In the remainder of the musical world of Western Europe, for reasons that are no longer clear, it became known as *tamburin* or *tambourin.* It is thus often confused with the Provençal tubular drum called *tambourin* in French (tabor in English) which is found in the works of French composers (see pp. 84f). In other words, when the term *tambourin* appears in French scores and parts it always means the *tambourin provençal.*

Construction. The tambourine is identical with the frame drum described on page 97. Its hoop is about 7 cm (2 3/4") wide and has a number of equidistant slots. In the middle of each slot is a stiff wire holding a pair of hammered brass jingles. Depending on the size of the hoops, whose diameters may vary from about 25 to 35 cm (10" to 14"), one may find as many as twenty such pairs of jingles. The narrow slots permit the small disks, which hang loosely on their wire axes, to jangle when the instrument is shaken or beaten. To enable the hand to hold the instrument, the hoop has no jingles along a space about the width of one hand, and it is usually equipped with an extra piece of wood to provide an even better grip.

The small jingles, about 5 cm (2") in diameter, have slightly bent rims and lie one upon the other in pairs. The typically high jingle sound has considerable carrying power. Small instrumental ensembles use tambourines with fewer jingles, while large orchestras, especially the percussion orchestras of Carl Orff, require large and brilliant orchestral tambourines.

Skin tension is effected through tensioning hoops or through nailing the skin to the outer rim of the hoop. The pitch of the skin sound is immaterial, for which reason -- in contrast to the frame drum -- there is no need for a tensioning mechanism. This makes the instrument lighter and frees the skin area closest to the rim for very soft playing.

Method of Playing. The tambourine is handled in various ways. Single beats as well as rhythmic patterns are produced with the tips of the thumb and middle finger, lightly pressed together, and occasionally with the addition of the index finger to increase the impact. The beating spot on the skin is opposite the holding hand, about 3 to 4 cm (1 3/16" to 1 5/8") from the rim. Very soft beats are produced at the extreme edge of the skin. To achieve the shortest and most precise sound possible the instrument must be held almost horizontally because in this way the jingles themselves are damped immediately after each beat by coming to rest upon one another. When the tambourine is moved gradually into a vertical position the jingle sound becomes less pronounced and softer while the skin sound becomes more prominent.

The skin sound of the tambourine can be strengthened by striking it with the heel of the hand, with the fist, or by beating the instrument against the elbow or knee. Rapid series of beats, too fast to be executed with one hand alone, must be played with the finger tips of both hands beating on the edge of the skin while the tambourine rests on the player's knees which are spread slightly apart. If necessary, the instrument can be held in place by pressing the forearms or the heels of both hands against it.

Although dancers shake the tambourine with one hand to produce a roll, the orchestral tambourine, as a rule, is set into rapid vibration by both hands holding the instrument vertically in front of the player. In this way rolls of any length and of contrasting dynamics can be executed. A considerably denser and more intense roll can be achieved by letting the moistened thumb tip stroke the skin. Such stroking begins at the lower edge of the skin and proceeds on a semicircular path upward along the edge of the rim, whereby the thumb, because of the moisture, vibrates in short, rapid skips along the skin, beating it like a drum roll, which, in turn, produces a dense rattling of the jingles. Here, too, different degrees of dynamics can be achieved by corresponding differences in finger pressure and by the way the tambourine is held: the more horizontal the position of the instrument, the more intense the rattling sound. Since the path of the skipping thumb is limited -- few players master the art of an uninterrupted roll by moving the thumb up and down without a break -- the roll can only be of short duration unless one is willing to have brief interruptions. A normal roll can thus last about three seconds if played loudly, and up to about eight seconds if played softly.

Use and Special Effects. One of the first appearances of the tambourine in the orchestra is found in Carl Maria von Weber's incidental music to *Preciosa* (1821). Wagner used it in the Italianate overture to *Das Liebesverbot* (1834), in the overture and *Bacchanal* of *Tannhäuser* (1845), and in the prelude to Act III of *Lohengrin* (1850). Berlioz used the *tambour de basque* in the *Roman Carnival* overture (1844); Bizet's *Carmen* (1875) contains a particularly characteristic use of the tambourine.

Verdi used the tambourine (together with castanets) to accompany the offstage chorus in *La Traviata* (1853) and *Don Carlos* (1867). Tchaikovsky used it in the *Nutcracker Ballet* (1892) and in the *Capriccio italien* (1880); Rimsky-Korsakov in *Sheherazade* (1888), and De Falla in *The Three-Cornered Hat* (1919).

In the 20th century the tambourine has become a regular orchestral instrument and a timbral component in its own right, divorced from its folkloristic connotations. This is evidenced, for example, in Richard Strauss's operas *Salome* (1905), *Elektra* (1909), *Der Rosenkavalier* (1911), *Ariadne auf Naxos* (1916), and *Die Frau ohne Schatten* (1919).

Berlioz, in his book on instrumentation, suggests using several tambourines together, and Orff took this suggestion in *Trionfi* and *Antigonae.* Henze uses three tambourines of different sizes and pitches in his opera *Elegy for Young Lovers.*

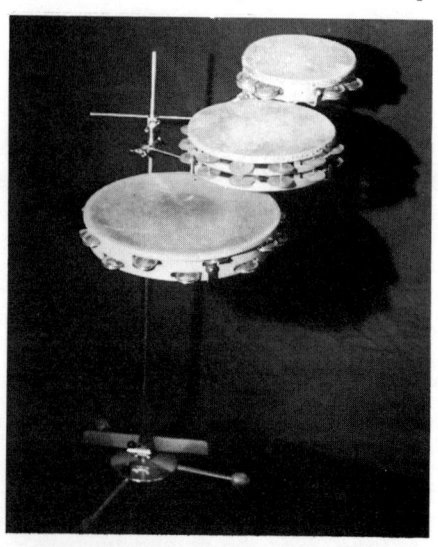

Three Tambourines Mounted on Stand

Stravinsky invented a special effect when at a dramatic point in *Petrouchka* a tambourine is to fall to the floor. He directs that it is sufficient, in this case, that the instrument be held only a few inches above the floor, so long as it hits the floor with its entire rim. Henze, in his opera *Il re cervo,* calls for an unusual technique of playing: the skin and one pair of jingles are struck alternately, the former with the thumb, the latter with the middle finger.

The most suitable beaters are those whose attack is hard and short, so that the jingles produce a precise sound: small drum sticks, small soft or hard-felt beaters, beaters for cymbals, xylophone, and triangle, metal beaters, knitting needles, and timpani mallets.

Examples -- Bo Nilsson: *Ein irrender Sohn* (Mus. Ex. 89); Stravinsky: *L'histoire du soldat;* Respighi: *The Pines of Rome;* Henze: *Elegy* (Mus. Exx. 38 and 66), *Antifone* (Mus. Ex. 67); Blacher: *The Moor of Venice.*

If the tambourine is to be played together with other percussion instruments by a single player, it is put on a stand (perhaps a snare drum stand) and struck with appropriate beaters. In Stravinsky's *L'histoire du soldat* there is one passage where small soft-felt beaters are used to play alternately on a tambourine, a side drum without snares, and a bass drum, and another passage where a triangle beater is used for the tambourine, triangle, side drum without snares, and bass drum.

If a score calls for several tambourines of different pitches, to be played by one player, it is of course necessary to use a special stand (see Ill. on p. 102).

If the tambourine is played with beaters rather than by hand, rapid successions of beats can be executed. Rolls played in the manner of timpani rolls, however, do not attain the density of those produced with the thumb or by shaking the instrument.

String or Friction Drums

Pasteboard Rattle (Waldteufel); Lion's Roar (Brummtopf)

The pasteboard rattle (*Waldteufel*, literally Forest Devil) may well once have been a ceremonial instrument of primitive tribes. Its origin seems to have been in India. It is known in Asia, Africa, North America, and Europe. In the last-mentioned area, however, it is found only as a toy instrument.

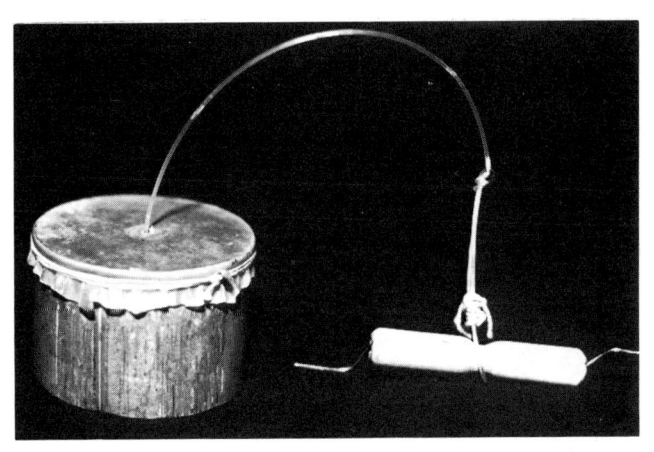

Pasteboard Rattle *(Waldteufel)*

Its construction is simple: one opening of a small tin cylinder, about 8 cm (3 3/16") in diameter and 6 cm (2 3/8") high, is covered with a thin skin membrane pierced in the center. A thin gut string, about 30 cm (12") long, is drawn through the hole and secured with a knot on the underside of the skin. The other end of the string is looped around a groove in a wooden handle. The player, holding one end of the handle, whirls the instrument round and round through the air, and the loop, sliding around the groove (which has been rosined), causes the string to vibrate. These vibrations are transmitted to the skin membrane causing it to produce a commensurate noise. Since the activation of the instrument in this manner requires a good deal of swing room a more practical way of playing has been invented for use in the orchestra: the cylinder acting as the resonator is held between the knees of the player, and the handle is replaced by a grooved, rosined, wooden rod which fits the loop and which is rotated with both hands by means of cranks attached to each end, while the string is pulled tight (see Ill. above). Timbre and dynamics can be adjusted in a limited way through faster or slower rotation of the rod, as well as through greater or lesser tension of the string.

The grotesquely comical sound of the *Waldteufel* has been used by Orff in his incidental music to Shakespeare's *A Midsummer Night's Dream* and by Kelemen in *Composé*.

The lion's roar *(Brummtopf)* is a string or friction drum operating on the same principle: it is the large version of the pasteboard rattle. As a folk and toy instrument it can be traced to Europe at the turn of the 17th century. It seems, however, to have originated in Africa. In the dance music of Latin America one frequently finds friction drums called *cuica, puita, roncador*, etc., in which the string is replaced by a rod.

Playing the Cuica

The shell of the lion's roar, depending on its place of origin, is a clay pot, a keg, or a cylinder of wood, cardboard, or tin, with a bottom. Similar to the pasteboard rattle, one opening of the resonator is covered with skin (originally with the bladder of an animal). The sound is generated by a gut string which protrudes from a hole in the center of the skin and is made to vibrate by a moistened piece of leather which is pulled along the string and away from the skin (see Ill.).

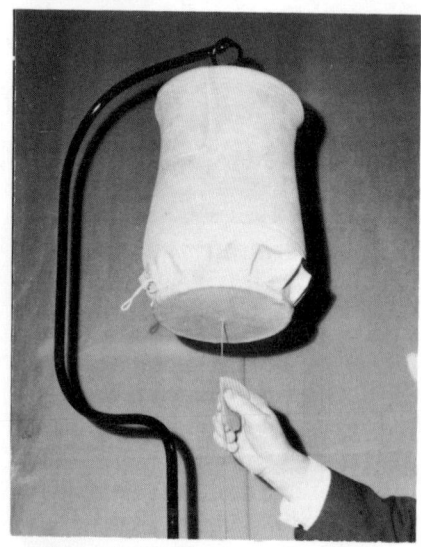

Suspended Lion's Roar (Brummtopf)

Standing Lion's Roar (Brummtopf)

Depending on the intensity of the string friction a muffled, growling noise is generated which can be increased to a rather high volume. (The English name *lion's roar* for the instrument thus is very appropriate.) If a lion's roar is to be used in the orchestra its cylinder, of wood or tin, should have the approximate size of a ten liter pail (2½ gallons), should be mounted on a wooden base, and should have its opening covered with thin skin. In the center of the skin a small hole is burnt with a red-hot needle, and a string is inserted. In order to avoid tearing the hole, a washer of heavier skin should be placed between the knot in the string and the drum skin.

Varèse used a string drum (which he called *tambour à corde*) in *Ionisation* (1931) where it must produce long drawn-out, swelling and fading sounds (Mus. Ex. 109). John Cage uses the lion's roar in the March of *Imaginary Landscape No. 2* (1942) and in *Third Construction;* Bert Alois Zimmermann uses it in *Die Soldaten.*

In the drum type called rod-friction drum, a wooden or bamboo stick replaces the string of the string-friction drum: this stick (or rod) is stood upright upon the drum's skin and stroked with the rosined hand to produce the characteristic friction sounds.

HAND DRUMS
Arabian Hand Drum (Darabucca); Bongo Drums; Congo Drums, also called Tumba or Tumbadora; Tablas

General Remarks. Skin-covered hand drums as primary musical instruments have been indigenous to primitive peoples of all continents. Of the various types -- identified by their shapes as conical, double conical, barrel-shaped, cylindrical, and hourglass drums -- several were taken over by Western civilization. Of these the instruments of the Latin American countries have become particularly popular and have been imitated widely due to the growing interest everywhere in South and Central American folk and dance music.

Arabian Hand Drum (Darabucca)

A hand drum called *darabucca* or *tambour arabe* and imported from Arabian countries consists of a vase-shaped resonator which grows wider toward the top. It is made of baked clay and covered with a sheepskin tightened by means of strings.

The dimensions of these hand drums range between 10 to 45 cm (4" to 18") in height and 8 to 30 cm (3 3/16" to 12") in the diameter of the drumheads.

Arabian Hand Drums *(Darabuccas)*

In the climate of European latitudes, primitive folk instruments can be used only within limits since the skins of the larger drums usually lose too much of their tension. In the countries of their origin, however, as well as in the United States, Arabian hand drums of several different sizes are used and are now constructed of metal and supplied with a skin-tensioning mechanism similar to that of the snare drum (see Ill. below). The only drawback is that instruments with a metal body unfortunately lose much of the specific timbre possessed by their clay forebears.

The player holds the drum in his bent arm, presses it against his body, and beats the center of the skin as well as the edge with his hand or with individual fingers. Drums with high skin tension sound very sharp and bright when played on both skin and rim simultaneously. Beating the center of the skin of larger instruments brings out the deep sound of the resonator, characterized by a short, strange upward glissando after a heavy beat.

Examples of the use of Arabian hand drums in European music are rare. A few French composers, such as H. Tomasi in his Concerto for Percussion and Orchestra, and A. Jolivet in his Concerto for Piano and Orchestra, have used these Arabian drums as additional membranophones in their percussion sections. In such situations these *tambours arabes,* in alternation with other drums, are played with small, soft or hard-felt beaters. It is necessary, however, that the drum be placed on a rack.

Orff, in *Prometheus,* uses hand-beaten *darabuccas* (Mus. Ex. 68).

Darabuccas with Tensioning-Screw Mechanisms

Bongo Drums

Construction. The bongo drums, or bongos for short, are the highest-pitched membranophones among the Latin-American hand drums. Their shells, used in pairs of different-sized drums, are conical in shape and made of several layers of hardwood veneer cut along the grain, glued together, and covered with goat skin membranes. In the original, primitive version the skin tension was achieved by nailing the skin to the wooden shell; modern bongos use tensioning screws to achieve the required pitches.

The diameter of the skin-side of the larger drum of a pair of bongos measures about 19 cm (7 5/8″) with a shell depth of about 14 cm (5 5/8″). The measurements of the smaller bongo drum are about 18 and 14 cm (7 3/16″ and 5 5/8″), respectively.

The so-called Mexican type differs from a normal bongo pair in that its measurements are smaller by 3 to 6 cm (1 3/16" to 2 3/8").

In contrast to drums played with sticks, the skin ring and pressure hoop of the bongo, as well as its tensioning screws, are situated below the upper rim of the shell so that the skin becomes the drum's highest point.

A normal-sized pair of bongos has the following average tuning ranges:
    Large bongos: $g - d^1$
    Small bongos: $a - e^1$
    Pairs of the latter may be tuned $c^1 - g^1$ and $d^1 - a^1$.

In general, tunings are not indicated in scores. Pitches are chosen merely to create clear differentiation in sound between the two bongos -- approximately a perfect fourth apart. It may be necessary, however, to adjust the bongo tunings to make them harmonize with other membranophones such as congas and tom-toms, or with other bongos.

Playing Technique. Because of the characteristic construction of all hand-drum types it is possible for the player to strike with his finger tips both the upper rim of the shell and the skin simultaneously. Sound produced in this way, which is based on the same principle as the rim shot of the snare drum, is considerably stronger than that resulting from striking only the skin. It is by this method, employing the inside of the knuckles of both index fingers, that distinct patterns and rolls are played. Bongo rolls demand extremely rapid successions of beats because of the very short, dry sound of the instrument.

Proficient players are able to produce timbral nuances by striking the rim as well as the center or the edge of the skin with single fingers, finger tips, or the entire hand. Other differentiations result if the fingers or the hand are left on the skin after the stroke (closed stroke) or if they are removed quickly (ringing stroke). Furthermore, one hand may muffle the skin, or increase its tension through pressure, while the fingers of the other hand strike the skin (muffled stroke).

If such subtleties in beating technique are considered essential by the composer or arranger, they should be notated with appropriate symbols and explained on the first page of the percussion part. Otherwise the player is likely to use only basic routines, possibly varying them according to his own judgment.

Suggested Symbols.

Rim Strokes:
    Skin and rim are struck sharply with the side of the index finger.
        a) ⊓ finger not lifted off after stroke -- closed or dead stroke;
        b) ⊓ finger lifted off immediately after stroke -- ringing or bounce stroke.

Center Strokes:
    1) Skin is struck in the center with the finger tip.
        c) • closed or dead stroke;
        d) ○ ringing or bounce stroke.
    2) A brisk thumb stroke flung from the wrist.
        e) ⌣ closed or dead stroke;
        f) ⌣ ringing or bounce stroke.
    3) Muffled stroke.
        g) ⋔ one hand is placed on the skin; the index finger of the other hand strikes the center of the skin.

Finely differentiated successions of strokes can be notated with the help of the symbols listed above. It should be noted in this connection that the rim strokes possess a wider dynamic range than the center strokes.

Examples of Bongo Notation with Stroke Indications:

In folk and dance music the players sit holding the bongo drums between their knees. This position is customary whenever the percussionist plays the bongos only with his fingers.

If the bongos are to be played together with other instruments they must be mounted in pairs on a stand.

If played with beaters, the numerous possibilities of finger beating outlined above are of course not applicable. Timbral differences in this mode of playing depend entirely on the kinds of beaters used, which include small soft-felt beaters, small hard-felt beaters, drum sticks, and similar beaters.

Examples – Varèse: *Ionisation* (Mus. Ex. 109); Egk: *Der Revisor, Variations on a Caribbean Theme;* Killmayer: *La buffonata, Orfeo,* Chamber Music for Jazz Instruments; Orff: *Astutuli, Weihnachtsspiel, Oedipus;* Boulez: *Le marteau sans maître;* Fortner: *In his Garden Don Perlimplín Loves Belisa* (5 bongos); Kotoński: *Musique en relief* (Mus. Ex. 77); Bo Nilsson: *Ein irrender Sohn* (Mus. Ex. 89).

Bongos

Conga Drums

History and Construction. The conga drum, also called tumba or tumbadora, evolved from the native African drum which consists of a longish, hollowed-out section of a tree trunk with a skin stretched over its upper opening.

Conga drums were brought to Latin-America, along with other instruments, by African slaves. There they became the typical rhythm instruments of rumba bands The hand drums which developed from them have the shape of an elongated barrel or a conical shell.

Like the bongo drums the conga drums are made of long strips of tough but very light wood, grooved and glued together. Their size and diameter vary according to their pitches which constitute a downward extension of the pitch range of the bongo drums.

Their skin tensioning, originally achieved with cords and later by nailing the skin to the drum, was eventually effected by means of a lug and pressure hoop mechanism. Thus the conga drums can be tuned in the same manner as the modern bongo drums. Three sizes have become the norm: small, medium, and large. Skin diameters of the drums measure anywhere from 23 to 29 cm (9 3/16″ to 11 5/8″), resulting in an approximate pitch range of $c - c^1$.

Mounted on three adjustable legs the instrument stands skin-side up in front of the player. Originally, however, it was suspended on a leather strap from the player's shoulder and played at hip level.

Conga Drums

Playing Technique. The native drummers, using the finger tips, knuckles, and heels of their hands, as well as their flat palms and fists, achieve through stupendous technical proficiency a comprehensive, subtly differentiated scale of dynamics and timbral nuances. The conga players of the Latin-American bands confine themselves mostly to an economical use of basic beats played with the entire hand, while finger patterns are left almost exclusively to the bongo players.

The drum is struck with the entire hand and with all fingers firmly held together but slightly curved. The following signs are the most commonly used to indicate the different manners of playing.

Rim Strokes:
    Skin and rim are struck.
        a) ⊓ hand remains on drum after stroke -- closed or dead stroke;
        b) ⊓ hand is lifted off immediately after stroke -- ringing or bounce stroke.

Center Strokes:
    1) Skin is struck in the center.
        c) • closed or dead stroke;
        d) ○ ringing or bounce stroke.
    2) Muffled stroke:
        e) ⌒ one hand strikes the center of the skin while the other is placed on the skin
            to dampen it or to tense it through pressure.
    Attacks (b) and (d) permit the execution of a roll.

In transparent, chamber-like instrumentation one may also use the single-finger technique common to bongos and tablas. For stronger accents, attacks with the backs of the fingers of the entire hand may be added. The use of beaters takes away much of the characteristic conga sound and is usually avoided.

Examples -- Liebermann: Concerto for Jazz Band and Symphony Orchestra (Mus. Ex. 104); Gershwin: *Porgy and Bess;* Egk: *Variations on a Caribbean Theme, Die Verlobung in San Domingo* (Mus. Ex 69); Orff: *Weihnachtsspiel, Oedipus, Prometheus* (Mus. Exx. 68 and 93); Britten: *The Prince of the Pagodes;* Killmayer: *Orfeo, Le petit Savoyard,* Chamber Music for Jazz Instruments; Kelemen: *Der neue Mieter, Radiant;* Werner Heider: *Konflikte;* Bo Nilsson: *Ein irrender Sohn* (Mus. Ex. 89).

Tablas and Banyas

The hand drums of India have gained the attention of the musical world through the many recent recitals by Indian musicians featuring their national instruments. In these ensembles the drums are used in pairs played by one player with spectacular virtuosity of finger technique, each hand playing its own drum throughout.

The shell of the tabla -- the drum on the right -- is usually made of wood, in the shape of a short cone flattened at the top. The drum on the left, the banya, has a shell more akin to a hemisphere and is made of metal. The height of both instruments is approximately 25 to 30 cm (10" to 12"); the diameter of their skins about 15 to 23 cm (6" to 9 3/16"). The tabla is tuned with small wooden blocks which are placed between the shell and the leather straps that hold the skin. They are moved up or down with a small hammer, thus adjusting the skin tension with great precision (see Ill. below). The pitch of the banya which acts as the bass drum is changed by tightening the leather straps which stretch the skin over the shell. A different, more sophisticated method of tensioning the skin permits gradual changes in pitch during performance by exerting varying degrees of pressure with the heel of the hand upon the edge of the skin. This action affects the skin tension because it presses the body of the drum down upon the bottom pad on which it rests and which is formed by the braided ends of the tensioning straps.

Banya   **Tabla**

The membranes of both of these drums consist of two pieces of skin: an outer piece with a large center hole, and a circular middle piece pasted onto the outer piece from the inside. Close to the center of the middle piece is a dark-colored circular spot of paste, about 7 to 8 cm (2 3/4" to 3 3/16") in diameter. The paste consists of various ingredients such as flour or rice and wax mixed together and hardened. Its origin goes back to ancient rituals. It has considerable influence on the tuning and timbre of the skin.

Needless to say, the refined finger technique of the Indian tabla player, attained through years of specialized training and practice, and his ability to produce up to 16 different, precisely defined pitches, can hardly be approached by a Western percussionist with his many and diverse professional tasks.

Berio uses tablas in *Circles* (1960) (Mus. Exx. 32 and 70); Henze uses an Indian hand drum in *Das Floss der Medusa* (1968).

TOM-TOMS

Chinese Tom-Toms

Common beaters: small soft-felt beaters

Less common: small hard-felt beaters
drum sticks

Japanese Barrel Drum--O-Daiko

Common beaters: felt-wound wooden beaters

Less common: round wooden sticks

Flat Japanese Skin Drum--Taiko

Beaters: round wooden sticks

Tom-Toms (modern version) and Roto Toms

Common beaters: jazz drum sticks

Less common: xylophone mallets
marimba mallets
hard-felt beaters
soft-felt beaters

History. When in the 19th century Afro-American music developed into jazz in North America, characteristic percussion combinations evolved, based on the percussion instruments used in the early wind bands and on those introduced by the Blacks. In the course of further development the instruments were refined and new ones were added. In the very early jazz bands percussionists used so-called African drums, but where these were prohibited because of the slave owners' fears that they might incite uprisings tubs, barrels, and similar articles were substituted. With the beginning of the Classical period of the Blues around the turn of the 20th century, snare and bass drums took on the role of providing the basic rhythms, a role they were already performing in the so-called street bands.

After the introduction of the bass-drum pedal, which made it possible for a single player to play both drums, the drummers began to add more and more instruments and the percussion sections grew into the kind that became typical of the fully developed jazz, swing, sweet, and other dance bands. In addition to cymbals and Chinese wood blocks, tom-toms in different sizes became standard components of the percussion section.

Chinese Tom-Toms

Until the end of the 1930's, tom-toms of Chinese origin or construction were preferred. They had wooden shells, typically lacquered in reddish-brown, and their skins were nailed to the shells and decorated with pictures of dragons or flowers. Larger instruments had the shape of small, pot-bellied kegs. They were placed vertically on their own stands and used mostly in shows with oriental atmosphere.

Their measurements were:
skin diameter ca, 30 to 40 cm (12" to 16")
depth of shell ca. 22 to 40 cm (9" to 16")
circumference of the widest part of the shell
ca. 140 to 160 cm (4'8" to 5'4").

Their pitch range presumably lay between ca. G and g.

Considerably more widespread and easier to handle are the Chinese tom-toms in the shape of a round of Swiss cheese. A ring with which they can be fastened to the bass drum is attached to their slightly bulging shell. One to three such tom-toms constitute a standard component of a percussion set.

The measurements of these shallow tom-toms are:
skin diameter ca. 25 to 38 cm (10" to 15 3/16");
depth of shell ca. 10 to 16½ cm (4" to 6 5/8")

Their pitch range lies roughly between c and c^1.

The tom-tom is usually played with a soft-headed beater striking the middle area of the skin and producing a dark sound which in the larger tom-toms almost resembles that of a kettle drum.

Chinese Tom-Toms

The characteristic sound of the instrument has been amplified by means of coil springs attached to the inside of the shell and vibrating freely when the drum is struck.

Tom-toms have appeared only sporadically in concert literature, and then without specific indications concerning sizes, desired timbres, or choice of beaters. The decision as to which instruments to use and how to use them depends on the percussionist's judgment and proficiency. If possible he will choose Chinese tom-toms of appropriate sizes and play them with small soft-felt beaters.

Examples -- Hindemith: *Symphonic Metamorphosis* (Mus. Ex. 71); Egk: *Die chinesische Nachtigall.*

O-Daiko

Orff, in *Prometheus,* premiered in 1968, introduced the large Japanese barrel drum O-Daiko into the orchestra. Its very compact cowhides (diameter ca. 80 to 100 cm -- 32" to 40") are nailed to the wooden shell under great tension. The shell itself may be as wide as one meter (40") or more.

O-Daiko

The drum, hanging freely from a hook in a wooden frame, is played with large beaters having felt-padded wooden heads, or with round wooden sticks. Its sound, similar to that of a kettle drum, has great volume and unusual precision.

In Buddhist practice, the O-Daiko, there called *Sodoku,* is played with two strong wooden sticks which strike the skin as well as the shell. A special scraping effect may be produced by running the sticks over the nails with which the skins are fastened.

Examples -- Orff: *Prometheus* (Mus. Exx. 68 to 72).

Taiko

In Orff's *Prometheus* appears yet another Japanese drum new to the musical scene: the Taiko.

Its flat shape, similar to the snare drum, is distinguished by the heavy cords with which its thick horse or cowhide membranes are stretched under extreme tension across the rims of its very solid wooden shell which is 16 cm (6 3/8") high and 34 cm (13 5/8") in diameter (see Ill. on p. 114).

The brightly penetrating sound of the skin with its somewhat crackling noise of impact is produced by two round wooden sticks which are always used one at a time.

Taiko

Examples -- Orff: *Prometheus* (Mus. Exx. 68, 93, and 98).

Modern Tom-Toms

Construction. With the increasingly preferred use of drum sticks among jazz drummers it has become necessary to abandon the sensitive, decorated skins of the Chinese tom-toms in favor of an instrument sufficiently robust to withstand the drummers' at times quite abusive treatment. This led to single-headed tom-toms with cylindrical plywood bodies in various sizes, equipped with the tensioning-screw mechanism of the modern drum. Soon the lower opening of the cylinder was also covered with skin so that a muffled but short, dry sound was achieved. This sound went well with other jazz drums, such as the bass drum with its damped reverberations, and the short, sharp sound of the snare drum. A damper inside the tom-tom, adjustable from the outside by a screw, can be pressed against the strong batterhead, thus damping off the upper partials.

At first glance, modern tom-toms look very much like the larger drum types with snares. However, while the dimensions and proportions of the shells of these snare drums and the toughness of their skins are designed to produce quick responses of the snare effect, the different dimensions of the tom-toms are designed to produce the greatest possible resonance and volume. Tom-toms are manufactured in sets of six different sizes which, by and large, have the following measurements: diameter 25 to 45 cm (10″ to 18″); depth 20 to 60 cm (8″ to 24″).

Modern Tom-Toms

The total pitch range usually extends from G - c^1.

The smaller tom-toms come either with attached stands or else are mounted on small drum racks; the larger ones have their own adjustable feet. The largest of the tom-toms (45 x 60 cm -- 18" x 24") approximates the measurements of a small bass drum.

Playing Technique. Since the modern tom-tom originated in the jazz percussion set its usual beaters are drum sticks. All the techniques and patterns customary in jazz-drum playing also suit the tom-toms. Rolls, however, are played only with single beats unless an imitation of the tenor drum is intended. The use of other beaters must be specifically indicated. A scale of timbres ranging from a large, full sound to gradually softer ones can be achieved with the successive use of wooden beaters, xylophone mallets, marimba mallets, small hard-felt beaters, and small soft-felt beaters.

Use. Tom-toms, under the name of jazz drums, were used by Hindemith in his opera *Cardillac* (1929) and by Berg in his opera *Lulu* (1933). In the former work they are even in three pitches. Since beaters are not indicated, the small soft-felt beaters which were customary at that time should be used. (Berg: *Lulu* -- Mus. Ex. 75)

Today, tom-toms are frequently used in combination with other skin drums. In this way an upward continuation of their pitch levels is achieved with the timbales (Hartmann: 7th Symphony -- Mus. Ex. 76) followed by smaller drums without snares, and finally with bongos, while downward pitch extensions lead to the lower conga drums, timpani, and bass drums.

Examples -- Hartmann: Viola Concerto, Piano Concerto, 7th Symphony (Mus. Ex. 76); Egk: *Irische Legende, Variations on a Caribbean Theme;* Gould: *Latin-American Symphonette;* Gershwin: *Porgy and Bess;* Killmayer: *La buffonata, Orfeo;* Revueltas: *Sensemayá;* Nono: *España en el corazon;* Henze: Symphonic Etudes, *Elegy* (Mus. Exx. 30 and 39), *Antifone* (Mus. Ex 67), *Il re cervo* (Mus. Exx. 9 and 73); Cage: *Amores* (9 tom-toms).

Roto Toms

Thanks to modern technology which has made fine-tuning of stretched skins possible, U.S. manufacturers have brought out sets of tunable skin drums (without shells) called roto toms (German *Tom-Tom-Spiel*) or bongo organs. The number of drums in such sets has so far ranged from 6 to 13 small-sized instruments (see Ill. below). Each of these can

Set of Roto Toms

be tuned up or down within the compass of a fifth by turning the drum on a central screw mechanism similar to that of the rotary-tuned timpani The highest possible pitch is in the vicinity of c^2, so that a chromatic scale of 13 such drums would reach down to c^1. If this kind of set were to be developed further, a total compass of skin-drum pitches could extend from about G to c^2.

Because these drums have neither a shell nor a bottom skin, their timbre in the highest registers is hard and terse, similar to that of the high-tensioned bongos. Instead of bottom skins, roto toms have wooden or metal disks which hold eight tensioning screws for fine-tuning of the skin, i.e., the batter head.

Drum or timbale sticks produce a sharp impact noise. Small hard or soft-felt beaters, on the other hand, result in correspondingly softer tones with a more precise pitch. The edge of the skin is raised above the rim and thus also permits various finger-playing techniques, similar to those used for hand drums.

Examples -- Colgrass: Variations for Four Drums and Viola; Cage: Quartet (Mus. Ex. 74).

Timbales

Common beaters: timbales sticks, ca. 30 cm (12") long and 1 cm (3/8") thick

Less common: wooden-headed beaters
xylophone mallets
marimba mallets
small hard-felt beaters
small soft-felt beaters

Timbales

Like the conga drums, the *timbales cubaines,* as they are also called, came from Africa to Latin-America by way of the slave trade. In their original form they were bowl-shaped, hollow pieces of wood over which animal hides were stretched, not unlike kettle drums. These "timpani" were struck with curved pieces of tree roots, thicker at the beater end.

In Afro-Cuban folk music this type of drum developed into the timbales which consist of two paired, very small timpani with hard, high-tensioned skins, sounding approximately a perfect fourth to a perfect fifth apart. They are played in many different ways with two small, light sticks. In Latin-American music they provide the rhythmic vitality that the snare drums provide in our dance bands.

Construction. Modern instrument manufacturers produce timbale pairs in the form of very small kettle drums whose bodies are made of metal and have a sound-hole at the bottom about the size of a man's hand. Simpler variations are not timpani-shaped but have cylindrical shells of plywood or sheet metal and a single skin. They come in two or three sizes and are mounted on a stand (see Ill. on p. 116). Their skin-tensioning mechanism is identical with the tensioning-screw devices of modern drums.

Skin diameters:
-- for the larger bowl-shaped or cylindrical instruments:
   ca. 35 cm (14")
   approximate pitch range: B - f
-- for the smaller bowl-shaped or cylindrical instruments:
   ca. 31 cm (12 3/8")
   approximate pitch range: d - a

Playing Technique and Use. In Latin-American bands the basic beats are performed with small timbale sticks:
  a) strike the center of the skin with the stick;
  b) rim shot: strike skin and rim simultaneously with the stick;
  c) strike skin with the curved hand while simultaneously striking the opposite rim with the stick held by the same hand;
  d) strike the outer wall of the bowl or shell with the tip of the stick or with its middle section;
  e) place one stick with its tip on the skin, or on skin and rim, and strike it with the other stick.

Timbales players in Latin-American bands occasionally enrich the large variety of sounds additionally by playing with the fingers and by adding one or two cowbells. However, the basic rhythms of the respective dances (Bolero, Guaracha, Rumba, Beguine, etc.) always persist unaltered, regardless of the many different possible timbres.

If the various manners of striking are to be notated, it is recommended that this be done with symbols.

In concert music the timbales are often scored as if they were high-pitched timpani to be played with soft felt beaters. It is possible, in fact, to assign specific pitches to them as long as the skins are struck near the rims. Beaters with small wooden heads or heads of hard felt may also be used, depending on whether a hard or a rather more muffled sound is desired.

If drum sticks are used, timbales sound not unlike undamped small tom-toms.

With a progressively scaled set of three or more timbales it is possible to create a wide, unbroken range of skin sounds from large tom-toms through timbales, to the smallest bongo drum.

Examples -- Hindemith: *Cardillac;* Sanjuan: *Liturgia negra* (Mus. Ex. 87); Killmayer: *La buffonata, Orfeo, Lorca-Romances,* Chamber Music for Jazz Instruments; Hartmann: 7th Symphony (Mus. Ex. 76); Kotoński: *Musique en relief* (Mus. Ex. 77); Foss: *Echoi* (Mus. Ex 82).

STRUCK IDIOPHONES

Triangle

Common beaters: metal rods

Less common: wooden beaters
leather beaters

General Information. Along with the cymbal and the bass drum the triangle entered the European orchestra in the 18th century by way of the Janissary music of the Turkish soldiers. It is not documented, however, whether the triangle at that time was still adorned with its original, loosely strung jingling-rings which gave the sound additional color. Today one expects from an orchestral triangle a fine, silvery-clear tone in which the numerous concordant and discordant partials blend with the fundamental sound of the instrument. The greater the thickness of the metal, the more prominent are the higher, more closely positioned overtones.

The fundamental of a triangle can be determined by striking it with a padded wooden beater while damping it slightly with the other hand.

Construction and Handling. Triangles made from a steel rod 1.5 cm (5/8") in diameter, with sides 25 cm (10") in length, and open at one angle, are best suited for the demands of a large orchestra. Their very high-pitched sound carries extremely well and easily cuts through the densest instrumentation. For thinner instrumentations, depending upon acoustics, one might use a lighter instrument with less volume.

The triangle is suspended from the first joint of the index finger by a thin gut noose. The noose is best made from a violin gut A-string and may be padded with a small piece of leather to protect the finger. The thumb and middle finger regulate the position of the instrument by means of gentle pressure on the string, but without touching the instrument itself. The triangle may, however, be hung from a stand to make quick changes to other instruments possible.

Method of Playing, Types of Beaters, and Characteristics of Sound. The choice of the best beating spot is of great importance. It is here that the tightly-knit higher partials arise and die down most evenly. In most triangles this spot is found in the upper third of the triangle's right side (see Ill. on p. 119). The beater must not strike the outer side of the instrument perpendicularly but instead must fall in a more grazing motion, at an inward angle. In this way the metal is set into vibration as gently as possible and with the least sound of impact.

The customary beaters are rods of iron, steel, or brass, varying in thickness from 2 to 6 mm (1/12" to 1/4"), and in length from 15 to approximately 20 cm (6" to 8"). Beaters of the French type with their strongly-weighted heads produce much more sonorous effects, but one must exercise extreme sensitivity in their use because with too heavy a touch they can cause the metal of the triangle to vibrate excessively, thus producing an unpleasantly loud sound. The stroke should always be carried out with the thickest part of the upper or pointed end of the beater. The beater is held between thumb and forefinger by its narrower middle section, while the lower, flatter end serves as a balance.

Although a drum stick or a wooden rod produces a weaker sound, it is nonetheless more bell-like. To reduce the clacking impact noise of the wooden beater the triangle should be struck near the tapering end of the open diagonal side.

Bartók calls for this effect in his Sonata for Two Pianos and Percussion. Pfitzner seeks an especially fine and ethereal effect in the second act of his opera *Palestrina* by asking that the triangle be struck with a small wooden rod. Here, too, a wooden beater with a weighted head is the best choice, such as the spoon-shaped beater of the four-row xylophone (Stravinsky: *Le Sacre du printemps* -- Mus. Ex. 35). Steel rods of small diameter--quite similar to knitting needles--should be used only when specifically indicated, because they produce a very thin tone which tends to rattle.

Triangle rolls are played inside the upper angle of the instrument by striking both triangle sides rapidly, back and forth, with a loose wrist.

All in all, the triangle player must not only acquire the technical discipline of playing but also the sensitivity and taste indispensible for suitable use of his instrument within the orchestral framework. If the triangle is used a great deal, as for example in certain works of the Classical and early Romantic periods, the performer must take special care to avoid penetrant ringing, by exercising the utmost restraint in dynamics.

Striking the triangle is often a problem when a performer must alternate quickly with other instruments, because its normal sound spectrum can be obtained only with a metal rod, and not with the more customary sticks and beaters.

In contemporary compositions one may find two or more triangles used in gradations of sound. Such differences between triangles are by nature very slight and are therefore effective only in a very transparent instrumentation.

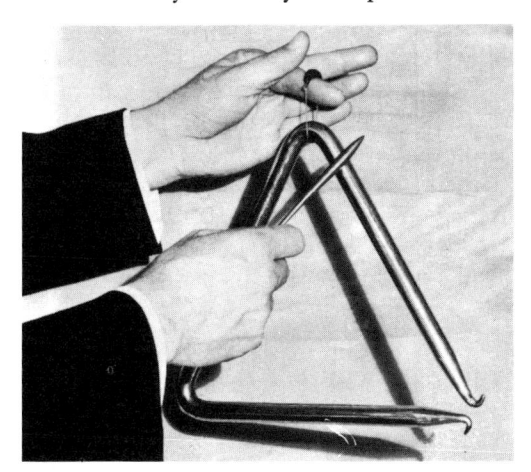

Holding the Triangle by Hand 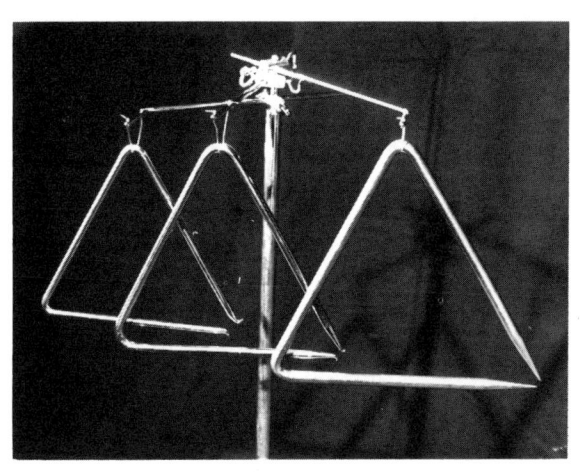   **Three Different Sizes of Triangles on a Stand**

Examples -- Armin Schibler: Concerto for Percussion and Orchestra; Henze: *Elegy* (three triangles of different sound and hung from a stand, as illustrated above), *Antifone* (four triangles -- Mus. Ex. 67); Nono: *The Red Cape* (six triangles); Zimmermann: *Die Soldaten* (nine triangles); Bo Nilsson: *Reaktionen* (Mus. Ex. 50), *Ein irrender Sohn* (Mus. Ex. 89).

Cymbals

Cymbals in pairs; Cymbals struck with beaters; Sizzle Cymbals; Cymbals struck by mechanical means (Hi-Hat); Chinese Cymbals

Beaters
Common for single cymbals: cymbal beaters (hardwood heads covered with leather)

Less common:	bass-drum beaters *(mailloche)*	drum sticks
	soft-felt beaters	triangle beaters
	hard-felt beaters	thin steel rods (knitting needles)
	rubber beaters	wire brushes
	vibraphone mallets	brushes of sheet-metal strips *(lamellae)*
	xylophone mallets	with the hand *(colla* or *con la mano)*

History. The first cymbals were crash (concussion) instruments in the form of small metal bowls with wooden handles. They originated in ancient Asia and were used in religious ceremonies by the more civilized peoples of antiquity. During the Middle Ages the Saracens brought them to Spain and southern Italy.

At the end of the 17th century, large cymbals of cast or hammered alloy, played in the Turkish Janissary manner, i.e., along with the bass drum, entered the military music of the Western courts. These cymbals had come with the music of the Turkish soldiers via eastern Europe. Their new sound, with its extraordinary ability to heighten rhythmic effects, eventually also gained entry into opera and concert music, at first only with the aim of imitating Turkish music, but soon also including any music of military character. Haydn's 11th Symphony (*Military,* 1794), Mozart's *Abduction from the Seraglio* (1782), and Beethoven's 9th Symphony (1824), all demonstrate this development. In the coda of the finale of Beethoven's 9th Symphony, however, there appear indications of a merging of percussion sounds with those of the orchestra proper, a trend which was to reach a high point in the music of the Romantic period.

Construction. The cymbal received its name from its shape*: a very shallow basin with a small round cup in the center. This cup has a drilled circular hole of approximately 1 cm (ca. 3/8″) in diameter, through which a leather loop is drawn, so that each hand can hold one of a pair of cymbals, and the two can be struck together. In Classical orchestrations, cymbals with a diameter of 39 cm (15 5/8″) are usually sufficient, since they still sound light and silvery-clear when played softly. As the density of the instrumentation and the size of the orchestra increase, cymbals with diameters of up to about 50 cm (20″) are required to produce sufficient sound without distortion. Top workmanship and proper quality and strength of the metal will assure a well-sounding crash in both forte and piano.

The use of a single cymbal, struck with beaters, became customary after cymbals began to become an integral part of the orchestra during the Romantic era. Before that time, a single cymbal, if needed, was hung from a music stand by a hook and struck with beaters. Thus one finds in many percussion parts the instruction *piatto sospeso* (suspended cymbal).

Method of Playing, and Sound. The custom of former days to borrow percussion players for the orchestra from military bands probably explains the combination of bass drums with pairs of cymbals, which was routine at that time. In any case the designation bass drum or *gran cassa* always implied the simultaneous use of a pair of cymbals. Only when the bass drum or the cymbals were to be played alone was *cassa sola* or *piatti sola* (sic) marked specifically, as for example in Verdi's *Un Ballo in maschera.* Moreover, it is understood almost to this day that if beaters are not specified, cymbals are always to be crashed in pairs.

There are exceptions, however. For example, in the works of Hindemith, instructions for beaters or for clashing are lacking and the choice is left, instead, to the performers who must of course be in good rapport with both composition and instrumentation.

The sparkling lustre of a big cymbal crash or the glistening sound of the cymbals played softly is achieved not only through the particular kind of metal used for the instruments, but also through sophisticated performance techniques. The execution of a fortissimo crash demands great exertion of strength as well as corresponding skill and sensitivity. Ugly sounds can be avoided only if the stroke causes the entire alloy to vibrate as much as possible, thus releasing sound from all fields of tension within the metal. Rigid, clamp-like holding of the cymbals as they collide, or clashing them with little energy, cause the opposite. Bringing the right-hand cymbal against the one in the left should be carried out in such a way that the two cymbals do not collide all at once, i.e., concentrically. Instead, the upper rims must touch a fraction of a second before the remainder to avoid compressing the air between the cymbals with a smack.

---

*Trans. note: the word "cymbal" is derived from the Greek kýmbe, meaning cup or bowl. The German name *Becken* is in fact synonymous with the German word for a shallow bowl, as is the Italian *piatto* with the word for (dinner) plate.

Some conductors demand that obvious cymbal crashes be executed by the performer standing in a grandiose pose in order to provide the audience with a visible aspect of the orchestral climax. This optical heightening of the crash loses its effectiveness if used for every forte stroke and should therefore be limited to true climaxes, if used at all. Gradations in dynamic range can be obtained by choosing cymbals of different sizes. Playing softly in regular, even beats requires the utmost control of the arm muscles, unless the cymbals are brought together at the outer edges, which is only done in the rarest instances when a particularly delicate pianissimo is wanted.

Pairs of Cymbals

Cymbal rolls *a 2* are produced by striking the plates together in the fastest possible succession, allowing the rims to separate only slightly. This rather noisy method of playing is used by Wagner, for example, in the climax of the *Bacchanal* in *Tannhäuser,* by Richard Strauss in the loudest part of *Josephslegende,* and by Bartók in a similar part in *The Miraculous Mandarin,* as well as by Mahler in his 6th Symphony (Mus. Ex. 79).

Usage. Striking a pair of cymbals, one of which is attached to the shell of the bass drum, and beating the bass drum at the same time, first became common practice in smaller wind and brass ensembles and was then adopted by minor orchestras to save expenses on musicians. That this was a coarse way of playing and to be rejected musically was the opinion not only of Curt Sachs in his *Handbuch der Instrumentenkunde,* but also of Berlioz (...*good enough to make a monkey dance....*).

Mahler (1st, 3rd, 5th, and 7th Symphonies), Berg (*Wozzeck,* see Mus. Ex. 78), and Werner Egk (*Die Zaubergeige* and *Die Verlobung in San Domingo*) expressly specify: "one cymbal mounted and struck by the other" or "cymbal attached to the bass drum." But even in these cases such instructions should be ignored and the cymbals played unattached to make possible a wider range of dynamic differentiation. On the other hand, in Berg's *Lulu,* the "large circus drum with attached cymbal," played by the Clown in the prologue, is a good example of intentional vulgarity. Several pairs of cymbals are used by Orff in *Antigonae* in a dynamic scale from pianissimo to the strongest fortissimo.

An effect seldom demanded, the *strisciatti,* is scored by Leoncavallo in *I Pagliacci* and by Dallapiccola in *The Prisoner.* While the left hand holds one cymbal vertically, the rim of the right-hand cymbal is run from the center outward across the narrow casting furrows on the inner surface of the left one, thus producing a sharp, hissing sound (Kagel: *Match for Three Players* -- Mus. Ex. 81).

Since a first-rate, select pair of cymbals represents a piece of valuable equipment often hard to replace, it is suggested that the cymbals not be robbed of their tension -- which slowly diminishes throughout their lifetime anyway -- by being played with beaters more often than absolutely necessary. In fact, suspended cymbals, i e., cymbals specifically designed for beater playing, actually sound better for such purposes. A single cymbal has sufficient sound only when the vibrations from a moderately strong stroke fade away very slowly instead of decaying rapidly.

The stronger and smaller the cymbal, the lighter the sound -- in large cymbals the low, long tones predominate. One can assemble a pitch scale by selecting single cymbals ranging from 25 to 71 cm (10" to 28 3/8") in diameter (see Ill. on p. 122).

Examples -- Debussy: *Jeux;* Orff: *Antigonae;* Nono: *España en el corazon, La terra e la compagna, Cori di Didone* (Mus. Ex. 80), *Canti di vita;* Henze: Symphonic Etudes, *Elegy, Antifone* (Mus. Ex. 67); Egk: *Irische Legende;* Killmayer: *Lorca Songs;* Armin Schibler: Concerto for Percussion and Orchestra; Haubenstock-Ramati: *Credentials;* Zimmermann: *Die Soldaten* (requires nine different cymbals); Kagel: *Match for Three Players* (Mus. Ex. 81); Orff: *Die Bernauerin* (Mus. Ex. 54).

Suspended (Single) Cymbals

In his opera *Cardillac* Hindemith chose the term *Zymbel* to indicate a strong, metallically clear-sounding cymbal of small diameter. It is to be struck with a drum stick or a felt beater while a steel rod (knitting needle) is held against the cymbal.

For general use a large orchestra needs a suspended cymbal of at least 46 cm (18 3/8") in diameter with corresponding thickness, which will be able to stand up to the most exacting demands. A cymbal that is too small or thin sounds cracked in fortissimo passages (such as are demanded in Wagner's *Götterdämmerung*), reminding one more of crackling tin than of gleaming gold. For chamber music and for microphone pickup, however, it is better to choose cymbals that speak more easily, i.e., correspondingly thinner cymbals. Jazz cymbals, so called by the jazz and dance band ensembles of the 1920's, are very thin small cymbals of approximately 22 cm (8 3/4") in diameter. They are completely lacking in the normally glistening sound. Their effect, when struck hard, is a quick, short, tinny hiss. A soft beater makes them give off a weak sound, similar to that of a small tamtam. Even so, these small or jazz cymbals are occasionally used in serious music.

Examples -- Hindemith: Chamber Music No. 1, *Symphonic Metamorphosis* (Mus. Ex. 71); Killmayer: Piano Concerto; Hartmann: *Simplicius Simplicissimus* and 6th and 7th Symphonies (Mus. Ex. 76).

Beaters. Beaters with leather-covered hardwood heads are used if nothing else has been specifically prescribed. For a soft sound, thin leather coverings should be used in order to make the impact sound of the stroke audible not only to the performer or conductor but also to the listeners who are farther away. The practice of using such beaters stems from the Classical and early Romantic periods when, generally, nothing existed other than the wooden, leather, and sponge beaters of the timpanists.

More recently there have been attempts to vary the methods of beating and to discover new ways of playing single cymbals, such as using hard-felt beaters for a soft tone. Also, beaters covered with a soft material are used, such as vibraphone or marimba mallets and timpani beaters.

Debussy, in *Jeux* and *La Mer,* called for heavy, gong-like sounds obtained by using the *mailloche,* a leather-headed bass drum beater, which agitates the cymbal down to its deepest metal tension. Hard strokes are obtained from the standard wooden-headed, leather-covered beaters, as well as from xylophone (glockenspiel) mallets.

By using small drum sticks, following the example of dance-band drummers, one can obtain various nuances of sound. Using these techniques and striking the cymbal near the edge with the heads of the sticks produces very light and pointed-sounding beats and rolls.

When the cymbal is struck near its heavy-walled center dome (bell cup), the sound takes on a more bell-like color.

Beats with drum sticks on the rim of the cymbal can be produced in dynamic ranges from pianissimo to fortissimo. Depending on the strength of impact, they activate the sounding material from the outside toward the inside, i.e., from the wide pitch spectrum of the outer edge to the large, more focused vibrations of the center. Metal beaters, such as steel knitting needles, triangle rods, and metal glockenspiel mallets produce a fine, glittering sound or a light, metallic accent, depending on thickness and weight. Here too, as discussed above, the beating spots also determine the differences in sound.

Examples -- Henze: *Elegy* (Mus. Exx. 10 and 30); Zimmermann: *Die Soldaten.*

Another variation is a roll played with a hard-felt beater while the point of a steel needle is held against the cymbal.

Examples -- Orff: *The Moon, Antigonae, Astutuli, A Midsummer Night's Dream;* Sutermeister: *Romeo und Julia;* Hindemith: *Sinfonia Serena, Cardillac.*

This effect is intensified by placing a small metal key chain (instead of the steel needle) on the cymbal, thus producing a still stronger jingling sound.

Bartók, in his *Dance Suite,* asks that the cymbal be struck with the hand *(colla mano),* using the middle knuckle of the bent index finger. In this case a cymbal that speaks easily should be used.

Schönberg, in the fourth of his Five Pieces for Orchestra, op. 16, wrote a cymbal tremolo to be produced with a cello bow on the edge of the cymbal. It is as good as impossible, however, even with a very thin cymbal, to develop by this method a crescendo to the indicated fortissimo level.*

The use of wire brushes has already been mentioned in connection with dance music: the impact of such a bundle of steel wires on the cymbal produces a fragile and blurred sound -- a useful *piano* effect.

Examples -- Gershwin: *Porgy and Bess;* Sutermeister: *Romeo und Julia;* Prokofiev: *Peter and the Wolf;* Hartmann: *Simplicius Simplicissimus;* Henze: *Elegy.*

A brush having strips of sheet-metal instead of thin wires elicits much stronger and more brilliant sounds from the cymbals, especially from the thick-walled, suspended stand-cymbals used in a large orchestra.

Two different cymbals and two tamtams, scraped at the edge with a metal nail file or equivalent, are used by Walter Haupt in his *Apeiron* (Mus. Ex. 22).

Modifications. Sizzle cymbal is the name given by jazz drummers to a cymbal having rivets loosely inserted into the rim, near the edge, at equal distances from one another. Like the key chain, the rivets produce a strong jingling sound.

Sizzle Cymbal

*Schönberg must have realized this himself, because in the later version of this piece, for small orchestra, the tremolo is scored for regular beaters, from *pp* to *fff*. (Trsl.)

Luciano Berio used two sizzle cymbals of different sizes in *Circles;* also Kagel used rivet cymbals in *Match for Three Players,* as well as W. Heider in *Konflikte* and Lukas Foss in *Echoi* (Mus. Ex. 82).

Recently the rivet holes in cymbals have occasionally been replaced by a movable metal arm which is attached to the top of the stand and allowed to jingle on the cymbal.

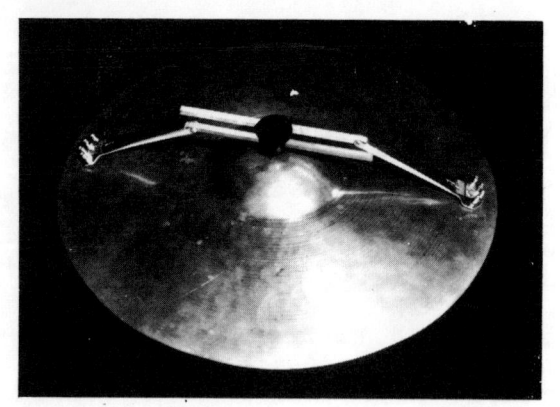

Jingling Arm on a Cymbal

The development of mechanical cymbal beating is a chapter all by itself. Originally invented for the purpose of freeing the performer's hands to play other instruments, it began with the slap-hand cymbals, an after-beat instrument of American jazz, emerging after World War I. With the help of a spring mechanism the player was able to beat two small cymbals together by using only one hand. However, he could also beat these cymbals with drum sticks.

Complete freedom for both hands was provided by the so-called Charleston machine which became widespread as an after-beat instrument of dance-band drummers in the 1920's during the vogue of the Charleston dance step.

From this machine developed the hi-hat with a stand that brings the cymbals up to the same height as the other instruments struck with drum sticks. The pedal of the hi-hat causes two jazz cymbals, each with a diameter of 30 to 36 cm (12" to 14 3/8"), to be beaten together. The sound is dry and very short because the cymbals, as they clash, remain together for a moment, thus preventing reverberations. From this style of playing, a techinque developed which is peculiar to jazz and dance-band drummers. It includes the use of partially or completely muted hi-hat cymbals as equal members of a group of different instruments beaten with drum sticks or wire brushes and designed to achieve quick successions of varying timbral nuances.

The hi-hat entered art music whenever the sounds of jazz were desired, as in Weill: *Lost in the Stars;* Jolivet: *Lone,* for Piano and Orchestra; Egk: *Die Verlobung in San Domingo;* Zimmermann: *Die Soldaten;* F. Zehm: *Capriccio* for Percussion Solo and Chamber Orchestra, or when a jazz ensemble was built into the music, as in Henze's *Maratona di danza* and Liebermann's Concerto for Jazz Band and Symphony Orchestra. The latter work employs the jazz band far beyond simple accompanying rhythms and requires a highly competent jazz drummer.

In *Circles,* Berio uses two hi-hats--one each for two players--in combination with numerous other percussion instruments (Mus. Ex. 32).

Bo Nilsson in *Reaktionen* calls for pedal cymbals struck "on the center" with xylophone mallets (Mus. Ex. 50).

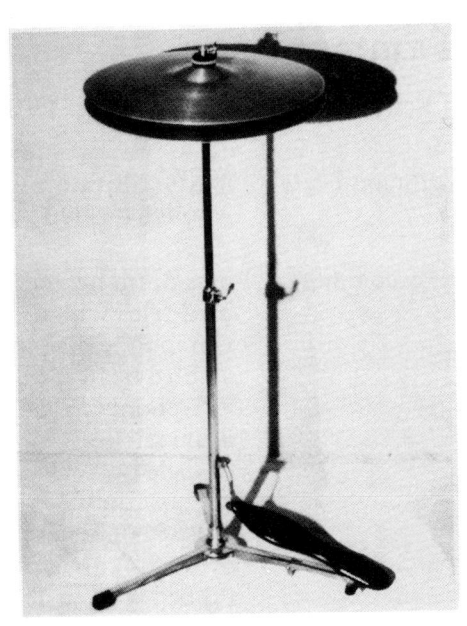

Hi-Hat

Another pedal device for cymbals was developed in the 1920's for small orchestral ensembles but has rarely been used since World War II because its sluggish mechanism, fitted with a pair of Chinese cymbals, did not allow enough variation in nuances of beating.

The primitive precursor of this machine consists of a cymbal screwed to the rim of a bass drum played by pedal. With the use of a combined beating mechanism the bass drum and the cymbal are struck simultaneously. Such a machine is used by Milhaud in his *La création du monde* with the designation *grosse caisse à pied avec cymbale*. Its player has to operate a large *batterie* along with it. (Mus. Ex. 83).

The so-called Chinese cymbals were occasionally imported during the last century, to be played as paired cymbals by military bands, but they are rarely used any longer. They differ in shape from Turkish cymbals by having slightly bent-up rims and round, pedestal-shaped centers with leather bands drawn through their domes as handles.

Chinese Cymbals

Chinese cymbals are made of hammered tin alloy and have a dull sound that varies little dynamically. Beaten as a single cymbal with a soft beater, the Chinese cymbal sounds similar to a small tamtam. Hard strokes produce unpleasant sounds.

Examples – Milhaud: Concerto for Percussion; Messiaen: *Turangalîla-Symphonie*; Varèse: *Ionisation* (Mus. Ex. 109); Jolivet: Concerto for Piano and Orchestra; Kotoński: *Musique en relief* (Mus. Ex. 77); Cage: *First Construction in Metal* (four separate Chinese cymbals); Orff: *Prometheus*.

Tamtams

Tamtam, Cast Tamtam, Water Gong, Sarténes; Tchanchiki

Common beaters: hard-felt beaters with leather covers
wooden-headed beaters with felt covers

Less common: bass-drum beaters
hard-felt cymbal beaters
vibraphone mallets
cymbal beaters (wooden heads covered with leather)
xylophone mallets
drum sticks
triangle beaters
wire brushes
brushes of sheet-metal strips *(lamellae)*
by hand *(con la* or *colla mano)*
rubbed with wine glass
rubbed with cardboard tube
with electric vibrator

Origin. Tamtam (Malaysian: *tammittam*) is a generic term for drum in the languages of several African peoples. It has been widely adopted to refer to the hammered, slightly arched bronze disk of Far-Eastern origin used in the orchestras of the West since the end of the 18th century.

Construction. The tamtam differs from the pitched, domed gong (or simply gong) by having no dome-like indentation in the center and thus having no definable pitch. As with the Turkish cymbal and the Javanese gong, the tamtam's alloy is difficult to duplicate, and even more so the method of working the bronze to produce tamtams that truly match their Chinese models. Current Western manufacture differentiates the cast bronze tamtam from the one of hammered sheet bronze. The former yields a sound of predominantly higher pitches because of its considerable amount of material and weight.

To attain the low sound necessary for use in the orchestra, an instrument with a large diameter of approximately one meter (40"), but in no case less that 75 cm (30"), must be chosen. The smaller the tamtam (down to about 35 cm -- 14"), the shorter the duration of its reverberations and the higher its predominant partials.

The tamtam is hung from a stand by means of a strong, twisted cord drawn through two holes at the rim of the instrument. Several tamtams of varying sizes can be hung on a special stand with movable arms (see Ill. on p. 127), thus making it possible for them to be played easily by one player, in combination with other percussion instruments.

Examples -- Henze: *Elegy* (Mus. Ex. 8), *Antifone* (Mus. Ex. 67); Nono: *Cori di Didone* (Mus. Ex. 80); Bo Nilsson: *Ein irrender Sohn* (Mus. Ex. 89); Varèse: *Ionisation* (Mus. Ex. 109).

Tamtams of cast alloy are suitable for loud passages, but in soft ones they speak with more difficulty and are hard to dampen. On the other hand, the thin sheet-bronze tamtams react considerably faster and develop more depth of tone, even with a smaller diameter. These, however, do not usually have the noble sound of the original type. The strong tensions in the material, resulting from the art of hammering it, cause it to release a multitude of partials when struck. The tamtam gives off a different tone color at each beating spot. Lighter colors predominate in the heavy-walled areas near the rim; towards the center lie the areas which, through vibration of the entire material, produce the greatest volume with the deepest, long-vibrating fundamental tones.

Example: Cage and Harrison: *Double Music* (Mus. Ex. 91).

Contemporary composers sometimes use the term gong to mean a very deep-sounding tamtam, which is apparent by its notation without clef and in a low position in the score (see Foss: *Echoi* -- Mus. Ex. 82). The small tamtams of the salon orchestras which occasionally appear in orchestra scores after World War I are, however, also often [erroneously] designated as "gongs."

Examples -- Hindemith: *Symphonic Metamorphosis* (Mux. Ex. 71); Berg: *Lulu* (Mus. Ex. 75); Foss: *Echoi* (Mus. Ex. 82).

Tamtams of Hammered Sheet Bronze

Cast Bronze Tamtams

Characteristics of Sound and Beaters. If struck softly the tamtam sounds dark and, in its lowest range, not unlike a large distant bell. Mussorgsky, for example, uses it in this way in *Boris Godunov*, as does Pfitzner in *Palestrina*.

Secco beats can be executed only on smaller instruments capable of quick damping by hand. Beats in too close succession, and not damped, cause the tones to run together since they do not have sufficient time, individually, to develop and decay.

Instruments strongly damped by being laid horizontally upon a cloth or being held between the knees, etc., produce a short, dry, somewhat tinny sound completely lacking the sparkle of the upper partials. Such an effect was intentionally scored by Orff in *Die Bernauerin* and *Antigonae*, and also by de Falla in *El Retablo de Maese Pedro*.

The tamtam beater has a round, hard-felt head usually covered with thin deerskin, its large size and weight corresponding to the diameter of the instrument. Its beat causes a relatively quick development of sound, desirable in rhythmically precise, accented styles of playing.

Cast tamtams, responding more slowly, are struck with a heavy beater whose head consists of a strong, felt-padded wooden disk.

A softly padded beater, such as a bass-drum or gong beater, produces a weaker tone on impact, but strong, more slowly developing reverberations. The vibrations here move gradually from the center outward to the rim, causing the sound to swell and then slowly die down.

Beaters with small, hard-felt heads (hard-felt cymbal beaters) or beaters covered with rubber mobilize only the higher-pitched area around the beating spot. Hard-felt cymbal beaters in pairs are also occasionally used for bright-sounding rolls where the score calls for timpani beaters (Mahler: 1st, 2nd, 3rd, and 6th Symphonies) or for sponge beaters (R. Strauss: *Macbeth*), since these beaters lack the heavy heads necessary for rolls on the tamtam. Still harder beaters, such as regular cymbal beaters, xylophone mallets, drum sticks, metal rods, and so forth, lead to high, shrill, metallic impact noises differing in loudness according to the density and weight of the respective beater.

Examples -- Stravinsky: *Petrouchka*; de Falla: *El Retablo de Maese Pedro*.

The instruction "rubbed with triangle beaters" is executed by rubbing both sides of the tamtam as rapidly and vigorously as possible with the tips of two heavy metal rods.

Examples -- R. Strauss: *Salome, Elektra*; Stravinsky: *Le Sacre du printemps*; Henze: *Il re cervo* (Mus. Ex. 9).

A dramatic highpoint in *Oedipus der Tyrann* by Orff is emphasized by beating the center of the tamtam with a cymbal, thus producing a hard and very strong mixture of the sounds of both metals (Mus. Ex. 84).

In playing the tamtam with a brush, it is best to use a large brush of sheet-metal strips. (The same is true for playing large cymbals.) Its strong steel lamellae produce a light-colored, hissing mixture of sound, down to a relatively low volume.

Example -- Killmayer: *La tragedia di Orfeo*.

Tones of extremely low audibility result from playing with finger tips on easily responding tamtams, the way Henze prescribes it (▽ *colla mano*) for the chamber music atmosphere of his *Elegy*:

A very unusual effect can be obtained by playing on the rim of the tamtam with the bow of a stringed instrument. A short, very high tone, comparable to that of a string harmonic, is the result.

Example -- Schönberg: *Die glückliche Hand*.

Water Gong

Water gong is the name given by John Cage to a tamtam about 30 to 40 cm (12" to 16") in diameter, which upon being struck is immediately immersed about halfway into a container filled with water. The water causes the pitch of the reverberations to slide down by about one fifth, producing a glissando similar to that of a beat on the pedal timpano. The reverse effect, a rising glissando, occurs if the instrument is struck while hanging in the water and then pulled out.

Examples – Cage: *First Construction in Metal* (Mus. Ex. 85); Cage and Harrison: *Double Music*.

Sarténes

The *sarténes*, belonging to the family of Latin-American folk instruments, exhibit a certain relationship to the high-pitched sets of gongs of the Far East.

Sarténes

Two or three steel frying pans of different sizes are inserted upside down, by their handles, into a gaily colored wooden block which serves as a stand (see Ill. above), and are beaten in the center of their bottom sides. Their clear, gong-like sound has a very definite pitch varying, according to the size of each pan, between a^1 and c^3. Best results are obtained with rubber-headed beaters (vibraphone mallets); harder beaters emphasize the pans' peculiar sheet-metal sound.

Example -- Angel Pena: *Igorot Rhapsody.*

Tchanchiki

Tchanchiki or *Atari-gane* is the name of a small Japanese gong of heavy brass alloy turned in the shape of a casserole. The outer side of the bottom is adorned with a number of engraved decorative grooves and acts as the beating surface. The instrument is suspended by soft cords which are attached to two handles on opposite sides of the rim or cylinder.

Tchanchiki

The shrill, very sharp sound is produced with a beater having a small, button-like head made of horn. The reverberations are short. The pitch of these instruments, which are used occasionally in modern Japanese music, ranges within the three-line octave. A *tchanchiki* in f^3 has a strike area of 10 cm (4"); its diameter at the open side, including the lip, is 12 cm (4 3/4"); and its depth is 2½ cm (1").

Examples -- Yuso Toyama: Rhapsody for Orchestra.

Animal Bells

Cow Bells, Herd Bells (Almglocken), Metal Block, Cencerro

Common beaters for Herd Bells *(Almglocken)*:	bell clappers
Beaters for Herd Bells, according to score instructions:	soft-felt mallets
	hard-felt mallets
	rubber mallets
	vibraphone mallets
	leather cymbal beaters
	xylophone mallets
	wooden mallets
	drum sticks
	metal rods
Common beaters for Cowbells:	drum sticks

Origin, Construction, Types. Ever since man has herded domestic animals, bells have been hung on them to identify their location by sound or to protect them from evil spirits Before metals were known, bells of wood were carved in the shape of broad trapezoids with one or several wooden clappers hung inside. Their sound resembled that of small slit drums. They were found in North India, ancient Persia, the Congo, and Estonia. In some places they are still used today.

In Africa the usual practice was to work fruit hulls into bells.

With the advent of ore mining, bells of bent and forged sheet-metal with rod-shaped inner clappers came into being. These bells were used singly, in pairs, or in bunches.

While the elongated, conical metal bells that originated in Africa and came down to us via Spain and Latin America have a clear, rather floating tone, the more pot-bellied bells common in the Alps sound duller and more muffled. In Switzerland such bells were also made of brass and used for ceremonial purposes; they have a maximum height of approximately 45 cm (18") and a circumference of approximately 150 cm (60") at their widest point.

By assembling a set of Alpine herd bells or *Almglocken*, from the largest to the smallest, a chromatic scale from about c to c^4 or even to g^4 may be obtained. It is necessary, however, to use a soft beater for the bells in the lowest octave to obtain a pitch.

Alpine Herd Bells

Chromatically tuned Alpine Herd Bells

The straight-walled bells, high, narrow, and clapperless, belong to the instruments characteristic of Latin-American folk and dance music (samba, beguine, rumba, conga, Afro-Cuban, and others). Called *cencerro*, they are beaten singly or in pairs with sticks and are woven into the rhythmic tapestry of the accompanying instruments. By varying the techniques of playing -- such as damping, letting them ring, changing the beating spot, i.e., rim, sidewall, inside, crown -- the player seeks the greatest possible number of differentiations in sound.

Examples -- Sanjuan: *Liturgía negra* (Mus. Ex. 87); Gould: *Declaration Suite* (Mus. Ex. 103).

In Western jazz and dance music such bells have become widespread under the name cowbell (also jazz cowbell). Their predominantly dry sound demands complete damping of all reverberations by inserting a piece of felt or similar material into the bell.

Cowbells Attached to the Bass Drum

Recently, manufacturers have developed a very short and dry-sounding instrument of strong tin, shaped like an angular trapezoid. It is attached to some other percussion instrument by a holder and is played with drum sticks by the drummer, along with his standard instruments: bass drum, snare drum, tom-tom, and cymbal. The instrument is often called metal block, because its sound is so far removed from that of the original cowbell.

Usage. In concert music of the late Romantic period the use of animal bells was limited to the musical depiction of grazing flocks, naturally without concern for exact pitches.

Examples -- R. Strauss: *Alpensinfonie;* Mahler: Symphonies No. 6 (Mus. Ex. 86) and No. 7.

For such use, bells of different sizes, selected from the higher pitches, are hung by their handles over a long wooden bar in rows of three or four (see Ill. on p. 130) and rung by the performer with care and discretion. To brighten the somewhat monotonous color of the sound, several small bowl-shaped bells *(Schalenglöckchen)* should be included.

For instrumental color, Webern, in his Five Pieces for Orchestra, op. 10, uses "several continous herd bells" and with them "some low bells" (tubular chimes) which should be barely audible. However, the dynamics in this instance do not permit the use of ordinary animal bells but require instead herd bells without clappers, fastened to a stand, and struck with rubber beaters.

When dealing with music having jazz-related elements the term metal block, already mentioned, is generally the more appropriate term for the short-sounding cowbell.

Examples -- Gershwin: *Porgy and Bess;* Milhaud: *La création du monde* (Mus. Ex. 58), Concerto for Percussion and Small Orchestra; Liebermann: Concerto for Jazz Band and Symphony Orchestra (Mus Ex. 104); Boulez: *"pli selon pli."*

Beaters, Characteristics of Sound. The herd bell, when struck with soft-felt beaters, has a smooth, clear, long-ringing tone which, when rolled, blends into a continuous sound. Hard-felt beaters, rubber covered wooden beaters, or vibraphone mallets produce a considerably stronger and more precise effect. Leather cymbal beaters or xylophone mallets, when used with a harder stroke, bring out metallically bright overtones. Wooden mallets or drum sticks produce a still stronger version of the bell's peculiarly tinny sound, while the use of metal rods results in sounds colored by a prominent admixture of hard, shrill, high-pitched components.

Examples -- Henze: *Elegy, Antifone;* Stockhausen: *Zyklus, Gruppen;* Bo Nilsson: *Reaktionen* (Mus. Ex. 50); Cage and Harrison: *Double Music* (water buffalo bells -- Mus. Ex. 91); Berio: *Circles* (Mus. Ex. 32), *Epifanie;* W. Heider: *Konflikte;* Cage: *First Construction in Metal* (8 oxen bells -- Mus. Ex. 85); Messiaen: *Sept Haïkaï* (*Jeu chromatique de cencerros* = 26 herd bells tuned chromatically from c^2 to c^4 -- see Mus. Ex. 88), *Couleurs de la Cité célesta* (27 herd bells tuned chromatically from c^2 to d^4).

Hand Bells and other Small Bells

Small Bowl-Shaped Bells; Hand Bells
Doorbells; Turkish Crescent; Bell Tree; Sanctus Bells;
Sarna Bell; Ship's Bell; Dobači

Small, even tiny bells with clappers have been in use among all peoples who could work metal. Such bells, equipped with handles, were known in China as early as around 1000 B.C. and became widespread in the Far East where they were used along with bowl-shaped cymbals and cast concussion bells.

In medieval Europe these small bells were called *crotalum* (from the Greek *krotalon*). When assembled into tuned sets of clapperless small bronze bells, they were called *cymbala.* The larger forms of these led to the development of the tower carillon, while the smaller types passed into non-musical usage with the emergence of the metal-bar glockenspiel which replaced them.

Today one finds small steel bells with handles used for various signaling purposes (dinner bells). In the theater they are often considered stage props, rather than musical instruments. Orff, on the other hand, uses a small, silvery-clear bell of this kind as an orchestral instrument in his music for Shakespeare's *A Midsummer Night's Dream.* De Falla rings in *El retablo de Maese Pedro* with a larger, louder handle bell (which may be of bronze). The so-called hand bells with which folk melodies are played in England consist of a set of small, tuned, cast bells covering about one octave in range.

Hand Bells

Two players hold two bells (with clappers) by leather straps in each hand: a total of eight bells. In this way they are able to assemble a melody from the eight pitches by adroitly turning the backs of their hands to cause only the correct bells to ring.

Benjamin Britten uses hand bells in his children's opera *Noye's Fludde* (1958). In

Match for Three Players (1964) Mauricio Kagel asks for three hand bells of different sizes but of unspecified pitches.

Example -- Egk: *Casanova in London* (hand bell, doorbell, ship's bell).

Doorbells and telephone bells are imitated by a spring-wound mechanism equipped with push buttons and small steel bells shaped like skullcaps (*calottes*). Such imitative effects have occasionally been used instrumentally.

Example -- Kagel: *Match for Three Players.*

The Turkish crescent (Ger. *Schellenbaum*) -- a staff adorned with eagles, stars, crescents, and/or horse tails and hung with small silvery bells -- is often carried ahead of uniformed marching bands as an emblem. It is of oriental origin and has been known in the West since the Turkish wars of the 16th century, although it has never played a musical role.

Bo Nilsson in *Ein irrender Sohn* (Mus. Ex. 89) uses a percussion instrument he calls *Schellenbaum* (bell tree), which consists of several small bells, including a few sleigh bells, attached to a wooden handle, or mounted on a metal ring, and shaken or struck (see Ill. below). The difference between the directions "middle" and "low" in the score determines the choice of smaller or larger bells.

Schellenbaum (Bell Tree)
used by Bo Nilsson

A much stronger sound is obtained from the Sanctus bells generally used in pairs in Roman Catholic churches. Three or four steel bells are solidly attached to metal crossbars, held by a handle, and shaken firmly. Egk uses them in his opera *Columbus* and in his ballet *Abraxas;* Kubelik does the same in his requiem *Libera nos.*

In *Gebrauchsmusik* (music for home and school) in the United States one occasionally finds an instrument of Far Eastern origin designated as bell tree. It consists of a number of small, *calotte*-shaped bells hung beneath each other on a string in descending order of size, thus forming a rope. By running a steel rod down the edges of the bells, a sound is obtained resembling that of a glockenspiel glissando made with a metal mallet.

Bell Tree of Far-Eastern Origin

The sarna bell (elephant bell) -- well known as dinner and ornamental bell, and a favorite export item from India -- is used by Henze in *Heliogabalus Imperator.*

Sarna Bell

The diameter of these spherical, thin-walled bells of brass alloy may range from 2 to 10 cm (3/4" to 4"). Their upper hemisphere extends into a handle, while the lower one has 8 to 10 claw-like, pointed prongs. Their sound has few overtones and is of a delicate timbre. Sarna bells are almost incapable of dynamic variations.

The well-known, heavy-walled, cast bronze bell known as ship's bell produces a penetrating, alarm-like ring. It has a clapper which, by means of a leather strap or thong attached to it, is pulled against the inner wall of the bell (see Ill. on p. 135).

The ship's bell may be used as an alarm or storm bell in the revolution scene in *Boris Godunov* by Mussorgsky, in scenes in Verdi's *Don Carlos,* and in other, similar situations.

Alarm Bell (or Ship's Bell)

    The Japanese temple bell, *Dobači,* is an upright, vessel-like bell of hammered bronze. Standing open-end-up on a padded base, it is struck on the inner rim with a rod-shaped, leather-covered beater.

    The size of such instruments, which are usually encountered singly, varies. Their diameter runs from about 10 to 60 cm (4″ to 24″); accordingly a scale from about c^1 to e^2 can be assembled. Their resounding tone, generating an additional sub-octave in larger bells, resembles in color that of a glass bell struck with the same kind of beater, but has a much greater volume. In his *Das Floss der Medusa,* Henze included two *dobači* of different sizes, designated as "temple bells." By rubbing the inner rim of the bell with the beater the instrument's low fundamental can be made to sound continuously as long as desired.

    Example -- Henze: *El Cimarron.*

Japanese Temple Bell *(Dobači)*

Anvil and other Heavy Metal Instruments

Metal Block

Common beaters: metal hammers

The metallic, short-sounding beat of the hammer on the anvil, with its unmistakable, penetrating, high partials, can be traced back to early medieval music. It re-appeared, much later, in opera scores. For example, anvils are beaten onstage by the *Gypsy Chorus* in Verdi's *Il Trovatore,* and Wagner has young Siegfried use the anvil in a rhythmically and dynamically varied manner during the *Forging Songs* in the *Ring.*

In the *Transformation Scene* of *Das Rheingold* one hears the tremendous crescendo of the anvil chorus of the Nibelungs offstage: a group of eighteen players beating eighteen anvils which are grouped, according to Wagner's directions, into three different sounds and sizes (Mus. Ex. 90). For the accented beats of the large, low-sounding anvil a heavy metal hammer is used; the higher-sounding anvils, beaten in a quicker rhythm, require correspondingly lighter hammers. The beating spot producing the best sound is found at the rounded tip of the anvil.

In our own century the anvil has become a musical instrument in its own right.

Anvil

Before the World Wars, salon orchestras and ensembles simulated the sound of an anvil by means of a piece of steel, such as a glockenspiel bar, which was mounted on a felt-covered base and beaten with a small metal hammer. Its muted sound resembled a small or far away anvil.

Example -- J. Strauss: *Feuerfest* Polka.

The glockenspiel bars may have led to the designation metal block, but today this term is easily confused with the jazz cowbell which occasionally is also called metal block (see p. 131).

Steel Plates (Steel Disks)

An anvil-like sound that is much bigger and richer in overtones than that of the glockenspiel bar is produced by steel plates (steel disks) placed on felt supports. These disks have a diameter of up to 20 cm (8″), a thickness of up to 3 cm (1 3/16″), and a weight of up to 5 kg (ca. 11 lbs.) -- (see Ill. on p. 137).

Steel Plates Lying on Felt Supports

In spite of the numerous, clearly audible partials, one can discern a distinctly focused pitch: the thicker the metal, the higher the frequencies of the sound spectrum. (A specific pitch -- a^4 -- is required for the anvil in Orff's *Antigonae*.)

Other examples -- Berlioz: *Benvenuto Cellini;* Gounod: *Philemon et Baucis;* de Falla: *La vida breve;* Varèse: *Ionisation* (Mus. Ex. 109); Britten: *The Prince of the Pagodes;* Copland: 3rd Symphony; Janáček: *Out of a Death-House;* Henze: *Elegy* (Mus. Ex. 8); Kelemen: *Der neue Mieter, Radiant;* Cage: *First Construction in Metal* (Mus. Ex. 85).

Steel plates or disks, if suspended from strings drawn through holes in their rims, produce freely floating tones. They also permit the assembly of a set of plates having a combined range of about a^3 to a^4, somewhat like a hanging version of the lithophone. A species of instrument has thus been developed whose prototypes already existed around the year 1000 B.C. in the ritualistic music of China. While those early, heavy, long-vibrating bronze disks were struck with wooden beaters, the modern steel plates are always struck with metal beaters or hammers. Softer beaters would make the massive material vibrate only slightly, and the sound of impact would be too prominent and annoying.

Example -- Kelemen: *Equilibres* (Mus. Ex. 34).

Automobile Brake Drums

Similar to the sound of steel plates is that of automobile brake drums from stripped-down junked cars (see Ill. below). Such instruments, with their many, varying sounds, are used occasionally in popular music. They have also been used by modern American composers, such as Harrison: *Canticle No. III;* Cowell: Symphony No. 14; Cage: *First Construction in Metal* (4 different brake drums), Cage and Harrison: *Double Music* (6 different brake drums -- Mus. Ex. 91), and Alvin Etler: Concerto for Brass Quintet, String Orchestra, and Percussion (1967).

Automobile Brake Drums

Switch

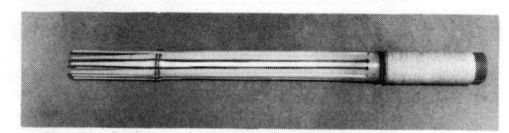

The Switch

The bent stick called switch was adopted from Janissary music at the time of Haydn and Mozart, but was then used only for accompanying beats on the bass drum (see also p. 94 of the bass-drum chapter).

In a few late Romantic works an independent instrument, also called switch, is used, which had its origin in the cults (exorcism of demons) of India, Asia, and Oceania. Made from a split section of bamboo, it served both as a beaten instrument and as a beater.

The orchestral beating switch was first used to portray the impression of the sounds of beating or whipping. Eventually its strange noise was also used as an abstract sound effect.

Examples -- R. Strauss: *Elektra, Die Frau ohne Schatten;* Mahler: 3rd and 6th Symphonies; Varèse: *Integrales;* Berg: *Wozzeck* (Mus. Ex. 92), *Lulu;* Othmar Schoeck: *Penthesilea;* Korngold: *Die tote Stadt.*

It is advisable to use several switches bound together, so that the listeners at a distance will be able to hear the swishing sound of the beating switch. For softer spots, birch branches or bunched bamboo strips, 50 cm (20") long, are best suited (see Ill. on p. 29, Nos. 3 and 4). The shell of a bass drum, or a thin-walled, empty box, provide the most resonant beating surfaces. A much louder noise can be produced with a bamboo section, about 40 cm (16") long and 4 cm (1 5/8") in diameter, which has been split into about twelve pointed switch tongues, about 30 cm (12") long (see Ill. above). Held by its handle and beaten against a hard surface, the sound of this switch easily cuts through a massive orchestration.

CLAPPERS

Hands; Clappers (Wooden Clappers, Slapstick, Whip); Small Boards (Bones); Strung Clappers (Bin-Zasara); Concussion Blocks (Hyoshigi); Concussion Sticks or Rods (Claves, Bamboos); Castanets; Finger Cymbals (Crotales); Cymbal Tongs (Castagnettes de fer--Gabelbecken)

Hands

The clapping of hands, either together or against the body, as well as the stamping of feet are the simplest and oldest means of rhythmic expression. They have remained an ever-recurring part of rites and dances of peoples on all continents.

In Orff's *Schulwerk* hand clapping is a part of fundamental rhythm training. There also are examples of its use in art music: Milhaud, in *Les choephores,* has the chorus clap and stamp according to rhythmic notation; Berio has the singer in *Circles* clap her hands in addition to beating time and giving entrance cues; in Satie's ballet *Parade,* and in Carlos Surinach's *Ritmo Jondo,* the members of the percussion section have to clap in accordance with precise rhythmic notation.

In Egypt, at the time of the Pharaohs, the clapping of hands was imitated by beating together small boards which had the outlines of hands and forearms carved on their outer surfaces.

Whip or Slapstick

In Adolphe Adam's opera *Le Postillon de Longjumeau* (1836) orchestral clappers had to underscore the cracking of the whips of the carriage drivers. Clappers were used in other stage works as well; for example in Weber's *Der Freischütz* (1821) and in Mascagni's *Cavalleria rusticana* (1890), as well as in numerous pieces of light music calling for such coloristic effects.

The clapper so used--the whip or slapstick--consists of two wooden boards, approximately 40 cm (16") long and 5 cm (2") wide, and connected at the insides of their narrow ends by a hinge. The boards are held by leather straps or wooden handles attached to their outer sides. To make it possible for the percussionist to operate the instrument with only one hand, lighter boards are used: one of them extended to act as a handle, the other mounted on it with a spring. These instruments produce a loud, slapping sound when whipped through the air and stopped suddenly.

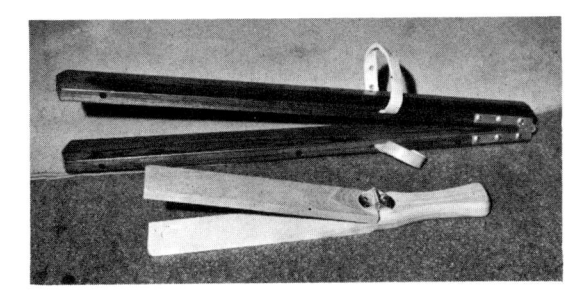

Whips or Slapsticks

In recent times, composers have included this instrument in scores for its sound as such, using the names of whip, slapstick, or simply clapper. Like the wooden clappers of their Far Eastern forebears, instruments for today's orchestra must be of hardwood, tough enough for heavy use, and capable of producing a sufficiently loud bang. The dimensions of such clappers are approximately 50 to 60 cm (20" to 24") in length and 1.5 cm (5/8") in thickness. Several precautionary cross-screws and rivets will provide the best protection against splitting of the wood. Their uses, like the clapping of hands, have natural limits. The faster the beats, the shorter the distance the boards may be separated from one another before striking again, and thus the lower the dynamic range possible.

Examples -- Pfitzner: *Von deutscher Seele;* Mussorgsky-Ravel: *Pictures at an Exhibition;* Ravel: Piano Concerto, *Air de feu, L'heure espagnole;* Varèse: *Ionisation;* Honegger: *La danse macabre;* Janáček: *Out of a Death-House;* Milhaud: *L'homme et son désir, La mort d'un tyran (Mus. Ex. 60);* Britten: *The Young Person's Guide to the Orchestra, The Rape of Lucretia, War Requiem;* Copland: 3rd Symphony; Egk: *Der Revisor;* Hindemith: Concerto for Orchestra.

Small Boards or Bones

Puccini, in his opera *Gianni Schicchi,* produces a whip-like effect with two drum sticks: the percussionist holds both sticks by their heads with one hand while beating their heavier opposite ends together in the cupped palm of his other hand. A similar effect can be produced with the small board clappers called bones, which consist of two oblong pieces of wood or bone struck together. Such a clapper is occasionally found in popular music.

Bones

Korean Multiboard Whip (or Rattle), Bak

The Korean multiboard whip, *bak,* appears as part of the percussion resources of Ysang Yun, for example, in *Dimensions, Träume* (Dreams), and *Sim Tjong.* In each instance, several *baks* are used.

A *bak* consists of six small, slightly convex hardwood boards or bars, 34 cm (13 5/8″) in length, 5½ cm (2 3/16″) wide at the bottom, and 4½ cm (1 3/4″) wide at the top. Their thickness is more or less comparable to that of marimba bars of similar length. At their upper ends the boards have two holes 8 cm (3 3/16″) apart, lengthwise. All six boards are connected loosely by a cord run through the holes.

Causing the boards to bang against one another produces a fast, penetratingly loud "arpeggio" of claps. This is done by first spreading the boards apart with both hands and then pushing them together at the required moment.

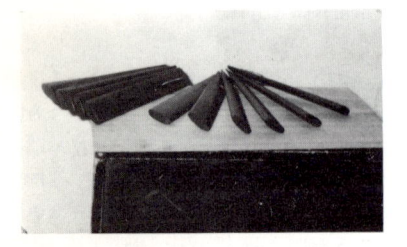

Korean Multiboard Whip *(Bak)*

Bin-Zasara

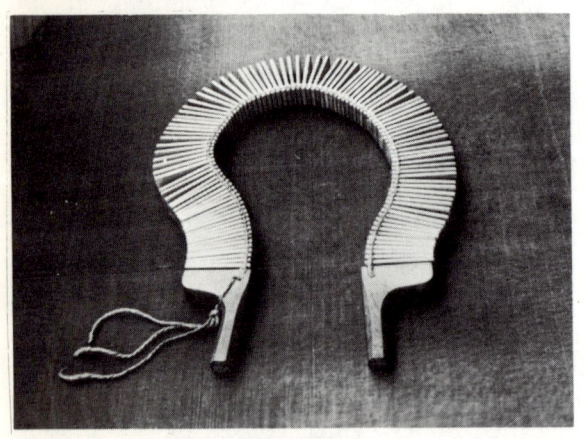

Bin-Zánsara

The strung clapper, Bin-Zasara, introduced from Japan by Carl Orff, consists of about ninety small boards each 10 cm (4") in length and 3 cm (ca. 1 3/16") in width, and tied together to form a rope approximately 120 cm (48") long (see Ill. on p. 140). A rapid, undulating movement of the handles attached to both ends causes a quick, successive beating-together of the little boards, thus producing a short, rattling noise similar to that of a ratchet. Orff included this clapper in *Prometheus* (see Mus. Ex 93).

Concussion Blocks (Hyoshigi)

In the music of the Chinese and Japanese theatres, redwood boards are clapped together giving important accents by their sharp and tremendously penetrating beats. Two longish, rectangular blocks are banged together strongly at a precise spot on their very slightly curved sides They must meet in exactly the right place to give the strongest possible clap.

Concussion Blocks (Hyoshigi)

In *Oedipus der Tyrann*, Orff calls these clappers *grosses Klappholz* (large wooden clappers). In *Prometheus*, he calls them by their Japanese name, *hyoshigi* (Mus. Ex. 98).

Claves, Bamboo Clappers

Claves

Simple stick clappers carved from sonorous hardwood are found as native rhythm instruments in the Far East as well as in Africa. They have come to Western music under the name claves, together with an entire group of other percussion instruments which originally came from Africa and which have permeated Latin-American folk and dance music (bongos, congas, maracas, etc.).

A pair of claves is made of two round hardwood sticks (ebony, rosewood, or similar wood), about 20 cm (8″) long and 2.5 to 3 cm (1″ to 1 3/16″) in diameter. While one clave rests on the finger tips and the pad of the thumb, above the cupped palm of the hand which serves as the resonator, it is struck at its mid-point with the other clave (see Ill. on p. 141).

The one-handed method of striking limits the rapidity of successive beats. Also, because both hands are needed to hold the claves, the player is not able to change quickly to other instruments unless, of course, he can beat the subsequent instrument with a clave, as for example in *Ionisation* by Varèse.

Examples -- Copland: 3rd Symphony, *Appalachian Spring;* Fortner: *Impromptus;* Henze: *Il re cervo;* Chávez: *Sinfonía India;* Sanjuan: *Liturgía negra;* Revueltas: *Sensemayá;* Killmayer: Chamber Music for Jazz Instruments, *Le petit Savoyard, La tragedia di Orfeo;* Zimmermann: *Dialoge;* Foss: *Echoi* (Mus. Ex. 106).

It takes dexterity to execute a claves roll. The beating stick, in a trembling motion, is played with both ends against the stationary stick; the thumb forms a central axis while the fore and ring fingers produce the roll by means of rapidly alternating pressure.

Example -- Berio: *Circles.*

The penetrating sound of the claves resembles that of a high tone on the xylophone, i.e., a pitch of the four-line octave. As long as specific pitches are not required, several different sounding pairs of claves (one pair per player) may be used together.

As a contrast to wooden claves, claves made of steel tubing, called steel sticks, have been used (along with wooden claves) by Zimmermann in *Die Soldaten.*

In areas where bamboo is available as material for instruments, it is natural to use it also for clappers. Like the claves, bamboo clappers produce high pitches which can be varied according to the size of the stick. Bamboo sticks, however, have less volume and produce a more pointed, noisy sound.

Examples -- Kazuo Fukushima: *Hi-Kio* for flute, strings, piano, and percussion; Orff: *Prometheus*

Castanets

History. Castanets, which may be classified as cup-shaped concussion clappers, demand a high degree of proficiency. Even in the days of Antiquity they were used only by professional dancers, as evidenced by representations on numerous art works. The prototype of the castanet is assumed to stem from Asia and existed in various shapes, of which that of a double-shelled mussel may have been one of the oldest. Semispherical, hollow pairs of carved wooden clappers resembling chestnut hulls were possibly responsible for the name *castañeta.* *

The form best known today was developed in Spain, a center of the art of dancing ever since Antiquity. There the virtuoso playing technique was perfected over a period of hundreds of years, along with the Spanish forms of dancing, elevating the castanets to the position of *the* national instrument. Southern Italy, under Spanish domination for several centuries, likewise absorbed castanets into its musical customs. Castanets did not become popular elsewhere because of the formidable difficulty of playing them. They were bound up with folklore and became separated from it only through their use in the orchestra.

Construction and Playing Techniques. The Spanish castanets consist of two carved shells, shaped like scallop or cockle shells, of very hard wood (such as grenadilla, ebony, rosewood), lying with the hollow parts against each other, and connected, hinge-like, by a

*Coming from the Latin *castanea,* meaning "chestnut." (Trsl.)

cord tied through holes at their upper rims.

The player holds in each cupped hand a pair of castanets hanging from the thumb by a string. Bending the thumb and thus tightening the string causes a slight opening of the shells. By successive tapping on the shells with the four fingertips of each hand, they click together and produce the precise, exciting rolls of the dance castanets. Complete mastery of the technique demands an unusually long period of intensive practice. For orchestral use it suffices if the player holds the nooses with the middle, ring, and little fingers of the closed hands, while the hinged ends of the castanets rest on the middle sections of the slightly bent index fingers and are kept in partially opened position through spring-like pressure by the thumbs (see Ill. below). Using this method, the player beats the prescribed rhythm on his knees, always alternating hands, similar to playing the timpani. Series of single beats, grace notes, shakes, and rolls can thus be executed in any dynamic shading. In order to make it possible to pick up the castanets quickly, it is helpful to sew a piece of leather around the string held by the fingers, thus making a handy grip.

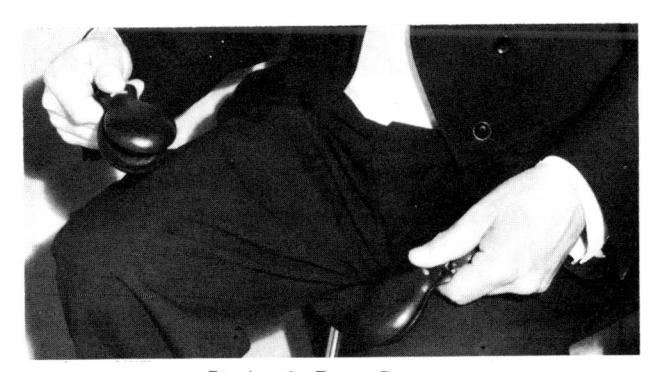

Playing the Dance Castanets

The so-called handle castanets were developed when the orchestral and ensemble percussionist was required to produce the sound of castanets. They were designed to make playing easier for the performer by providing a handle whose other end consists of a flat piece of wood of the same kind and contour as the castanet shells, extending between the shells and thus serving as a clapping wall for them.

Handle Castanets

The shells are hinged to the divider by a piece of gut. Handle castanets, usually played in pairs, are only moderately satisfactory when used for clear rhythms and dynamic gradations. On the other hand, they are very suitable for massive castanet rolls produced by intense shaking, as in Orff's *Antigonae* and *Oedipus der Tyrann* where several handle castanets produce the large volume of sound called for. Smaller handle castanets with their brighter, more chattering sound caused Richard Strauss to choose them for sounds illustrating smacking lips and clicking tongues in *Der Rosenkavalier* and in *Elektra*. It would be wrong, therefore, to use dance castanets in these spots.

Even though the individual pitches are not very clear, the difference between the larger instruments with deeply hollowed shells and the smaller ones with shallower shells is easily discernable. The pitches obtainable lie roughly between e^3 and e^4.

In contrast to the Spanish dancer who with a larger castanet in his left hand produces accents and with a smaller, higher sounding one in his right beats the rhythmic patterns, the orchestral percussionist, because of his different way of handling castanets, uses a pair in equal tuning.

Use. In the following works the use of castanets still underlines the typical Spanish flavor -- Bizet: *Carmen;* de Falla: *The Three-Cornered Hat;* Debussy: *Iberia Suite;* Ravel: *Rhapsodie espagnole, Alborada del gracioso.* However, Wagner, in the *Bacchanal* of the Parisian version (1861) of *Tannhäuser,* has a rhythmically dance-like part for the castanets which leads to the orgiastic climax of the ballet scene. Richard Strauss considerably weakened their connotations as dance instruments by using castanets purely for the color of their sound *(Salome, Die Frau ohne Schatten).* In this abstract role the castanet sound has appeared in numerous contemporary scores.

Examples -- Varèse: *Ionisation* (Mus. Ex. 109); Egk: *Joan von Zarissa, Peer Gynt, Die chinesische Nachtigall;* Orff: *Carmina Burana, Die Kluge, Antigonae* (Mus. Ex. 37), *Oedipus.*

Two differently pitched pairs of castanets are used by Bo Nilsson in *Ein irrender Sohn,* indicated as high and very high (Mus. Ex. 89).

In the ballet *The Red Cape,* Luigi Nono wrote for four differently pitched castanets, indicated as soprano, alto, tenor, bass (see Mus. Ex. 94). Execution by one player is made possible through the use of a castanet holder originally developed in the United States. Two to four single castenets, different in size and sound, are attached to the holder in such a way that striking them with the finger or with a soft-headed beater is entirely sufficient to produce rhythmically precise clapping.

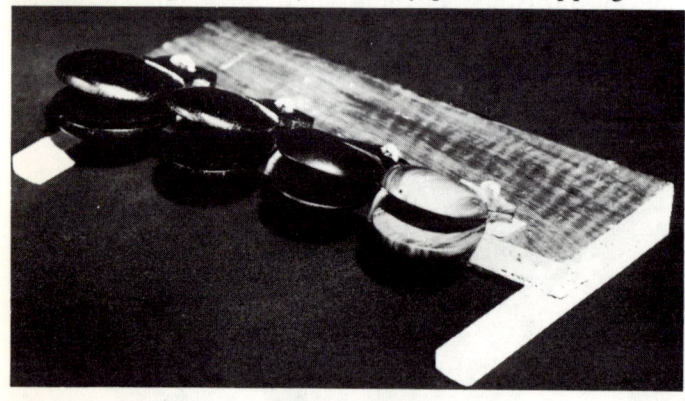

Castanet Holder

Finger Cymbals,[*] Cymbal Tongs (Castagnettes de fer--Gabelbecken)

In addition to wooden clappers, finger cymbals -- dance clappers made of metal alloy -- have been known since Antiquity. These are the smallest and weakest-sounding members of the cymbal family. Their diameters range from 4 to 5 cm (1 5/8" to 2"). They are still used today by female dancers in the Near East and are played in a manner remotely resembling that of playing castanets, thus earning for them the name *castagnettes de fer*

---

[*]Often called crotales, although smaller and without definite pitch (see crotales).

(iron castanets) in France. The technique of playing the finger cymbals requires a nimble beating together of two pairs of cymbals, attached with leather loops, one cymbal each, to the thumbs and middle fingers. The flat inner sides of the cymbals are then clapped together rhythmically.

Very fast rhythms, for which the finger dexterity of the orchestral player is insufficient, are executed with only a single pair of finger cymbals; the hand with the cymbals beats against the knee to produce the first beat, after which a second beat is accomplished by striking with the free hand against the thumb which holds one of the cymbals, causing the two of them to clap together once more. After each beat the cymbals are immediately separated by the thumb which acts as a spring. With this technique very fast series of beats are possible.

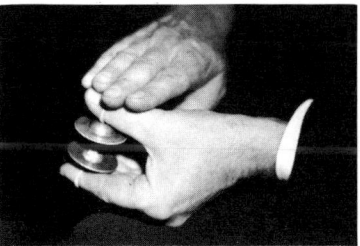

Finger Cymbals

Examples – Berio: *Circles;* Ulvi C. Erkin: *Senfoni II.*

In order to simplify playing, the pairs of cymbals may be attached to springlike tongs made of heavy steel wire. These cymbal tongs (*Gabelbecken*) originated in the Orient. By closing the tongs, the inner plates of the cymbals clash together and immediately separate again because of the tension of the spring. Series of beats are played alternately by the left and right hands, thus producing a ringing metallic clatter.

Cymbal Tongs (Castagnettes de fer – Gabelbecken)

Examples – Charpentier: *Louise* (1900); Milhaud: *L'homme et son désir* (Mus. Ex. 95).

WOODEN DRUMS
Tubular Wood Blocks; Rectangular Wood Blocks; Temple Blocks; Mokubio; Slit Drums; Log Drum; Wood Plate Drum; Wooden Barrel (Sake Barrel); Wooden Board; Hammer

Origin. The predecessors of the various forms of wooden drums known to us were part of the instrumental resources of many peoples. Small, high-pitched wooden drums predominate in the traditional theatrical music of China and Japan, which is rich in percussion sounds, while the temple blocks stem from the Buddhist and Confucian cultures of Eastern Asia.

Slit drums in all sizes are found in Africa, Asia, the South Pacific, and the Americas.

These instruments are used both ceremonially and as talking drums for the communication of news events. The so-called Chinese wood blocks, and later the Chinese or Korean temple blocks, became known in the musical world of the West through instrumental groups which evolved from early jazz.

In the 1920's, contemporary composers, such as Ravel, Milhaud, Honegger, Hindemith, Gershwin, introduced the new sounds of wooden drums into orchestral scores, often in connection with jazz elements.

Wooden drums used to be employed sparingly because of their obvious and noisy effects. Today, however, they are standard components of the percussion section.

Tubular Wood Blocks

The tubular wood block (see Ill. below) probably was developed after World War I in an attempt to produce a small, light, two-toned instrument for dance bands and light-classical ensembles. Its prototype may have been the ancient bamboo slit drum. The tubular wood block is made from a round piece of hardwood about 25 to 30 cm (10" to 12") long and 5 to 6 cm (2" to 2 3/8") in diameter. It is partially hollowed out from both ends toward the middle, each side having a different depth, and it has slits at each opening to increase the vibrations. Today it has almost completely disappeared from the orchestral percussion section because its low dynamic level is considered unsatisfactory. If it does occur in an orchestra score it is usually replaced by a rectangular wood block.

Tubular Wood Block

Rectangular Wood Blocks

Construction. The term wood block indicates the shape of the instrument: a long, rectangular hardwood block of rosewood or a similar wood, with a deep resonating chamber cut into each of its long sides. Its pitch is determined by the size of the block, the size of the resonating chamber, and especially by the thickness of the wooden ceiling above the chamber. It is difficult to determine the exact pitch at first hearing because the short, sharp, penetrating wooden tone has a dominant noise factor. A wood block offers two beating areas (the wide sides), each producing a different sound, about a second or a third apart in pitch. The instrument is mounted so that the surface chosen for beating lies on top.

It is possible to produce wood blocks with pitches varying from g^2 to c^4. To achieve clear contrasts in pitch, however, no more than three to four different blocks should be used.

Measurements of wood blocks (between c^3 and c^4) range from 26 to 18 cm (10 3/8" to 7 3/16") in length, 10 to 6 cm (4" to 2 3/8") in width, and 7 to 4 cm (2 3/4" to 1 5/8") in height, respectively.

Smaller wood blocks, attached to a pronged holder, can be fastened to a music stand, a bass drum, or another suitable place. Larger blocks, or a group of blocks, are placed on a soft base or a special stand (see Ill. on p. 147).

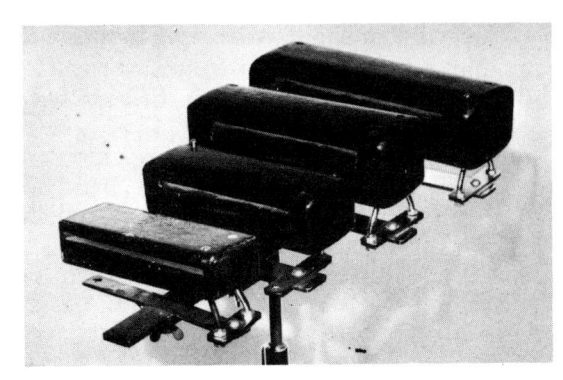

Four Wood Blocks of Different Pitches on a Special Stand

Beaters and Method of Playing. Wood blocks are struck on the spot which produces the strongest resonance, usually the mid-point of either of the wide surfaces. The technique of beating is similar to that which is normally used with heavy-headed beaters; rhythmic passages as well as rolls are executed with alternating strokes, as on the wood and metal-bar instruments. Beaters are usually of hard materials; the dance-band drummer generally uses drum sticks. In the orchestra, glockenspiel mallets produce the greatest possible volume. When scored along with other percussion instruments the wood block is normally played with whatever beaters are in use, such as wooden cymbal beaters or xylophone mallets.

Examples – Milhaud: *La création du monde* (Mus. Ex. 58); Bo Nilsson: *Ein irrender Sohn* (Mus. Ex. 89).

Rubber covered, wooden headed beaters produce a timbre approximating that of high-pitched temple blocks.

Examples -- Milhaud: *La création du monde;* Varèse: *Ionisation* (Mus. Ex. 109); Orff: *Trionfi;* Cage: *Amores* (7 wood blocks); Foss: *Echoi* (Mus. Ex. 106); Kagel: *Anagrama* (Mus. Ex. 44).

Temple Blocks

Construction. The temple blocks of China, Indo-China, and Japan provide variations of the standard wood-block sound because of their special timbres and richer dynamic gradations. Their shape resembles a pot-bellied herd bell or the mouth of a fish -- in fact, they are called "wooden fish" in China. They are carved from a piece of camphor wood which is hollowed out with special knives. Their large resonating chambers produce sounds of dark color and good carrying power in the lower range. The tone, however, seems almost as diffuse as that of the wood block and is not perceived as a definite pitch. Present manufacture is limited to sets of blocks ranging from about c^2 to g^3 in pitch.

Temple Blocks

The ball-like shape of temple blocks necessitates their being attached to a special stand capable of holding sets of from three to five blocks (see Ill. on p. 147).

Beaters. The most suitable beaters have wooden heads covered with rubber, such as marimba mallets. Hard beaters, like those used for wood blocks, produce a leaner, thinner sound, but also a more precise knock.

Usage. The popular and dance band music of the 1930's used the temple blocks to suggest exotic local color or to imitate hoof beats. In the United States, composers of light music of a higher level introduced temple blocks into orchestral scores, and soon they also made their appearance in serious contemporary music.

Examples – Berg: *Lulu;* Walton: *Facade* (ballet); Gershwin: *Porgy and Bess;* Gould: *Latin-American Symphonette;* Messiaen: *Oiseaux exotiques, Réveil des oiseaux, Turangalîla-Symphonie;* Egk: *Allegria, Der Revisor, Die Verlobung in San Domingo;* Killmayer: *La tragedia di Orfeo;* Armin Schibler: Concerto for Percussion and Orchestra; Carter: Double Concerto (five temple blocks); N. Mamangakis: *Konstruktionen* (six temple blocks – see Mus. Ex. 96); Hartmann: Concerto for Viola and Orchestra; Foss: *Echoi* (Mus. Ex. 106); Haubenstock-Ramati: *Vermutungen über ein dunkles Haus* (Mus. Ex. 41).

Mokubio (Mokugyo)

Mokugyo is the name of a Chinese (Japanese) wooden drum used by Buddhist priests. Its shape and sound are the same as those of the Korean temple blocks. The mokubio, on the other hand, is a wooden drum of Japanese origin.

The drum consists of a disk-shaped, turned block of camphor wood with a circular opening at the bottom that becomes wider, conically, as it deepens: the resonance chamber. The remaining "ceiling" is ca. 1 cm (3/8") thick. In the center of the top side is a raised, round disk, just a few millimeters high: the strike area. The box-shaped instrument stands on three short, wooden, glued-on feet.

Mokubios

Beaters. Mallets with hardwood heads are used (possibly also xylophone mallets).

The pitch-levels of these wooden drums, depending on size, range from the three-line octave to approximately the middle of the four-line octave. The sound quality of the drums is similar to that of claves or xylophones.

An instrument in bb^3 has the following measurements:

    Upper diameter: 15 cm (6")
    Diameter of the strike area: 10.5 cm (4 3/16")
    Lower diameter: 16 cm (6 3/8")
    Height: 7 cm (2 3/4")
    Height of feet: 2.5 cm (1")
    Diameter of the bottom opening: 7.3 cm (about 3")
    Diameter of the hollowed-out bottom: 11 cm (4 3/8")
    Depth of the resonator space: 6 cm (2 3/8")

Use of mokubios in modern Japanese music generally is limited to single drums. Example -- Yuso Toyama: Rhapsody for Orchestra.

Slit Drums

A slit drum is made from a section of a tree trunk of suitable exotic wood. The section is hollowed out by a length-wise cut which provides an effective resonating chamber. Ethnomusicological findings indicate that some of these wooden drums may be as long as 4 m (13'4") in the Cameroon region of West Africa, 6 m (20') in Brazil, and as much as 7 m (23'4") in Assam, although the predominant types are much smaller and thus easier to carry and to handle.

The thinner the walls toward the edges of the slits -- which also function as beating spots -- the lower and darker the sound, provided the size of the resonating chamber is correspondingly large. Usually the rims are of different thickness, thus making it possible to produce two different tone qualities.

The extraordinary carrying power of the sound of this drum explains why primitive peoples use it for conveying messages by means of a system similar to Morse code. Strong hardwood sticks or small club-shaped beaters are used for this purpose.

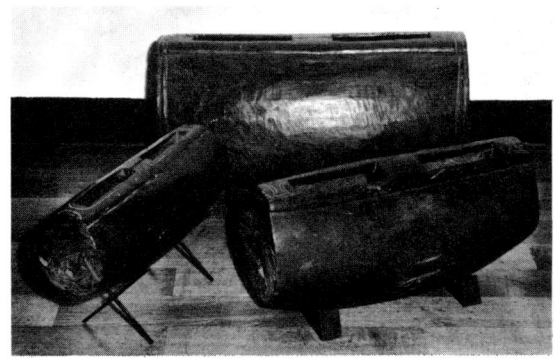

Native Slit Drums

Slit drums from 50 to 80 cm (20" to 32") in length, obtained from museums and private collections, have entered Western art music. Carl Orff was the first to include a slit drum in his stage works *Die Bernauerin* and *Antigonae.* Later Stockhausen used slit drums in *Gruppen for Three Orchestras* and *Zyklus for one Percussion Player.*

Heavy hard-felt beaters bring out the low, hollow sound of the slit drum by activating the entire resonating chamber, while hard, wooden beaters produce a lighter, noisier sound.

Further examples -- Nono: *Composizione per orchestra* No. 2 (four slit drums); Cage: *Third Construction;* Kelemen: *Radiant;* Orff: *Antigonae* (Mus. Ex. 97), *Weihnachtsspiel* (Mus. Ex. 110).

Log Drum

The bass instruments among the wooden drums -- long drum and rhythm log -- were developed in the U.S. and are based on the same principle of sound production as that of the old Mexican wooden drum, *teponaztli,* which is beaten with padded beaters on two tongues cut into the drum's top surface. Variations in thickness and length of the tongues produce clear differences in pitch.

The resonating chamber of the log drum consists of a long, rectangular wooden box. A freely vibrating tongue is cut into the lid of the box which is 2 cm (3/4") thick (see Ill. below). The length of the lid determines the pitch of the instrument. The pitch can be altered, however, if a hole is cut into the lid. The closer the hole is positioned toward the base of the tongue, the shorter will be the vibrating section behind it, and thus the higher the pitch of the fundamental tone.

Log Drums

The measurements of a log drum -- for instance one with a pitch of C -- are 76 cm (30 3/8") in length and 14 cm (5 5/8") in height and width, respectively. A set of log drums can have a range of approximately G to c. Their present use in American educational music is limited, however, to just a few random pitches or series of pitches, because it is still difficult to place a large number of log drums in sufficiently close proximity to make easy manipulation possible.

The log drum's sonority is comparable to that of the bass trough xylophone. It is determined by the proportions of the resonator box which lies lengthwise on its back. The carrying power of the log drum, like that of the low-pitched wood-bar instruments, is not great.

Beaters used are either the heavy, hard-felt type, or the bass xylophone mallets of solid rubber covered with soft felt.

Examples -- Berio: *Circles, Passaggio;* Henze: *El Cimarron.*

Wood-Plate Drum (Wooden Tom-Tom); Wooden Barrel (Sake Barrel)

A set of tom-toms can be converted to wood-plate drums by replacing their batter heads with thin lids of wood and by also removing their bottom skins, as directed in Nono's *Diario polacco '58* and Stockhausen's *Kontakte* (see Ill. on p. 151).

This type of instrument originated with the wooden boards of the Far East and the Japanese wooden barrels (such as those used for sake) whose wooden staves are held together without glue or nails by braided natural fibers (see Ill. on p. 151).

The somewhat darker sound of the ca. 60 cm (24") high wooden barrel is produced by striking its head, in a succession of single beats, with round, wooden sticks approximately 43 cm (17 3/16") long and 3 cm (1 3/16") in diameter.

Wood-Plate Drum (Wooden Tom-Tom) 　　　　　Wooden Barrel (Sake Barrel)

Wooden Board

A wooden board, 67 cm (26 3/4") long, 36 cm (14 3/8") wide, and 2.3 cm (ca. 1") thick, produces a light, clapping, wooden sound whose character varies considerably depending upon whether the board is struck at the edge or in the middle.

Carl Orff uses a wooden board as well as a wooden barrel in *Prometheus:* the wooden board, lying on a kettle drum (see Ill. below), and another kettle drum are beaten alternately, as are a wooden barrel *(barile di legno)* and a taiko bass drum (Mus. Ex. 98).

Wooden Board

Hammer

A wooden box acting as a resonator and beaten with a hammer has long been known as a ceremonial instrument in China and Japan.

An oblong, hanging board called *semanterion* and struck with a hammer, has for centuries been used in religious rites in the monasteries of the Greek Orthodox church.

Hammer

Among the compositions in which the sound of such a board has been employed, are Mahler: 6th Symphony; Milhaud: *L'homme et son désir, Les choephores;* Othmar Schoeck: *Penthesilea;* Berg: Three Pieces for Orchestra; and Schönberg: *Die glückliche Hand.*

Striking a cantilevered wooden floor with heavy blows of a large-headed wooden hammer (one with a large striking area) can be extraordinarily startling, exciting, and purposely different from the music being performed around it.

SCRAPED INSTRUMENTS
Ratchet; Guíro (Gourd Scraper); Sapo Cubana or Bambú Brasileño (Bamboo Scraper); Reco-Reco (Wooden Scraper); Washboard; Metal Rasp (Metal Scraper)

General Information. Sticks, plates, tubes, and other vessels with a cross-grooved or notched surface may be scraped with a suitable object to produce a crackling, scratching, or even clattering sound.

The simplest types of scrapers used by primitive peoples were notched bones or wooden sticks. Louder scraping sounds with a greater range of nuances are produced by hollowed-out gourds, bamboo tubes, clay vessels, and wooden boxes.

Ratchet

The approximate date of the transition to the swung ratchet is obscure. The prototype of the European form of the instrument presumably came from India. In medieval Europe the small ratchet turned from church use to becoming a children's toy (Leopold Mozart: *Toy Symphony,* see Mus. Ex. 107).

In Catholic areas one often finds a large ratchet fastened to a wooden saw horse and operated by a hand lever. During Holy Week, when church bells must be silent, ratchets of this kind ("church ratchets") take their place. Beethoven may have thought of such a giant ratchet for his *Wellington's Victory.* Carl Orff used the same instrument offstage in the church scene of *Die Bernauerin.*

The percussionist of the salon orchestra had long ago included the small ratchet in his set of sound effects (Joseph Strauss: *Plappermäulchen* Polka). In symphonic music the small ratchet seems to have appeared for the first time in *Till Eulenspiegel* by Richard Strauss, and has been used occasionally ever since.

The ratchet consists of a wooden cogwheel around whose axis rotates a rectangular wooden frame. To the far end of the frame are attached one or more light-wood tongues which reach into the gaps between the cogs. The hub of the cogwheel is lengthened into a handle by which the ratchet is swung rapidly in the air to rotate the frame with the tongues around the cogwheel. The tongues, thus, scrape under tension across the cogs, snapping against them as they go past, and producing a dense, loud, rattling noise.

In the *cranked* ratchet, adopted for orchestral use in the 1930's, the operation is reversed: the frame is stationary while the cogwheel is turned. Here the hub of the cogwheel terminates in a hand crank by which it is rotated, while the frame with the scraping tongues is either held by the player or fastened down with a screw clamp, as desired. This mechanism allows the production of rhythmically precise, snare-like rolls of any duration. Dynamics can be changed by varying the turning speed or by changing the pressure of the scraping tongues with the fingers of the hand holding the instrument.

The cranked ratchet, thus, is similar to the church ratchet mentioned above.

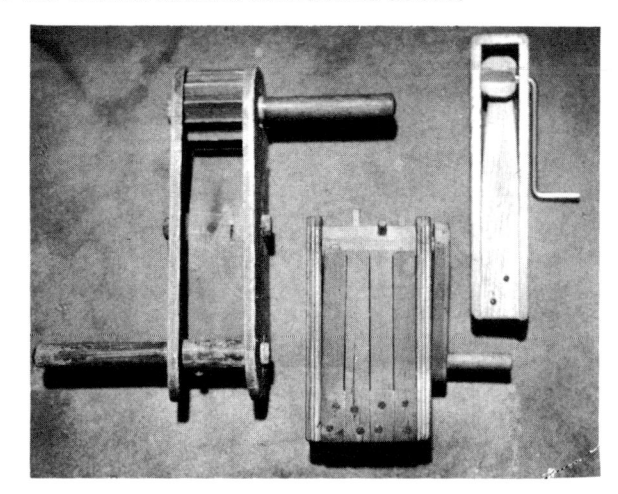

Ratchets

Examples -- Janáček: *Out of a Death-House;* R. Strauss: *Don Quichote, Der Rosenkavalier;* Schönberg: *Gurrelieder;* Ravel: *L'heure espagnole, Air de feu, L'enfant et les sortilèges;* Mussorgsky-Ravel: *Pictures at an Exhibition;* de Falla: *El Retablo de Maese Pedro;* Respighi: *The Pines of Rome;* Honegger: *Jeanne d'Arc au Bucher;* Milhaud: *La mort d'un tyran;* Orff: *The Moon, Die Kluge, Carmina burana, Die Bernauerin, A Midsummer Night's Dream;* Egk: *Die chinesische Nachtigall;* Jolivet: Concerto for Piano and Orchestra; Killmayer: *La tragedia di Orfeo;* Morton Gould: *Declaration Suite* (Mus. Ex. 103).

Guíro (Gourd Scraper)

Among the instruments which were introduced with the music of Latin America is a scraped instrument called guíro, made from a hollow gourd. It is approximately 60 cm (24") long and 40 cm (16") in circumference at its widest point. Its elongated, pot-bellied body, with ca. 12 cm (4 3/4") wide scrape-notches cut into its upper surface, forms a natural and effective resonator (see Ill. on p. 154). The player holds the instrument by inserting his thumb and middle finger into two holes drilled into its bottom. A small stick -- preferably a Chinese chopstick -- is used as a scraper. Several nuances of sound may be obtained: scraping with the tip of the stick produces light timbres; the more the stick is used towards its middle the deeper and more sonorous are the sounds; the deepest sounds are obtained by using the scraper's square-edged handle.

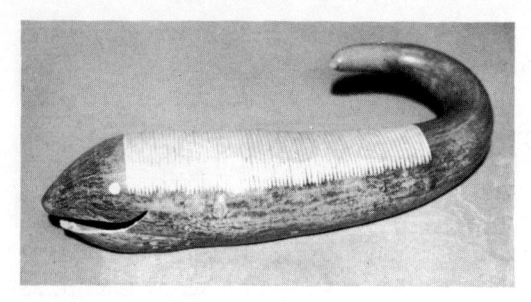

Guíro (Gourd Scraper)

Since the guíro is used mostly in the samba it is often called "samba cuke." The player, by using an upward motion of the arm that holds the guíro, produces a counter pressure on the scraper. The scraping thus becomes faster and more intense and the sound louder. The resulting accents are applied to specific beats in the measure. The back and forth movements of scraping are executed legato without lifting the scraper from the instrument. Differentiations in sound, in addition to those already mentioned, are possible by using strokes of greater or lesser length and of varying pressure.

Examples of Latin-American rhythms:

⊓ = Downstroke (outward)
V = Upstroke (inward)

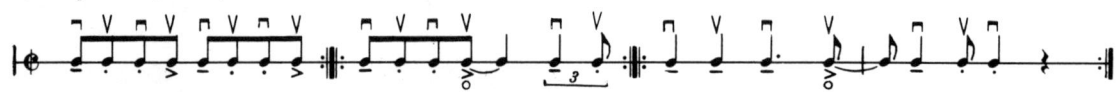

o = Counter pressure by the arm holding the instrument

Examples in concert works with Latin-American traits -- Villa-Lobos: *Uirapurú;* Morton Gould: *Latin-American Symphonette;* Sanjuan: *Liturgía negra;* Milhaud: *Saudades do Brasil.*

The guíro has also been used for its purely instrumental sound without folkloristic implications. In such cases it usually is scraped in the simplest manner. The earliest example is found in Stravinsky's *Le Sacre du printemps* (Mus. Ex. 99). Additional examples are – Varèse: *Ionisation;* Copland: *Billy the Kid* (ballet); Sanjuan: *Liturgía negra* (Mus. Ex. 87); Carter: Double Concerto; Birger-Blomdahl: *Play for Eight;* Aldo Clementi: *Informel No. 1;* Donatoni: *For Grilly, Puppenspiel;* Kotoński: *Musique en relief* (Mus. Ex. 77); F. Manino: *Mario e il Mago;* Y. Matsudaira: *Figures sonores;* Kelemen: *Equilibres;* Berio: *Circles;* Chávez: *Sinfonía India;* Orff: *Weihnachtsspiel* (Mus. Ex. 110), *Oedipus, Prometheus* (Mus. Ex. 93).

Sapo Cubana or Bambú Brasileño (Bamboo Scraper)

A smaller and more manageable scraped instrument, the sapo cubana or bambú brasileño, can be made from a hollow bamboo section about 6 cm (2 3/8") in diameter and 35 cm (14") in length. While one end of the section is closed by a botanical node, the other provides an opening to the resonating chamber. A frequent variation of the resonator opening is a lengthwise slot cut along a band of furrows carved into the bamboo section. The band is scraped with a thin metal rod or with a piece of split Tonkin bamboo (see Ill. on p. 155).

Sapo Cubana or Bambú Brasileño

Compared to the guíro, the sapo cubana sounds scratchier and less sonorous. It is useful, however, as an easy-to-handle rhythm instrument for smaller dance bands and combos. Unfortunately the bamboo tube tends to split easily with temperature changes, which impairs its durability in northern latitudes.

Reco-Reco (Wooden Scraper)

The fragility of bamboo led to the production of a scraper made of wood, the reco-reco, which has a resonator similar in convexity to that of the guíro. The body, approximately 40 cm (16″) long, provides the scraping surface by having a band of notches attached or cut into it. Scrapers may be small sticks, knitting needles, or a split piece of bamboo leaf. Deep notching produces a strongly resonant but none too variable scraping sound useful for rhythmic passages with strong, short, quickly changing accents.
Example -- Villa-Lobos: *Choros No. 8* (Mus. Ex. 100).

Reco-Reco (Wooden Scraper)

In the Confucian temples of China an instrument with this type of sound is used for ceremonial purposes: the *reposing tiger,* made of painted wood and having a notched back which is scraped with a bamboo switch having twelve splits in one end.

Other forms, for instance a serrated wooden box or a notched stick (the so-called stick scraper), are found in African cultures and among American Indians. The notched stick is easily produced. (At times it is used to replace the *râpe à fromage* (cheese grater) in Ravel's *L'enfant et les sortilèges.*)

Washboard; Metal Rasp (Metal Scraper)

The washboard of North-American Negro music is an actual household washboard scraped rhythmically across its surface of furrowed tin with a stick or with finger nails or finger tips covered with thimbles.

A metal rasp, likewise borrowed from non-musical sources, is used in Satie's ballet music *Parade* to simulate the rattling *roue de la loterie* (lottery wheel).

In his opera *Out of a Death-House,* Janáček scores, in addition to the noises of the prisoners' work tools, a rhythmically notated saw. A bamboo or stick scraper may be used in this case.

RATTLING INSTRUMENTS

The group of instruments producing rattling sounds when beaten or shaken is divided into four categories:

I. Beaten rattles whose rattling bodies sound by being struck on their frames, holders, or resonators:
   Sistrum
   Spurs
   Pandereta brasileño
   Wasamba
   Jawbone *(Quijada)*
   Cabaza (Gourd rattle)
   Angklung
   Rattle drum

II. Container rattles which consist of a container with small rattling bodies inside:
   Sleigh bells
   Maracas
   Metal rattles
   Shakers
   Sandbox or sand rattle
   Marbles

III. Row rattles whose rattling bodies are mounted in certain arrangements and rattled against one another:
   Hanging rattles
   Chains
   Hanging bamboo chimes
   Hanging glass chimes

IV. Foil rattle:
   Metal foil

Primitive rattles are among the oldest instruments of mankind. Curt Sachs in *Die Musikinstrumente Indiens und Indonesiens* has observed: "Due to its nature, only crude rhythms are served satisfactorily by a rattle. Any finer rhythms demand an instrument that functions precisely and reliably through direct control from the brain of the performer to the vibrating instrumental body."

Today's percussionist faces the problem of having to elicit from all sorts of different rattle instruments precisely notated beats and series of beats, which have to be performed in an exact manner, i.e., in the "finer rhythm" as Sachs calls it. This demands absolute precision in starting and stopping the rattle sounds, which can only be achieved through skillful manipulation, adapted to whichever rattle is used at any given moment.

BEATEN RATTLES

In the ancient Egyptian temples of Isis the unique rattle of the sistrum was used to capture the attention of the worshippers, as well as to drive away evil spirits.

A frame of iron or precious metal in the shape of a horseshoe or in an eliptical shape and provided with a handle, had closely attached to it two to four small metal rods going across from side to side through holes in the frame. The ends of the rods were bent so that when shaken they beat with a metallic rattling against the outer walls of the frame.

During Antiquity, as the instrument spread throughout the Mediterranean countries, a variation was developed: rings or perforated metal disks were strung on its small crossrods thus increasing the rattle effect and making it sound somewhat like clattering coins.

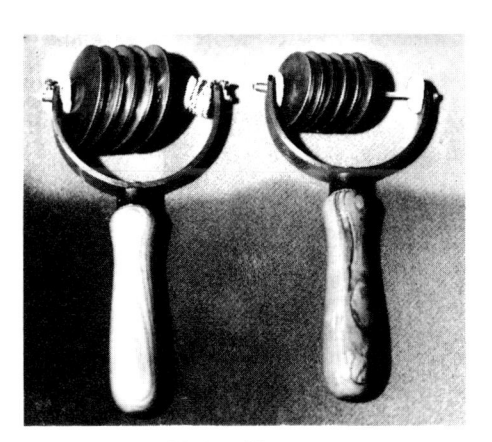

Modern Sistrum

Spurs

Sistrum; Spurs

The orchestral sistrum consists of a metal hoop on a handle and one or two crossbars, each carrying four to six disks made of bronze alloy. The disks may have a diameter of about 4 to 5.5 cm (1 5/8" to 2 3/16") and a thickness of 3 mm (1/8"). As they are shaken the disks crash not only against each other but also back and forth from one inner wall of the frame to the other. If small pieces of felt are strung between them, the jingling disks can vibrate longer and reverberate like small bells. Without these felt pieces the disks are muted by their own mass and produce a more rattling noise (see Ill. above).

Differences of sound are obtained with larger or smaller and thicker or thinner bronze disks. The smaller the diameter and the thicker the metal, the higher the pitch. For shaken rolls the sistrum must be held vertically so that the disks jingle evenly. Single beats are performed by holding the instrument horizontally and moving the forearm in short up-and-down motions. This throws the disks slightly upward and, when they come down again, produces a precise impact noise with which a given beat in a measure may be accented.

The Italian name *sistro (sistre)* which appears occasionally in older orchestral parts -- as a rule notated in G-clef -- denotes a set of small bells (cymbala) which stems from the medieval forerunners of the keyboard glockenspiel (see p. 55f).

When Rossini indicated *sistro* in the score of *The Barber of Seville*, it is assumed that he had in mind such bells made of bronze. He notated them without clef, but their pitch must of course fit the prevailing harmony.

Today, crotales or glockenspiels are used as good substitutes.

Medieval tracts mention a *sistrum* that seems to have been a triangle with jingle rings.

Carl Orff rediscovered the sistrum for his *Oedipus*, where it appears both alone and in groups (Mus. Ex. 47). Other examples: A. Clementi: *Informel No. 1;* Y. Matsudaira: *Figures sonores;* Kagel: *Match for Three Players;* Cage and Harrison: *Double Music* (2 sistrums -- Mus. Ex. 91).

Similar to the sistrum are the spurs which were part of the equipment of the percussionist in early salon and operetta music. With them the performer produced the sounds of the spurs of a horseback rider.

Six to eight slightly arched coin-sized disks, made of sheet steel 1 mm (1/25") in thickness, are strung loosely on a metal rod with a wooden handle. When the rod, held vertically, is moved up and down in even rhythm the disks clang together with a bright sound resembling the noise of walking in spurred boots (see Ill. on p. 157).

Another instrument producing the sound of spurs consists of a wooden handle with curved holders attached to both its ends. A wire with five to six jingling disks is strung across the ends of each holder, as in a sistrum.

Examples -- J. Strauss: *Die Fledermaus* and *The Gypsy Baron*.

Pandereta Brasileño

An instrument whose sound resembles that of the sistrum is the pandereta brasileño, which may occasionally replace the tambourine in Latin-American music. Its frame, in the shape of a longish rectangle with a handle at one end, is made of small bamboo sticks. Two cross wires between the longer sides of the frame each hold two pairs of disks of hammered sheet brass, which serve as rattles similar to tambourine jingles.

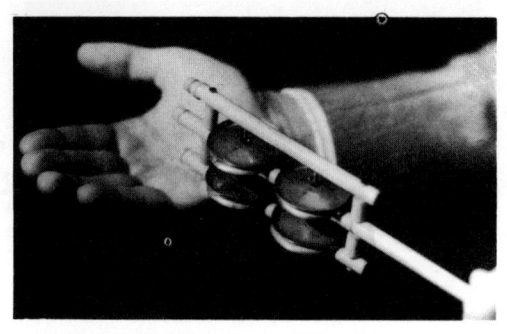

Pandereta Brasileño

The stereotyped rhythm of the pandereta brasileño, like that of the maracas, is used occasionally in the samba and the conga, as well as in Calypso music. Its jingling is similar to that of the tambourine, though darker in timbre. However, since it lacks the powerfully resonant skin of the latter, its volume is much weaker and its reservoir of playing modes quite small. The pandereta brasileño is generally limited to simple beat patterns. Because it is played like the maracas it, too, can produce accents by being beaten against the palm of the hand.

Wasamba Rattle

Wasamba Rattle

The wasamba rattle, an African gourd sistrum, consists of an angular section of a tree branch of which one part serves as the handle, while on the other part 10 to 15 disks cut from fruit husks are strung loosely. Wasambas are used in pairs or in choirs. By shaking the wasamba rattle back and forth, the disks bang together giving off a light clatter (see Ill. on p. 158).

Carl Orff used the instrument in the orchestra of *Prometheus* (Mus. Ex. 93).

Jawbone (Quijada); Vibra Slap

Among the numerous Latin-American instruments which arose largely from improvisation and which owe their origin almost exclusively to the influence of African folk music is a beaten rattle called jawbone or *quijada*.

It is nothing more than the colorfully painted lower jawbone of an ass or a zebra, with all the teeth loose in their sockets.

Jawbone (Quijada)

A light blow with the fist on the outer wall of the forked bone makes it vibrate, which in turn causes the teeth to produce a short rattle. This peculiar and somewhat low, almost buzzing sound is used now and then for economically spaced-out simple series of added accents in rumba or conga rhythms, thus introducing a new color into the tapestry of percussion accompaniments.

Cage uses the jawbone in his *Third Construction*.

American instrument makers have developed a substitute for the jawbone, called vibra slap, which consists of a thin, bent steel tube. Fastened to it at one end is a small wooden box containing short, loosely attached metal rods, while a wooden ball is attached to the other end. The player thrusts the ball into the palm of his hand or against his fist, thus causing the steel tube to vibrate. The vibrations, in turn, cause the short metal rods in the box to be thrown against its inner walls. The rattling noise that results is practically identical with that of the original jawbone. The advantage of this new instrument is its almost unlimited durability as compared to the jawbone which usually turns brittle after a short period of time.

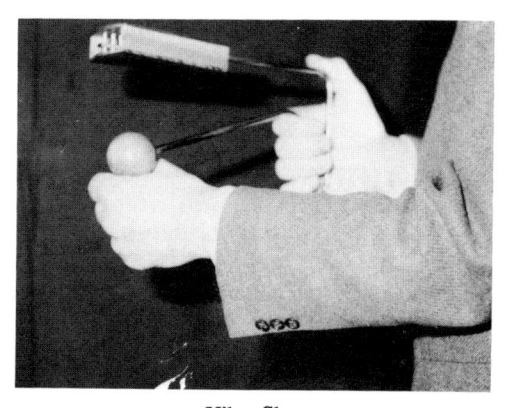

Vibra Slap

Cabaza

The African rattle called cabaza consists of a gourd with a wide-meshed net of strands of very hard, pearl-sized seeds wound loosely around it.

Native Cabaza

Modern Cabaza

Its round or sometimes pear-shaped body, with a circumference of as much as 80 cm (32"), is held by an attached wooden handle (see Ill. of native cabaza above).

The technique of playing the cabaza in Brazilian samba music is based on a succession of four basic motions, all within one measure:
1. Beat with the open hand against the body of the instrument and the strands of seeds;
2. The hand, with outstretched fingers, briefly strokes the loosely attached strands, causing the seeds to rub against the body of the gourd;
3. The body of the gourd is turned clockwise while the hand, after sharply beating the gourd, continues to rest on the seeds, again producing friction between the seeds and the gourd;
4. A counter-clockwise turn returns the body of the gourd to the beginning position; the hand continues to rest on the seeds.

Changes in the style and fashion of playing dance music also affect the execution of the cabaza rhythm.

The cabaza roll, produced by rapidly rubbing the seeds against the gourd, is executed by a quick, short, turning motion, back and forth, of the hand that holds the instrument in vertical position.

As in the case of the jawbone, the cabaza's gourd body was replaced by instrument makers with a modern equivalent. Around a cylinder of serrated light metal are slung, close together, 10 to 13 loops of ball chains. By turning the cylinder abruptly with the help of a handle, the chains rub against it in cabaza fashion. The sound produced by this type of instrument is a good deal higher and brighter than that of the original cabaza, and has a more sharply penetrating effect.

The cabaza is rarely used in serious music. Orff employed it advantageously as a rattle in *Die Bernauerin* and *Trionfi*, where it adds a round, full-sounding timbral element, especially if several cabazas are used.

Angklung

The angklung, made of bamboo, is found exclusively in Java and Bali.

Into a lattice frame are hung two or three bamboo tubes of different lengths, tuned in octaves, whose prongs, cut out of their lower ends, reach into slots in the bottom cross-tube of the frame. When the instrument is shaken the suspended tubes act like pendula, their prongs banging against the walls of the slots (see Ill. on p. 161).

Natives shake large numbers of angklungs for their traditional dances. However, sets of these rattles, shaken in melodic succession by individual players, have also been developed. They are comparable to the sets of cowbells used in alpine pageants, or to the English hand bells.

Although the angklung sounds mostly like rattling bamboo, its pitch is clearly discernible. The possible pitch range lies within the two and three-line octaves, but very large specimens sound lower.

Examples -- Orff: *Catulli carmina, Weihnachtsspiel* (Mus. Ex. 110 -- both examples use several angklungs without indication of specific pitches), *Prometheus* (two angklungs tuned to g♭ and b♭).

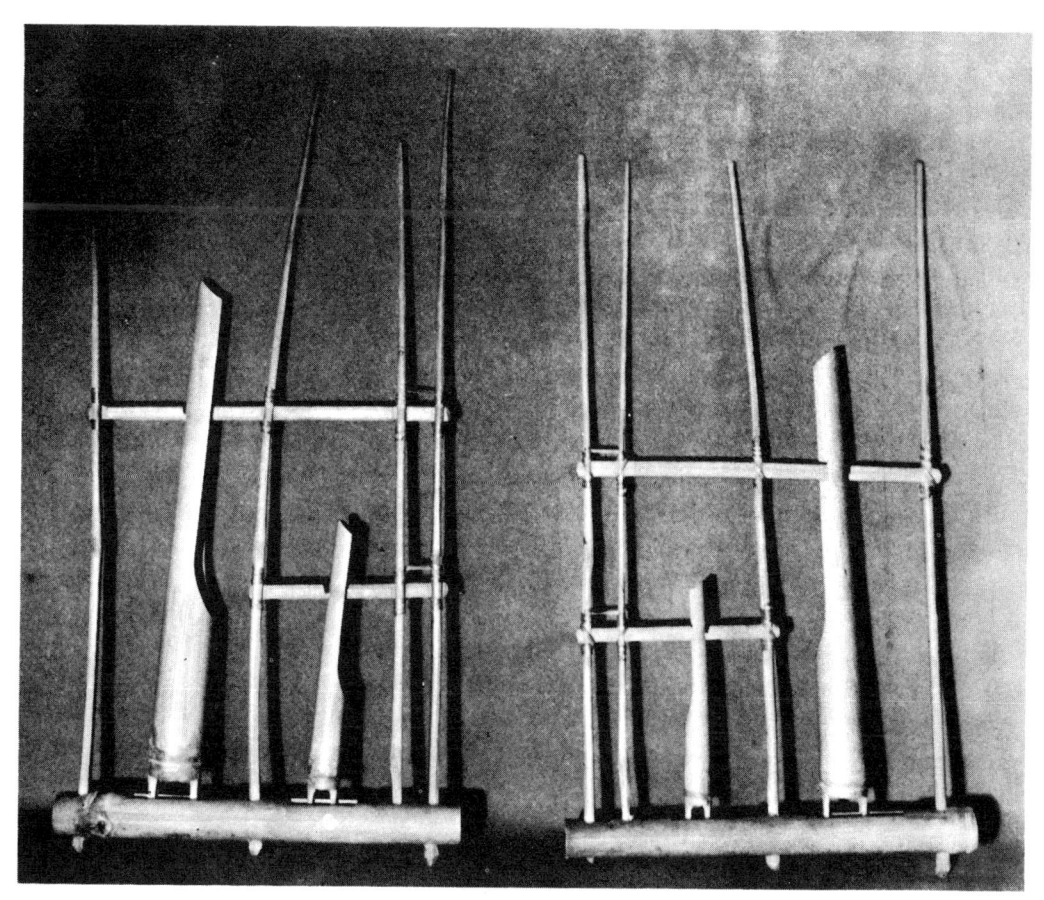

Angklung

Rattle Drum; Chinese Paper Drum

The rattle drum is a two-headed frame drum to which are attached small wooden or metal balls hanging from strings. When the drum is turned quickly on its axis, the balls are flung against the drumheads and produce a rattling sound.

A rattle drum in the shape of an hourglass and presumably coming from Tibet was originally made of two human skulls. The modern version with string-tensioned drumheads permits changes of tuning while being played, by varying the pressure on the tensioning strings with the hand that holds the instrument (see Ill. on p. 162).

The Chinese version of this type of rattle drum, also called Chinese paper drum, has a handle. Its diameter measures ca. 6 to 11 cm (2 3/8" to 4 3/8" -- see Ill. on p. 162).

Examples -- Kagel: *Match for Three Performers* (indicated in the score as Chinese paper drum -- Mus. Ex. 101).

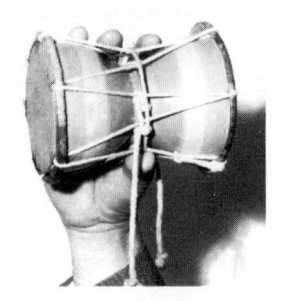

Tibetan Rattle Drum

Chinese Rattle Drum
(Chinese Paper Drum)

CONTAINER RATTLES

Round Bells

Small round bells, such as sleigh bells, apparently originated in Asia and have been known to metal-working peoples since ancient times. Hollow, spherical, elongated, or flattened bodies with narrow, slit-like openings enclose small, freely rolling metal balls. The bodies are made of bronze alloy or tin; their various sizes may range from those of cherry pits to a man's fist.

Round bells are derivations of the ordinary small bell and may be considered as belonging to the container rattles. They are encountered in many contexts, such as bells mounted on the rims of the circular rattles used in the cultic ceremonies of Asiatic peoples and in Antiquity. In the Middle Ages such bells were occasionally found attached to hand drums with one or two heads. In the 14th century round bells became fashionable affectations as accessories for elegant clothing, and somewhat later they became part of carnival and jesters' costumes.

On the Turkish crescent of military bands the round bell was barely audible, compared to the other small bells; it served mainly as decoration. On the other hand, the tinkling of the round bells on teams of horses became so well established that the bells' musical use automatically conveyed the impression of a sleigh ride.

Bunched Sleigh Bells

Round Bells (Sleigh Bells)

Sleigh Bells

Sleigh bells are fastened to a circular leather strap, a plate, or a rod equipped with a handle. A rattling roll is produced by shaking the bells; simple rhythms by beating them. Best suited are bells made of cast alloy, generally with a diameter of 20 to 30 mm (3/4" to 1 3/8"). With such measurements their pitches fall within the four-line octave. Grouped in a random variety of pitches they fit into any tonality as a mixed sound.

On the other hand, Mozart's *Schlittenfahrt* from his *German Dances* requires five small groups of tuned bells to make possible the playing of the notated pitches c, e, f, g, and a (Mus. Ex. 102).

Even though in the Romantic orchestra sleigh bells were used simply as another color in the steadily expanding palette of sound, they never completely lost their traditional connotations.

Examples -- Charpentier: *Louise;* Mahler: 4th Symphony; Pfitzner: *Palestrina;* R. Strauss: *Intermezzo, Der Rosenkavalier, Arabella;* Orff: *Die Kluge, Carmina burana.*

Sleigh bells appear as a purely abstract sound in Varèse's *Ionisation.* Kagel wrote for two large sleigh bells with a diameter of about 5 cm (2") as well as for a *Schellenbündel* (bunched sleigh bells) in *Match for Three Players.*

The sleigh bells' peculiar mixture of tinkling metallic sounds and hollow rattles lacks the bright overtones of freely vibrating small bells, because the metal balls that rattle inside the sleigh bells also act as dampers.

Bunched sleigh bells are used by Ysang Yun in *Sim Tjong.* Six such bunches are called for, each consisting of numerous round bells with diameters from 1 to 1½ cm (3/8" to 5/8"), attached like bunches of grapes to the ends of wires which are gathered in a handle (see Ill. on p. 162).

In this instrument the tinkling sound effect of the original sleigh bells has given way to a dense hissing because of the thin-walled bell metal.

By using different sizes of bells it is possible to achieve minor differentiations in pitch from bunch to bunch.

Ghungrü (Indian Bell Strap)

The Indian bell strap, *ghungrü,* has slightly more volume because the bells are made of a higher grade metal (hardened sheet brass). They are only 1 cm (5/8") in diameter and have crosswise slits. Each leather strap has from 16 to 32 bells attached to it, depending on its width.

Ghungrü

Indian ritual dancers wear *ghungrü* straps around their ankles. The current trend toward Indian instruments in popular music has brought about a fairly wide distribution of this type of bunched bells.

Gerald Hummel uses them in his ballet music *Die Folterungen der Beatrice Cenci* (The Tortures of Beatrice Cenci).

Maracas

Among the numerous types of related container forms, the maracas are the most widely used. Maracas are obligatory in the percussion accompaniment of many Latin-American dances and became very popular together with the rumba.

The maraca consists of a round or somewhat oval hollow gourd with stem, filled with a small number of fruit pits, pebbles, or buckshot. Modern manufactured maracas come in pairs and are of wood or plastic. They have a diameter of about 5 to 15 cm (2" to 6").

The differences in size and in the type of filling determine the nuances of sound which can range from a light hiss to a coarse rattle. Maracas with fine-grained filling are preferred for small instrumental ensembles, while larger instruments with coarser and heavier filling are more appropriate for orchestral use.

In Latin-American music and its derivatives, maracas are normally used only for the precise beating of simple rhythms, while modern composers also use them, often in groups, to obtain the sound of shaken rattles.

Maracas

Playing the maracas consists of a stereotyped shaking motion so that the enclosed particles are flung, in a bunch, against the inner walls of the rattle. A very soft sound can be obtained by holding the maracas horizontally and, using a very light movement of the arm, throwing the filling up noiselessly, thus producing a short, marked rattle precisely on the notated beat when the filling falls down again. This method of playing is performed with two instruments alternately and requires that the moment of impact be calculated sensitively and timed correctly. Rolls are produced with circular motion causing rapid rotation of the filling.

Examples -- Sanjuan: *Liturgía negra* (Mus. Ex. 87); Orff: *Weihnachtsspiel, Catulli Carmina* (Mus. Ex. 25), *Antigonae;* Egk: *Joan von Zarissa;* Prokofiev: *Romeo and Juliet;* Messiaen: *Turangalîla-Symphonie;* Boulez: *Le marteau sans maître;* Varèse: *Ionisation* (high and low maracas -- Mus. Ex. 109); Henze: *Ode an den Westwind;* Kotoński: *Musique en relief* (Mus. Ex. 31).

Mexican Bean

Berio, in *Circles,* uses a rattle called Mexican Bean. This instrument consists of a dried bean pod ca. 30 cm (12") long and filled with seeds which produce a rattling noise.

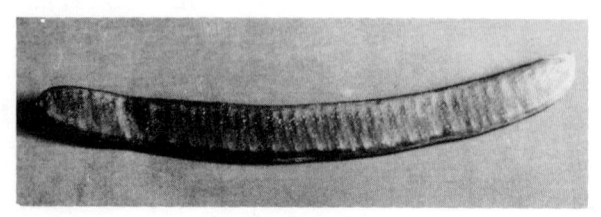

Mexican Bean

Metal Rattles

The metal rattles used by Indians living on the islands of Central America consist of canister-shaped tin containers with handles and filled with pebbles. The sound is loud and metallic. Modern replicas may be fashioned by filling tin cans or tin spheres with pebbles or metal pieces.

Examples — Villa-Lobos: *Emperor Jones;* Chávez: *Sinfonia India;* Gould: *Declaration Suite* (Mus. Ex. 103); Carter: *Pocahontas* (Mus. Ex. 65); Orff: *Die Bernauerin* (Mus. Ex. 54).

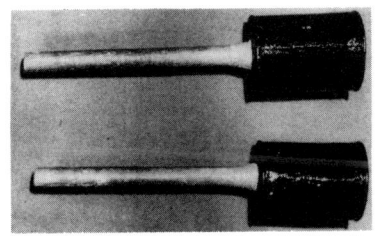

Metal Rattles

Chocallos (Tubular Rattles)

Chocallos (Tubular Rattles); Ganza

The tubular rattle, also called *chocallo (chocalho)*, like the maraca, was originally an instrument of primitive tribes. It is a container rattle consisting of a hollow, closed section of bamboo approximately 40 cm (16″) long and about 5 cm (2″) in diameter. Inside is a fine-grained filling which produces a light hissing sound when the rattle is shaken. In addition to bamboo, tubular rattles may also be made of tubes of wood or tin whose open ends are covered with skins or similar materials. Of these rattles, the metal ones produce an especially penetrating, sharp, high clatter (see Ill. above).

The chocallo is typical of the samba in which it is used to play a stereotype eight-note pattern that runs through the entire piece:

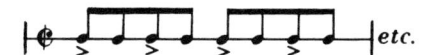

For such a passage the ends of the tube (which is shaken intensely) either are held between the palms of both hands, or the tube is held in its middle by one hand. Other simple rhythms are executed with the technique already described for the maracas.

Examples -- Liebermann: Concerto for Jazzband and Symphony Orchestra (ca. 6 tubular rattles in the orchestra -- Mus. Ex. 104); Villa-Lobos: *Momo Precoce* (*"chucalhos"* of both wood and metal).

In *Bachianas Brasileiras No. 2*, Villa-Lobos used a tubular metal rattle called *ganza*, which in this instance provides an excellent imitation of a locomotive letting off excess steam after coming to a halt. The *ganza* is ca. 7 cm (2 3/4″) in diameter, ca. 30 cm (12″) long, and filled with small pebbles.

Sandbox; Sand Rattle

The sandbox *(arenaiuolo)*, scored by Richard Strauss in the ballet *Schlagobers* and by Hindemith in Chamber Music No. 1, as well as the sand rattle in Orff's opera *Die Kluge*, are tin rattles with fine-grained fillings. An ordinary metal rattle or tubular metal rattle may be used.

Marbles

A type of rattle which appears from time to time in amateur productions and vaudeville, especially in English-speaking countries, is one containing glass or china balls. The "marbles" are made to rotate in bottles or bowls whose own sounds determine the respective pitches of the rattle noise. The jingling coins of variety-show performers and clowns produce a similar effect: here coins are twirled on their edges in bowls.

ROW RATTLES

Row rattles consist of suspended strands of small hard objects, such as wooden balls, fruit husks (see Ill.), cocoons, snail shells, sea shells, animal horns, claws, or teeth.

Fruit-Husk Rattle

Chains

In his *Sinfonía India*, Carlos Chávez includes numerous Indian percussion instruments, among them row rattles of deer hooves, wooden balls, and strung butterfly cocoons. The last named produce a uniquely soft and subdued-sounding rattle noise.

Chains; Chain Rattles

Iron chains offer a row rattle which, with its unmistakable sound, conveys to the listener very graphic images. For example, their use as a background sound in Weber's *Der Freischütz*, when the wild huntsmen pass through the Wolf's-Glen, is well known. Similarly, Milhaud calls for rattling chains in *Les choephores* (1919); Schönberg uses them -- probably for the first time for their sound-quality as such -- in the *Gurrelieder* (1911).

Further examples -- Janáček: *Out of a Death-House;* Jolivet: *Cinq danses rituelles;* Varèse: *Intégrales.*

Another chain rattle, produced along the lines of a prototype said to have originated in Persia, has two strings of chains, each 80 cm (32") in length, whose individual links are about 5 cm (2") long and 6 mm (1/4") thick (see Ill.). The chains are tied by their centers to a handle so that the four ends hang freely, forming a chain whip which may be beaten against either a strong steel plate or a sort of rug formed of heavy chains lying closely together on a blanket-covered support. Such an arrangement not only produces the desired noise of rattling chains but also eliminates the disturbing extraneous noises that result from beating against the wooden floor. Rhythms like those written by Janáček in the opera *Out of a Death-House* may be performed successfully with a pair of such chain whips whose ends should touch a metal base briefly and in alternation. Rolls are produced by shaking the chains while they touch the metal plate or chain rug.

Japanese Wood Chimes; Bamboo Chimes

Small bunches of bamboo or glass rods suspended on strings or rods are used occasionally as door chimes. According to an old superstition they are supposed to ward off evil spirits, in the same manner as the hanging door bells one sometimes finds.

The Japanese wood chimes, an instrument of suspended bamboo sticks clapping together, serve the same function. Six to eight bamboo sticks, each ca. 15 cm (6") long and about 2 cm (3/4") in diameter, hang with their openings down from strings about 15 cm (6") long. They are spaced short distances apart along a crossbar about 30 cm (12") long (see Ill.). By slapping the sticks that hang at either end of the row more or less forcefully, a clatter results from all the sticks banging together which lasts as long as they continue to swing.

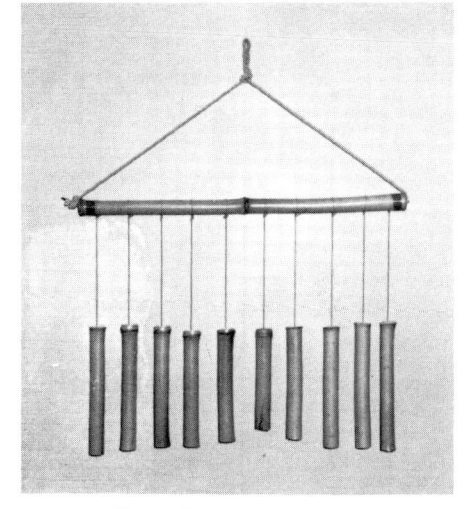

Suspended Bamboo Chimes

Examples -- Kelemen: *Equilibres, Radiant, Der neue Mieter.*

Grasping the bamboo sticks energetically with both hands makes the bunch bang together vigorously with a strong, brightly accented beat. When the grip is loosened, a prolonged clatter follows as their pendulum motion gradually dies down.

Examples -- Stockhausen: *Kontakte;* Berio: *Circles;* Foss: *Echoi* (Mus. Ex. 106).

By suspending two or three metal hoops, one inside the other, and using them as holders, it is possible to assemble a larger number of bamboo sections (see Ill. on p. 168). Differences in the lengths of the sticks produce a distinct mixture of sound: longer sticks give lower pitches, shorter ones give correspondingly higher pitches. Thus it is possible to produce bunches of bamboo sections on approximately four clearly distinguishable pitch levels.

Glass Chimes; Shell Chimes

Instruments consisting of suspended glass rods (glass chimes) instead of bamboo sections function according to the same laws of length versus pitch, as do sticks of wood. Naturally, their fragile material demands gentle handling. The sound of glass chimes is weaker but is distinguished by a remarkably delicate glassy rustling.

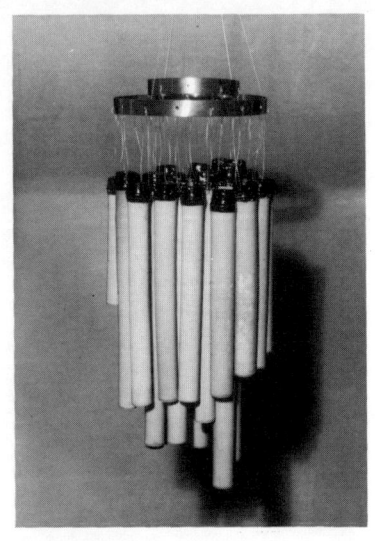

Suspended Bunched Bamboo Chimes

Suspended Glass Chimes

Examples -- Berio: *Circles, Passaggio;* Pousseur: *Euer Faust.*

Small, suspended glass disks instead of rods produce a more tinkling sound reminiscent of clinking wine glasses. Variations may be obtained by varying the sizes and shapes of the disks.

Example -- Foss: *Echoi* (Mus. Ex. 106).

Suspended pieces of flat, pressed sea shells, produced in Hongkong and called shell chimes, give a noisier clatter (see Ill.).

Example -- Henze: *Das Floss der Medusa.*

Shell Chimes

Foil Rattle

FOIL RATTLES

A sheet of very thin and light metal, when shaken by an attached handle or two, produces a rattling sound similar to, but much stronger than, the common kitchen aluminum foil (see Ill. above). The larger the sheet, the lower and stronger the crackling. Noisiest of all is the thunder sheet, well-known as a backstage property (see thunder sheet, p. 173).

Examples -- Cerha: *Spiegel V;* Haubenstock-Ramati: *Vermutungen über ein dunkles Haus;* Cage: *First Construction in Metal* (5 graduated thunder sheets -- Mus. Ex. 85).

BUMBASS

The bumbass, also called devil's violin, is probably the oldest and most primitive form of a one-man percussion band.

Construction. A pole about 2 m (6'8") tall has one or two small cymbals stuck loosely on top. Farther down a circle of small sleigh bells is attached to the pole to increase the jingling and rattling. A skin-covered wooden or metal hoop, or preferably a small drum, is attached to the side of the pole approximately 60 cm (24") up from its lower end, i.e., at about the height of the bridge of a double bass. A thin wire is strung from the top of the pole, crossing the drum head, and fastened to the pole below the drum. Fastened to the wire is a small beater which hits the drum.

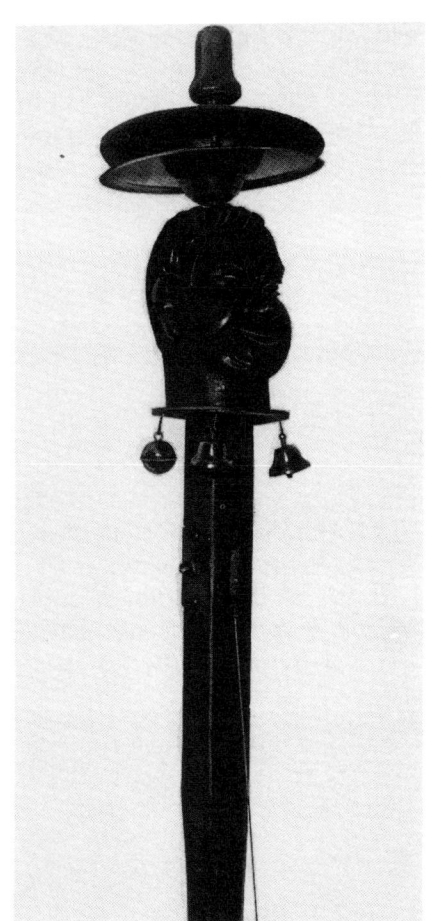

Bumbass Top

Bumbass Drum

Method of Playing. The player scrapes the string and beats the drumhead with a serrated stick, imitating the rolls and beats of a snare drum's simple rhythm accompaniment. At the same time, the basic rhythm is beaten in a bass-drum-and-cymbal manner by stamping pole and all on the wooden floor.

Usage. The bumbass has been used for centuries by street musicians and unskilled amateurs. In times of war it frequently served the soldiers as a home-made percussion accompaniment for their small, impromptu instrumental groups.

In Kelemen's score *Composé,* which is unusually rich in percussion instruments, there is a short, rhythmic passage for the bumbass. It is notated as follows: the full-size, down-stemmed notes indicate stamping, while the smaller, up-stemmed notes indicate beats with the stick, for example:

IMITATIVE INSTRUMENTS

The use of imitative instruments is not limited to mere imitation. Often their sounds or noises are used musically, i.e., they are employed as purely abstract, instrumental effects.

The cuckoo call, which appeared as a simple, two-toned whistle flute tuned g^3 - e^3 as early as in Leopold Mozart's *Toy Symphony,* is best produced by an instrument consisting of two stopped wooden pipes sounded by bellows. Their air columns can be shortened or lengthened by moving the end-stoppers; thus it is possible to tune the pipes to specific pitches and intervals within a range of about $b\flat^1$ - c^3.

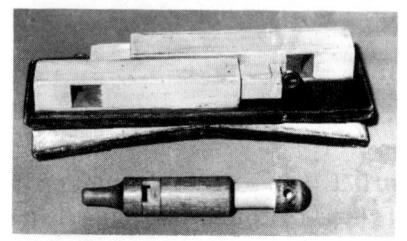

Cuckoo Calls

Examples -- J. Strauss: *Im Krapfenwaldl* Polka (f♯ - d♯); Humperdinck: *Hänsel und Gretel* (d - b♭); Reznicek: *Traumspiel-Suite* (b - g♯); Messiaen: *Réveil des oiseaux.*

The nightingale whistle, sometimes simply called bird whistle, is the instrument most commonly used for imitating bird calls. It is made of metal and resembles a small tobacco pipe. When its bowl is partially filled with water a bird-like twittering can be produced through sensitive blowing and tonguing.

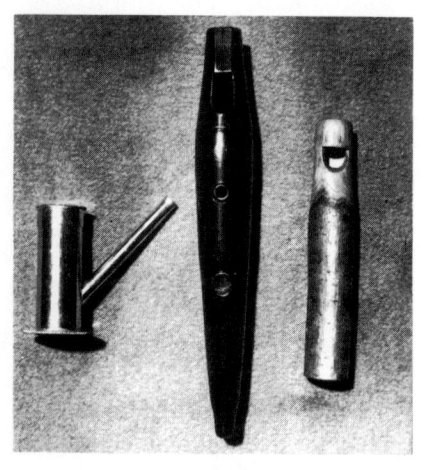

Bird Whistles

Examples -- L. Mozart: *Toy Symphony* (Mus. Ex. 107); J. Strauss: *Dorfschwalben aus Österreich;* Puccini: *Madama Butterfly.*

For Respighi's *The Pines of Rome* a recording of very delicate and economically spaced nightingale songs is available. If it is used in concert performances there must, of course, be good reproducing equipment. If no recording is available the effect can be produced by covering a bird whistle with cloth to obtain the required effect of distance.

The quail call in Leopold Mozart's *Toy Symphony* can be produced by blowing short bursts of air into a slide whistle while simultaneously pulling out the plunger.

The so-called gag instruments of the silent film era also included a number of blown instruments which were used, more or less successfully, to imitate voices of animals such as frogs, ducks, roosters, sheep, goats, cows, horses, etc. They are rarely used anymore.

Another gag instrument is the "hoofbeats" consisting of two halved, scraped-out coconut shells. They have knob handles at the crown and their rims are beaten together in the rhythm of a trot or gallop, thus imitating the noise of horses' hoofs on stone pavement.

The toy trumpet and the *Rufhorn* (a larger reed trumpet) are instruments whose tone is produced by blowing against a metal tongue, as in the harmonica.

Examples -- L. Mozart: *Toy Symphony* (trumpet in g^1); J. Strauss: *Der Vergnügungszug* Quick Polka (train-conductor's horn in e^1).

The so-called sand blocks were used to imitate the sound of steam engines in silent films. Two rectangular wooden boxes each have sandpaper glued over one entire surface. By rubbing these rough surfaces together rhythmically a short, hissing noise results similar to that of a steam locomotive in motion.

Example -- Gershwin: *Porgy and Bess.*

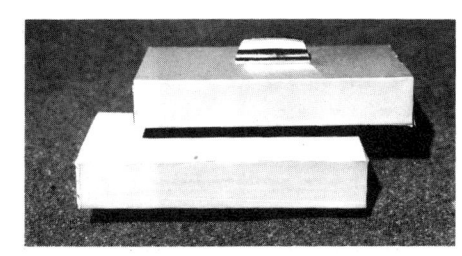

Sand Blocks

A similar effect, but with far less volume, is produced by a wire brush rubbing against a drumhead in the same rhythm.

Example -- Weill: *Lost in the Stars.*

Morton Gould uses sand blocks in his *Spirituals* and, to imitate dancing feet, in his *Minstrel Show;* Lukas Foss uses them as an abstract sound in *Echoi* (Mus. Ex. 106), as does Luciano Berio in *Circles.*

Imitating automobile horns also falls to the percussionist, especially since Gershwin scored them in *An American in Paris.* For this composition four automobile horns are needed, tuned a^1, $b\flat^1$, c^2, and d^2. The kind of horn intended is that with rubber bulb and membrane which was used on the first automobiles. The sound is short and barking and today has a comical effect (see Ills. on p. 172 and Mus. Ex. 108).

The *klaxon à manivelle,* once popular in France, is a hand-cranked automobile warning device producing a very peculiar, croaking noise.

Example -- Françaix: *Les Zigues de Mars.*

Signal whistles are short whistle flutes, 5 to 10 cm (2" to 4") long, made of metal, wood, or horn. They come singly or in twos or threes, mounted together, and blown through a single mouthpiece. They thus have one, two, or three pitches. Single whistles may have a finger hole giving them two alternating pitches (see Ill. on p. 172).

The pea whistle or police whistle has a small, light ball enclosed in the hollow space where the air vibrates.

Automobile Horns  **Signal Whistles**  **Pea Whistles**

Examples -- Ibert: *Divertissement, Suite symphonique;* Poulenc: *Le bal masque.*
Whistles of various types are used by Milhaud in *Les choephores* and in *L'homme et son désir.*

The mouth siren consists of a metal cylinder, approximately 6 to 10 cm (2 3/8" to 4") long, with a mouthpiece (see Ill. below). Blowing causes a fan disk to rotate and produce a clear, howling glissando which can reach c^4 if one blows hard enough. If the blowing is stopped suddenly, the tone ceases. If, however, the air pressure falls gradually, the sound slides gradually to its lowest pitch, somewhere between c^2 and g^1.

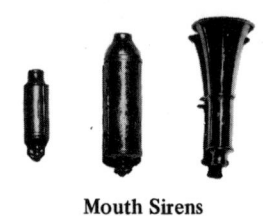

Mouth Sirens

The mouth siren was obligatory as a gag instrument in accompaniments for silent films and vaudeville, and there are even examples of its use in concert music.

Examples -- Hindemith: Chamber Music No. 1; Milhaud: *Les choephores, L'homme et son désir;* Richard Mohaupt: *Die Gaunerstreiche der Courasche;* Norbert Schultze: *Schwarzer Peter;* Gavin M. Gordon: *The Rake's Progress;* Ernst Toch: *Bunte Suite.*

The howling of ordinary sirens has also been used in music. Handdriven or electric machines are suitable, provided the rise and fall of the pitch can be controlled and the sound stopped at will.

Examples in concert music are -- Satie: *Parade (sirène aigue);* Milhaud: *Les choephores;* Varèse: *Ionisation (sirène claire, sirène grave* -- Mus. Ex. 109). Pfitzner uses a rising siren-tone onstage in his opera *Das Herz.*

A ship's whistle or fog horn, the phonetic signalling device of ocean vessels, was what Satie intended in *Parade* by the designation *sirène grave.* This instrument, which imitates the typically rough, hoarse sound of the ship's whistle, is made of three rectangular wooden pipes bunched together and blown through a common mouthpiece. (Although called *sirène*, it has no glissando. -- Trsl.)

Stage effects have long included the reproduction of sounds of thunder, wind, and rain.

Richard Strauss was probably the first to bring the wind machine into the orchestra in *Don Quichote* (1889), *Josephslegende* (1914), *Alpensinfonie* (1915), and *Die Frau ohne Schatten* (1919).

Additional examples -- Milhaud: *L'homme et son désir;* Ravel: *L'enfant et les sortilèges, Air de feu, Daphnis et Chloé;* Orff: *The Moon, Astutuli, Weihnachtsspiel* (Mus. Ex. 110), *Prometheus.*

The sound of the wind machine is generated through the friction created by a strip of coarsely woven or ribbed material rubbing against a rotating cylinder made of sharp-edged boards.

Wind Machine

The cylinder is about 80 cm (32") long and has a diameter of about 70 cm (28"). The ends of its axle rest on a rack, and it is turned by a hand crank. The cloth, laid over the cylinder, is tensed by being tied to the rack, and the turning of the cylinder produces the sound of wind blowing. The rate of speed at which the cylinder is rotated determines the volume of sound.

In the theater, bamboo sticks are also used to imitate the noise of wind. The sticks turn through the air like the arms of a windmill, usually powered by a motor, and produce a whirring noise of considerable volume, comparable to that of the ancient bull roar or thunder stick, an instrument consisting of a wooden slat hanging from a string. When whirled through the air the slat produces noises ranging from the gentle hum of a light breeze to the thundering roar of a hurricane.

Examples -- Cowell: *Ensemble* (1925) for two violins, two celli, and thunder sticks, 11th Symphony.

The thunder sheet, once used only to imitate the sound of a thunderstorm or an unleashed body of water, is now also used as a sound-source in its own right. It consists of a tin sheet 1 mm (1/24") thick and measuring about 1 x 2 m (3'4" x 6'8"). Handles are welded to one of the longer edges of the sheet, so that it may be held vertically and shaken. Its sound is that of a metallic, crackling, roaring din, depending in volume upon the intensity of the shake. Today, in large theaters, rolls of thunder are produced with a gigantic drum hanging in the fly loft. For instrumental effects in the orchestra, however, one still uses the thunder sheet (see also foil rattle, pp. 168f).

Examples -- Krenek: *Karl V;* Searle: *The Riverrun;* Niccoló Castiglioni: *Ode;* Orff: *Weihnachtsspiel* (Mus. Ex. 110).

The rain machine, a large revolving drum of wood and screen wire, containing little pea-sized balls that tumble around inside it, is an old, established theatrical property (Rossini: *The Barber of Seville* -- see Ill. on p. 174). Another easy method of imitating the sound of rain showers consists of rubbing a brush against the head of a bass drum.

Rain Machine

Cannon shots in the theater, such as those fired onstage in the first act of Verdi's *Otello,* are produced by the property man who explodes gunpowder in a special shooting device.

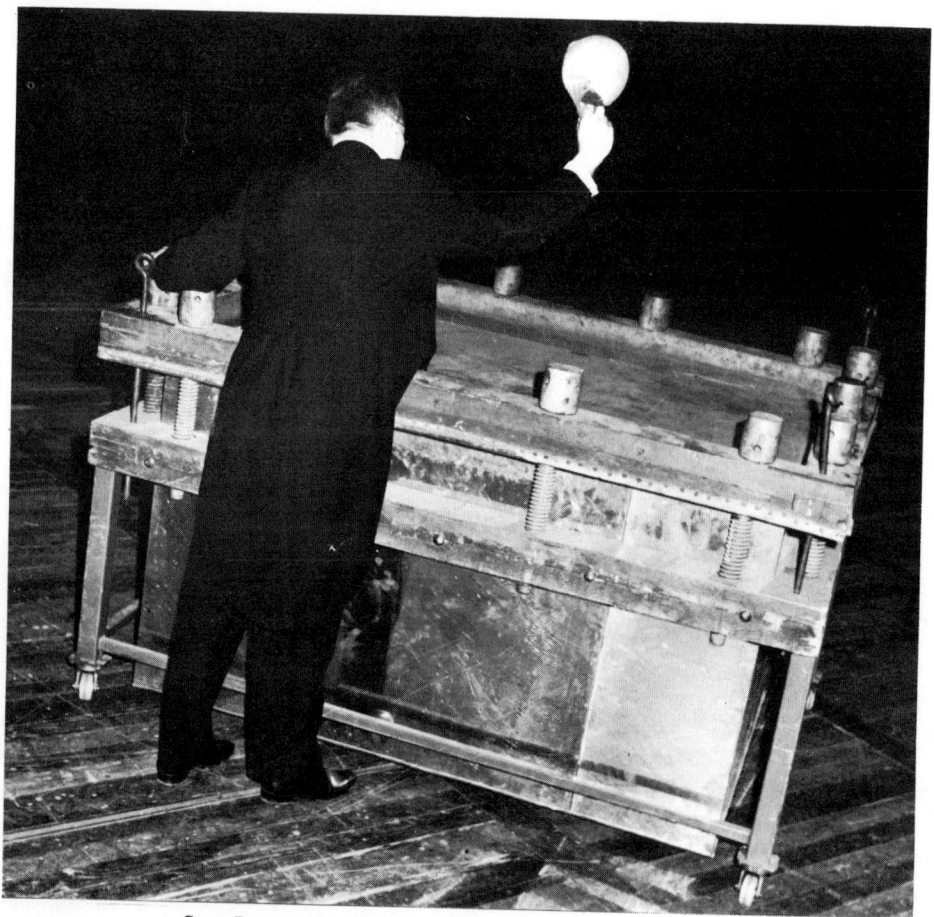

Stage Property for imitating Cannon Shots (Skin Instrument)

Cannon shots are seldom used in concert music (Beethoven: *Wellington's Victory;*

Tchaikovsky: *Overture 1812*). When they *are* called for, a bass drum, as large as possible, with one drumhead removed, may be substituted. All the following works, thus, include a bass drum marked *quasi cannone* in the percussion section of the orchestra -- Mussorgsky-Ravel: *Pictures at an Exhibition;* Puccini: *Madama Butterfly;* Rimsky-Korsakov: *The Legend of the Tsar Saltan.* In Puccini's operas *Madama Butterfly* and *Tosca* the cannon shots offstage must be performed in measured beats. For this effect an apparatus especially built for stage purposes is used: an unusually large tanned skin is stretched over a rectangular frame measuring 150 x 190 cm (60" x 76"). The whole is then mounted horizontally over a resonator box of the same proportions and of a height of about 100 cm (40"). This oversized drum is beaten with a heavy, leather-padded wooden ball held by a leather strap that is nailed to it. Thanks to the extraordinary resonance of the box and of the large backstage area, the audience receives the impression of cannon shots fired at a distance (see Ill. on p. 174).

Rifle and pistol shots fired onstage, along with their corresponding hand weapons, also are among the responsibilities of the property man.

Examples -- Weber: *Der Freischütz;* Lortzing: *Der Wildschütz;* Berg: *Lulu;* Egk: *Die Verlobung in San Domingo.*

Shots to be sounded in the orchestra require a 9 mm (.36) calibre, six-chambered revolver loaded with blank cartridges.

Examples -- J. Strauss: *Auf einer Jagd* Quick Polka; Satie: *Parade.*

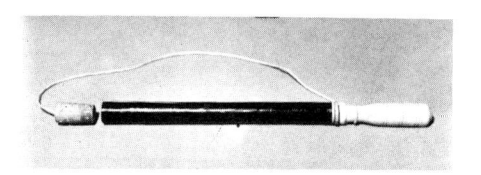

Popgun (Instrument for Popping Bottle Cork)

Another sharp noise, much softer than a pistol shot, yet quite unmistakable, is produced by a cork popping out of a champagne bottle. Ever since this special effect was accorded a solo role by Johann Strauss in his *Champagner-Polka* and by H. C. Lumbye in his *Champagner-Galopp,* it has become customary to have a small popping-apparatus available in the orchestra. A metal tube, closed at one end by a cork, contains a piston with an airtight head of leather disks, such as used in bicycle pumps. By pushing the piston towards the cork, the mounting air pressure forces the cork out of the tube with a loud pop (see Ill. above).

Occasionally, noises and sounds of tools and appliances from everyday life are also included in concert music. For example, the clatter of office machines, used by Satie in the ballet *Parade* (1917), and by George Antheil in *Ballet mécanique* (1925), must either be produced in rhythms as notated, or treated as a rhythmtically undefined background sound.

In recent North American compositions one also finds such unusual implements as iron pipes, packing crates, automobile brake drums, lids of garbage cans, and kitchenware (china and glass dishes), all used as percussion instruments. (See, for ex., Henry Cowell's 11th Symphony -- Mus. Ex. 105 -- where 4 glass or china bowls in various tunings are used.)

Ligeti, in *Aventures,* includes noises such as "plucking four rubber bands above a resonator;" "quickly thumbing through the pages of a large, thick book;" "beating a pillow with a rug beater;" "bursting a blown-up paper bag;" "rubbing a suitcase with sandpaper;" and so forth. In *Apparitions* for orchestra he indicates at one particular spot that a sack filled with small medicine bottles (glass) be smashed. Berio, in *Epifanie,* uses automobile coil springs of about finger-thick steel in three different sizes. When beaten with a small metal hammer they sound not unlike triangles, though much stronger. Penderecki, in *Fluorescences,* requires the rhythmical sawing of wood in different gradations of sound. In Ernst Toch's 3rd Symphony the hissing of a compressed air blower is used.

In 1963 Rolf Liebermann created his *Composition for Machines,* which consists of the sounds and noises of 156 modern machines and appliances in rhythmical, metrical, and dynamic differentiations. This commissioned work was played on the occasion of the exhibition *Les Echanges* in Switzerland. It is notated on perforated tape and performed "live" by a mechanical orchestra "conducted" by a computer, thus obviating the need for human performers.

The imitation of natural sounds, as well as of those of musical instruments, can be accomplished more or less successfully by electronic means. When such sounds are mixed with live music, however, listeners find them inferior by comparison: their sound quality is perceived as an artifical and alien intrusion -- "loudspeaker music."

Thus, wherever the interpretation of serious music demands a high level of quality one observes a return to the use of non-electronic sound sources.

List of Latin-American Percussion and Noise Instruments and their Possible Substitutions

NAME (Brazilian/Indian)	KIND	SUBSTITUTE INSTRUMENT(S)
Timbales	Small Kettle Drums	
Carrilhão	Glockenspiel	
Campãnuela Sineta	Small Bells	
Campainha Sino	Bell	
Marimbula Sansa (Zanza) Sandi Lun Etingili	Plucked Idiophone	
Caixa de campanha	Field Drum	Long Drum
Caixa de rufo Timbalão	Tenor Drum	Long Drum without snares Tenor Drum without snares
Tambor Caixa	Snare Drum	
Palillos	Sticks or Rods Drum Sticks	
Bombo Tambora (Spanish)	Bass Drum	
Tamburine	Frame Drum (without jingles)	
Cabaquinha	Square-Shaped Frame Drum	
Pandeiro (Portuguese)	Tambourine	
Cuíca Puita Roncador Onca Boi Zubumba	Friction Drum (String Drum)	Lion's Roar

NAME	KIND	SUBSTITUTE INSTRUMENT(S)
Tartaruga	Friction Instrument (Tortoise shell treated with oil or other substance, and rubbed with hands)	
Huehuetl Tlapanhuehuetl Caxambu Carimbo Tambu (Tambi-Tambu) Tambula Bambola Tambor-de-Crioulo Tumba	Large hollowed-out tree trunk with leather or parchment membrane	Muffled Bass Drum Low Conga Drum
Surdo	Large Tom-Tom	
Ferrinho	Triangle	Triangle, hand-damped
Prato Platillo (Spanish)	Cymbal	
Tantã	Gong	
Gangarria Chocalho de metal	Cowbell	
Agógo	Iron Double Bell (two pitches)	Two Cowbells sounding one third apart
Jicara de aqua	Small Cup (bright-sounding rhythm instrument)	China Cup or Plate
a) Tabletas a) Tablillas a, b) Matraca a, b) Carraca	a) Wooden Rattle consisting of two or three small boards that are shaken together b) Swing Ratchet	a) Handle Castanets (flat) b) Ratchet
Castanhetas	Castanets	
Caixeta	Wood Block	
Trocano Torocano Teponaztli Toponaztle	Large Wood Block or Wood Drum (Hollowed-out tree trunk, up to 3 m (10′) long, with resonance slits and holes, and struck with a leather-wound club. It is used by Indians for drum signals.)	Low Slit Drum

NAME	KIND	SUBSTITUTE INSTRUMENT(S)
Caracacha Caracaxà Caraxa Cataca Reque-Reque Guitcharo	Scraped Instrument	Bamboo Scraper Guíro Reco-Reco
Cabaza Afoxe Afoche	Rattle: a hollow gourd with a beaded net (seeds or pearls) around it	Metal Cylinder Cabaza
Cascavels Cascabeles (Spanish)	Jingles	
Ganzá Xucalho Chocalho Chocalho de madeira Maruga	Metal or Wooden Container Rattle filled with seeds or small pebbles	Chocallo (Tubular Rattle) Maracas
Ayacaxtli	Gourd or Clay Vessel with handle, filled with buckshot or equivalent	Container Rattle with coarse filling
Tenabari	Row Rattle of strung butterfly cocoons.	Shallow cardboard box with rattle filling (dark timbre)
Maceta	Mallet	Bass Drum Mallet

Appendix

batteria I

3 tomtom (piccolo, medio, grande) · tamburo militare con la corda (c. c.) · tamburo militare senza la corda (s. c.) · wood-block · metal-blocks (da percuotere con bacchette di xilofono)

batteria II

3 crotali (ca. [notation])· 3 piatti sospesi (piccolo, medio, grande) · 3 triangoli (piccolo, medio, grande). 3 campane de gregge (piccolo, medio, grande)

batteria III

3 tamtam (piccolo, medio, grande) · gran cassa · maracas · 3 tamburi baschi (piccolo, medio, grande) · 3 bongo (acutissimo, più acuto, medio) · 6 campane tubolari ([notation 1 2 3 4 5 6])

Explanation of Signs for Beaters:

bacchetta di triangolo ⌂ · di feltro ♀ · di metallo ● · di legno ⊓ · di xilofono ✱ · spazzola metallica da jazz Y · pelle ⊗ · gomma ⊞ · mano Y · unghia △

The strings may also be played in choirs, in which case the instructions in parentheses must be followed. All instruments sound as notated, except the Ottavino (Piccolo), Campanelli a tastiera (Keyboard Glockenspiel), and Celesta, which sound one octave higher, and the Chitarra (Guitar) and Contrabasso, which sound one octave lower.

    Ex. 1: Grouping of Percussion Instruments and Explanation of Signs for Beaters, etc. (Hans Werner Henze: *Elegy for Young Lovers*)

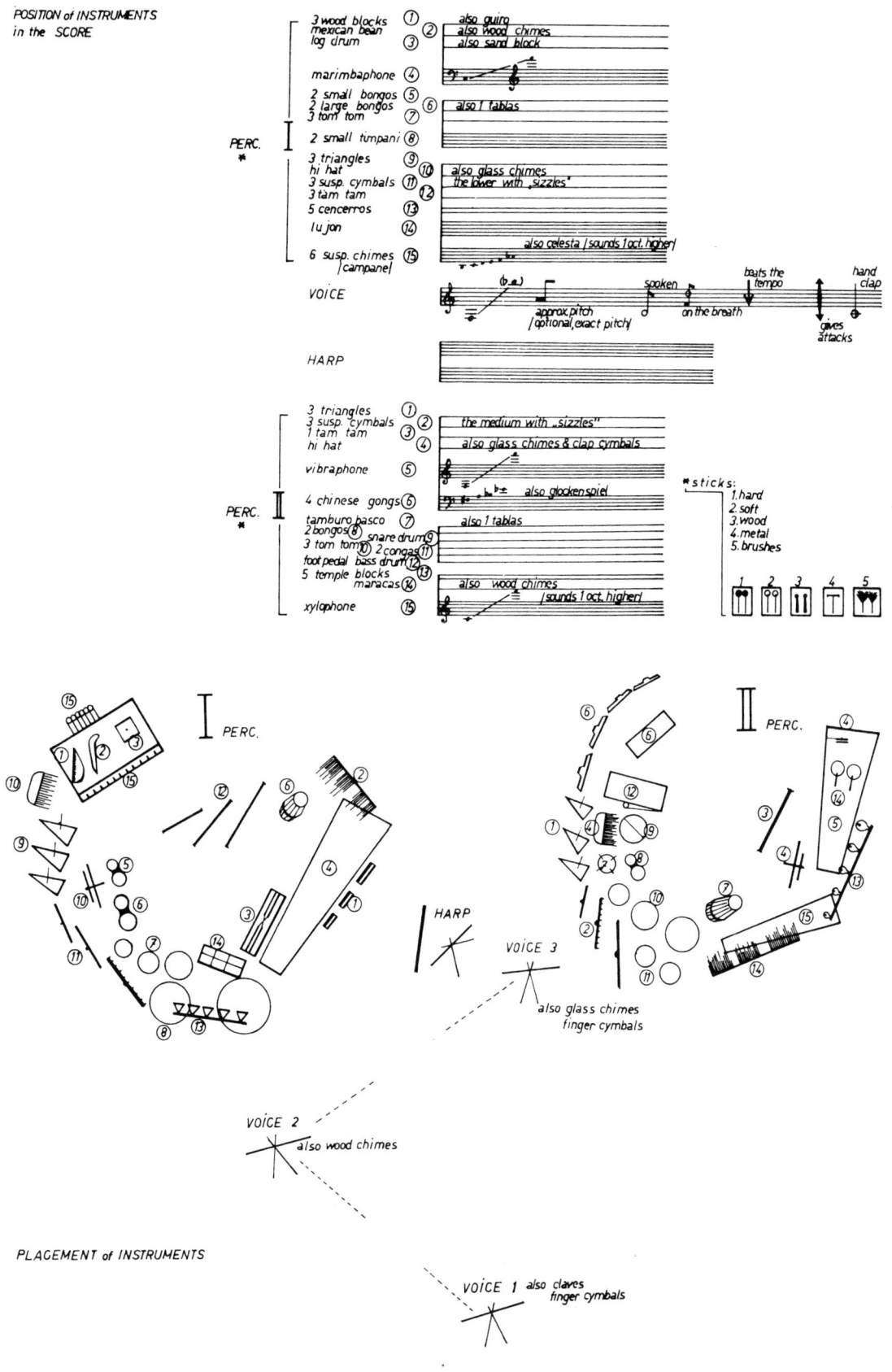

Ex. 2: a) Grouping of Percussion Instruments in the Score, for Two (Three) Performers;
b) Placement of Instruments on Stage.
(Luciano Berio: *Circles*)

Disposizione dell' orchestra

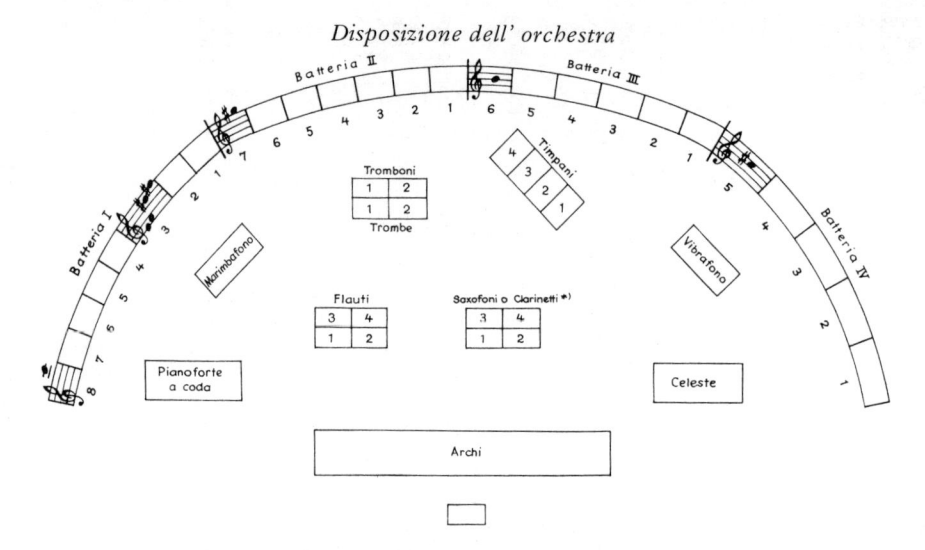

Instruments of the Four Rear Sections

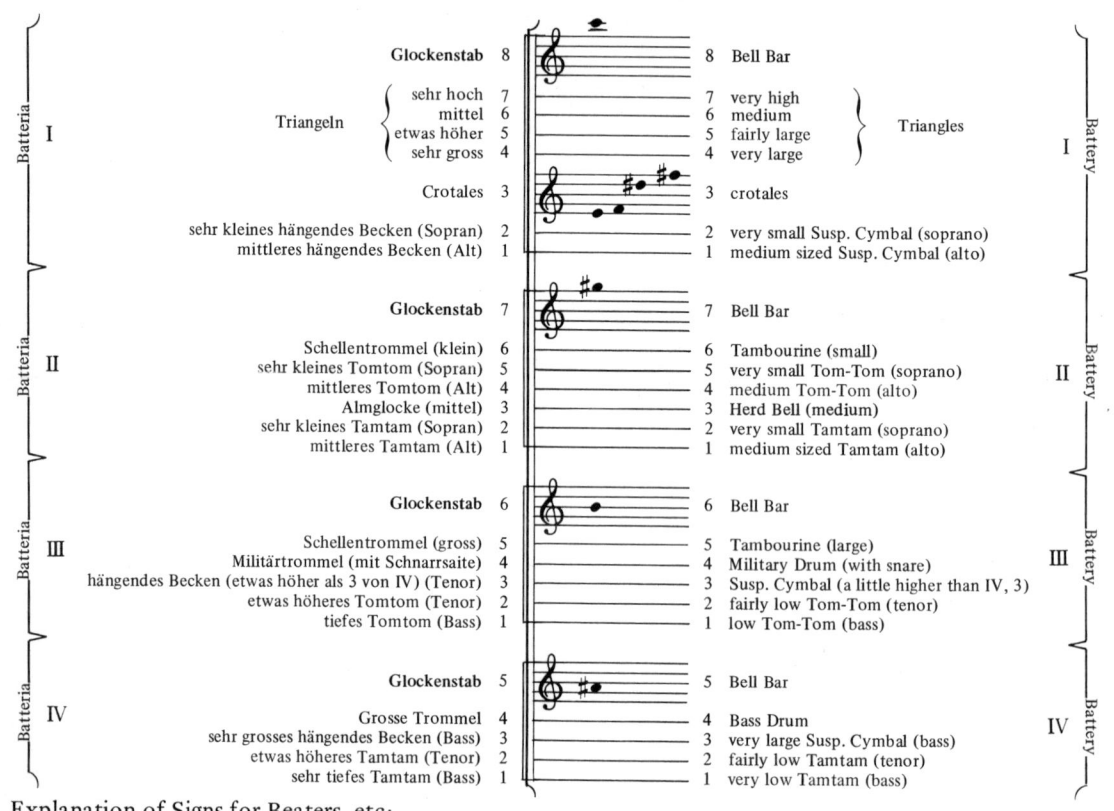

Batteria I / Battery I
Glockenstab	8	8	Bell Bar
Triangeln { sehr hoch	7	7	very high } Triangles
mittel	6	6	medium
etwas höher	5	5	fairly large
sehr gross	4	4	very large
Crotales	3	3	crotales
sehr kleines hängendes Becken (Sopran)	2	2	very small Susp. Cymbal (soprano)
mittleres hängendes Becken (Alt)	1	1	medium sized Susp. Cymbal (alto)

Batteria II / Battery II
Glockenstab	7	7	Bell Bar
Schellentrommel (klein)	6	6	Tambourine (small)
sehr kleines Tomtom (Sopran)	5	5	very small Tom-Tom (soprano)
mittleres Tomtom (Alt)	4	4	medium Tom-Tom (alto)
Almglocke (mittel)	3	3	Herd Bell (medium)
sehr kleines Tamtam (Sopran)	2	2	very small Tamtam (soprano)
mittleres Tamtam (Alt)	1	1	medium sized Tamtam (alto)

Batteria III / Battery III
Glockenstab	6	6	Bell Bar
Schellentrommel (gross)	5	5	Tambourine (large)
Militärtrommel (mit Schnarrsaite)	4	4	Military Drum (with snare)
hängendes Becken (etwas höher als 3 von IV) (Tenor)	3	3	Susp. Cymbal (a little higher than IV, 3)
etwas höheres Tomtom (Tenor)	2	2	fairly low Tom-Tom (tenor)
tiefes Tomtom (Bass)	1	1	low Tom-Tom (bass)

Batteria IV / Battery IV
Glockenstab	5	5	Bell Bar
Grosse Trommel	4	4	Bass Drum
sehr grosses hängendes Becken (Bass)	3	3	very large Susp. Cymbal (bass)
etwas höheres Tamtam (Tenor)	2	2	fairly low Tamtam (tenor)
sehr tiefes Tamtam (Bass)	1	1	very low Tamtam (bass)

Explanation of Signs for Beaters, etc:

↑ Triangle Beater (*Triangelschlägel*)
♀ Soft Felt Beater (*weicher Filzschlägel*)
⚥ Hard Leather Beater (*Schlägel aus hartem Leder*)
● Metal Beater (*Metallschlägel*)
⊤ Wooden Mallet (*Holzschlägel*)
Y Wire Brush (*Jazzbesen*)

∧ With the Hand (*mit der Hand*)
+ With the Fingernail (*mit dem Fingernagel*)
ı Knitting Needle (*Stricknadel*)

Ex. 3a: Grouping of Percussion Instruments for Several Performers. (Hans Werner Henze: *Antifone*)

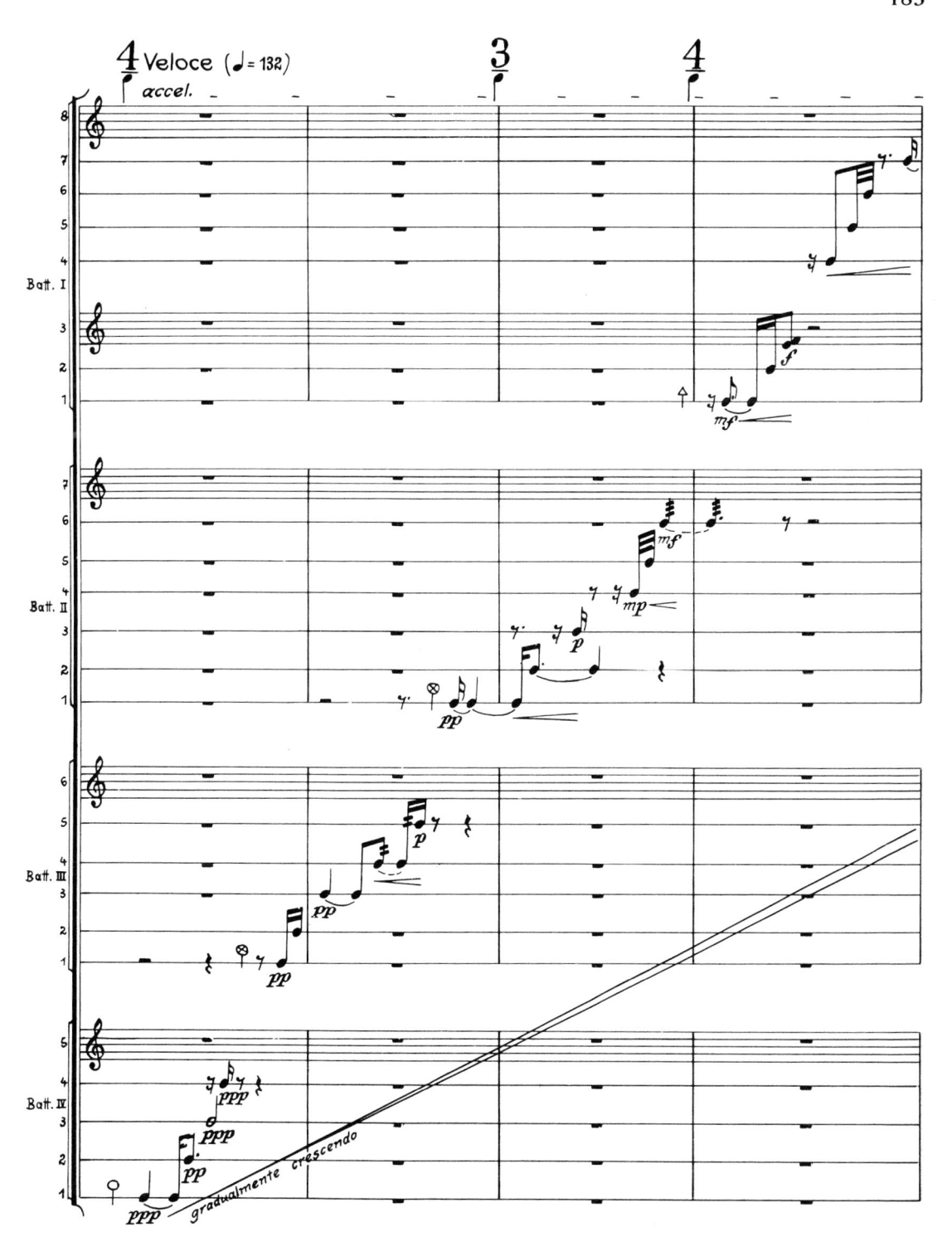

Ex. 3b: Score Page Illustrating Ex. 3a.
(Hans Werner Henze: *Antifone*)

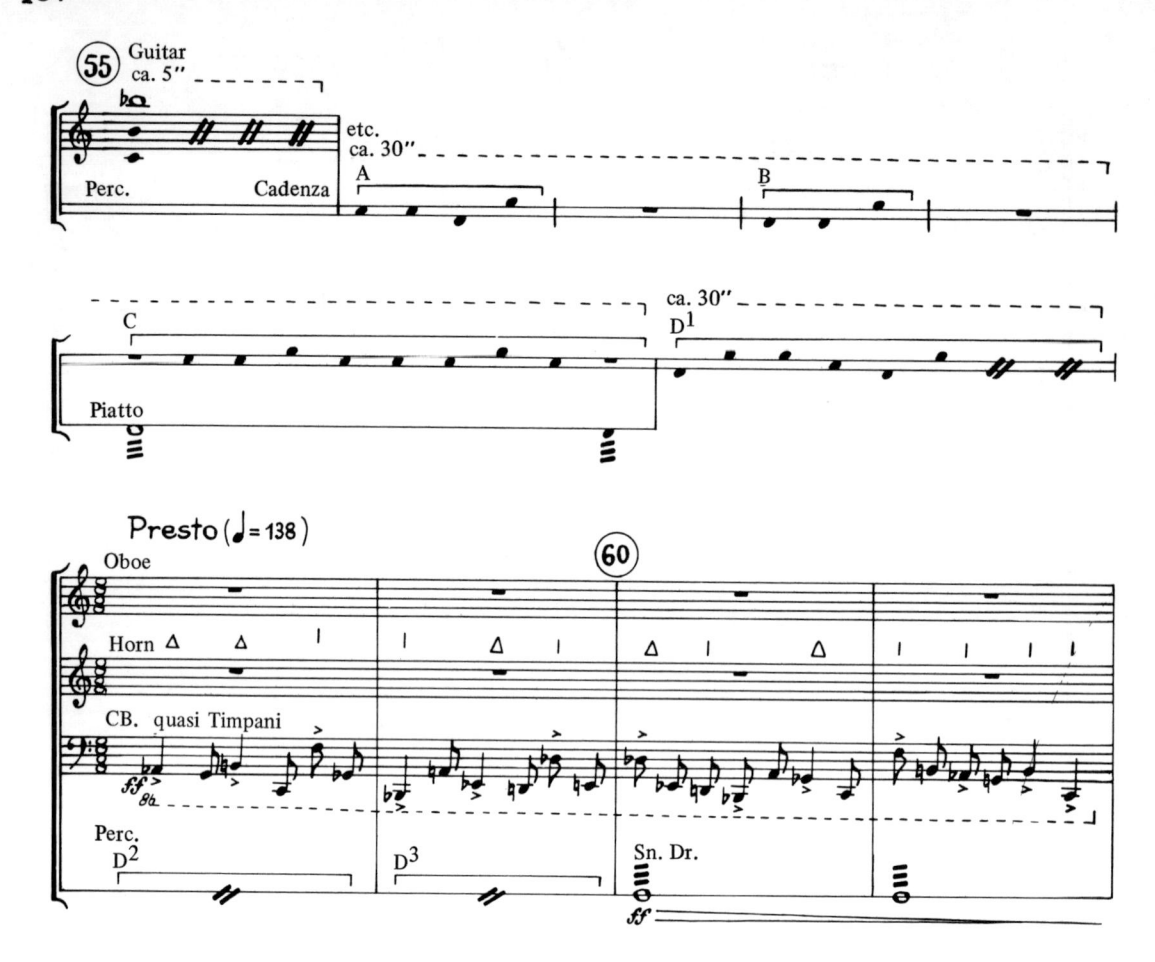

Ex. 4: a) Choice of Percussion Instruments from Three Groups, to be used by one percussionist during his improvised cadenza;
b) Playing Instructions for a).
(Theodor Antoniou: *Epilogue for Soprano, Oboe, Horn, Double Bass, Guitar, Piano, and Percussion*)

Playing Instructions for Ex. 4:

A = Improvisation with wooden percussion instruments (Wood Block; Temple Blocks).
B = Improvisation with skin instruments (Drums).
C = Improvisation with metal instruments (Cymbals, Tamtam, Metal Blocks, etc.).

Throughout the performance of sections A, B, and C. there must be a steady crescendo, and the rests between sections must grow progressively shorter.

D^1 = First Variation: to be played on one of the three groups of instruments -- A, B, or C.
D^2 = Second Variation: to be played on instruments from any two different groups.
D^3 = Third Variation: to be played on all three instrument groups.

Durations of A-B-C, as well as of D^1, 30 seconds each.

For Improvisations A, B, and C, the choice of beaters should depend on their appropriateness for the instruments selected.
From D^1 on, drum sticks must be used in anticipation of the drum-roll entrance in measure 60.

Ex. 5: 4 Timpanists.
(Hector Berlioz: *Symphonie fantastique*)

Ex. 6: 5 Timpani (2 players); Tamtam, Bass Drum (Gr. C.).
(Igor Stravinsky: *Le Sacre du printemps*)

Ex. 7: 2 Timpanists.
(Karl Amadeus Hartmann: *8th Symphony*)

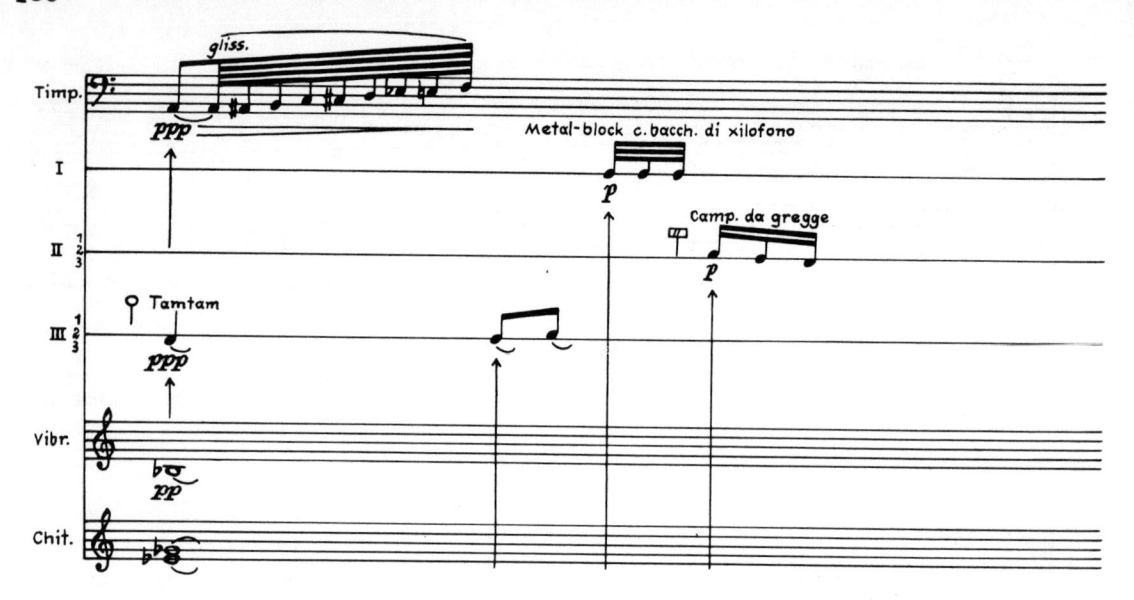

Ex. 8: Timpani glissando (strike; then raise pitch with pedal); 3 Tamtams, with soft mallet ♀ ; Metal Block, with xylophone mallet; Herd Bells (*Camp. da gregge*), with rubber beater ⌶ ; and others.
(Hans Werner Henze: *Elegy for Young Lovers*)

Ex. 9: Timpani glissando downward (rolled); Military Drum; 3 Tom-Toms; Tamtam glissando.
(Hans Werner Henze: *Il re cervo*)

Ex. 10: 4 Timpani; Metal Block; 3 Suspended Cymbals *(Piatto sosp.)*, struck with wooden mallet ⊓ ; 6 Tubular Bells *(Camp. tub.)*, struck simultaneously with a wooden cross bar.
(Hans Werner Henze: *Elegy for Young Lovers*)

Ex. 11: 6 Timpani--2 low and 2 high, plus 1 each in E and A, among other instruments.
(Karl Amadeus Hartmann: *7th Symphony*)

Ex. 12: Cymbal; Snare Drum (C. cl.); Bass Drum (G. C.); 3 Timpani (2 of them above b: d^1 and $f\sharp^1$)--see page 36.
(Darius Milhaud: *La création du monde*)

Ex. 13: Timpani, with wooden mallets *(mit Holzschl.)*; Cymbal, with sponge beater *(mit Schwammschl.)* or felt beater.
(Gustav Mahler: *7th Symphony*)

Ex. 14: Timpani in Music of the Baroque Era, usually played with wooden beaters.
(Jacques Philidor le cadet: *Partition de plusieurs marches*–1705)

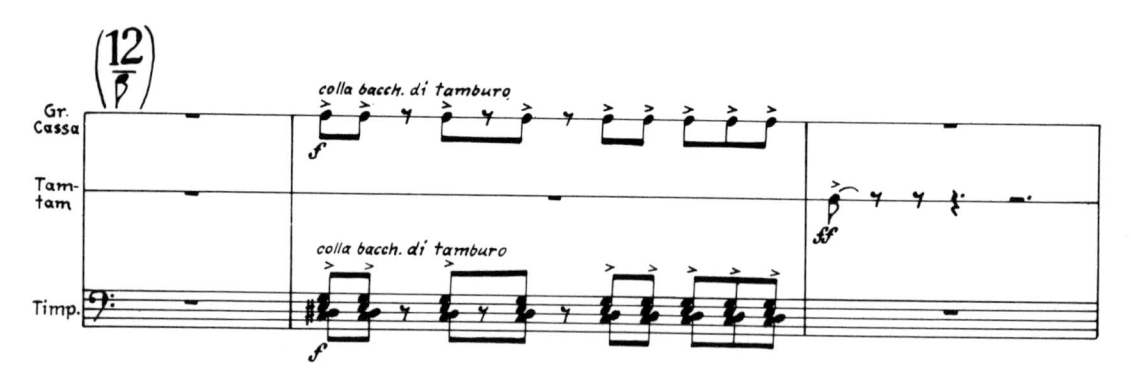

Ex. 15: Bass Drum, with drum sticks; Tamtam; Timpani, with drum sticks.
(Carl Orff: *Trionfi*)

Ex. 16: Soloistic Use of Timpani.
(Benjamin Britten: *Nocturne for Tenor Solo, Seven Obbligato Instruments, and String Orchestra, Op. 60*)

Ex. 17: Soloistic Use of 6 Timpani, Snare Drum *(kl. Tr.)*, Cymbal *(Bck.)*, and Bass Drum *(gr. Tr.)*.
(Karl Amadeus Hartmann: *6th Symphony*)

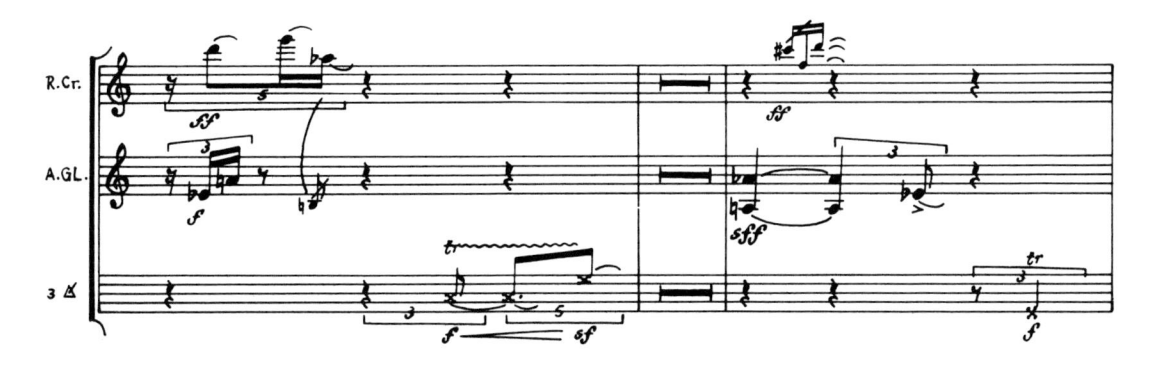

Ex. 18: Descant Set of Tubular Chimes *(R. Cr.)*, Set of Herd Bells *(A. Gl.)*, and 3 Triangles (△).
(Michael Gielen: *Ein Tag tritt hervor, Pentaphonie*)

Ex. 19: Timpani, Xylophone, Tambourine, Snare Drums (*C. cl., Tmb.*) with and without snares on, Bass Drum (*Gr. C.*).
(Igor Stravinsky: *Les noces*)

Ex. 20: Glockenspiel, Xylophone, Triangle, Snare Drum (*kl. Tr.*), and Celesta.
(Karl Amadeus Hartmann: *6th Symphony*)

Ex. 21: Keyboard Xylophone.
(Béla Bartók: *Bluebeard's Castle*)

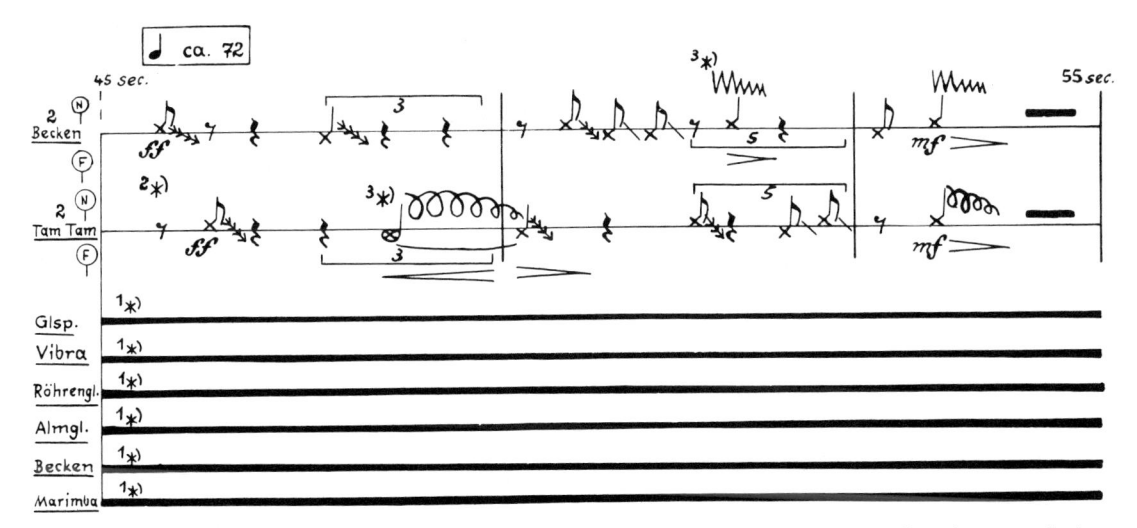

1*) constant motion or dense roll (Sound Panel: Glockenspiel, Vibraphone, Tubular Bells, Herd Bells, Cymbal(s), Marimba).
2*) stroke the rim of the cymbal with a small file (nail file).
3*) fast circular or rubbing motion.

⊕ = needle
\ = stroke from center to rim.
⊕ = small file

Ex. 22: 2 different Cymbals *(Becken)* and 2 Tamtams stroked or rubbed with a needle or with a small file; homogeneous sound-panel produced with the other instruments. (Walter Haupt: *Apeiron*)

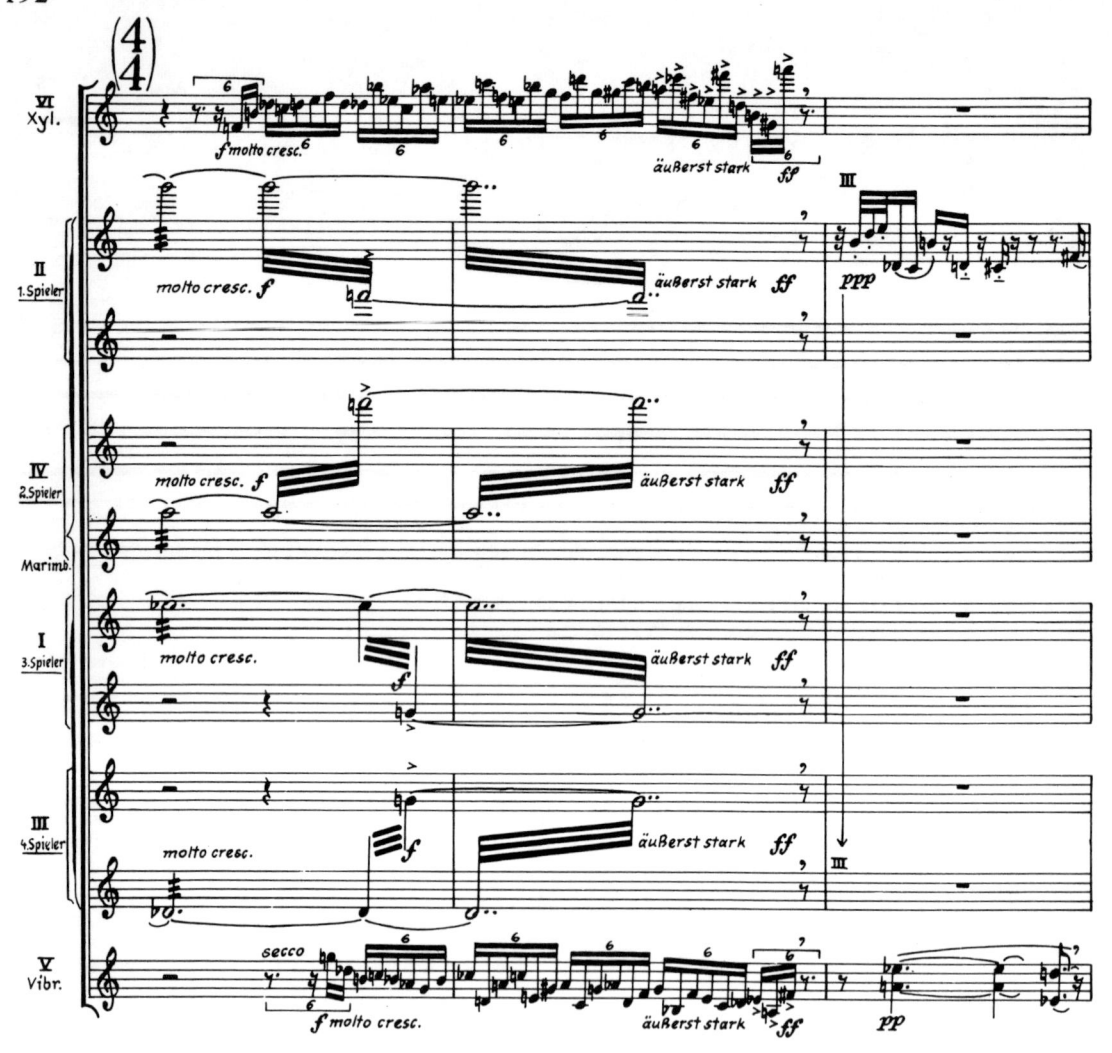

Ex. 23: Xylophone, 4 Marimbas for 4 players (actually, only 2 marimbas with 2 players each are needed), Vibraphone.
(Karl Amadeus Hartmann: *8th Symphony*)

Ex. 24: Bass Xylophone (3 players), Bass Drum (2 players). First player strikes the left head of the bass drum (with timpani sticks); second player strikes the right head (with wooden beaters, at the edge of the skin).
(Carl Orff: *Die Bernauerin*)

Ex. 25: Maracas, Tenor Trough Xylophone (glissandi), Metallophone, Clash Cymbals, Bass Drum, Timpano.
(Carl Orff: *Catulli Carmina*)

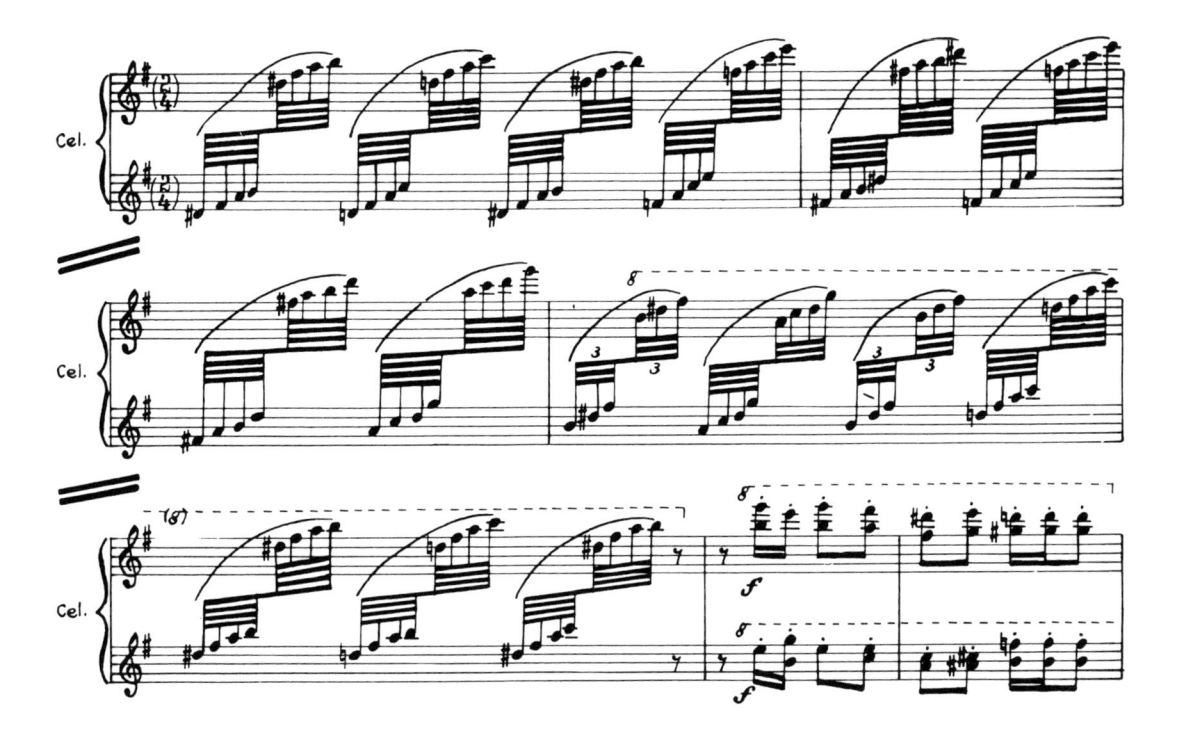

Ex. 26: Celesta.
(Peter I. Tchaikovsky: *Nutcracker Suite*)

Ex. 27: Glockenspiel, Xylophone, 2 Marimbas, Vibraphone, Celesta.
(Karl Amadeus Hartmann: *8th Symphony*)

Ex. 28: 2 Glockenspiels played with the longer edge of 2 glockenspiel bars, Keyboard Glockenspiel *(mit Tasten)*, Lithophone *(Steinspiel)*, Xylophone, Cymbal *(Beck.)* played with wooden beater, Tubular Chimes *(Röhrenglocken)* played with the longer edges of 2 wooden bars.
(Carl Orff: *Oedipus der Tyrann*)

Ex. 29: Keyboard Glockenspiel, Xylophone.
(Olivier Messiaen: *Oiseaux exotiques*)

Ex. 30: Timpani played with wooden beaters, 3 Tom-Toms and 3 Suspended Cymbals (*Piatti sosp.*) played with snare-drum sticks, Tubular Chimes (*Camp. tub.*), Keyboard Glockenspiel (*Camp. a tast.*), Celesta, Marimba, Vibraphone (to f♯ ^{3}).
(Hans Werner Henze: *Elegy for Young Lovers*)

*) Vb. ⌐ ¬ = with half pedal.

**) 𝄋 = move larger maraca [with right hand] in circular motion, and produce irregular accents (> approximately as notated) by beating it against the left hand.

Ex. 31: Glockenspiel, Maracas, Marimba, Vibraphone with half pedal.
(Wlodzimierz Kotoński: *Musique en relief*)

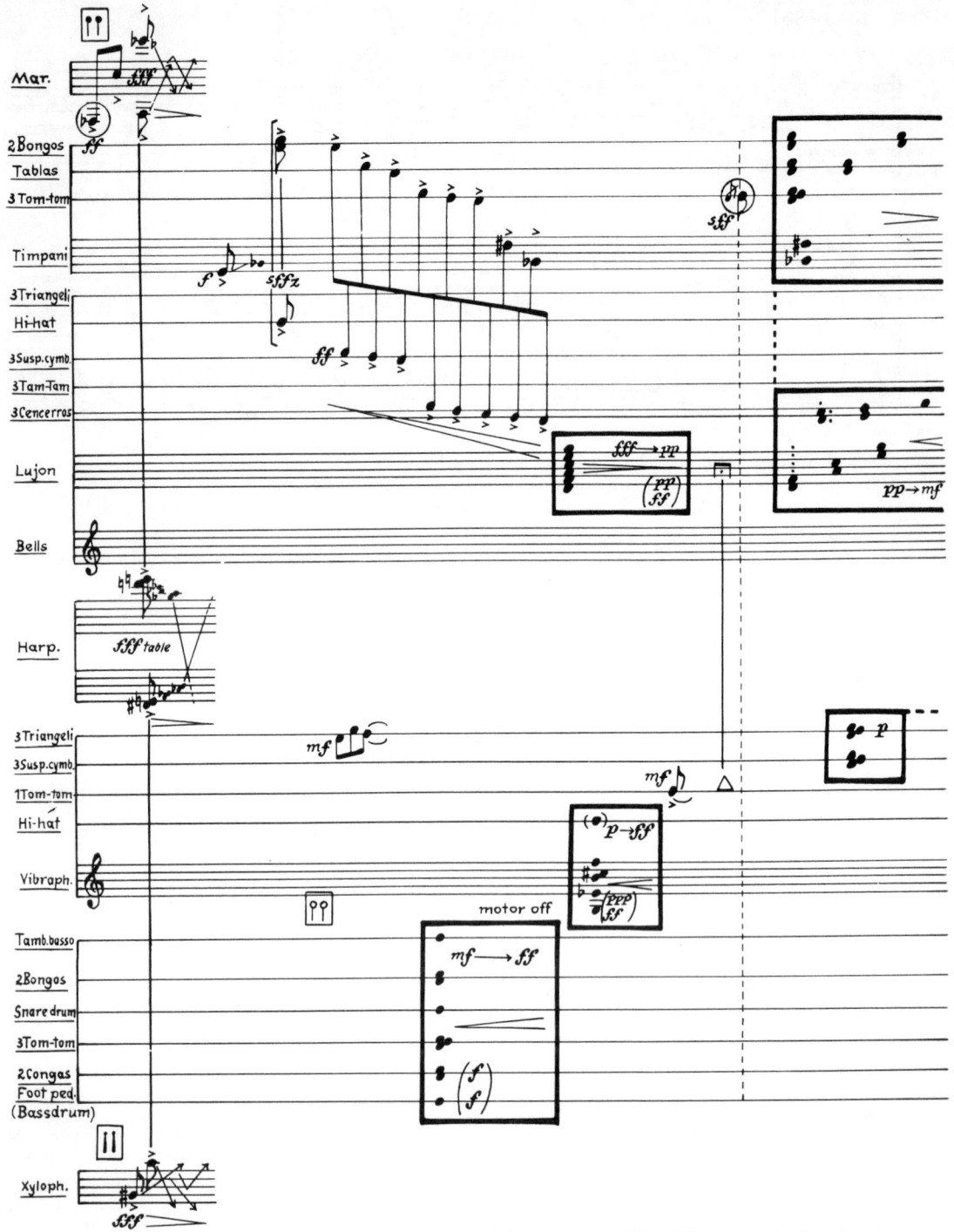

Ex. 32: Loo-Jon, 5 Cencerros, Tablas, Hi-Hat, and other instruments. (Luciano Berio: *Circles*)

Ex. 33: Lithophone *(Steinspiel)* (sounds 2 octaves higher than notated), Timpano *(Pk.)*. (Carl Orff: *Antigonae*)

Ex. 34: 3 Stone Disks (*Steinplatten*), Bamboo Sticks suspended from strings, 3 Metal Plates.
(Milko Kelemen: *Equilibres*)

Ex. 35: Timpani, Triangle played with wooden beater, Antique Cymbals.
(Igor Stravinsky: *Le Sacre du printemps*)

Ex. 36: 2 Crotales, Bell.
(Igor Stravinsky: *Les noces*)

Ex. 37: Dance Castanets, Xylophone played with wooden mallets, Trough Xylophones played with rubber beaters, Crotales *(Cymb.)*, Timpani *(Pk.)* played with wooden and felt beaters (3 players).
(Carl Orff: *Antigonae*)

Ex. 38: Crotales played with triangle beaters (⌂), 2 Tambourines *(Tamb. baschi)* played with felt beaters (♀).
(Hans Werner Henze: *Elegy for Young Lovers*)

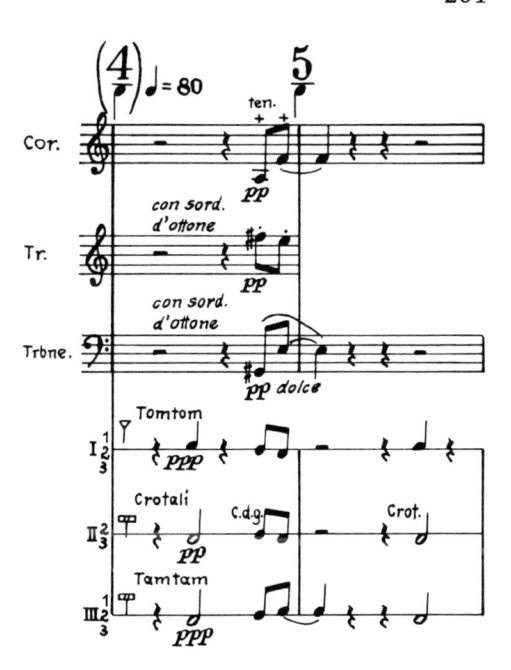

Ex. 39: 3 Tom-Toms played with fingers (𝄆), Crotales and Herd Bells *(C. d. g.)*,
3 Tamtams played with rubber beaters (𝄇).
(Hans Werner Henze: *Elegy for Young Lovers*)

Ex. 40: Domed Gongs *(Gong Chin.)*.
(Giacomo Puccini: *Turandot*)

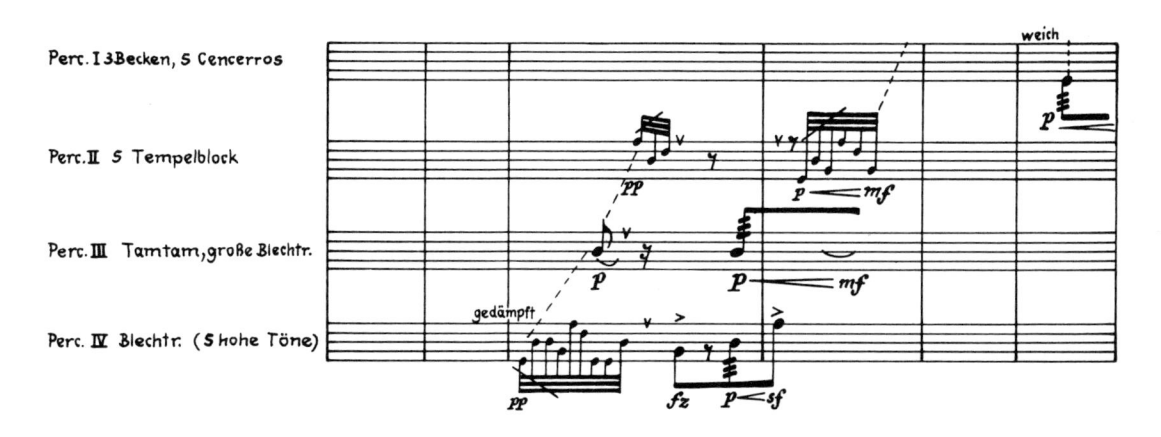

Ex. 41: Perc. I: 3 Cymbals, 5 Cencerros
Perc. II: 5 Temple Blocks
Perc. III: Tamtam, large Steel Drum (Calypso Drum)
Perc. IV: Steel Drum(s) (5 high pitches)
(Roman Haubenstock-Ramati: *Vermutungen über ein dunkles Haus*)

Ex. 42: 5 Large Bells *(Glocken)*.
(Richard Strauss: *Der Friedenstag*)
© 1938 by Richard Strauss

Ex. 43: Tubular Bells *(Campane tubolari)* played with felt-padded mallets (instead of the indicated vibraphone mallets) to achieve the *ff*.
(Hans Werner Henze: *Elegy for Young Lovers*)

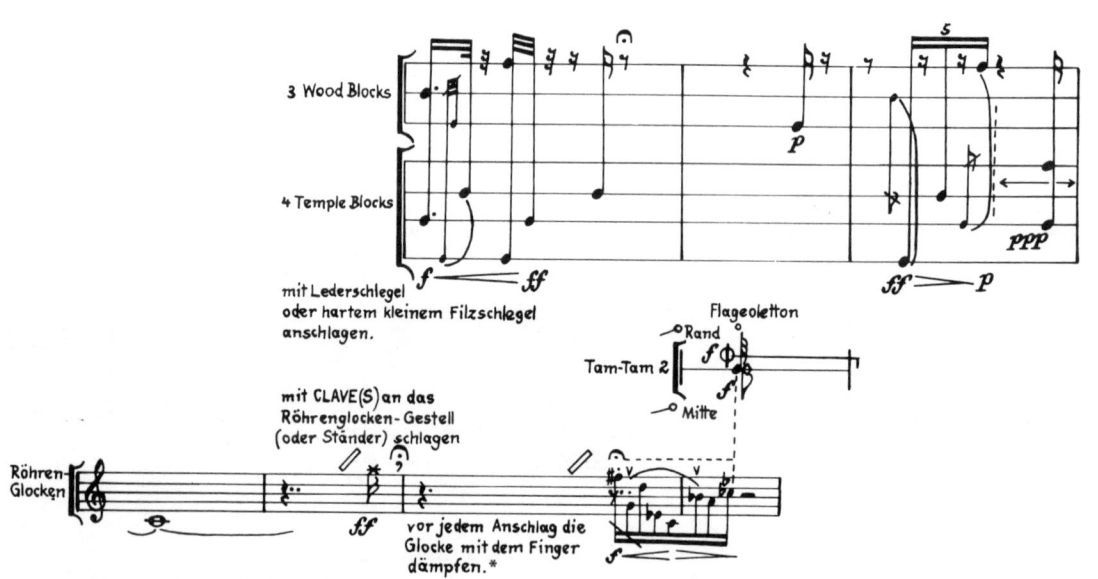

*damp chimes with finger before each stroke.

Ex. 44: 3 Wood Blocks and 4 Temple Blocks played with leather beaters or small, hard-felt beaters, 2 Tamtams played at rim *(Rand)* and center *(Mitte)*, Tubular Chimes *(Röhrenglocken)*, Chime Frame or Stand stuck with clave(s).
(Mauricio Kagel: *Anagrama*)

Ex. 45: Tubular Chimes (high chimes) notated in G-clef, Bell Plates (low chimes) notated in bass clef.
(Hans Werner Henze: *Il re cervo*)

Ex. 46: Tubaphone.
(Aram Khatchaturian: *Gayané*)

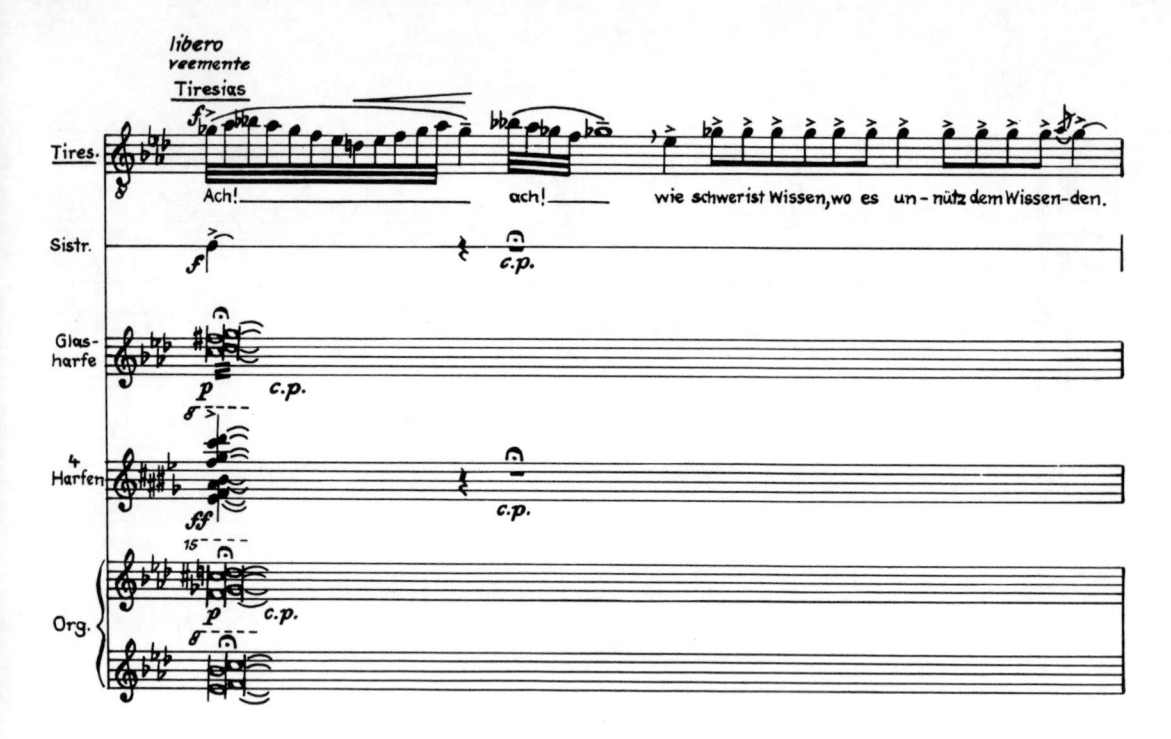

Ex. 47: Sistrum, Glass Harp (4 players), and other instruments.
(Carl Orff: *Oedipus der Tyrann*)

Ex. 48: Solo for a Set of Glasses (played with beaters).
(Carl Orff: *The Moon*)

Ex. 49: Set of 15 Tuned Bottles.
(Eric Satie: *Parade*)

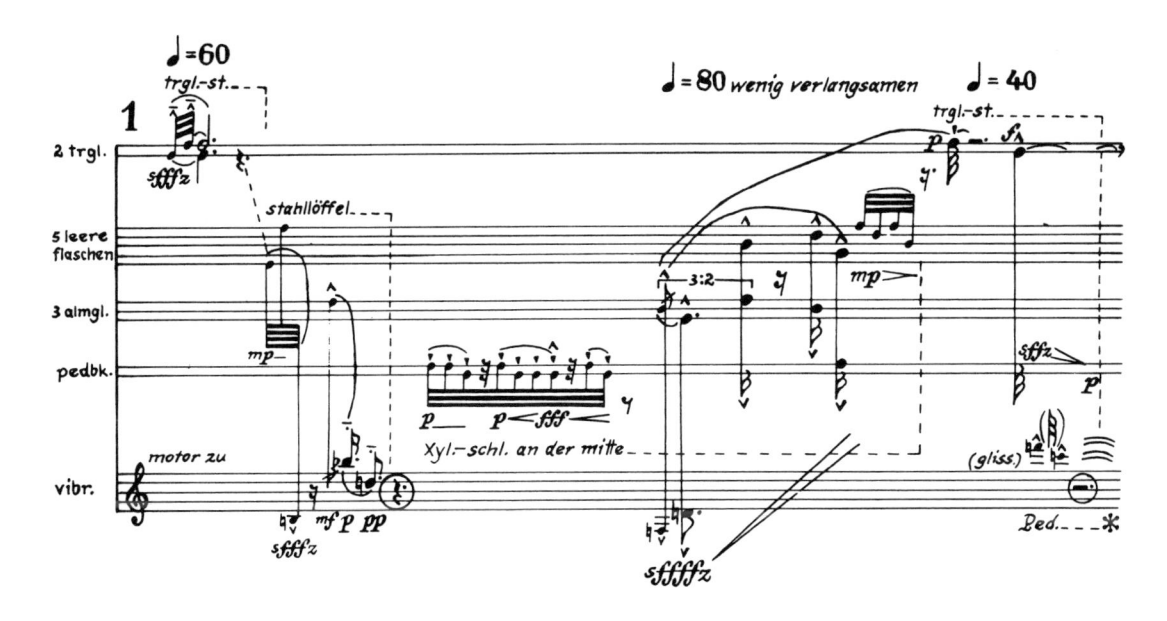

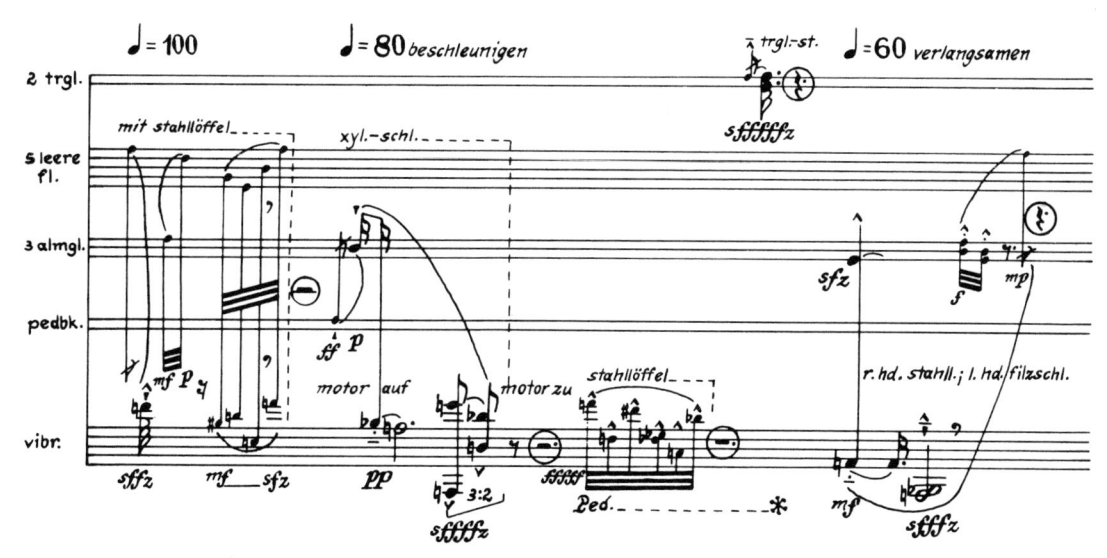

Ex. 50: 2 Triangles *(trgl.)*, 5 Empty Bottles *(leere flaschen)*, 3 Herd Bells *(almgl.)*, 2 Hi-Hats *(pedbk.)*, Vibraphone with motor on and off; Beaters: triangle stick *(trgl.-st.)*, steel spoons *(stahllöffel)*, xylophone mallets *(xyl.-schl.)*, triangle stick for glissando, felt beater *(filzschl.)*.

(Bo Nilsson: *Reaktionen*)

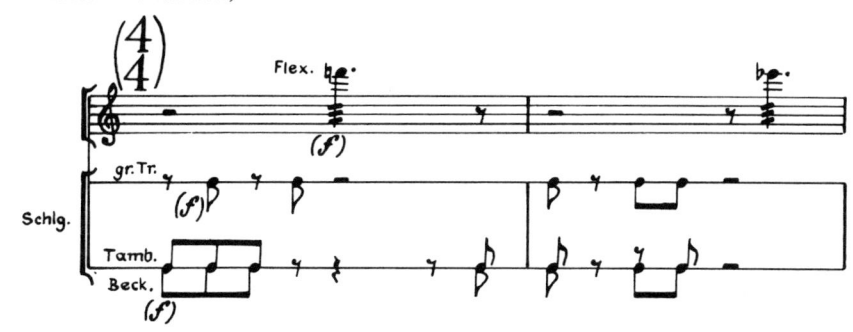

Ex. 51: Flexatone and other percussion instruments.
(Arnold Schönberg: *Moses and Aaron*)

Ex. 52: Flexatone.
(Aram Khatchaturian: *Piano Concerto*)

Ex. 53: Slide Whistle.
(Maurice Ravel: *L'enfant et les sortilèges*)

Ex. 54: 2 Small Timpani *(Kl. Pk.)* played with hands *(colla mano)* by 2 players, Single Cymbals *(Beck.)*, Metal Rattles *([Metall]rasseln)*, Slit Drum *(Schlitztrommel)*, rolls with timpani sticks on piano strings (2 pianos; 4 players).
(Carl Orff: *Die Bernauerin*)

Ex. 55: Piano Strings played with felt beaters (*Filzschlägel*) and wooden beaters (*Holzschlägel*), 2 Bass Xylophones.
(Carl Orff: *Antigonae*)

Ex. 56: Offstage:
Snare Drums *(kl. Tr.)*, Tenor Drum *(Rührtr.)*, Bass Drum *(gr. Tr.)*;
In the Orchestra:
Timpani *(Pk.)* played with hard beaters, and other percussion instruments.
(Carl Orff: *Die Bernauerin*)

Ex. 57: Timpani *(Timb.)*, Snare Drum *(C. cl.)*, *Tambour provençal*, 2 Cymbals.
(Darius Milhaud: *Suite provençale*)

Ex. 58: Cowbell *(B. métal)*, Wood Block *(B. bois)*, Cymbal, Snare Drum *(C. cl.)*, *Tambour provençal* *(T.in)*, Bass Drum *(G. C.)*, Timpani *(Timb.)* (2 players).
(Darius Milhaud: *La création du monde*)

Ex. 59: *Basler Trommel.*
(Rolf Liebermann: *Geigy Festival Concerto*)

Ex. 60: Whip *(Fouet)*, Tambourine *(Tambour de basque)*, Cymbals (1 pair; 1 suspended cymbal), Snare Drum *(Caisse claire)*, Tenor Drum *(Caisse roulante)*, *Tambourin provençal*, etc.
(Darius Milhaud: *La mort d'un tyran*)

Ex. 61: Timpani, Triangle, Cymbals (*Piatti/Becken*), Bass Drum (*G. C.*) played with beater and switch (*Verga/Rute*), other Janissary percussion instruments (not shown).
(Josef Haydn: *11th ["Military"] Symphony*)

Ex. 62: Cymbal (*Cymbale*) played with wooden beater (*bois*) or beater handle, Bass Drum (*Grosse Caisse*) played with bass-drum (*mailloche*) in the center (*au milieu*) and at the rim (*au bord*).
(Igor Stravinsky: *L'histoire du soldat*)

Ex. 63: Bass Drum (Gr. Tr.) played on rim with small wooden stick.
(Gustav Mahler: *6th Symphony*)

Ex. 64: Frame Drum tuned to d^1.
(Jacques Chailley: *La Dame à la Licorne*)

Ex. 65: Xylophone, Timpani, Tin Rattle, Snare Drum, Small Indian Drum, Large Indian Drum, Bass Drum.
(Elliott Carter: *Pocahontas*)

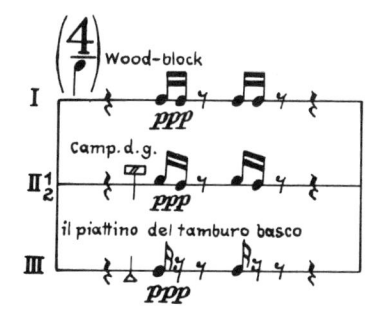

Ex. 66: Wood Block, Cowbells *(Camp. d. g.)* played with rubber beater (⃫), Jingles of a Tambourine struck with a needle (⋏).
(Hans Werner Henze: *Elegy for Young Lovers*)

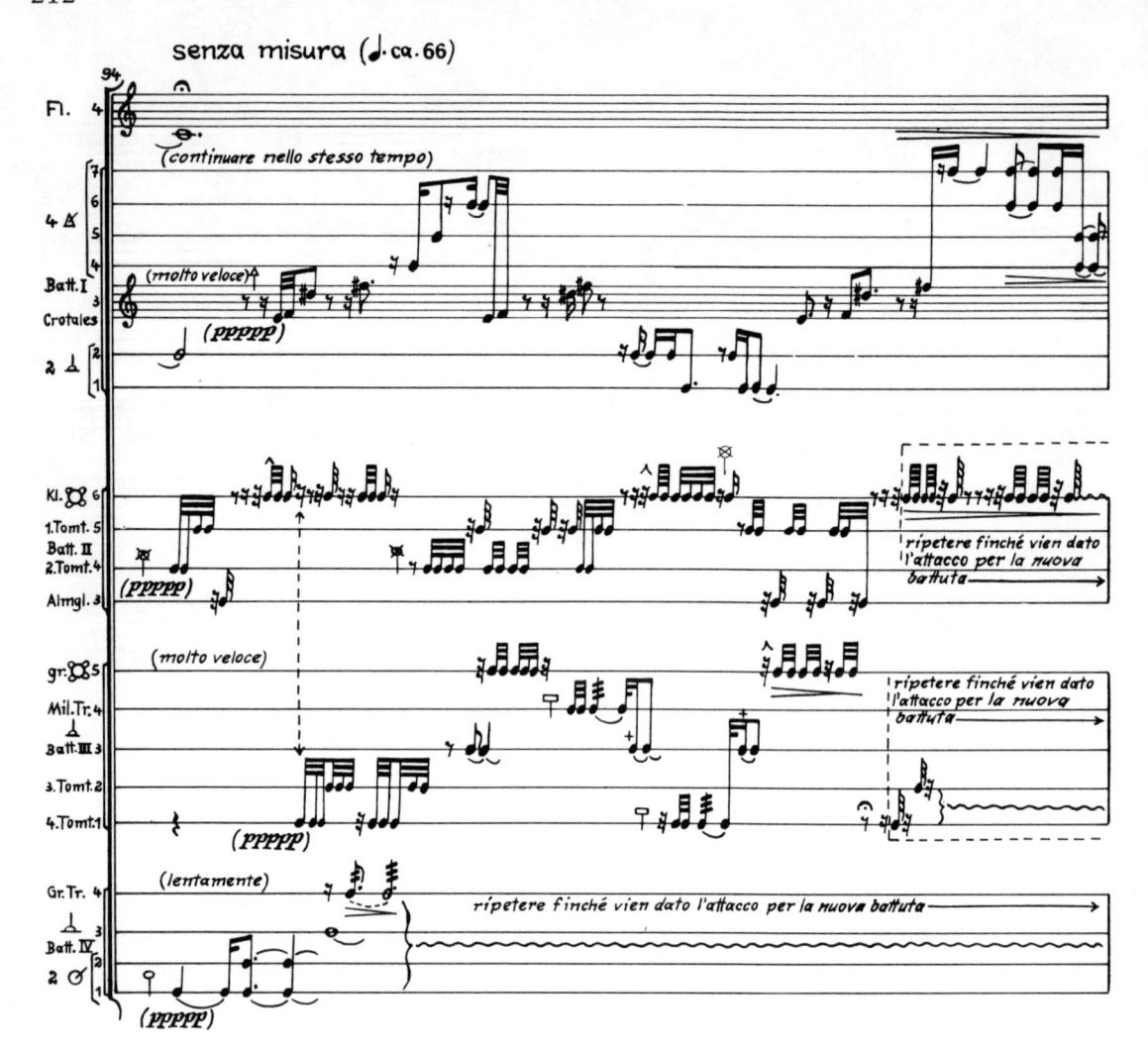

Ex. 67: 4 different Triangles (△) and Crotales played with triangle rod (⇧), 4 different Suspended Cymbals (⊥), Small and Large Tambourine (✡) played with the hands (∧) or with a leather beater (✤), 4 different Tom-Toms, Herd Bell *(Almgl.)*, Military Drum, Bass Drum *(Gr. Tr.)*, 2 Tamtams (♂). (For beater symbols see Ex. 3.)

(Hans Werner Henze: *Antifone*)

Ex. 68: Darabucca, O-Daiko played with soft beater, Taiko played with round wooden rods, 2 Congas struck in the middle *(in centro)* and at the rim *(in margine)*.
(Carl Orff: *Prometheus*)

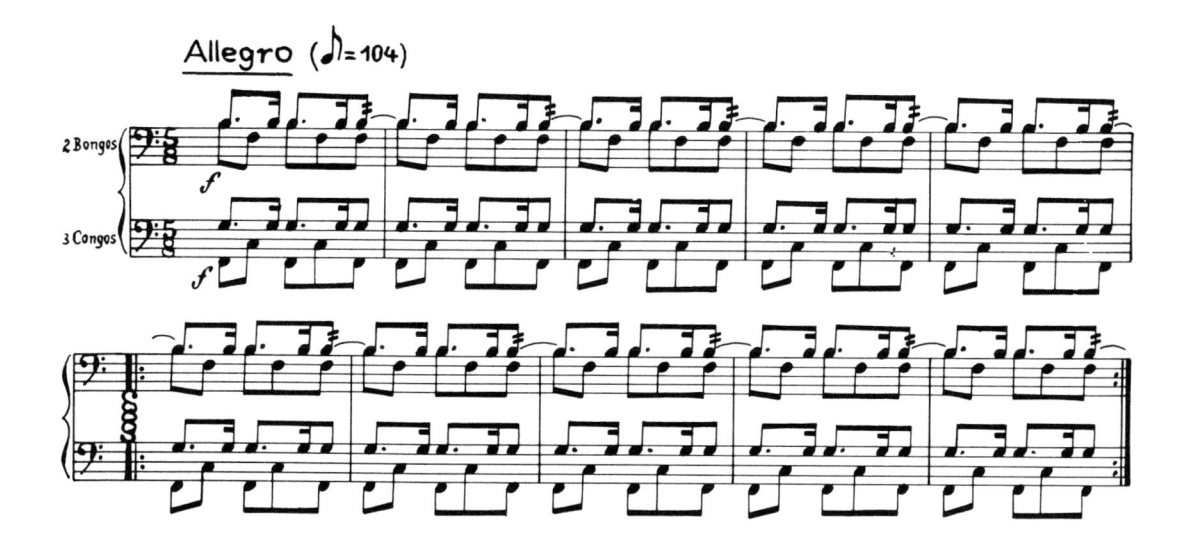

Ex. 69: 2 Bongos, 3 Congas.
(Werner Egk: *Die Verlobung in San Domingo*)

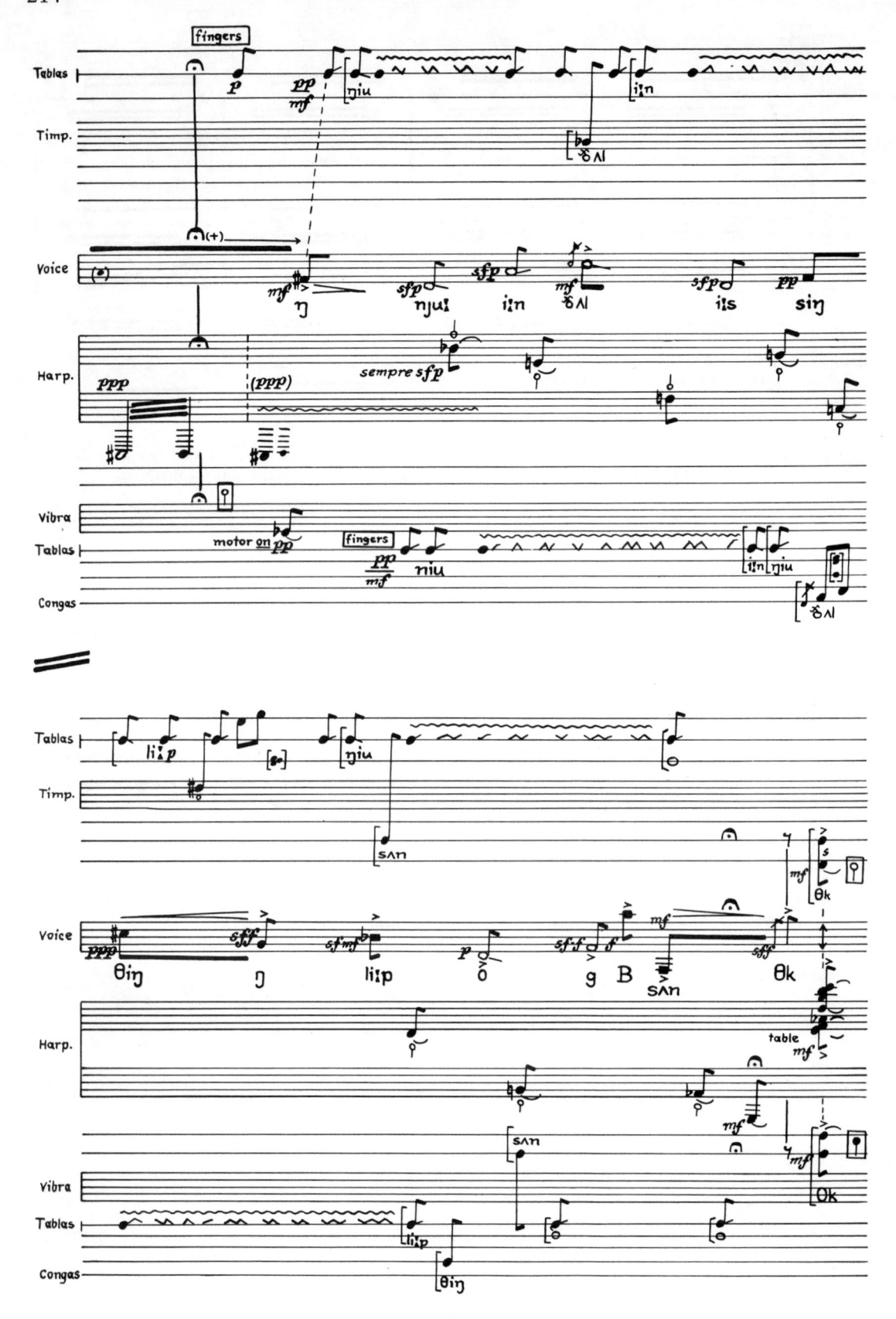

Ex. 70: Tablas and other percussion instruments.
(Luciano Berio: *Circles*)

Ex. 71: 4 Timpani *(Pk.)*, Tubular Chimes *(Glocken)*, Triangle, Tom-Tom (Chinese), Wood Block *(Holzblock)*, Small Cymbal *(Kl. Becken)*, Small Gong or Tamtam.
(Paul Hindemith: *Symphonic Metamorphosis*)

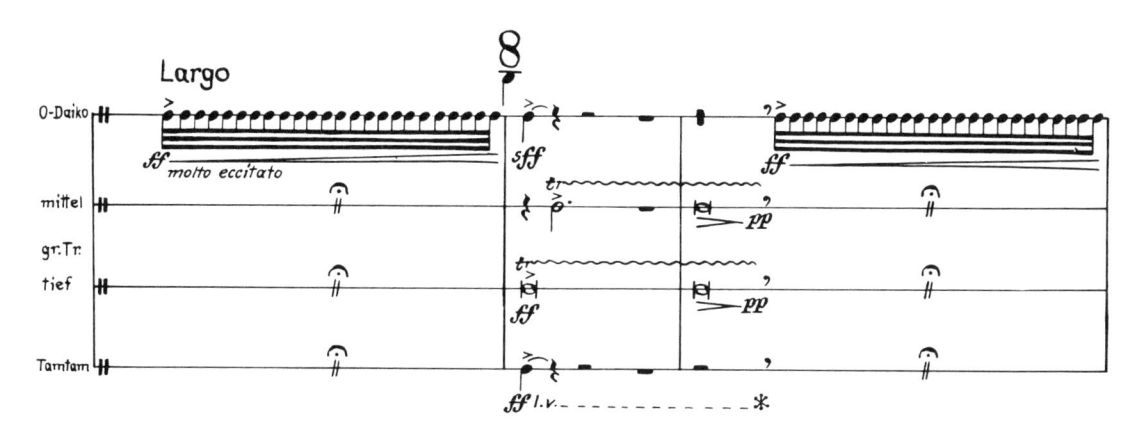

Ex. 72: O-Daiko played with round wooden rods, Bass Drums *(gr. Tr.)* medium and low *(mittel, tief)*, Tamtam.
(Carl Orff: *Prometheus*)

Ex. 73: High Tom-Tom *(Tomtom alto)*, Military Drum *(Tamb. mil.)*.
(Hans Werner Henze: *Il re cervo*)

Ex. 74: Set of 12 Tom-Toms.
(John Cage: *Quartet*)

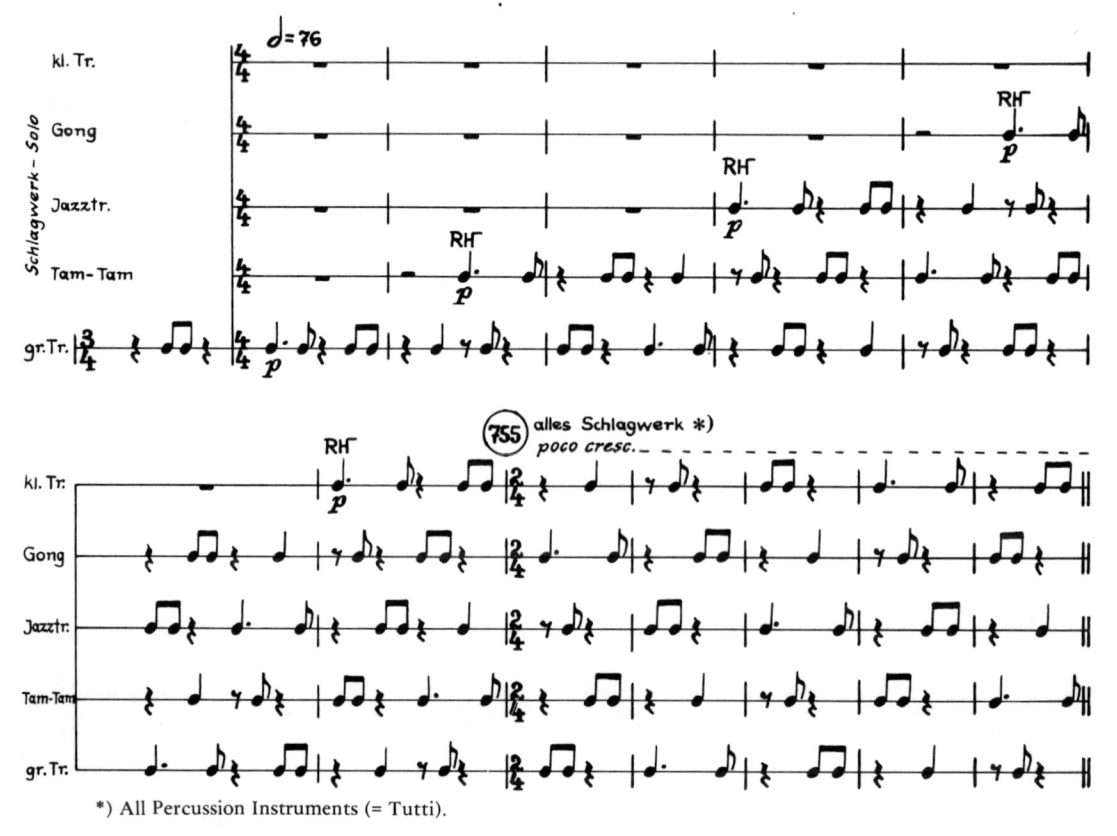

*) All Percussion Instruments (= Tutti).

Ex. 75: Percussion — Soli:
Snare Drum *(kl. Tr.)*, Gong (Small Tamtam), Jazz Drum, Tamtam, Bass Drum *(gr. Tr.)*.
(Alban Berg: *Lulu*)

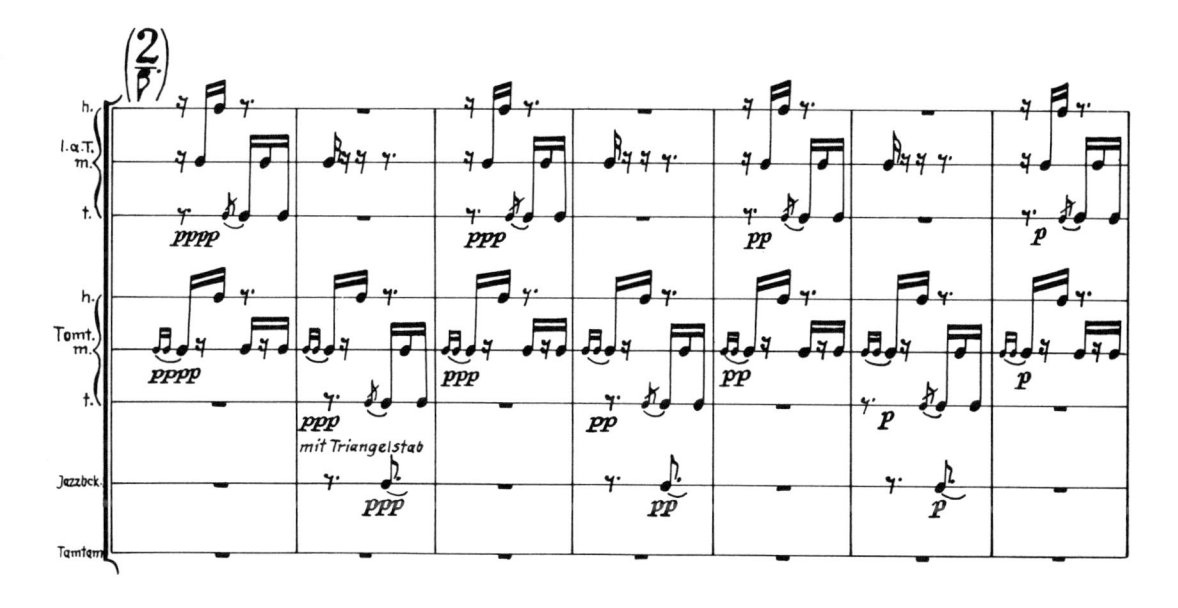

Ex. 76: 3 Timbales (Latin-American) high, medium, low *(h., m., t.)*, 3 Tom-Toms high, medium, low, Jazz Cymbal *(Jazzbck.)* played with triangle beater.
(Karl Amadeus Hartmann: *7th Symphony*)

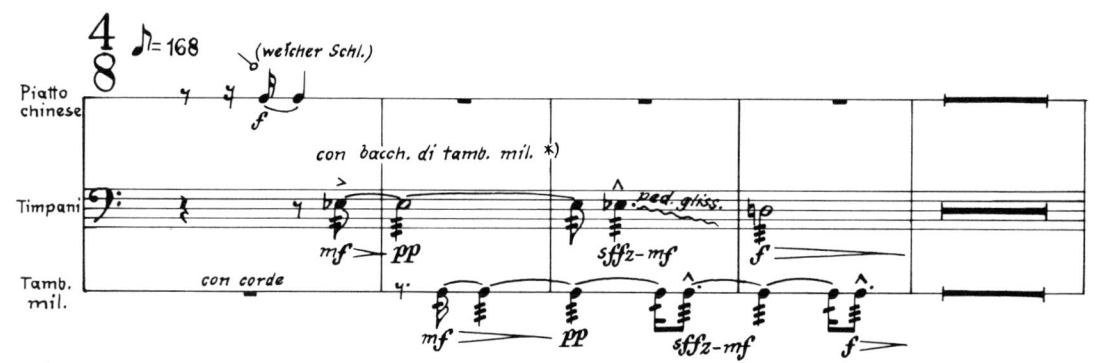

*) Double-stroke roll with drum sticks, played like a drum.

*) Hold left stick against center of skin; strike edge of skin with right stick.

**) On the rim; without skin.

(continued on next page)

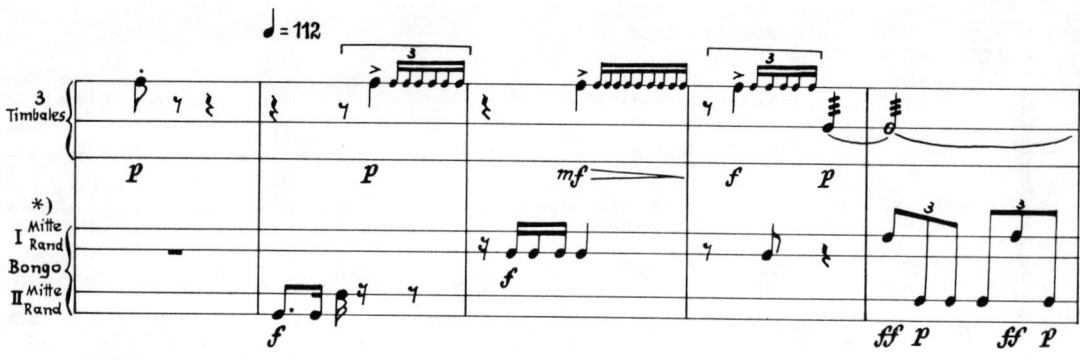

*) Mitte = center; Rand = rim

*) The glissando on the small Timbale or Bongo is produced by gradually covering the skin with the flat hand and the opening of the shell with the knee.

Ex. 77: Chinese Cymbal played with soft beater, Guiro, Timpani glissando downward (with snare-drum stick), Military Drum, 3 Timbales, 2 Bongos, Snare Drum (Tamburo). (Wlodzimierz Kotoński: *Musique en relief*)

Ex. 78: Cymbal mounted on Bass Drum (in actual performance to be played separately). (Alban Berg: *Wozzeck*)

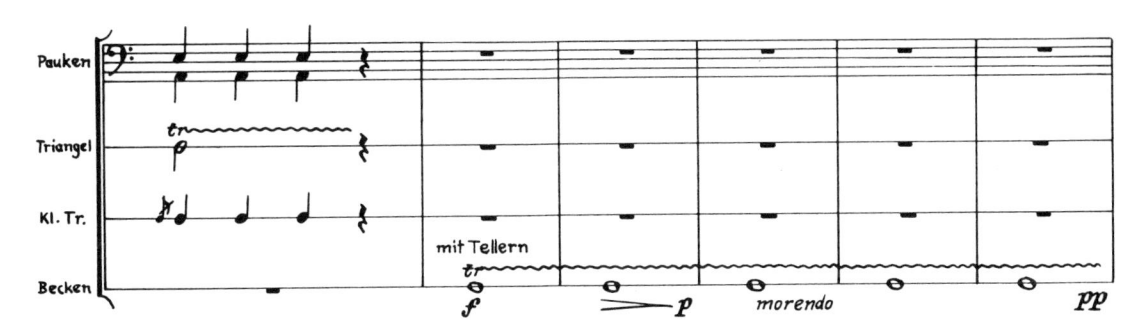

Ex. 79: Cymbal roll with 2 Cymbals (cymbal against cymbal), other percussion instruments.
(Gustav Mahler: *6th Symphony*)

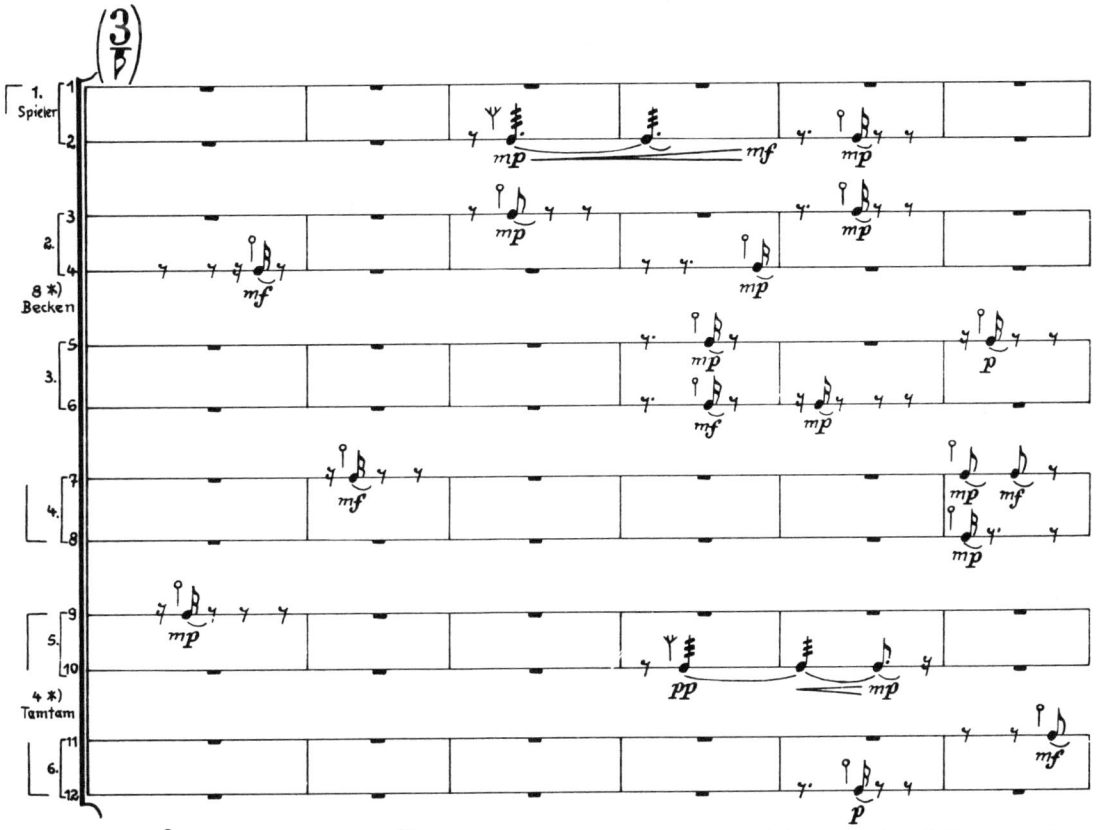

*) ♩ = with felt beater; Y = with wire brush (*Jazzbesen*); Cymbals (*Becken*) and Tamtams of different sizes: first Cymbal = highest pitch; last Tamtam = lowest pitch.

Ex. 80: 8 different Cymbals, 4 different Tamtams, played with felt beaters and wire brushes by 6 performers.
(Luigi Nono: *Cori di Didone*)

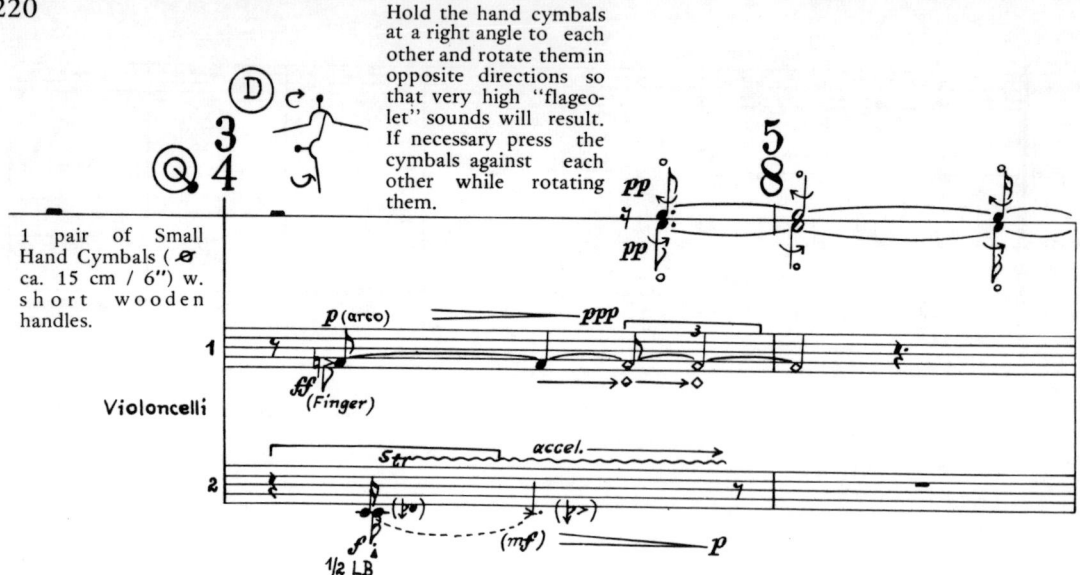

Ex. 81: Pair of Small Cymbals.
(Mauricio Kagel: *Match for Three Players*)

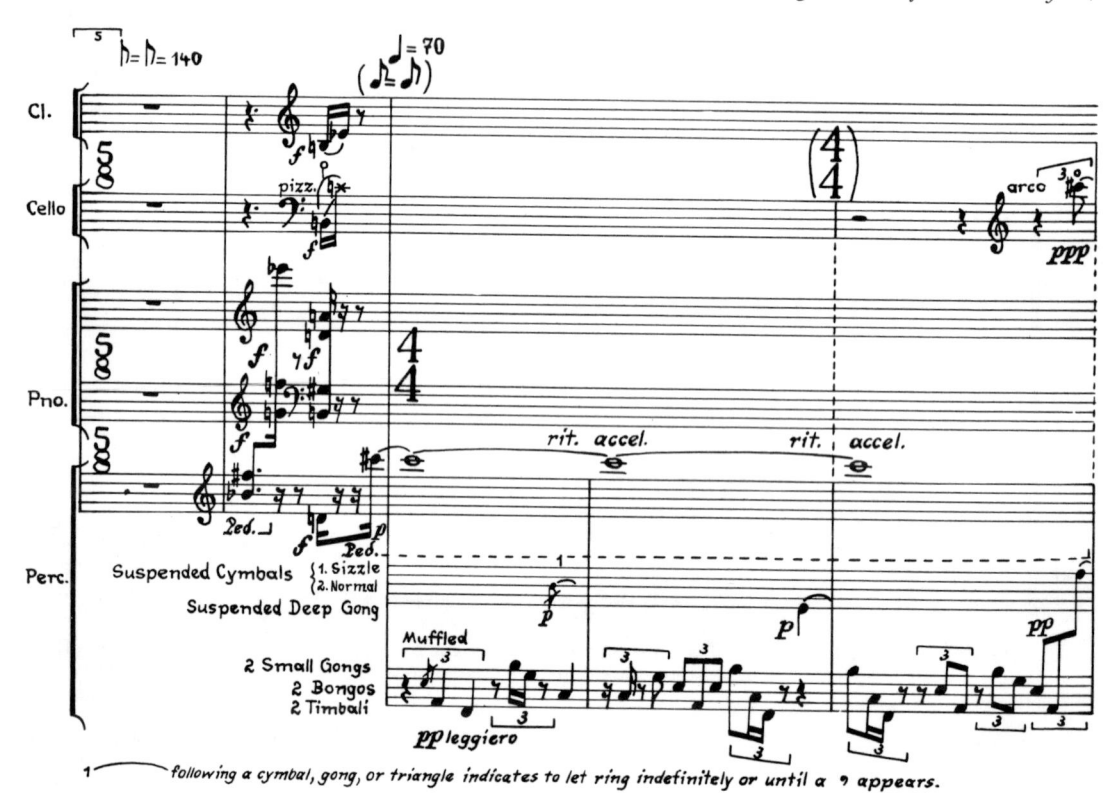

Ex. 82: Suspended Cymbals, Sizzle Cymbal, Suspended Deep Gong (or Tamtam), 2 Small Gongs (or Tamtams) muffled, 2 Bongos, 2 Latin American Timbales, etc.
(Lukas Foss: *Echoi*)

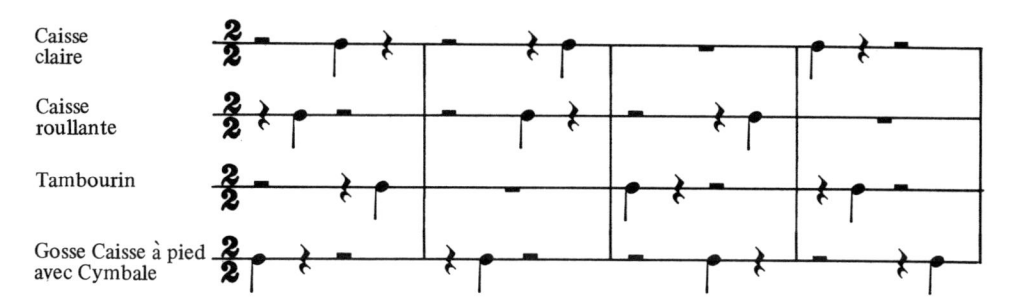

Ex. 83: Bass Drum and Cymbal played simultaneously with a pedal (*Grosse caisse à pied avec cymbale*), and other percussion instruments.
(Darius Milhaud: *La création du monde*)

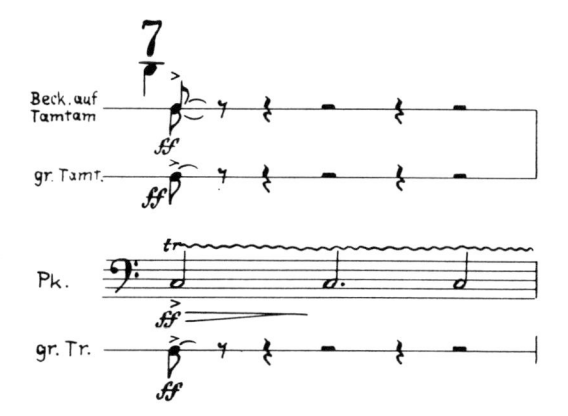

Ex. 84: Strike Tamtam center with a Cymbal (*Becken auf Tamtam*), other percussion instruments.
(Carl Orff: *Oedipus der Tyrann*)

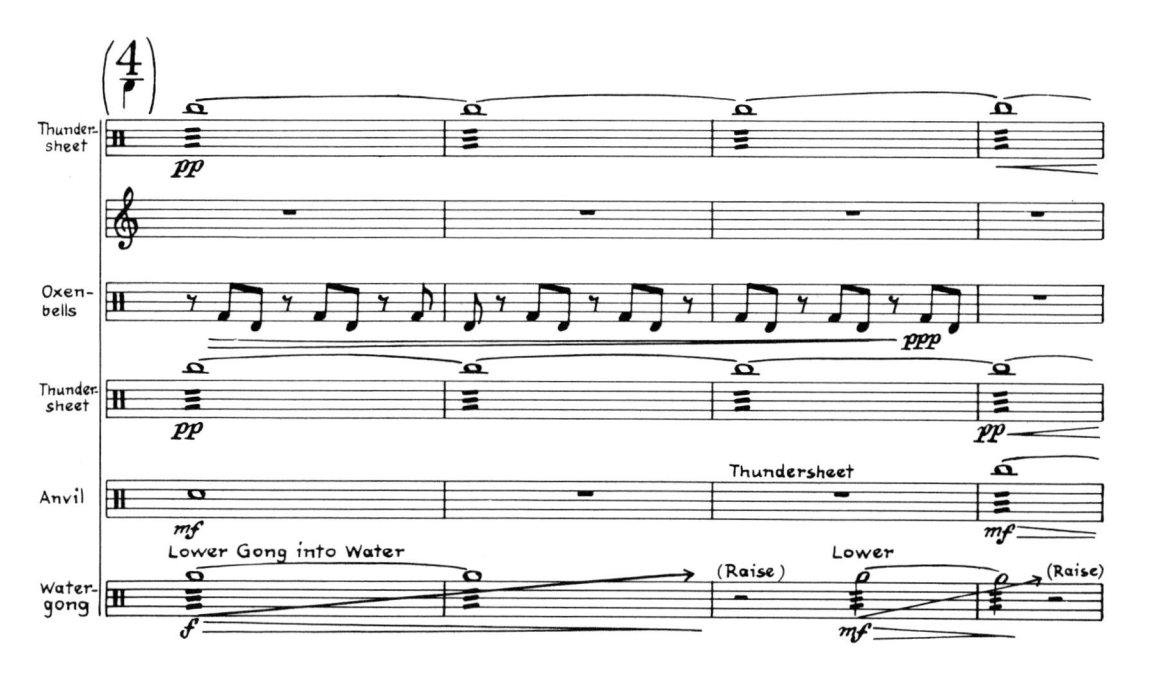

Ex. 85: 3 graduated, suspended Thunder Sheets, Oxen Bells, Anvil, Water Gong (12″ 16″), Chinese Gong (Tamtam) gradually lowered into tub of water during tone production).
(John Cage: *First Construction in Metal*)

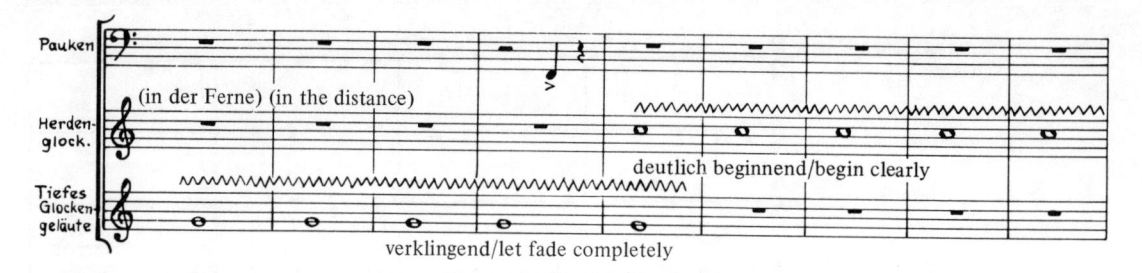

Ex. 86: Timpani *(Pauken)*, Herd Bells *(Herdenglocken)*, Low Tolling of Bells *(Tiefes Glockengeläute)*.
(Gustav Mahler: *6th Symphony*)

Ex. 87: Cencerro, Timbales, Maracas, Guíro, and others.
(Pedro Sanjuan: *Liturgía negra*)

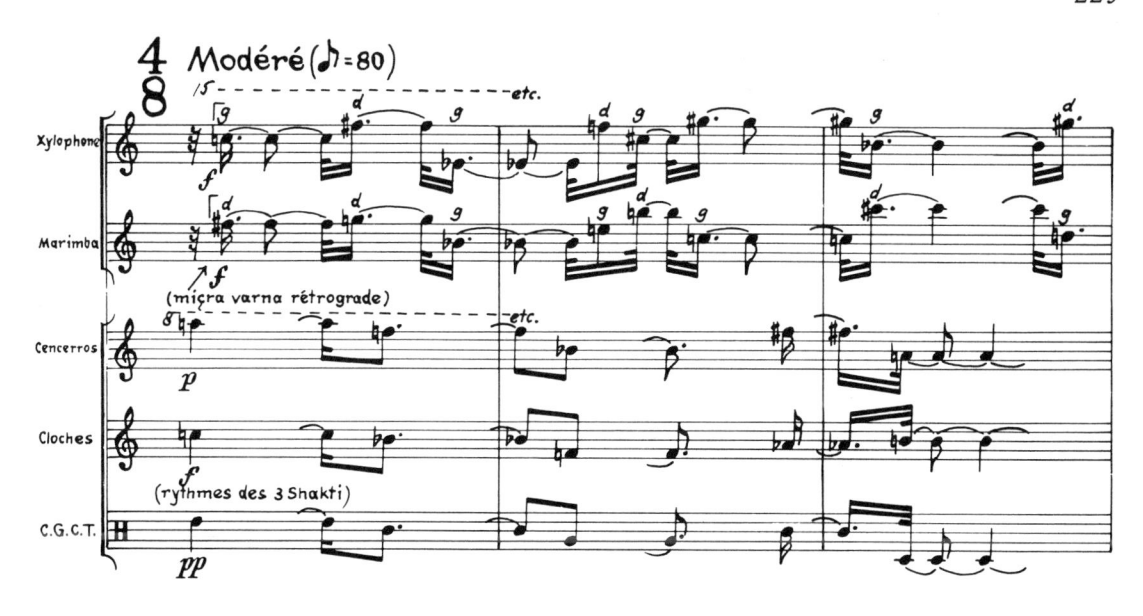

Ex. 88: Set of Herd Bells *(Cencerros)*, Set of Tubular Chimes *(Cloches)*, 2 Small Turkish Cymbals *(C.)*, 2 Small Tamtams *(G.)*, 1 Chinese Cymbal *(C.)*, 2 Tamtams *(T.)*, and others.
(Olivier Messiaen: *Sept Haïkaï*)
© 1967 by Alphonse Leduc

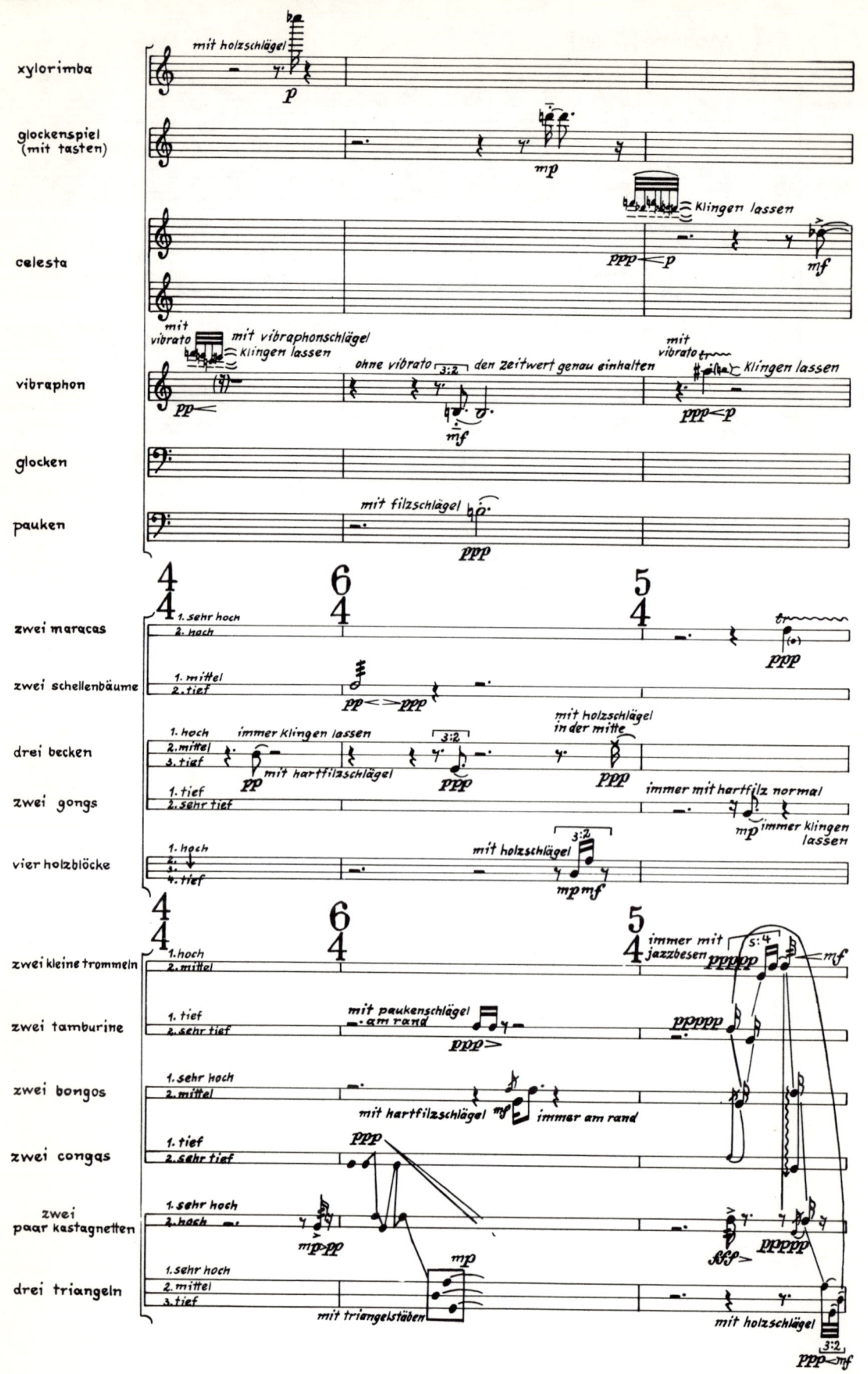

Ex. 89: *(continued on next page)*:

2 Maracas, very high and high;
2 Bell Trees *(Schellenbäume)*, medium and low;
3 Cymbals *(Becken)*, high, medium, low, always let ring *(immer klingen lassen)*, play high cymbal with wooden beater in center; hard-felt beater for the others;
2 Tamtams *(Gongs)*, low and very low, played with hard-felt beater and let ring;
4 Wood Blocks *(Holzblöcke)*, from high to low, played with wooden beater;
2 Snare Drums *(kleine Trommeln)*, high and medium, played with wire brush *(Jazzbesen)*;
2 Tambourines, low and very low, played at rim with timpani stick;
2 Bongos, very high and medium, played with hard-felt beater, always at rim;
2 Congas, low and very low;
2 pairs of Castanets, very high and high;
3 Triangles, very high, medium, and low, first played with triangle rods, then with wooden beaters;
Xylorimba, played with wooden beater;
Keyboard Glockenspiel *(Glockenspiel mit Tasten)*;
Celesta (let ring);
Vibraphone, played with vibraphone mallets: with vibrato—let ring; without vibrato—observe time-values precisely; etc.;
Chimes *(Glocken)*;
Timpani *(Pauken)*, with felt beaters.

(Ex. 89:   Bo Nilsson: *Ein irrender Sohn*)

Ex. 90:   18 Anvils in various locations backstage.
(Richard Wagner: *Das Rheingold*)

Ex. 91: 6 Automobile Brake Drums, 2 Sistrums, Water Buffalo Bells, Japanese Temple Gong, Muted Gongs, Tamtam struck at the edge and in the center.
(John Cage and Lou Harrison: *Double Music*)

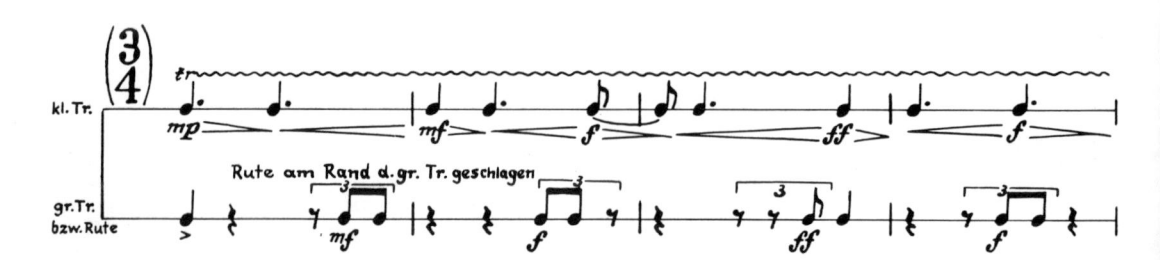

Ex. 92: Snare Drum with snares off (muted), Switch beaten against the shell of a Bass Drum.
(Alban Berg: *Wozzeck*)

227

Ex. 93: Wasamba Rattle, Guíro, Bin-Zasara, Rattles, Taiko, 2 Congas.
(Carl Orff: *Prometheus*)

Ex. 94: 4 Castanets (different sounds).
(Luigi Nono: *The Red Cape*)

Ex. 95: Castanets--wooden (*de bois*) and metal (*de fer* = Cymbal Tongs).
(Darius Milhaud: *L'homme et son désir*)

Ex. 96: Glockenspiel *(Gl.)*, Triangle (△), Suspended Cymbal (⊥), 2 Tamtams (♂ & ♀), 6 Temple Blocks, 15 Tubular Bells *(Röhrenglocken)*.
(Nikos Mamangakis: *Konstruktionen*)

Ex. 97: Large, low, wooden Slit Drum *(grosse tiefe Holztr.)*, Timpani, muffled *(coperti)*; Bass Drum, muffled *(coperto)*.
(Carl Orff: *Antigonae*)

Ex. 98: Hyoshigi, Taiko, Wooden Barrel *(Fass)*, Timpani *(Pk.)*, Wooden Board *(Schlagbrett)*.
(Carl Orff: *Prometheus*)

Ex. 99: Guiro and other percussion instruments.
(Igor Stravinsky: *Le Sacre du printemps*)

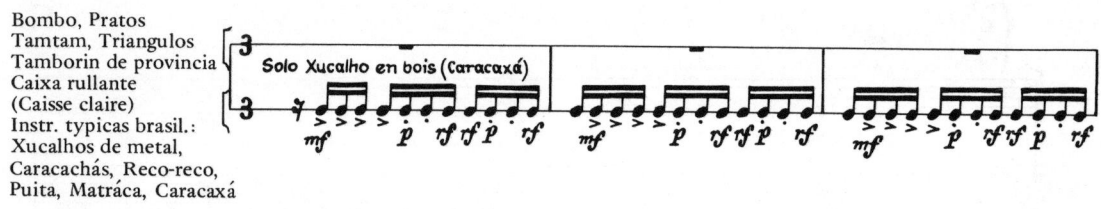

Bombo, Pratos
Tamtam, Triangulos
Tamborin de provincia
Caixa rullante
(Caisse claire)
Instr. typicas brasil.:
Xucalhos de metal,
Caracachás, Reco-reco,
Puita, Matráca, Caracaxá

Ex. 100: Caracaxá (scraper of serrated wood), see list of Latin-American Percussion Instruments on page 179.
(Heitor Villa-Lobos: *Choros No. 8*)

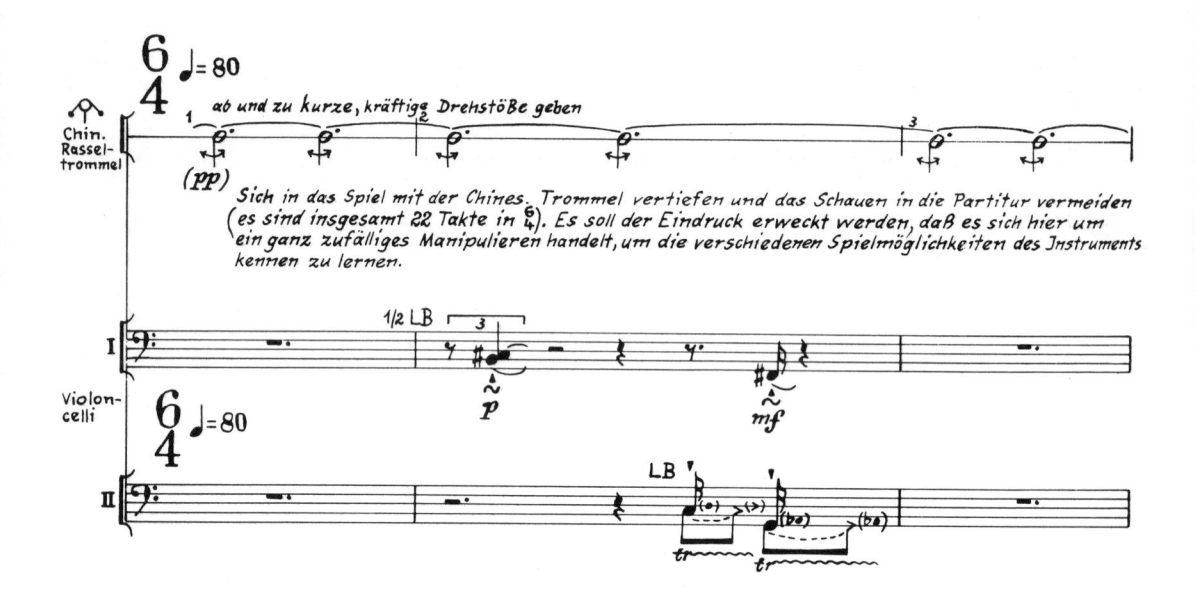

Ex. 101: Chinese Paper Drum and other instruments.
(Mauricio Kagel: *Match for Three Players*)

Ex. 102: Sleigh Bells (*Schellen*), tuned.
(W. A. Mozart: *Schlittenfahrt*)

231

Ex. 103: Timpani, Tubular Chimes, Snare Drum (with rim shots), Bass Drum, Ratchet, Tin Horn (metal rattle), Cowbell.
(Morton Gould: *Declaration Suite*)
© 1956 by G. & C. Music Corporation.

Ex. 104: Jazz Percussion: Drums, Cowbell (= bell without clapper), Tumba, Tubular Rattle (*Rohr*).
(Rolf Liebermann: *Concerto for Jazz Band and Symphony Orchestra*)

Ex. 105: 4 Timpani played at the rim with hard sticks, Xylophone, 4 Bowls of different sizes (glass or china kitchen bowls with a live sound may be used), 4 Small Suspended Cymbals (heavy Balinese cymbals about 6" across were originally used, but 4 metal pipes of different sizes, suspended or laid in cradles, or a Trinidad steel drum, or anything else that will produce light, metallic sounds of different but not precise pitch levels may be used instead of the cymbals).
(Henry Cowell: *Symphony No. 11*)

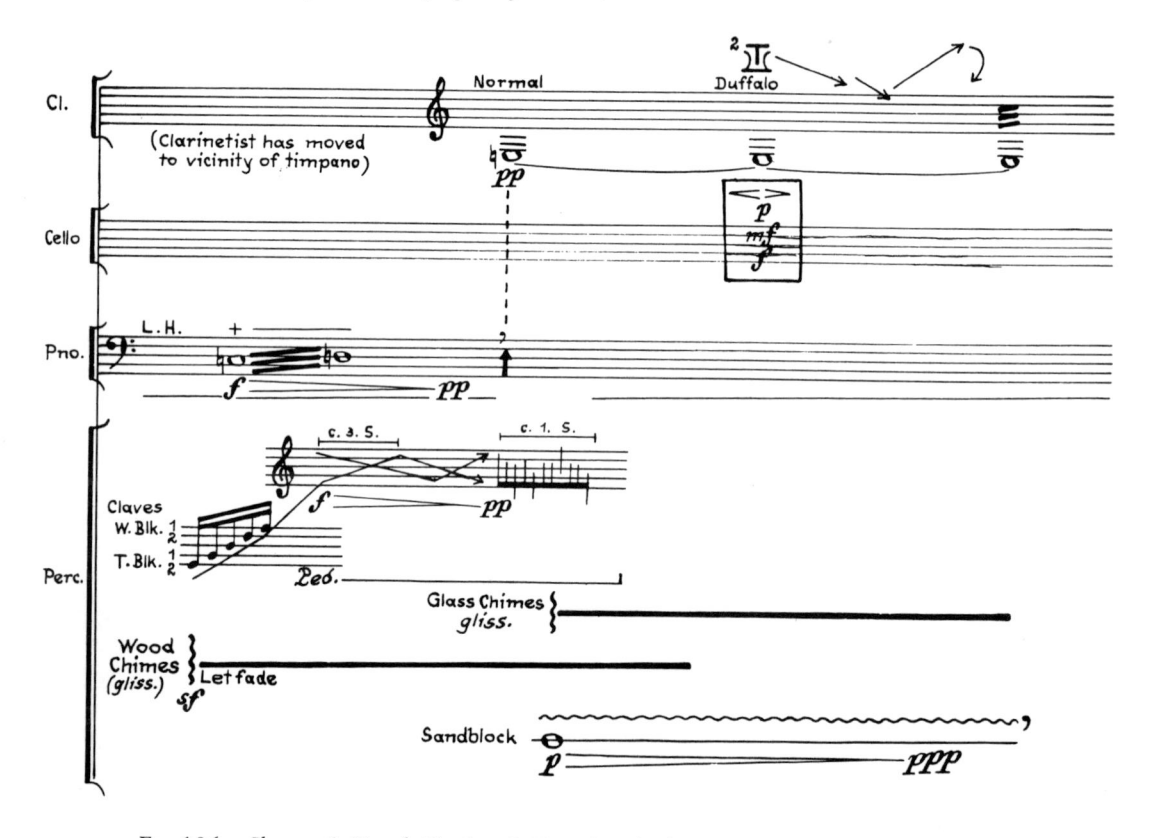

Ex. 106: Claves, 2 Wood Blocks, 2 Temple Blocks, Glass Chimes (suspended glass rods or plates), Wood Chimes (suspended bamboo sections), Sandblock, and other instruments.
(Lukas Foss: *Echoi*)

Ex. 107: Bird Calls: Quail *(Wachtel)*, Nightingale *(Nachtigall)*, Cuckoo *(Kuckuck)*; Ratchet *(Knarre)*, Triangle, Toy Trumpet and Drum *(Trompete u. Trommel)*, other instruments.
(Leopold Mozart: *Toy Symphony*)

Ex. 108: 4 Taxi Horns.
(George Gershwin: *An American in Paris*)

Ex. 109: 1) Crash Cymbal (*Grande cymbale chinoise*), Very Low Bass Drum (*Grosse caisse, très grave*); 2) Gong, High Tamtam (*Tamtam clair*), Low Tamtam (*Tamtam grave*); 3) 2 Bongos, high & low (*clair & grave*), Tenor Drum* (*Caisse roulante*), 2 Bass Drums laid flat, medium & low (*2 Grosses caisses à plat, moyenne & grave*); 4) Military Drum (*Tambour militaire*), Parade Drum* (*Caisse roulante avec cordes*); 5) High *Sirène claire*, Lion's Roar (*Tambour à corde*); 6) Low *Sirène grave*, Slapstick or Whip (*Fouet*), Guíro; 7) 3 Chinese Wood Blocks, high, medium, & low (*Blocs chinois, clair, moyen, & grave*), Claves, Triangle; 8) Snare Drum with snares released (*Caisse claire, détimbrée*), 2 pairs of Maracas, high & low (*clair & grave*); 9) Tarole Drum (a very shallow snare drum), Snare Drum (*Caisse claire*), Suspended Cymbal

©1934 by Franco Colombo Inc., New York.   *(continued on next page)*

*Tenor Drum is translated in the front matter of the published score as "Slide-Drum"--probably an error, since footnote *d* (same score page) includes "tenor drum," (though it does *not* include "parade drum"). This is a typical example of the confusion that encumbers the percussion field and its terminology. (Trsl.)

(Cymbale suspendue); 10) Sleigh Bells *(Grelots)*, Cymbals; 11) Guíro, Castanets; 12) Tambourine *(Tambour de Basque)*, Anvils, 1st very high *(Enclumes, 1er plus aigue)*; 13) Piano, Slapstick or Whip *(Fouet)*.
(Edgard Varèse: *Ionisation*)

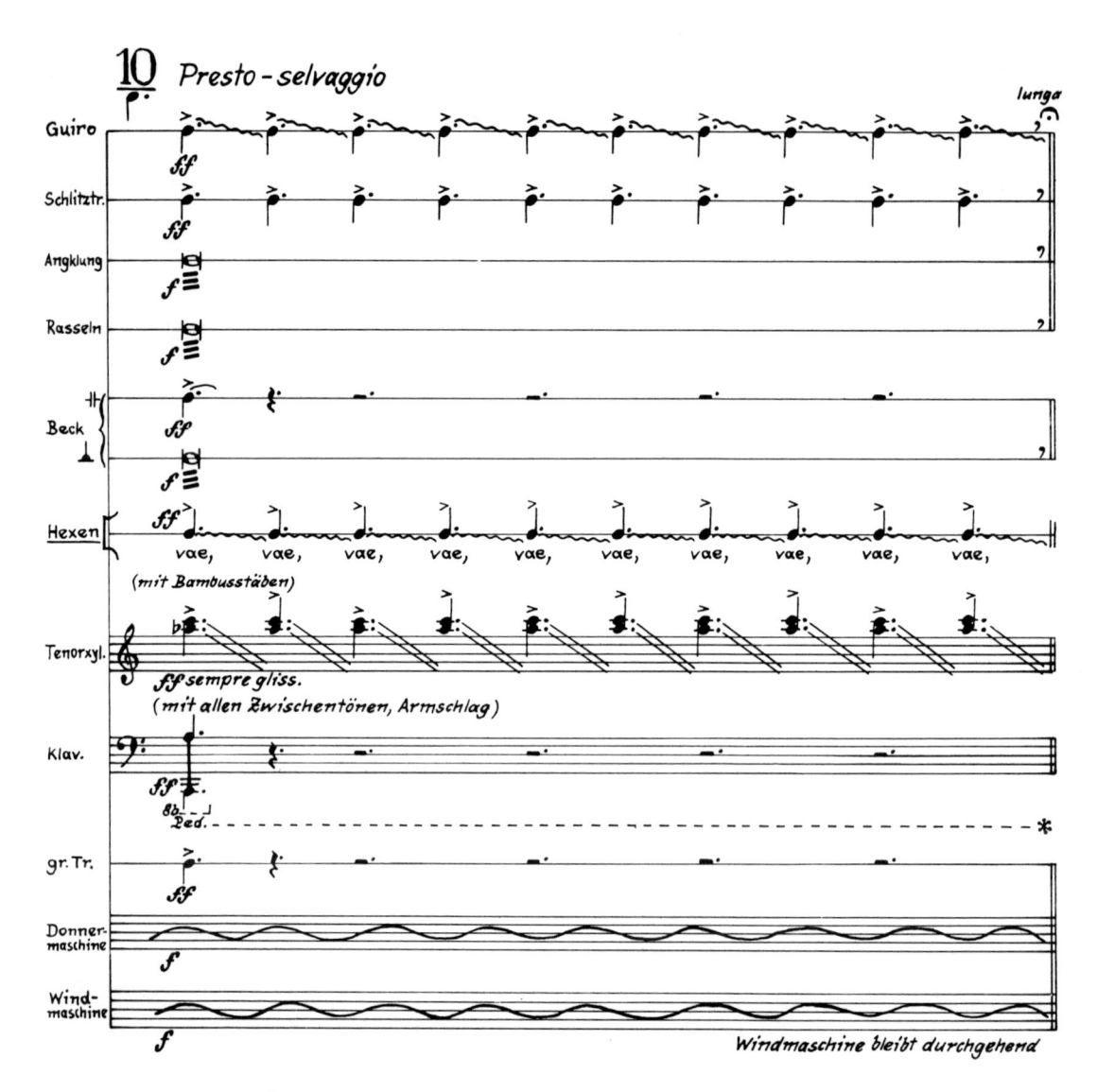

Ex. 110: Guíro, Slit Drum *(Schlitztrommel)*, Angklung, Rattles *(Rasseln)*, Cymbals *(Becken)*, Tenor Xylophone, Piano *(Klav.)*, Bass Drum *(gr. Tr.)*, Thunder Sheet *(Donnermaschine)*, Wind Machine continues throughout *(Windmaschine bleibt durchgehend)*.
(Carl Orff: *Weihnachtsspiel*)

237

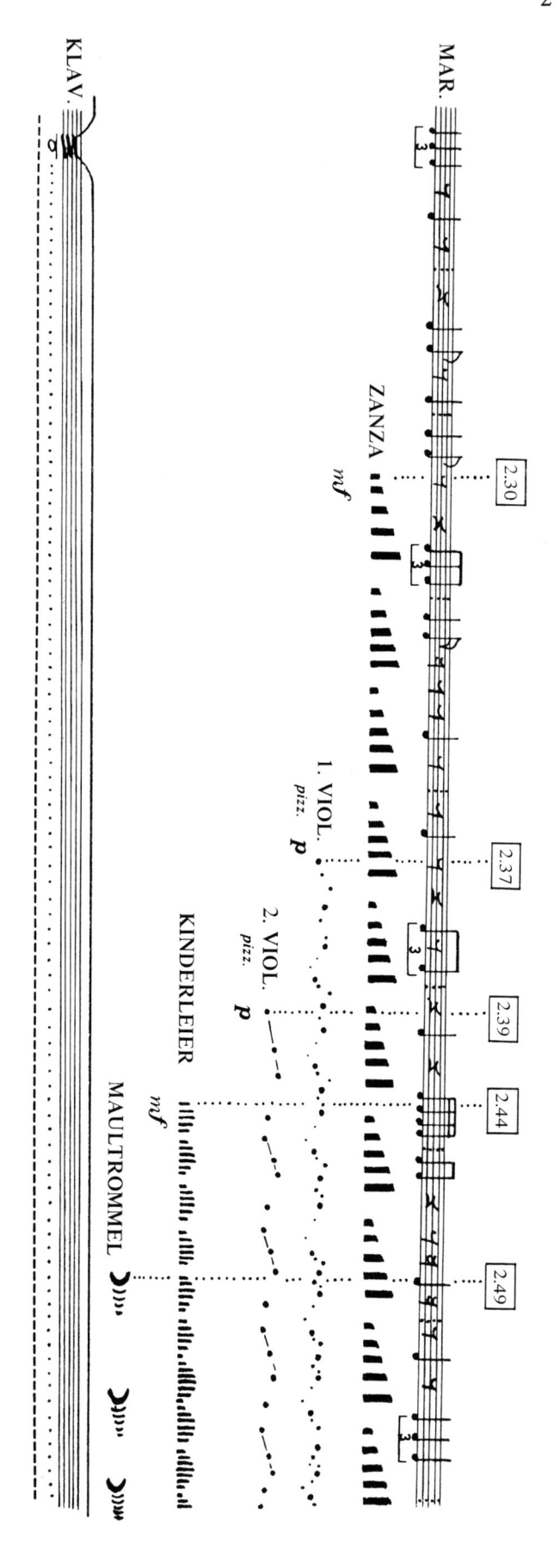

Ex. 111: Marimba, Sansa (*Zanza*), 1st and 2nd Violins, Toy Hurdy-Gurdy (*Kinderleier*), Jew's-Harp (*Maultrommel*), Piano (*Klav.*)
(Walter Haupt: *Lasermusik*)

Bibliography

Avgerinos, Gerassimos — Lexikon der Pauke
Frankfort 1964

-- — Handbuch der Schlag- und Effektinstrumente
Frankfort 1967

Blades, James — The Orchestral Instruments of Percussion, in *Musical Instruments through the Ages* (ed. Anthony Baines)
London and Baltimore 1961

-- — Percussion Instruments and their History
New York 1970

Buchner, Alexander — Musical Instruments through the Ages, trsl. Iris Urwin
London 1956

Casella, Alfredo and Mortari, Virgilio — La tecnica dell'orchestra contemporanea
Milan 1950

Caskel, Christoph — Schlaginstrumente, in *Musik in Geschichte und Gegenwart*, Vol. XI
Kassel 1965

Dauer, Alfons M. — Der Jazz
Kassel 1958

Kotoński, Wlodzimierz — Schlaginstrumente im modernen Orchester (orig. in Polish)
Mainz 1968

Ludwig Drum Company — The Ludwig Drummer
Chicago 1964

Malm, William P. — Japanese Music and Musical Instruments
Tokio and Rutland, Vt. 1959

Marfurt, L. — Musik in Afrika
Munich 1957

Prieberg, Fred K. — Lexikon der Neuen Musik
Freiburg/Munich 1958

Read, Gardner — Thesaurus of Orchestral Devices
New York 1953

Reinhard, Kurt — Chinesische Musik
Kassel 1956

Sachs, Curt — Reallexikon der Musikinstrumente
Berlin 1913

Sachs, Curt *(Cont'd)*	Handbuch der Musikinstrumentenkunde Leipzig 1920
--	Die Musikinstrumente Indiens und Indonesiens Berlin 1923
--	Geist und Werden der Musikinstrumente Berlin 1929
--	The History of Musical Instruments New York 1940
Valentin, Erich	Handbuch der Instrumentenkunde Regensburg 1954
White, Charles L.	Drums through the Ages Los Angeles 1960

Index

Page numbers in italics indicate main entries; an asterisk (*) following a page number indicates an illustration (picture); an x following a page number indicates a musical illustration.

Abbreviations (instruments), 17
Adam, A.
   Le Postillon de Longjumeau, 139
Aelophon, 16
Aerophones, 31
Afoche, 179
Afoxe, 179
African Drums, 12, 108, 111
African Gourd Sistrum, 158
Afro-Cuban Dances, 131
Agógo, 178
Alarm Bell, 13, *134f, 135**
Alarmglocke, 13
Albero di sonagli, 13
Almglocken, 13, 32, *130ff*
Alpine Herd Bells, 13, *130**
Ambira, 76
Amboss, 13
American Indian Drums, 12, *98*f*
Amplification, 83
Angklung, 15, 83, 156, *160f, 161**
Animal Bells, 13, *130ff*
Animal Voices, 171
Antheil, G.
   Ballet mécanique, 175
Antique Cymbals, 10, 55, *60f*
Antoniou, Th.
   Epilogue for Soprano and Chamber Ensemble, 33, *184x*
Anvil, 13, 32, 83, *136**
Applikatur, 91
Arabian Hand Drum, 12, *105*f*
Arabische Trommel, 12
Arenaiuolo, 15, *165*
Armonica di vetro, 11
Atari-gane, *129f*
Auber, D. F.
   Fra Diavolo, 87
Autohupe, 16
Automobile Brake Drums, 13, *137**, 175
Automobile Coil Springs, *175f*
Automobile Horn, 16, *171f, 172**
Ayacaxtli, 179

Bacchette di vetro sospese, 16
Bach, J. S.
   Schlage doch, gewünschte Stunde, 53
Backbone, *35,* 37, 39
Baguettes de verre suspendus, 16
Bak, *140**
Balais de metal, 57
Bambola, 178
Bamboo, 138, *142*
Bamboo Brush, *29**
Bamboo Chimes, hanging, 156
Bamboo Chimes, suspended, 15, *167**
Bamboo Clappers, 141, *142*
Bamboo Rattle, 15
Bamboo Scraper, 15, 152, *154f,* 179
Bamboo Shaker, Brazilian, 15
Bamboo Slit Drum, 146
Bamboo Sticks to imitate noise of wind, *173*
Bamboo Strips, 138
Bamboo Tubes, 152
Bambou brésilien, 15
Bambou suspendu, 15
Bambù brasileño, 15, 152, *154,* 155*
Bambù brasiliano, 15
Bambù sospeso, 15
Bambusraspel, 15
Bambusrohre, hängend, 15
Bambustrommel, 12
Banya, *110*f*
Baril de bois, 14
Barile di legno, 14, *151*
Barile di sake, 14
Bar Instruments of the Orff *Schulwerk, 80ff*
Barra di sospensione con i sonagli, 13
Barrel, *150f,* 151*
Barrel Drum, 14
Barrel-Shaped Hand Drums, 105
Bartók, B.
   Bluebeard's Castle, 47, 190x
   Dance Suite, 123
   The Miraculous Mandarin, 46, 96, 121
   Music for Strings, Percussion, and Celesta, 38, 40, 46
   Sonata for Two Pianos and Percussion, 38, 40, 46, 90, 96, 118
   Violin Concerto, 38f
   The Wooden Prince, 46
Basel Technique [of drumming], *91f*
Basler Trommel, 11, 84, *86f,* 87*
Bass Drum, 12, 33f, 83, 90, *94ff,* 95*, 103, 111, 114f, 118, 120, 131, 138, 177
Bass Drum and Cymbal, 121
Bass Drum Mallets, 27*, 179
Bass Drum, muffled, 178
Bass Drum Pedal, 96
Bass Drum Players, 94
Bass Drum Tuning, 95
Bass Drum with Pair of Cymbals, 120
Bass Metallophone, *58,* 80
Bass Timpano, 36
Bass Xylophone, 10, 41f, *48*ff,* 80
Bass Xylophone Mallets, *22**
Basse de flandres, 16
Bayreuth, 66f
Beaten Rattles, *156ff*
Beaters for *Schulwerk* Instruments, 80*
Beaters, measurements, 20-30
Beaters, specified, 33
Beaters, Table of, *19-30*
Beating-Noises, 33
Becken, 120
Becken, chinesisches, 13
Becken, hängend *or* auf Ständer, 13
Becken mit Fussmaschine, 13
Becken, paarweise, 13
Beethoven, L. van, 73
   Egmont, 87
   Symphony No. 9, 120
   Wellington's Victory, 87, 152, 174
Beguine, 117, 131
Beinklapper, 14
Bell, 10, 31, 33, *64f,* 177
Bell Casting, *64f*
Bell Clapper, metal, *29**
Bell Lyra, 53

Bell of cast bronze, 134
Bell Piano, 66
Bell Plate Mallets, *28**
Bell Plates, 11, 65, *67ff*, 70
Bell Plates, set of, 69
Bell Plates with Resonators, 63, *68**
Bell Strap, Indian, 15, *163**
Bell Substitutes, *65f*, 70
Bell Tree, 13, 132f, *133**
Bell Tree, Far-Eastern, 134*
Bells, bowl-shaped, 131f
Bells, electro-acoustical, 64, 66
Bells, electro-mechanical, 66
Bells of wood, 130
Bells on tape, 64, 67
Bells, semispherical, 66
Berg, A.
   Lulu, 57, 115, 121 (prologue), 127, 138, 148, 175, 216x
   Three Pieces for Orchestra, 40, 45, 57, 75, 152
   Der Wein, 55
   Wozzeck, 40, 45, 121, 138, 218x, 226x
Berger, Th.
   Concerto manuale, 46, 58
   Symphonie chronique, 70
Berio, L.
   Circles, 33f, 58, 111, 124, 132, 138, 142, 145, 150, 154, 164, 167f, 171, 181x, 198x, 214x
   Epifanie, 132, 175
   Passaggio, 150, 168
Berlioz, H., 33, 61, 121
   Requiem, 40, 88
   Roman Carnival, (overture), 102
   Symphonie fantastique, 39f, 94, 185x
   Symphonie Roméo et Juliette, 61
   A Treatise upon Modern Instrumentation and Orchestration, 102
Bicchieri di vetro, 11
Big Drum, 12
Bin-Zasara, 14, 138, *140*f*
Birch Branches, 138
Birch Brush, *29**
Bird Calls, 32, *170f*
Bird Whistle, 16, *170*f*
Birger-Blomdahl, K.
   Play for Eight, 154
Bizet, G.
   L'arlésienne suite, 85
   Carmen, 102, 144
   Farandole and Pastorale, 85
Blacher, B.
   The Moor of Venice, 103
Bladder and Strings, 16
Blechtrommel, 11
Bloc chinois, 14
Bloc de bois, 14
Bloc de bois cylindrique, 14
Bloc de métal, 13
Bloc en bois, 14
Blocco di legno, 14
Blocco di legno coreano, 14
Blocco di metallo, 13
Block, Korean, 14
Board Clappers, 14

Boards, small, *138ff*
Boi, 177
Boito, A.
   Mefistofele, 66
Bolero (dance), 117
Bombo, 177
Bones, 14, 138, *139f*, 140*
Bones, notched, 142
Bonghi, 12
Bongo Drums, 12, 36, 83, 99, *105ff*, 108*, 115, 142
Bongo Drums, Mexican, *106f*
Bongo Drums, notation, 108
Bongo Drums, playing technique, *107f*
Bongo Organs, 115
Bongo-Trommeln, 12
Bongo Tunings, 107
Boobam, 12, 83, *99*f*
Boobam Set (bamboo) in keyboard order, 99*
Boobam Set (rectangular) in keyboard order, 100*
Bottiglia, suono di, 11
Bottles, tuned, 11, *73f*, 74*
Boulez, P., 56
   Le Marteau sans maître, 45, 48, 58, 108, 164
   "pli selon pli," 47f, 61, 69f, 131
   Le visage nuptial, 61
Bounce Stroke (Hand Drums), *107, 109*
Bourdon, 12
Bouteillophone, 11, *73f*, 74*
Bowed Idiophones, 31
Bowl-Shaped Bells, small, 32, 83
Bozza, 40
Brake Drums, Automobile, 13, *137**, 175
Brass Hammers, small, *23**
Brazilian/Indian Instruments, 177
Brazilian Samba Music, 160
Brettchenklapper, 14
Britten, B.
   Nocturne for Tenor Solo and Chamber Ensemble, 40, 188x
   Noye's Fludde, 132
   The Prince of the Pagodes, 36, 46, 58, 61, 88, 110, 137
   The Rape of Lucretia, 139
   The Turn of the Screw, 70
   War Requiem, 139
   The Young Person's Guide to the Orchestra, 139
Bronze-Bar Instruments, 53
Bronze Bells, 32, *64f*, 83
Bronze Disks, Chinese, 137
Bruckner Beaters, 39
Bruit de sonnailles des troupeaux, 13
Bruit de tôle, 16
Brummtopf, 12, *103f*, 104*
Brushes, 19
Brushes, birch or split bamboo, *29**
Brushes, sheet-metal strips or wire, *30**
Buckelgong, 11
Bumbass, 16, *169*f*
Bumbass, notation, 170x
Bunched Bamboo Chimes, suspended, 168*
Bunched Sleigh Bells, *162*f*
Butterfly Cocoons, 179
Buttibu, 12
Büttner, F., 40

Cabaquinha, 177
Cabaza, 15, 156, *159f*, 160*, 179
Cabaza, modern, 160*
Caccavella, 12
Cage, J., 79, 128
   Amores, 115, 147
   First Construction in Metal, 125, 128, 132, 137, 169, 221x
   Imaginary Landscape No. 2, 105
   Quartet, 116, 216x
   Third Construction, 105, 149, 159
Cage, J., and Harrison, L.
   Double Music, 63, 127f, 132, 137, 157, 226x
Caisse claire, 12, *89f*
Caisse claire détimbrée, 90
Caisse claire sur le bois, 94
Caisse roulante, 11, *88**, 90
Caisse roulante avec cordes, 11
Caisse roulante avec timbre, 90
Caixa, 177
Caixa da rufo, 177
Caixa de campanha, 177
Caixeta, 178
Calotte-Shaped Bells, 133
Calottes, 64, *66*, 132
Calypsotrommel, 11
Campainha, 177
Campana d'allarme, 13
Campana di legno, 14
Campana grave, 11
Campana in lastra di metallo, 11
Campanaccio di metallo, 13
Campane, 70
Campane da pastore, 13
Campane tubolari, 11
Campanelle da messa, 13
Campanelli, 10, 32, 53, 55
Campanelli a tastiera, 10
Campanelli giapponese, *58**
Campanello d'allarme, 13
Campãnuela, 177
Cane Switch, *29**
Cannon Shot, 16, *174*f*
Caracacha, 179
Caracaxà, 179
Caraxa, 179
Cardboard Box, shallow, 179
Cariglione, 10
Carillon, 10, 46, 53, 55, 132
Carimbo, 178
Carraca, 178
Carrilhão, 177
Carta sabbiata *or* vetrato, 16
Carter, E.
   Double Concerto for Harpsichord and Piano with Two Chamber Orchestras, 148, 154
   Eight Pieces for Four Timpani (one player), 40
   Pocahontas, 98, 165, 211x
Cascabeles, 179
Cascavels, 179
Cassa chiara, 89
Cassa di legno, 14
Cassa rullante, 11
Cassa sola, 94, 120

Cassettina di legno, 14
Cast Bronze Bell, *65**, 134
Cast Tamtam, 126
Castagnette de fer, 14, 138, 144f, 145*
Castagnette di ferro, 14
Castanea, 142
Castanet Holder, 144*
Castañeta, 142
Castanets, 14, 33, 102, 138, *142ff*, 143*, 178
Castanhetas, 178
Castiglioni, N.
   Ode, 173
Cataca, 179
Catena, 15
Catuba, 12
Caxambu, 178
Celesta, 10, 46, 51f, *56*,
Cencerro, 13, *130f*
Center Dome (of Gong), 63
Cerha, F.
   Spiegel V, 169
Chabrier, E./Française, I.
   Souvenir de Munich, 79
Chailley, J.
   La Dame à la Licorne, 83, 97, 210x
Chain Rattles, *166*
Chain Whip, *166*
Chaîne, 15
Chains, 15, 156, *166**
Chapeau chinois, 13
Charleston Beckenmaschine, 13
Charleston Machine, 124
Charpentier, G.
   Louise, 56, 87, 145, 163
Chávez, C.
   Sinfonía India, 98, 142, 154, 165f
   Toccata for Percussion Instruments, 90, 98
Cheese Grater, 155
Chestnut, 142
Chimes, 10, *64f*
Chimes, Bamboo, 15, 156, *167**, *168**
Chimes, Glass, *167f*, 168*
Chimes, Shell, 16, *167f*, 168*
Chimes, Wood, *167f*
China Cup *or* Plate, 178
China Dishes, 175
Chinese Bronze Disks, 137
Chinese Cymbals, 13, 119, *125**
Chinese Paper Drum, *161f*, 162*
Chinese Rattle Drum, *161f*, 162*
Chinese Tom-Toms, 12, *111ff*, 112*
Chinese Wood Blocks, 112, 146
Chocalho, 15, *165*, 179
Chocalho de madeira, 179
Chocalho de metal, 178
Chocallo, 15, *165**, 179
Chopstick, Chinese, 153
Chordophones, 31
Chucalho, 15, 165
Church Bells, 11, *64*, 70
Church Ratchet, *152f*
Cimbali antichi, 10
Cimbalini, 14
Cinelli, 13

Circus Drum, 121
Clacson, 16
Clapper, Metal, 19
Clapper (of Bell), 65
Clapper, strung, 14, 138, *141*
Clapper, wooden, 14, *138f*
Clappers, 31, *138ff*
Clappers, orchestral, 139
Claves, 14, 138, *141*f*
Claves made of steel, 142
Clay Vessels, 152, 179
Clementi, A.
    Informel No. 1, 154, 157
Climatic conditions, 35, 38
Cliquette, 14
Cloche en lame de métal, 11
Cloche, grande, 11
Clochette, 13
Clochettes à mains, 13
Clochettes pour la messe, 13
Close Roll, 92
Closed Stroke (Hand Drum), *107, 109*
Coconut Shells, 16, 171
Cocteau, J., 74, 97
Coins, Jingling, 166
Colgrass, M.
    Variations for Four Drums and Viola, 116
colla mano, *21**, 39, 73
con la mano, *21**
Concert Snare Drum, 89
Concussion Bells, cast, 132
Concussion Blocks, 14, 138, *141**
Concussion Sticks *or* Rods, *138*
Conga (dance), 131
Conga Drum, low, 178
Conga Drums, 12, 99, 105, *107ff*, 115, 142
Conga Drums, playing technique, *109f*
Conga(-Trommel), 12
Conical Hand Drums, 105
Container Rattles, 156, *162ff*, 179
Copland, A.
    Appalachian Spring, 85, 142
    Billy the Kid, 154
    Symphony No. 3, 70, 88, 93, 137, 139, 142
Coquilles noix de coco, 16
Corde di pianoforte (percosse) *or* (battute), 11
Cordes du piano (frappées), 11
Cork-Headed Mallet, *27**
Cork, popping, *175*
Corne d'appel, 16
Coucou, 16
Coup de bouchon, 16
Coup de marteau, 14
Coup de pistolet, 16
Coupes de verre, 11
Cowbells, 13, 32, 83, 117, *130*f*, 131*, 178
Cowbells, set of, 161
Cowell, H., 40, 79
    Ensemble for Strings and Thunder Sticks, 173
    Symphony No. 11, 173, 175, 232x
    Symphony No. 14, 137
Cranked Ratchet, *153*
Crécelle, 15
Crescent, Turkish, 13

Cross-Support Xylophone, 44
Crotales, 10, 14, *60*f*, 80, 138, 144, 157
Crotali, 10, 14
Crotalophone, 61
Crotalum, 132
Crown (of Bell), 64f
Cuban Sticks, 14
Cuban Tom-Tom(s), 12
Cuckoo Call, 16, 170*
Cucolo, 16
Cuica, *104**, 177
Cup (of Bell), 64
Cylindrical Hand Drums, 105
Cymbal Crash, *120f*
Cymbal played with cello bow, 123
Cymbal played with nailfile, 123
Cymbal played with wire brush, 123
Cymbal Set, 62*
Cymbal, single, 31
Cymbal, single, suspended, 122*
Cymbal, Slap-Hand, 124
Cymbal, suspended, 13, 112, *121f*, 122*
Cymbal Tongs, 14, 138, *144*, 145*
Cymbal with Jingling Arm, 124*
Cymbal with Key Chain, 123
Cymbala, 132, 157
Cymbale chinoise, 13
Cymbale suspendue, 13
Cymbales (a 2), 13
Cymbales à pédale, 13
Cymbales antiques, 10, 61
Cymbalphone, 61
Cymbals, 20, 33f, 39, 53, 61f, 92, 94, 112, *118ff*, 131, 178
Cymbals, bowl-shaped, 132
Cymbals, Chinese, 13, *125**
Cymbals, Crash *or* Clash, 13
Cymbals, Hi-Hat, *124f*, 125*
Cymbals, Jazz, 122
Cymbals, method of playing, *120ff*
Cymbals, pair of, 13, 31, 94, 119, *121**
Cymbals, pitch scale, *121f*, 122*
Cymbals struck by mechanical means, 119
Cymbals struck with beaters, 119
Cymbals, Turkish, 125f
Cymbals, use of beaters, *122f*

Dallapiccola, L.
    The Prisoner, 58, 121
Damper, cloth, 96
Damper, felt, 96
Damper Pedal on Vibraphone, 57
Dance Castanets, *143**
Dance Drum, 12, 97
Darabucca, 12, *105*f*
Darabuccas with tensioning-screw mechanisms, 106*
David, J. N.
    Violin Concerto, 61
De Falla: see Falla, M. de
Dead Stroke (Hand Drums), *107, 109*
Debussy, C.
    L'après-midi d'un faune, 61
    Fêtes, 88
    Iberia Suite, 88, 144
    Jeux, 122
    La Mer, 122

243

Delerue, 40
Delibes, L.
    Coppelia, 61
Dense Roll, 92
Derbouka, 12
Derbuka, 12
Dervaux, 40
Desportes, I., 40
Dessau, P.
    In memoriam Bert Brecht, 86
Devil's Violin, 169
Diable des bois, 12
Diavolo di bosco, 12
Dinner Bell, 13, 132, 134
Dinner Gong, 63
Disk-Shaped Mallets, *28**
Djimba, 76
Dobači, 13, 132, *135**
Domed-Gong Mallets, *28**
Domed Gongs, *63*, 126
Donatoni, F.
    Concertino for Solo Timpani, Strings, and Winds, 40
    La fille du régiment, 87
    For Grilly, 154
    Puppenspiel, 154
Donnerblech, 16
Door Chimes, 167
Doorbells, 132, *133*
Double Bell, iron, 178
Double-Bounce Strokes, 92
Double Conical Hand Drums, 105
Drag, 92fx
Drum Guilds of Basel, 86, 91
Drum Heads, synthetic, 89
Drum Sticks, *26**, 177
Drum Sticks, plastic, *26**
Drum Sticks, wooden, *26**
Drums, 31, *84ff*
Drums, African, 108, 111
Drums, Bavarian, 87
Drums, muffled, *89f*, *90**
Drums of American Indians, *98**
Drums without Snares, 33
Dukas, P.,
    L'apprenti sorcier, 54
Dulcimer, 66

Edge (of Bell), 65
Egk, W.
    Abraxas, 70, 133
    Allegria, 148
    Casanova in London, 133
    Die chinesische Nachtigall, 38, 57, 63, 90, 113, 144, 153
    Columbus, 49, 63, 67, 98 (revised version), 133
    French Suite, 63
    Irische Legende, 57, 90, 115, 122
    Joan von Zarissa, 46, 55, 58, 63, 144, 164
    Peer Gynt, 46, 55, 67, 70, 144
    Der Revisor, 108, 139, 148
    Variations on a Caribbean Theme, 57, 108, 110, 115
    Die Verlobung in San Domingo, 57, 110, 121, 124, 148, 175, 213x
    Die Zaubergeige, 57, 70, 86, 121

Einem, G. von
    Dantons Tod, 97
Ekende, 76
Electric Bass, 31
Electric Chimes, 31
Electric Guitar, 31, 75
Electro-Acoustic Amplification, 100
Electro-Acoustical Bells, *67**
Electronic Amplification, 31
Electronic Sounds, 176
Electrophones, 31
Elefantenglocke, 13
Elephant Bell, 13, 134
Elongated Heads on Wooden Mallets, *27**
Enclume, 13
Eoliphone, 16
Éperons, 15
Erkin, U. C.
    Senfoni II, 145
Etingili, 76, 177
Etler, A.
    Concerto for Brass Quintet, String Orchestra, and Percussion, 137
Exorcism of Demons, 138

Falla, M. de
    El Retablo de Maese Pedro, 97, 127f, 132, 153
    The Three-Cornered Hat, 102, 144
    La vida breve, 137
Feet, stamping, 138
Felt Beaters, hard, *21**
Felt Beaters, soft, *20**
Ferrinho, 178
Field Drum, 11, *87f*, 177
Fifes, 84f
Fifes and Drums, 91
Finger Cymbals, 14, *60f*, 138, 144, *145**
Fingerzimbeln, 14
Fischietto a pallina, 16
Fischio, 16
Fischio sirena, 16
Five-Stroke Ruff, 92fx
Flam, 92fx
Flannel-Disk Beaters, *20**
Flaschenkorkenknall, 16
Flaschenspiel, 11
Flauto a culisse, 11
Flessatono, 11
Flexatone, 11, *74f*, 75, 79
Fog Horn, 16, *172*
Foglio di metallo, 16
Foil Rattle, 16, 156, *168*f*
Foot Cymbal(s), 13
Fortner, W.
    The Creation, 88
    Impromptus, 142
    In his Garden Don Perlimplin Loves Belisa, 108
    Symphony, 46
    Der Wald, 58
Foss, L.
    Echoi, 117, 124, 127, 142, 147f, 167f, 171, 220x, 232x
Fouet, 14
Foundry Bells, 53

Four-Note Grace, 92fx
Four-Row Xylophone, *43*f,* 71
Four-Stroke Ruff, 92fx
Frame Drum, 12, 83, 95, *97f,* 98*, 101
Frame Drum, square-shaped, 177
Frame Drum without Jingles, 177
Française, I., 79
Françaix, J.
    Les Zigues de Mars, 171
Franklin, B., 73
Friction Drum(s), 12 31, *103ff,* 177
Fruit-Hust Rattle, 166*
Frusta, 14
Frying Pans, 129
Fukushima, K.
    Hi-Kio, for Flute, Strings, Piano, and Percussion, 142
Fundamental (of Bells), 65
Fussbecken, 13

Gabelbecken, 14, 138, 144, *145**
"Gag" Instruments, 78, *171f*
Galoubet Pipers, *84*
Gambang Gangsa, 53
Gamelan Instruments, 44*
Gamelan Orchestra, 53, 63
Gangarria, 178
Ganza, *165,* 179
Gariglione, 10
Gegenschlagblöcke, 14
Gegenschlagstäbe, 14
Geläute, 13
Gershwin, G., 146
    An American in Paris, 171, 234x
    Piano Concerto in F, 46
    Porgy and Bess, 46, 91, 96, 110, 115, 123, 131, 148, 171
Gerster, O., 40
Ghungrü, 15, *163**
Giant Ratchet, 152
Gielen, M.
    Pentaphonie, 70, 189x
Gitterrassel, 15
Gläserspiel, 11
Glasharfe, 11
Glass-Bell Instruments, 72, 135
Glass Bowls, tuned, 73
Glass Chimes, 16
Glass Chimes, suspended, 156, *167f,* 168*
Glass Dishes, 175
Glass Disks, suspended, 168
Glass Harmonica, 11, 31f, *73*
Glass Harp, 11, *72*
Glasses, tuned, 11
Glasstäbe, hängend, 16
Glazunov, A. K.
    Violin Concerto, 54
Glockenspiel, 10, 32, *51ff,* 80, 132, 157, 177
Glockenspiel à clavier, 10
Glockenspiel, alto-soprano, *81**
Glockenspiel Bar as Anvil, 136
Glockenspiel Beaters, *23*

Glockenspiel, soprano, *80**
Glockenspiel with Pedal Damper, 54*
Gluck, W. von
    Iphigenie en Tauride, 88
Goldenberg, M.: *Modern School for Xylophone,* 46
Gong, 31ff, *62*f,* 126f, 178
Gong, Chinese, 63
Gong, domed, 11, 32, *63*
Gong Drum, 12, 95
Gong, Far-Eastern, 128
Gong giapponese, 63
Gong, Japanese, 129
Gong, Javanese, 63, 126
Gong Sets, 63
Gordon, G.
    The Rake's Progress, 39, 79, 91, 172
Gould, M.
    Declaration Suite, 93, 131, 153, 165, 231x
    Latin-American Symphonette, 38, 48, 93, 115, 148, 154
    Minstrel Show, 171
    Spirituals, 171
Gounod, Ch.
    Faust, 87
    Philemon et Baucis, 137
Gourd, 15, 152
Gourd, hollow, 179
Gourd Rattle, 15, *156*
Gourd Scraper, 15, *152f,* 154*
Gourd Sistrum, African, 158
Gourd Vessel, 179
Gourd Xylophone, 44
Grabmann, M., 77
Grace Notes (Drum), 92f
Grail Bells, *66*,* 79, 84
Grancassa *or* gran cassa, 12, 90, *94,* 120
Grancassa a una pelle, 12
Gran cassa e piatti, 94
Gran tamburo vecchio, 11
Grand tambour, 11
Grande cloche, 11
Grande xylophone, 47
Graphic Notation, 77
Greek Cymbals, 10
Grelots, 15
Grido di corno, 16
Grosse caisse, 12
Grosse caisse à pied avec cymbals, 125
Grosse caisse à une seule peau, 12
Grosse Trommel, 12
Grosse Trommel, einfellig, 12
Grosses Klappholz, 141
Guaracha, 15, *117*
Guiro, 15, 152, *153f,* 154*, 179
Guitcharo, 15, *179*

Hammers, 14, 19, *22*, 23*, 24*, 29,* 145, 151f, *152**
Hammerschlag, 14
Hand Bells, 13, *132*f*
Hand Drums, *105ff*
Hand Drums, Arabian, *105*f*
Hand Drums, playing technique, *107ff*
Hand-Screw Timpani, 36
Handel, G. F.
    Saul, 53

Handglockenspiel, 13
Handle Bell, 132
Handle Castanets, *143*f*
Handle Castanets, flat, 178
Hands, 21
Hands, clapping, *138f*
Hanging Board, oblong, *152*
Hard-Felt Beaters, *21**
Hard-Rubber Mallets, *24**
Hardwood Hammers, small, *29**
Harmonica de verre, 11
Harness Bells, 15
Harrison, L.
   Canticle No. III, 137
   Double Music, see: Cage J. and Harrison L.
Hartmann, K. A.
   Concerto for Piano and Orchestra, 115
   Concerto for Piano, Winds, and Percussion, 46, 48, 58, 90
   Concerto for Viola and Orchestra, 48, 58, 115, 148
   Gesangsszene, 48
   Simplicius Simplicissimus, 46, 90, 122f
   Symphony No. 2, 46, 58
   Symphony No. 3, 46
   Symphony No. 6, 40, 46, 48, 56, 58, 90, 122, 189x, 190x
   Symphony No. 7, 36, 46, 48, 55, 58, 70, 90, 115, 117, 122, 187x, 217x
   Symphony No. 8, 40, 46 48, 55f, 58, 70, 185x, 192x, 194x
Haubenstock-Ramati, R.
   Credentials, 122
   Vermutungen über ein dunkles Haus, 64, 148, 169, 201x
Haupt, W.
   Apeiron, 123, 191x
   Lasermusik, 77, 237x
Haydn, J., 138
   Military Symphony, 94, 112, 210x
Heider, W.
   Konflikte, 110, 124, 132
Henze, H. W.
   Antifone, 33f, 48, 58, 61, 90, 103, 115, 119, 122, 126, 132, 182x, 183x, 212x
   El Cimarron, 78, 135, 150
   Elegy for Young Lovers, 33, 38ff, 48, 56ff, 61, 70, 75, 102f, 115, 119, 122f, 126, 128x, 132, 137, 180x, 186x, 187x, 196x, 200x, 201x, 202x, 211x
   Das Floss der Medusa, 111, 135, 168
   Heliogabalus Imperator, 78, 134
   Maratona di danza, 124
   Ode an den Westwind, 48, 90, 164
   Il re cervo, 38, 70, 92x, 102, 115, 128, 142, 186x, 203x, 215x
   Symphonic Etudes, 58, 115, 122
Herd Bells, 13, *130**
Herd-Cowbells, 13, 32
Herdenglocken, 13
Hertel, J. W.
   Symphony with 8 Timpani, 40
Hi-Hat, 13, 119, *124f*, 125*
High Drums, 33

High-Hat, 13
Hindemith, P., 120, 146
   Cardillac, 115, 117, 122f
   Chamber Music No. 1, 46, 54, 122, 165, 172
   Concerto for Orchestra, 139
   Die Harmonie der Welt, 70
   Mathis der Maler, 86, 94
   Sinfonia Serena, 123
   Symphonic Metamorphosis, 70, 90, 113, 122, 127, 215x
Hip (of Bell), 65
Hoffmann, G. M., 53
Holmxylophon, 44
Holzblock, 14
Holzblocktrommel, 14
Holzfass, 14
Holzplattentrommel, 14
Holzraspel, 15
Holz-Tom-Tom, 14
Holztrommel, 14
Homs, J.
   Musica per A 6, 79
Honegger, A., 146
   Antigone, 75
   Danse macabre, 139
   Deliciae Basilienses, 87
   Le dit des jeux du monde, 74
   Jeanne d'Arc au Bucher, 67, 153
   Pacific 231, 88
   Le roi David, 85
Hoofbeats, 16, 148, *171*
Hoop-Crack, 93
Horn-Tipped Beater, *23**
Hourglass Hand Drums, 105
Huehuetl, 178
Hufgetrappel, 16
Hummel, G.
   Die Folterungen der Beatrice Cenci, 163
Humperdinck, E.
   Hänsel und Gretel, 43, 170
   Die Königskinder, 43, 67
Hyoshigi, 14, 138, *141**

Ibeka, 76
Ibert, J.
   Divertissement, 172
   Suite symphonique, 172
Idiophone, plucked, 177
Idiophones, 31
Idiophones, struck, of indefinite pitch, 83
Imitative Instruments, *170ff*
Incudine, 13
Indian (American) Drums, 98f
Indian Bell Strap, 15, *163*
Indian Drum(s) (Tablas), 12
Indianische Trommel, 12
Instruments with Definite Pitch, *35ff*
Instruments with Indefinite Pitch, *83ff*
Iron Bells, 53
Iron Chains, 15, *166*
Iron Double Bell, 178
Iron Pipes, 175

Janáček, L.
  Jenufa, 48
  Kátja Kabanová, 46
  Out of a Death-House, 67, 69, 137, 139, 153, 155, 166
Janissary Music, 94, 101, 118, 120, 138
Janissary Switch, 29*
Japanese Barrel Drum (O-Daiko), 111, *113**
Japanese Metal-Bar Instrument, 58
Japanese Skin Drum, flat, 111, 113
Japanese Temple Bell, *135**
Japanese Wood Chimes, 15
Javanese Gong, *63*, 126
Jawbone, 15, 156, 159*f
Jazz Cowbell, 136
Jazz Cymbals, 122, 124
Jazz Drum, 115
Jazz Tom-Tom, 12
Jazzo-flûte, 11
Jeu chromatique de cencerros, 132
Jeux de timbres, 10, 32
Jeux de timbres à clavier, 10
Jew's-Harp, 31, 77
Jicara de aqua, 178
Jingles, 83, 101, 179
Jolivet, A.
  Cinq danses rituelles, 166
  Concerto for Ondes Martenot and Orchestra, 99f
  Concerto for Piano and Orchestra, 54, 57, 61, 81, 106, 124f, 153
  Lone, for Piano and Orchestra, 124
Jones, D.
  Sonata for Timpani [Solo], 40
Jungle Wood Drum, 14

Kagel, M., 79
  Anagrama, 70, 147, 202x
  Match for Three Players, 121f, 124, 133, 157, 161, 163, 220x, 230x
Kalimba, *76f*, 77*
Kankobele, 76
Kanone, 16
Kasanga, 76
Kastagnetten, 14
Kazoo, 31
Kelemen, M.
  Composé, 96, 104, 170
  Equilibres, 60, 137, 154, 167, 199x
  Der neue Mieter, 110, 137, 167
  Radiant, 110, 137, 149, 167
Kesselpauke(n), 10
Kettenrassel, 15
Kettle Drums, 10, 32, *35ff*, 94, 151
Kettle Drums, small, 177
Keyboard Glockenspiel, 10, 46, 51, *55**f, 157
Keyboard Xylophone, 10, 41 *46f*, 47*
Khatchaturian, A.
  Gayane, 46, 71, 203x
  Piano Concerto, 75, 206x
Killmayer, W.
  La buffonata, 108, 115, 117
  Chamber Music for Jazz Instruments, 48, 108, 110, 117, 142

Killmayer, W. (Cont'd)
  Lorca-Romances, 117, 122
  Le petit Savoyard, 110, 142
  Piano Concerto, 122
  Rêveries, for Soprano, Piano, and Percussion, 91, 93
  La tragedia di Orfeo, 58, 90f, 93, 96, 108, 110, 115, 117, 128, 142, 148, 153
Kinderleier, 77
Kindertrompete, 16
Kitchenware, 175
Klapper, 14
Klappholz, 14
Klaviaturglockenspiel, 10
Klaviaturxylophon, 10
Klaviersaiten, geschlagen, 11
Klaxon, 16
Klaxon à manivelle, *171*
Kleine Trommel, 12, 89
Knarre, 15
Knochenklapper, 14
Kodály, Z.
  Háry János, 46
Kokosnuss-Schalen, 16
Konietzny, H.
  Concertino for Solo Timpani and Percussion, 40
Köper, K. H., 40
Korean Block, 14
Korean Multiboard Rattle, *140*
Korean Multiboard Whip *140**
Korean Temple Blocks, 146
Korngold, E. W.
  Die tote Stadt, 138
Kotoński, W.
  Musique en relief, 38, 58, 88ff, 108, 117, 125, 154, 164, 197x, 217/218x
Kramer, G., 36
Krauss, C., 66
Kremlin Bell, *64*, 67
Krenek, E.
  Karl V, 173
  Der Zauberspiegel, 62
Krotalen, 14
Krotalon, 132
Kubelik, R.
  Libera nos, 133
Kuckucksruf, 16
Kuhglocke(n) ohne Klöppel, 13
Kürbisraspel, 15
Kýmbe, 120

Lalo, E.
  Le roi d'Ys, 88
  Symphonie espagnole, 88
Landsknechtstrommel, 11
Lastra dal tuono, 16
Lastra di metallo, 13
Lastra di sasso, 10
Latin-American Folk and Dance Music, 131, 142
Latin-American Folk Instruments, 128, *177ff* (list of)
Latin-American Rhythmic Sequences, 92x, 154x
Latin-American Timbales, 83

Leather-Covered Mallets, *27**
Leather-Wound or Banded Wooden Beaters, *20**
Legnetti, 14
Leoncavallo, R.
   I Pagliacci, 70, 121
Lero lero, 15
Lever Timpani, *36f, 37**
Lids of Garbage Cans, 175
Liebermann, R.
   Composition for Machines, 176
   Concerto for Jazz Band and Symphony Orchestra, 110, 124, 131, 165, 231x
   Geigy Festival Concerto for Drum (Basler Trommel) and Orchestra, 87, 91, 209x
Ligety, G.
   Apparitions, 175
   Aventures, 175
Likembe, 76
Lilimba, 76
Lion's Roar, 12, *103ff,* 177
Lion's Roar, standing, 104*
Lion's Roar, suspended, 104*
Lip (of Bell), 64f
Lithophone, 10, *59f,* 60*, 137
Litofono, 10
Log Drum, 14, 83, 145, *149f,* 150*
Long Drum, 84, *85*f,* 87, 95, 149, 177
Long Drum (Provençal), 32
Long Drum with snares, 11, *85*f*
Long Drum without snares, 84, 177
Loo-Jon, 10, *58f,* 59*
Lortzing, A.
   Der Wildschütz, 175
Lotos Flute, 11, *78f*
Lottery Wheel, 155
Lotusflöte, 11
Lully, J.-B.,
   Amadis, 85
Lully School, 84
Lumbye, H. C.
   Champagner-Galopp, 175
   Traumbilder, 43
Lun, 76, 177

Macchina da scrivere, 16
Macchina dal vento, 16
Maceta, 179
Machine à écrire, 16
Machine à vent, 16
Mahler, G.
   Symphony No. 1, 121, 128
   Symphony No. 2, 128
   Symphony No. 3, 121, 128, 138
   Symphony No. 4, 163
   Symphony No. 5, 121
   Symphony No, 6, 67, 94, 121, 128, 131, 138, 152, 210x, 219x, 222x
   Symphony No. 7, 39, 121, 131, 188x
Mailloche, *27**, 90, 96, 122
Malaysian-African Tammittam, 32
Mallets, 19, *27**, 179
Mamangakis, N.
   Constructions, 70, 148, 228x

Manino, F.
   Mario e il Mago, 154
Maraca de métal, 15
Maraca di metallo, 15
Maracas, 15, 142, 156, 158, *163f,* 164*f, 179
Marais, M.
   Alcyone, 84
Marbles, 156, *165f*
Marimba, 10, 31ff, 41, 44, *47ff,* 76
Marimbafono, 10
Marimbaphone, 10
Marimbula, 31, *76f, 78**, 177
Marteau, 14
Martello, 14
Martin, F.
   Der Cornet, 87
Maruga, 179
Mascagni, P.
   Cavalleria rusticana, 70, 139
   Iris, 58
Mascella d'asino, 15
Massenet, J.
   Le Cid, 85
Matraca, 178
Matsudaira, Y.
   Figures sonores, 154, 157
Maultrommel, 77
Mayuzumi, T.
   Tonepleromas 55, 75
Mbira, 76
Measurements of Beaters, 20-30
Membrane(s), 32
Membranophones, 31f, 35, 83
Membranophones with pitched skin sounds, 83
Mercenary Soldiers, 85, 90f
Mercenary Soldiers' Drum, 11
Messiaen, O.
   Couleurs de la Cité céleste, 132
   Oiseaux exotiques, 46, 54, 56, 148, 195x
   Réveil des oiseaux, 148, 170
   Sept Haïkaï, 62, 70, 132, 223x
   Turangalîla-Symphonie, 57, 61f, 85, 125, 148, 164
Messklingel(n), 13
Metal-Bar Instruments, 31, *51ff*
Metal Block, 13, 32, 83, *130f, 136*
Metal Castanets, 14
Metal Clapper(s), 19, *29**
Metal Container Rattle, 15, 179
Metal Cylinder Cabaza, 179
Metal Disk, 13
Metal Foil, 156
Metal Hammers, *29**
Metal-Head Mallets, *23**
Metal Instruments, heavy, *136f*
Metal Plates, 66
Metal Plates, tuned, 68
Metal Rasp, 152, *155*
Metal Rattles, 15, 156, *165**
Metal Rattles (Central American), *165**
Metal Rods, *25**
Metal Scraper, 152, *155*
Metallfolie, 16
Metallgefässrassel, 15
Metallkastagnetten, 14

Metallofono, 10
Metallophone, 10, 51f, *58f*
Metallophone, alto, *82**
Metallophone, alto-soprano, *82**
Metallophone, bass, *58, 82**
Metallophone, Japanese, *58*
Metallophone, soprano, *82**
Metallplatte(n), 13
Metallraspel, 15
Mexican Bean, 15, 163*, *164*
Mexican Bongos, 106f
Meyerbeer, G.
    L'africaine, 40
    Le prophète, 40
    Robert le diable, 40
Microphone Beaters, 39
Milhaud, D., 90, 146
    Les choephores, 138, 152, 166, 172
    Concerto for Percussion and Small Orchestra, 85, 125, 131
    Concerto for Vibraphone and Orchestra, 57
    La création du monde, 36, 85, 125, 131, 147, 187x, 208x, 221x
    L'homme et son désir, 139, 145, 152, 172, 227x
    La mort d'un tyran, 85, 139, 153, 209x
    Salade, 85
    Saudades do Brasil, 154
    Suite française, 85
    Suite provençale, 85, 88, 208x
Militärtrommel, 11
Military Drum, 11, 84, 87f, 88*, 90f
Military Drum on stage, 92
Mirliton, 31
Mixtur-Trautonium, 67, 75
Modern Tom-Toms, 111, *114*f*
Mohaupt, R.
    Die Gaunerstreiche der Courasche, 172
Mokubio, 145, *148*f*
Mokugyo, *148*
Moscow Bell, 64
Motor Horn, 16
Mouth (of Bell), 65
Mouth Sirens, *172**
Mozart, L.
    Toy Symphony, 152, 170ff, 233x
Mozart, W. A., 73, 138
    Abduction from the Seraglio, 94, 120
    Contra Dances, 87
    The Magic Flute, 55
    Schlittenfahrt, 163, 230x
    Serenade K. 187/188, 40
Muffled Drum, *89f*, 90*
Muffled Stroke (Hand Drums), *107, 109*
Musical Clock, 53
Musical Glasses, *72**
Musical Saw, 11, 31, *74f*
Mussorgsky, M.
    Boris Godunov, 134 (revolution scene), 66, 67 (coronation scene), 127
Mussorgsky, M./Ravel M.
    Pictures at an Exhibition, 94 (Dance of the Chicks in their Shells), 139, 153, 175
Mussorgsky, M/Rimsky-Korsakov, N.
    Khovanshtchina, 66f

Mustel, A., 56

Nacchera cilindrica, 14
Nacchere, 14
Nachtigallenschlag, 16
Nebelhorn, 16
Nightingale, 16
Nightingale Song (recording), 171
Nightingale Whistle, *170f*
Nilsson, Bo
    Ein irrender Sohn, 56, 58, 91, 102, 108, 110, 119, 126, 133, 144, 147, 224/225x
    Reaktionen, 58, 74, 119, 124, 132, 205x
Noce di cocco, 16
Nono, L.
    Canti di vita, 90, 122
    Composizione per orchestra No. 2, 149
    Cori di Didone, 122, 126, 219x
    Diario polacco '58, 150
    España en el corazon, 115, 122
    The Red Cape, 119, 144, 227x
    La terra e la compagna, 122
Notation: Condensed [percussion] Score, 34
Notation: Five-Line Staff, *33f*
Notation: General, *33f*
Notation, Graphic, 77
Notation of Beaters, 33
Notation of "Dry" Instruments, 33
Notation of Instruments with Definite Pitch, 34
Notation of Instruments with Indefinite Pitch, 34
Notation of "Ringing" Instruments, 33
Notation of Snare Drum, 33f, 93x
Notation of Timpani, 36
Notation: Pitch, 32f
Notation: several players, 34
Notched Bones, 152
Nsimbi, 76

O-Daiko (Japanese), 12, 111, *113**
Office Machines, 175
Old Parade Drums, 86*
Onca, 177
Ondes Martenot, 31, 67, 75
One-Man Percussion Band, *169*
Open Roll, 92
Orchestra Bells, 10, 51, *53ff*
Orchestral Chimes, *69f*
Orchestral Clappers, 139
Orchestral Glockenspiel, *53ff*, 54*, 56
Orchestral Sistrum, *157*
Orchestral Tambourin Provençal, 85*
Orchestral Tambourine, 101
Orchestral Triangle, 118
Orchestral Tubular Chimes, *69**
Orchestral Xylophone, *45**
Orff, C., 49, 60
    Antigonae, 36, 39f, 46, 48ff, 54f, 60f, 63, 70, 79, 95f, 102, 121ff, 127, 137, 144, 164, 198x, 200x, 207x
    Astutuli, 60, 73, 108, 123, 172

Orff, C. (Cont'd)
   Die Bernauerin, 36, 39, 49, 55, 58, 60, 70, 79 (witch's scene), 86, 95f, 122, 127, 149, 152f, 160, 165, 192, 206x, 208x
   Carmina Burana, 144, 153, 163
   Catulli Carmina, 50, 58, 161, 164, 193x
   Die Kluge, 60f, 144, 153, 163, 165
   A Midsummer Night's Dream, 104, 123, 132, 153
   The Moon, 55, 61, 72, 123, 153, 172, 204x
   Nänie und Dithyrambe, 61
   Oedipus der Tyrann, 36, 46, 48f, 54, 56, 60f, 63, 70, 73, 79, 95f, 108, 110, 128, 141, 144, 154, 157, 195x, 204x, 221x
   Percussion Orchestras, 101
   Prometheus, 49, 63, 73, 79f, 95, 106, 110, 113f, 125, 141f, 151, 154, 159, 161, 172, 213x, 215x, 227x, 229x
   Das Schulwerk, 72, 97
   Schulwerk Beaters, *80*
   Schulwerk, Hand Clapping, 138
   Schulwerk Instruments, *80ff*
   Trionfi 36, 39f, 48, 54f, 60f, 70, 96, 102, 147, 160, 188x
   Weihnachtsspiel 50, 73, 108, 110, 149, 154, 161, 164, 172f, 236x
Ornamental Bell, 134
Oxen Bells, 132

Packing Crates, 175
Palillos, 177
Pandeiro, 177
Pandereta, 101
Pandereta Brasileño, 15, 156, *158**
Pandéros, 97
Paper Drum, Chinese, *161f, 162**
Papier de verre, 16
Papua, 78
Parade Drum, 11, 84, *86f,* 87*
Parade Drum with snares off, 88
Paradetrommel, 11
Paradiddle, *92*
Parris, R., 40
Parsifal Bells, 66
Partials (in Bells), 65
Pas de cheval, 16
Passerone, 40
Pasteboard Rattle, 12, *103*ff*
Pauken, 10
Pea Whistle, 16, *172**
Pedal Cymbal, 13, *125*
Pedal Mechanism (Bass Drum), 96*
Pedal Timpani, 37*f
Peitsche, 14
Peitschenknall, 14
Pena, A.
   Igorot Rhapsody, 129
Penderecki, K.
   Fluorescences, 176
Petit, 40
Pfitzner, H.
   Das Herz, 172
   Palestrina, 61, 67, 69, 118, 127, 163
   Die Rose vom Liebesgarten, 43, 89
   Von deutscher Seele, 69, 139

Philidor, Jacques, le cadet
   Partition de plusieurs marches, 39, 188x
Piano as Percussion Instrument, *79f*
Piano-String Bells, 64
Piano Strings, struck, 11, 63, *79f*
Piatti (a 2), 13
Piatti a pedale, 13
Piatti sola, 112
Piatto, 92, 94, 120
Piatto cinese, 13
Piatto sospese, 13, 112
Piccolo Timpano, *35f*
Pictograms (instruments), *17*
Pioggia di effetto, 16
Pistol Shot, 16, 175
Pistolenschuss, 16
Pistolettata, 16
Piston, W.
   Violin Concerto, 36
Pitch, definite, 31, 35
Pitch, indefinite, 31f
Pittrich, 37
Plaque de métal, 13
Plastic Beaters, *23**
Plastic Sticks, small, *26**
Platillo, 178
Plattenglocke, 11
Plucked Idiophones, 31, 177
Pluie, de prisme, 16
Pokido, 76
Police Whistle, 16, *172*
Polizeiflöte, 16
Popgun, 16, *175**
Popping Bottle-Cork, *175**
Poulenc, F.
   Le Bal masque, 172
Pousseur, H.
   Euer Faust, 168
Prato, 178
Prepared Piano, 79
Press Rolls, 93
Primitiv Rattles, *156*
Prisme de pluie, 16
   Alexander Nevsky, 46
   Peter and the Wolf, 123
   Romeo and Juliet, 164
   Symphony No. 7, 46
Provenzalische Trommel, 11
Puccini, G.
   La Bohème, 43, 70, 87 (drums on stage)
   Gianni Schicchi, 139
   Madama Butterfly, 58, 63, 171, 175
   Tosca, 67, 69, 87, 175
   Turandot, 49, 63, 70, 175
Puita, 104, 177

Quail Call, *171*
Quasi cannone, 175
Quijada, 15, 156, *159**

Raganella, 15
Rahmentrommel, 12

Rain Machine, 16, *173f*, 174*
Râpe à fromage, 155
Râpe de bois, 15
Râpe de métal, 15
Rasp, 15, 31
Raspa di metallo, 15
Raspador metal, 15
Ratchet, cranked, *153**
Ratchets, 15, 31, 141, *152f*, *153**, 178
Ratsche, 15
Rattle Drum, Tibetan, *161f*, 162*
Rattle Instruments, 32, *156ff*
Rattle(s), 31, 83, *165f*, 179
Rattles, beaten, 83
Rattles of Indefinite Pitch, 83
Ravel, M., 146
   Air de feu, 139, 153, 172
   Alborada del gracioso, 61, 88, 144
   Bolero, 88
   Daphnis et Chloë, 90, 94, 172
   L'enfant et les sortilèges, 79, 153, 155, 172, 206x
   L'heure espagnole, 70, 139, 153
   Piano Concerto, 139
   Rhapsodie espagnole, 144
Reco-Reco, 15, 152, *155**, 179
Recorder, 78
Rectangular Wood Block, *146f*, 147*
Reed Organ, 73
Reed Trumpet, 171
Regenmaschine, 16
Regenprisma, 16
Reibtrommel, 12
Reihenklapper, 14
Reposing Tiger, 155
Reque-Reque, 179
Reso Reso, 15
Resonanzkastenxylophon, 10
Resonaphone, 32
Resonator Barrels, 66
Resonator Tubes (Bass Trough Xylophone), 50
Respighi, L.
   The Fountains of Rome, 55
   The Pines of Rome, 55, 103, 153, 171
Revolver, 16
Revueltas, S.
   Sensemayá, 98, 115, 142
Reznicek, E. N. von
   Traumspiel-Suite, 170
Rhythm Log, 149
Riedl, J. A.
   Piece for Percussion, 70
Rifle Shots, 175
Rim Shot, *93*
Rim Strokes (Hand Drums), *107*, *109*
Rimsky-Korsakov, N.
   Capriccio espagnol, 87
   The Legend of the Tsar Saltan, 175
   Shéhérazade, 87, 102
Ringing-Stones, 60
Ringing Stroke (Hand Drums), *107*, *109*
Rivoltella, 16
Rod Friction Drum, *105*
Rods, 19, 177
Röhrenglocke(n), 11
Röhrenglockenspiel, 11
Röhrenholztrommel, 14

Rolliertrommel, 88
Rolls (Drum), *92f*
Rollschellen, 15
Rolltrommel, 11
Roncador, *104*, 177
Rossini, G.
   The Barber of Seville, 153, 173
   La gazza ladra, 87
Rotary-Tuned Timpani, *37**
Roto Toms, 111, *115**f
Roto Toms, set of, 115*
Roue de la loteri, 155
Roulette Wheel, 74
Round Bells, *162**f
Round Wooden Sticks, *26**
Roussel, A.
   Suite in F, 45
Row Rattles, 156, *166ff*, 179
Rubber Bands, 175
Rubber Mallets, *24**f
Rufhorn, 16, *171*
Ruff (Drum), *92fx*
Rührtrommel, 11
Rührtrommel ohne Saiten, 11
Rumba, 117, 131, 163
Rumba Bands, 108
Rumbakugeln, 15
Rute, 13

Sablier, 15
Sachs, C., 44, 53, 64, 74
   Handbuch der Instrumentenkunde, 121
   Die Musikinstrumente Indiens und Indonesiens, 156
   Reallexikon der Musikinstrumente, 12
Saint-Saëns, C.
   Danse macabre, 43
   La princesse jaune, 63
Sake Barrel (Drum), 14, 145, *150f*, 151*
Sakefass, 14
"Samba Cuke", *154*
Samba (dance), 131, *154x*, 158, *160*, *165x*
Sanctus Bells, 13, *132f*
Sand Blocks, 16, *171**
Sand Paper, 16, 171
Sand Rattle, 156, *165*
Sandblöcke, 16
Sandbox, 15, 156, *165*
Sandi, 76, 177
Sandpapier, 16
Sandrassel, 15
Sanjuan, P.
   Liturgía negra, 117, 131, 142, 154, 164, 222x
Sansa, 31, *76f*, 177
Sanza, *76f*, 177
Sapo cubana, 15, 152, *154f*, 155*
Sarna Bell, 13, 132, *134**
Saron, 53
Sarténes, 13, 126, *128f*, 129*
Satie, E.
   Parade, 74, 138, 155, 172, 175, 204x
Saw, musical, 11, 31, *74f*
Saw, noise of, 155

Scampanellio da gregge, 13
Schalenglöckchen, 13, 32, 83, 131
Schellen, 15
Schellenband, Indian, 15
Schellenbaum, 13, *133**
Schellenbündel, 15, 163
Schellentrommel, 12
Schibler, A.
    Concerto for Percussion and Orchestra, 46, 90f, 93, 96, 119, 122, 148
Schiffsglocke, 13
Schlagbrett, 14
Schlagrassel, 15
Schlitztrommel, 14
Schnarre, 15
Schoeck, O.
    Penthesilea, 138, 152
Schönberg, A.
    Five Pieces for Orchestra, Op. 16, 123
    Die glückliche Hand, 69, 128, 152
    Gurrelieder, 166
    Moses and Aaron, 75, 205x
Schotenrassel, 15
Schreibmaschine, 16
Schultze, N.
    Schwarzer Peter, 172
Schulwerk Beaters, 80
Schulwerk Instruments, *80ff*
Schüttelrohr, 15
Scie musicale, 11
Scraped Idiophones, 31
Scraped Instruments, *152ff,* 179
Scraper, cane, *26**
Scraper, metal, 15
Scraper, wooden, 15
Scratcher, wooden, 15
Screw Timpani, *36**
Scriabin, A.
    Le poème de l'extase, 70
Searle, H.
    The Riverrun, 173
Sega (cantante), 11
Semanterion, 152
Shaken Idiophones, 31
Shakers, 156
Shell Chimes, 16, *167f,* 168*
Ship's Bell, 13, 132, *134f,* 135*
Ship's Whistle, *172*
Shostakovich, D.
    Symphony No. 5, 46
    Symphony No. 6, 46
    Symphony No. 7, 46
Shoulder (of Bell), 65
Side Drum, 11, 84, *89*
Side Drum without snares, 103
Sifflet à coulisse, 11
Sifflet à roulette, 16
Sifflet d'oiseau, 16
Sifflet imité du rossignol, 16
Sifflet signal, 16
Sifflet sirène, 16
Signal Bells of electrical appliances, 66
Signal Whistle, 16, *171f,* 172*
Signalpfeife, 16

Silofono, 10
Silofono a tastiera, 10
Silofono basso, 10
Silomarimba, 10
Sineta, 177
Singende Säge, 11
Single Grace Note, 92fx
Single-Stroke Roll, 92
Sino, 177
Siren, Police, 16
Sirena bassa, 16
Sirene, 16
Sirène, aigue, 16
Sirenenpfeife, 16
Sirens, 16, 172
Sistra, 15, 55
Sistre, 157
Sistro, 32, 55, 157
Sistrum, 15, 55, *156f,* 157*f
Sistrum, notation, 157
Sizzle Cymbal, 119, *123**f
Skin Membranophone, *83ff*
Skins, circular, 32
Slap-Hand Cymbal, 124
Slapstick, 14, 138, *139**
Slate Disks, 60
Sleigh Bells, 15, 32, 133, 156, *162**f
Sleigh Bells, bunched, 15
Slide Whistle, 11, 32, *78f,* 79*
Slit Drums, 14, 83, *145f, 149**, 178
Small Bell, *132*ff*
Small Bell, bowl-shaped, 13
Small Bells, European, 52f
Small Bells, set of, 157
Snare Drum, 12, 33, 84, *88ff,* 89*, 111, 113f, 131, 177
Snare Drum, concert, 89
Snare Drum (salon and dance orchestras), *88f*
Snare-Drum Sticks, see Drum Sticks
Snare Drum Technique, *91ff*
Snares of wire spirals, 89
Sodoku, 113
Soft-Felt Beaters, *20**
Solnhofener Platten, 60
Sonagli a mano, 13
Sonagliera, 15
Sonaglio, 13
Soneria di campane, 10
Sonnette de table, 13
Sound Bow (of Bell), 65
Speroni, 15
Spielsäge, 11
Sponge Beaters, *20,* 33
Spontini, G.
    La Vestale, 94
Spoon Beater, *22**
Sporen, 15
Sproni, 15
Spurs, 15, 156, *157**f
Square-Shaped Frame Drum, 177
Stabglockenspiel, 10
Stabpandereta, 15
Stahltrommel(n), 11
Stamping, 138

Stappare la bottiglia, 16
Steam-Engine Sound, 171
Steel Disks, *136f*
Steel Drums, 11, *63f,* 64*
Steel Plate, 13, *136f*
Steel Plates lying on felt supports, 137*
Steel Rods, square, 65
Steel Sticks, 142
Steeple Bell, 11
Steinspiel, 10
Stempelflöte, 11
Stick over Stick, *93*
Stick Rim Shot, *93*
Stick Scraper, 155
Sticks, *19*, 177
Sticks, plastic *or* wooden, 26*
Sticks, round, wooden, 26*
Stockhausen, K.
   Gruppen for Three Orchestras, 132, 149
   Kontakte, 150, 167
   Zyklus for one Percussion Player, 132, 149
Stone-Disk Instruments, *59f*
Stone Disks, 10
Storm Bell, 13, 134
Strauss, Johann
   Auf einer Jagd, 175
   Champagner-Polka, 175
   Dorfschwalben aus Oesterreich, 171
   Feuerfest (Polka), *170*
   Die Fledermaus, 158
   The Gypsy Baron, 158
   Im Krapfenwaldl (Polka), *170*
   Der Vergnügungszug (Quick Polka), 171
Strauss, Josef
   Plappermäulchen (Polka), 152
Strauss, R., 55
   Alpensinfonie, 131, 172
   Also sprach Zarathustra, 69
   Arabella, 163
   Ariadne auf Naxos, 102
   Don Quichote, 153, 172
   Elektra, 39, 102, 128, 138, 144
   Die Frau ohne Schatten, 58, 63, 73 (last scene), 102, 138, 144, 172
   Friedenstag, 67, 69, 86, 202x
   Intermezzo, 163
   Josephslegende, 61, 121, 172
   Macbeth, 128
   Der Rosenkavalier, 39, 86, 102, 144, 153, 163
   Salome, 39, 43, 56, 102, 128, 144
   Schlagobers, 46, 165
   Die schweigsame Frau, 46, 70
   Till Eulenspiegel, 86, 152
Stravinsky, I.
   The Firebird, 39, 46, 96
   L'histoire du soldat, 90 (March Royale), 96, 102f, 210x
   Les noces, 35, 46, 61, 90, 190x
   Petrouchka, 46, 85, 102, 128
   Le Sacre du printemps, 35, 40, 61, 83, 96, 119, 128, 154, 185x, 199x, 229x
Street Bands, 111
Street Drum, *87f*
Striegler, K., 40
Striking Note (of Bells), 65

String Drums, 12, 31, *103ff,* 177
String-Friction Drum, 105
Strisciatti, 121
Stroked Idiophones, 31
Struck Idiophones, *118ff*
Strung Clapper, 14
Stumpff, J. C. N., 37
Sturmglocke, 13
Sul palco (on stage), 92
Suono di bottiglia, 11
Suono di osso, 14
Surdo, 178
Surf Machine, 16
Surinach, C.
   Ritmo Jondo 138
Suspended Cymbals, 112, 121, *122*f*
Sutermeister, H.
   Raskolnikov, 46, 96
   Romeo und Julia, 123
Swanee Piccolo, 11
Swanee Whistle, 11, *78f*
Swing Ratchet, 178
"Swiss" [Drums], 91
Switch, Bamboo, 138
Switches, 13, 19, *29*, 138**
Symbols for Beaters, 33
Symbols for Instruments, *17*
Synthetic Mallets, 24*
Synthetizer(s), 31

Tabella, 14
Tabla, 12, 105, *110*f*
Tabla-Trommel(n), 12
Table de bois, 14
Tabletas, 178
Tablette, 14
Tablillas, 178
Tabor, 11, *84f,* 101
Taiko, 12, 111, *113,* 114*
Taiko Bass Drum, 151
Taletta, 14
Talking Drums, 146
Tambi-Tambu, 178
Tambor, 177
Tambor-de-Crioulo, 178
Tambora, 177
Tambour, 87, 90
Tambour à corde, 12, 105
Tambour à friction, 12
Tambour arabe, 12, *105f*
Tambour d'acier, 11
Tambour de basque, 12, 32, *101f*
Tambour de bois africain, 14
Tambour d'empire, 11
Tambour en peau de bois, 14
Tambour, grand, 11
Tambour indien (américain), 12
Tambour militaire, 11, 90
Tambour roulant sans timbre *or* sans cordes, 11
Tambour sur cadre, 12, 97
Tambourin, 32, 101
Tambourin grave, 85
Tambourin moyen, 85

Tambourin provençal, 11, *84f*, 85*, 90, 101
Tambourine, 12, 32f, 97, *100ff*, 102*, 158, 177
Tambourine, orchestral, 101
Tambourine without Jingles, 12, *97*
Tambourines mounted on stand, 102*
Tambourins (French, without snares), 84
Tambu, 178
Tambula, 178
Tamburello (basco), 12
Tamburi con corde, coperti, 90x
Tamburi senza corde, 90
Tamburin ohne Schellen, 12
Tamburino, 12, 32, 177
Tamburino senza cimbali, 12
Tamburo, 32
Tamburo alto *or* chiara, 12
Tamburo arabo, 12
Tamburo basco, 12
Tamburo basso, 11
Tamburo d'acciaio, 11
Tamburo di Basilea, 11
Tamburo di frizione, 12
Tamburo di legno africano, 14
Tamburo di legno pelle, 14
Tamburo indiano (d'America), 12
Tamburo militare, 11
Tamburo piccolo, 12, 32, *89*
Tamburo provenzale, 11
Tamburo rullante con corde, 11
Tamburo rullante senza corde, 11
Tammittam, 32, *126*
Tamtam, 32ff, 63, *126ff*, 127*
Tamtam, large, 63
Tamtam, low, 66
Tamtam, Malaysian, 13
Tamtam Mallets, *28**
Tamtam of cast bronze, *126f*, 127*
Tamtam of hammered sheet bronze, *126f*, 127*
Tamtam, playing modes, *127f*
Tamtam, small, 63, 122
Tantā, 178
Tapan, 96
Tarol, 90
Tartaruga, 178
Tavola da lavare, 15
Tavola di legno, 14
Taxi Horn, 16
Tchaikovsky, P.
   Capriccio italien, 102
   Nutcracker Ballet, 102
   Nutcracker Suite, 56, 193x
   Overture 1812, 175
Tchanchiki, 126, *129*f*
Tcherepnin, A., 40
Telephone Bells, 133
Tempelglocke, 13
Temple Bell, Japanese, 13, *135**
Temple Block, 14, 33, 83, 145, *147*f*
Temple Blocks, Chinese *or* Korean, 146
Tenabari, 179
Tenor Drum, 84, *88**, 94, 177
Tenor Drum without snares, 11, 84, *88*, 177
Tenor Trough Xylophone, *49**
Tenortrommel, 11, *88*

Teponaztli, *149*, 178
Teschio cinese, 14
Thärichen, W., 40
   Timpani Concerto, 39
Thimbles, 155
Three-Note Grace, *92f*, 93x
Three-Stroke Ruff, *92f*, 93x
Thunder Sheet, 16, *168*f*, 173
Thunder Sticks, *173*
Tibetan Rattle Drum, *161f*, 162*
Tiefe Glocke, 11
Timbalão, 177
Timbale Sticks, *26**
Timbale(s), 10, 12, 83, *115ff*, 116*, 177
Timbales cubaines, 12, *116f*
Timbales latino-americani, 12
Timbres à clavier, 10
Timbres, jeu de, 10
Timpanetti, 12
Timpani, 10, 17, 31ff, *35ff*, 36*, 37*, 38*, 115
Timpani, backbone, *35*, 37, 39
Timpani Beaters, *20**
Timpani coperti, 39
Timpani, glissandi, 38
Timpani in Baroque music, 39, 188x
Timpani in Classical music, 40
Timpani in Contemporary music, 40
Timpani, notation, 36
Timpani, playing technique, *39f*
Timpani rolls, 40
Timpani setups, 40
Timpani, sound factors, *38f*
Timpani, staccato, 40
Timpani, tuning, *36ff*
Timpano, bass, 36
Tin Rattle, 15
Tischglocke, 13
Tlapanhuehuetl, 178
Toch, E.
   Bunte Suite, 172
   Symphony No. 3, 176
Tocsin, 13
Tôle pour imiter le tonnere, 16
Tomasi, H., 40
   Concerto for Percussion and Orchestra, 106
   Don Juan de Mañara, 56
Tom-Tom, Chinese, *111ff*, 112*
Tom-Tom (chinois), 12
Tom-Tom cinese, 12
Tom-Tom Damper, 114
Tom-Tom (Jazz), 12
Tom-Tom, large, 178
Tom-Tom, modern, 12, 88f, 111, *114*f*
Tom-Tom Set, 83
Tom-Tom, single-headed, *114*
Tom-Tom-Spiel, *115*f*
Tom-Tom, wooden, 14, *150f*, 151*
Tom-Toms, 12, 84, 86, 90, 92, 107, *111ff*, 131
Tom-Toms, tuned, 83
Tonkin Bamboo, 154
Tonkinese Cane, 46
Top Plate (of Bell), 65
Toponaztle, 178
Torocano, 178

Tortoise Shell, 178
Tower Carillon, 132
Toy Hurdy-Gurdy, 77
Toy Trumpet, 16, *171*
Toyama, Y.
    Rhapsody for Orchestra, 130, 149
Train-Conductor's Horn, 171
Trautonium, 31
Tree Trunk, hollow, 178
Triangel, 13
Triangle 13, *118f*, 119*
Triangle, hand-damped, 178
Triangle, playing technique, *118f*
Triangle with jingle rings, *118*, 157
Triangolo, 13
Trillerpfeife, 16
Trinidad, 63
Trinidad Gongtrommel(n), 11
Trocano, 178
Trogxylophon, 10
Trompe d'auto, 16
Trompe de brume, 16
Trough-Shaped Metallophones, 53
Trough Xylophones, 10, 42, 44, *48ff*, 49*
Trough Xylophone, bass, 150
Tubaphone, 11, *71**
Tube(s) de cloche(s), 11
Tubi di bambù, 15
Tubo, 15
Tubofono, 11
Tubular Bell(s), 11
Tubular Chime Hammers, *24**
Tubular Chimes, 11, 65, *69f*, 131
Tubular Drum (provençal), 101
Tubular Rattles, *165**, 179
Tubular Wood Blocks, 14, *146**
Tubuscampanophon, 11
Tubuscampanophone, *71*
Tumba, 12, 105, *108ff*, 178
Tumbadora, 12, 105, *108ff*
Tuned Bottles, 11, *73f*, 74*
Tuned Glasses, set of, *72*f*
Tuned Gongs, 66
Tuned Musical Glasses, 11, *72*f*
Tuoni, 16
Turkish Crescent, *132f*, 162
Turkish Cymbals, 125f
Turkish Drum, 94
Turkish Janissary Music, 94
Turmglockenspiel, 10
Two-Note Grace, *92f*, 93x
Two-Toned Whistle, 170
Two-Row Xylophone, *44*
Typewriter, 16

Uccelli, 16
Upbeat Rolls, 93
Usignuolo, 16

Varèse, E.
    Intégrales, 138, 166
    Ionisation, 88, 90, 93, 95, 105, 108, 125f, 137,
        139, 142, 144, 147, 154, 164, 172, 234-236x

Verdi, G.
    Un Ballo in maschera, 70, 94, 120
    Don Carlos, 67 (in front of the church), 102, 134
    Otello (first act), 174
    Rigoletto, 94
    La Traviata, 94, 102
    Il Trovatore, 69, 70 (scene I), 94, 136 (Gypsy Chorus)
Verga, 13
Verge, 13
Verres choqués, 11
Vibes, 10
Vibra Slap, *159**
Vibrafono, 10
Vibraharp, 10
Vibraphone, 10, 46, 48, *51f, 56ff*, 57*, 70
Vibraphone Mallets, *24**
Vibraphone with two players, 73
Villa-Lobos, H.
    Bachianas Brasileiras No. 2, 165
    Choros No. 8, 155, 230x
    Emperor Jones, 165
    Momo Precoce, 165
    Uirapurú, 154
Vogelpfeife, 16

Waist (of Bell), 65
Wagner Beaters, 39
Wagner, R.
    Götterdämmerung, 122
    Das Liebesverbot, 102
    Lohengrin, 40, 86, 102
    Die Meistersinger, (on stage), 86
    Parsifal, 40, 66f, 86 (on stage)
    Das Rheingold, 136 (Anvil Chorus), 225x
    The Ring, 40, 136 (Forging Songs)
    Tannhäuser, 102, 121, 144
    Die Walküre, 86
Waldteufel, 12, *103*ff*
Walton, W.
    Facade (ballet), 148
Wasamba Rattle, 15, 156, *158*f*
Waschbrett, 15
Washboard, 15, 152, 155
Water Buffalo Bells, 132
Water Gong, 126, *128*
Weber, C. M. von
    Der Freischütz, 139, 166 (Wolf's-Glen), 175
    Preciosa, 102
Webern, A.
    Five Pieces for Orchestra, 131
    Six Pieces for Orchestra, 69f
Weill, K.
    Lost in the Stars, 91, 124, 171
Whip, 14, *138f*, 139*
Whistle Flutes, 171
Whistle, Slide, 11
Wind Chimes, glass, 16
Wind Chimes, shells, 16
Wind Chimes, wood, 15
Wind Machine, 16, *32, 172f*, 173*
Windglocken, Glas, 16
Windglocken, Holtz, 15

Windglocken, Muscheln, 16
Wirbeltrommel, 11, *88**
Wire Brush, *30**, 91
Wire Spirals as snares, *89*
Wood and Straw Instrument, 43, 45
Wood Block, bass (tuned), 83
Wood Block, large, 178
Wood Blocks, 14, 31, 33, *146f*, 147*, 178
Wood Blocks, Chinese, 14, *146*
Wood Blocks, rectangular, 14, *146f,* 147*
Wood Blocks, tubular, 14, *146**
Wood Chimes, Japanese, *167*
Wood-Plate Drum, 14, 145, *150f,* 151*
Wooden-Bar Instruments, 31, *41*
Wooden Barrel, 14, 145, *150f,* 151*
Wooden Beaters, 33
Wooden Board, 14, 145, *150f,* 151*
Wooden Board on Kettle Drum, 151*
Wooden Boxes, 152
Wooden Clappers, 138
Wooden Container Rattle, 179
Wooden Drum, Chinese, 148
Wooden Drum, Japanese, 148
Wooden Drum, large, 178
Wooden Drum, Mexican, 149
Wooden Drums, 14, *145*
Wooden Fish, 147
Wooden Hammer, small, *22**, *23**
Wooden Mallets, *27**
Wooden Mallets with leather-covered plastic heads, *27**
Wooden Rattle, 178
Wooden Scraper, 152, *155**
Wooden Sticks, *26**, 152

Xilofono, 10

Xilofono a tastiera, 10
Xilofono basso, 10
Xilofono in cassetta di risonanza, 10
Xucalho, 179
Xylomarimba, 10
Xylophone, 10, 17, 31, 33, *41ff,* 43*, 44*, 45*, 47*, 48*, 49*, 50, 80, 142
Xylophone à cassette-résonance, 10
Xylophone à clavier, 10
Xylophone, alto, *81**
Xylophone, alto-soprano, *81**
Xylophone, bass, *82**
Xylophone basse, 10
Xylophone Mallets (Beaters), *22**, 46
Xylophone Resonators, 44
Xylophone, soprano, *81**
Xylorimba, 10, *41f,* 46f, 47*
Xylorimba (five-octave type), 47*

Yun, Ysang
   Dimensions, 140
   Sim Tjong, 140, 163
   Träume (Dreams), 140

Zanza, 76f
Zehm, F.
   Capriccio for Percussion Solo and Chamber Orchestra, 124
Ziehpfeife, 11
Zimbel(n), 10
Zimbelspiel, 62*
Zimmermann, B. A.
   Dialogue, 48, 142
   Die Soldaten, 56, 105, 119, 122ff, 142
Zubumba, 177
Zymbel, 122

Acknowledgments

Universal Edition
Editions Max Eschig, Paris
Boosey & Hawkes Music Publishers Ltd., London
J. & W. Chester Ltd., London
Edition Modern, Munich
C. F. Kahnt, Lindau
C. F. Peters Corp., New York
Associated Music Publishers, Inc., New York
Carl Fischer, New York / B. Schott's Söhne, Mainz
G. Ricordi & C. S. p. A., Milan
Editions Salabert, Paris
Musikverlage Hans Sikorski, Hamburg
Bote & Bock, Berlin
Le Chant du Monde, Paris
Chappell & Co. Ltd., London
Durand & Cie, Paris
Les Nouvelles Editions Meridian, Paris
Musikverlag Hans Gerig, Cologne
Alphonse Leduc, Paris
Henry Litolff's Verlag / C. F. Peters, Frankfort, London, New York

Table of Rar[

PAGE	INSTRUMENT	
35	Timpani	
45	Xylophone	1 o
47	Xylorimba	
47	Marimba	
48	Bass Xylophone	
50	Soprano Trough Xylophone	1 o
50	Tenor Trough Xylophone	
53	Glockenspiel or Orchestra Bells	2 (
55	Keyboard Glockenspiel	1 o
56	Celesta	1 o
56, 58	Vibraphone and Metallophone	
59	Lithophone (Stone Disks)	1 (
60	Crotales, Antique Cymbals	2 o
62	Gong	
64	Chimes (Large Bells)	
67	Bell Plates	
69	Tubular Chimes	
71	Tubaphone	2 o
72	Musical Glasses	
73	Tuned Bottles (Flaschenspiel)	1 o
74	Flexatone and Musical Saw	
78	Slide Whistle	
79	Piano Strings	

Concert pitch (actual pitch) of percussion instruments with definite pitch.

269021107

AUG 1 8 1980

269021107

HEWLETT-WOODMERE PUBLIC LIBRARY

FOR REFERENCE
Not to be taken from this room